Economics

S. F. Goodman

MACMILLAN
Business

First published 1998 by
MACMILLAN PRESS LTD
Houndmills, Basingstoke, Hampshire RG21 6XS
and London
Companies and representatives throughout the world

ISBN 0–333–67397–2 paperback

A catalogue record for this book is available
from the British Library.

This book is printed on paper suitable for recycling and
made from fully managed and sustained forest sources.

10   9   8   7   6   5   4   3   2   1
07   06   05   04   03   02   01   00   99   98

Editing and origination by
Aardvark Editorial, Mendham, Suffolk

Printed in Malaysia

To Francis and Tom

Contents

List of Tables and Figures

Tables

Figures

Acknowledgements

The author and publishers wish to thank the following for permission to reproduce copyright material:

The Bank of England for Tables 15.1, 15.2, 23.1 and Figure 20.1; the OECD for Tables 9.1, 21.1, 23.2, Figures 3.1 and 10.1 and the 'Focus' items on The Sahel and Fishing; the Office for National Statistics for Tables 2.1, 3.1, 3.3, 3.4, 12.1, 14.1, 14.2, 16.1, 17.1, 19.1, 21.2 and Figures 3.2 and 19.3; the Office for Official Publications of the European Communities for Tables 3.2, 3.5, 19.2 and 19.3.

I would like to thank my wife, Lindsay, for her help with the index and for her encouragement and my son Francis for his computing advice. My students at several institutions over the years and currently at Kings Langley School and Roundwood Park School have been a constant source of inspiration and challenge. I owe particular thanks to Ben Brewer, Natalie Broome, Stuart Flint, Andrew Henderson and Chris Hopper who have acted as constructive critics of some of the material and ideas. I hope they and my other students will remember the subject with pleasure.

Preface

Economics is a subject that has fascinated me since I was a teenager and I continue to enjoy the insights that it gives on the way the world works. I hope that this book will stimulate an interest in others and give them a similar enjoyment through their lives.

This book is inevitably something of a compromise. It recognises that students need an understanding of the basic currency of the subject in terms of theory but that many do not find the theory very satisfying. When the theory has become a dull and possibly painful memory I hope that the reader will retain a way of looking at the world with economic insights. Most modern economic textbooks are formidably long and are often written by teams or pairs of authors. This book has become much more detailed than intended but I have found that it is the detail that makes topics interesting and useful. There is already too much superficiality in the world of two-minute sound bites so this book tries to withstand the tide. Some venerable topics have been treated very scantily but others reappear in several contexts because I think they are more useful over one's lifetime. The book largely ignores indifference curve analysis and the behaviour of demand but spends a lot of space on government policies and contemporary events and issues. It is, in any case, sound advice to students never to rely entirely on one book so you should read as widely as possible from a variety of sources.

If you have studied economics before you can skip the first two or three chapters and possibly the price theory and the first chapter on degrees of competition. If you are new to the subject do a fast scan read through the whole book before going back and reading selected chapters slowly. The exercises are mainly to give you food for thought and to stimulate arguments. Economics is best studied in a group of argumentative, fairly sceptical friends.

S. F. GOODMAN

1 Introduction to Economics

Aims of the chapter

To:
- explain the subject matter and definition of economics;
- outline the nature of the economic problem;
- refer to the main alternative methods of approaching the solution of the economic problem;
- discuss the problem of economic jargon;
- explain the distinction between positive and normative approaches to the subject.

1.1 The Subject Matter of Economics

'Economics is the study of the way in which mankind organises itself to tackle the basic problem of scarcity' according to the *Macmillan Dictionary of Modern Economics*. There are a number of different versions of this definition but they all emphasise the fact that human wants exceed the resources available to satisfy them. Some definitions refer to 'competing ends' as, for example, 'economics is the science that studies the allocation of scarce resources among competing ends'. Not everyone understands the use of the word 'ends' in this context and it may help to substitute 'uses' instead. The word 'science' is important in this definition and its significance is discussed at the end of this chapter.

Exercise I

What enables people to claim economics is a science?

The scarcity of resources in relation to demand, which is wants backed by the willingness and ability to pay, leads to three central questions or economic problems:

1. What to produce;
2. How to produce;
3. For whom to produce.

The subject matter of economics is best understood by scanning the contents pages and index of this book and other general textbooks. Some books concentrate mainly upon a theoretical approach to the topics whereas others have applied economics as their main emphasis. Having said that, most 'applied' economics has a very strong underpinning of theory as well as analysis of an industry or economic activity in descriptive terms. The impression is often given that economics starts at a beginning and works towards an end, that is that it is a linear subject, but many of the ideas in the topics that are usually dealt with at the end of textbooks are essential for a full understanding of the topics at the beginning. A few brave souls have tried to reverse the order of presentation but in doing so simply reverse the problem. The best advice is to skim quickly through these basic texts and then go back over the ground more slowly. This book tries to introduce ideas as they naturally occur whatever the main topic, usually in a brief fashion, rather than keep them rigidly in a 'box' in a specific chapter. The difficulty with this approach is that the same points may be made more than once.

Economics has developed over a long period of time and is like a house with many attics full of lumber. We are happy for most of the time with the main rooms and their contents because they fit in with our modern-day society and way of living. Occasionally, however, someone ventures into an attic and brings out some long discarded piece of furniture or a toy. The furniture may be elevated to the status of a desirable antique and placed in a position of importance. The toy may be played with again with greater pleasure than it gave its original owner. Modern economics, therefore, sometimes resurrects ideas and theories that were once buried or discounted or even sneered at. These ideas, such as those of the classical school, the monetarists and Pareto may be taken up enthusiastically, not only by economists but also by politicians. At this point we may observe a common phenomenon that politicians either do not fully understand the ideas or simply take over the bits that suit their predilections. The old furniture, or even some of the more modern, may be sent back to the attic but we can never be sure that an economic idea is completely buried for ever. This tendency for death and resurrection may stimulate your interest in the subject or simply leave you bewildered and sceptical about its value. It should stimulate you because it shows that the subject is not fossilised. If you accept the idea that the subject matter and its theoretical basis is forever changing you will discover that the study of economics is, for the most part, fun.

1.2   The Nature of the Economic Problem

The problem has been stated as scarcity of resources in relation to human wants and as three subdivisions of that. Chapter 3 discusses various underlying forces such as population change that have a bearing on the depth of the problems and Chapter 24 discusses the associated problems of economic growth and the environment. At the core of the economic problem is choice and the need to allocate scarce resources. The economist approaches this core with what is called the concept of opportunity cost, that is that one course of action has an economic cost in terms of the opportunities that have to be sacrificed in order to pursue it. As a society we have to chose whether to use resources to build hospitals or the Eurofighter. If we choose to open a new prison every week we forgo the chance of building schools or housing. Opportunity cost is dealt with in Chapter 2. If we look at the three problems listed above we gain some insight into the overall economic problem.

What to produce is obviously a choice facing society because there are insufficient supplies of land, labour and capital to produce everything our population would like. In a free market system the choices are made in response to the willingness and ability of buyers to pay and the suppliers' ability to satisfy the buyers' wants within their own cost and profit constraints. The phrase 'allocative efficiency' is applied to the best or optimal combinations of outputs arising from the most efficient combination of inputs.

How to produce is not so obviously a matter for the economist but when the question is examined it is clear that how to produce involves many economic choices of the combination of resources and the quantities used. The 'how to produce' question is ultimately about the best cost combination of resources so it is an economic question. The answers to the question how to produce are constantly changing as technology and the supply, demand and price of resources alter.

For whom to produce is a fundamental economic question that is often relegated to the background but the concept of distributional equity is of great importance because it deals with the justice of the distribution of the nation's output among individuals. Not all economists like to introduce the word justice into the discussion because it smacks of value judgements. Economic systems provide different solutions to the problem according to the structures and policies adopted and economists are interested in the impact of these alternative policies.

Exercise 2

Why is 'how to produce' an economic question?

If you have studied economics before you will be familiar with the approach contained in the three traditional questions dealt with above but there is an alternative approach.

An alternative approach to the economic problem is to see the subject in relation to important world issues which, almost inevitably, are also classified into three:

- The first is how to achieve **economic stability**. This covers a wide variety of topics such as controlling the business cycle and avoiding slumps and booms and the very important one of controlling the general price level, that is inflation and deflation.

- The second covers all the topics associated with the issues of **economic growth**, both national and international. In this area we can also discuss the fundamental problems of how to manage the world economy in order to achieve sustainable development, that is we can consider the environmental aspect of policies.

- The third covers the problem of **distribution of income and wealth** but in a more universal fashion because it involves an analysis of the relationship between income groups and wealth holders not just within one nation but among nations. The traditional approach of 'for whom to produce' is a rather cosy justification of the *status quo*, that is it concluded that if you wanted something and could afford it you should have it. It ends up justifying the existence of an industry making mink coats for poodles while people a short distance away die of hypothermia. The newer approach asks about the longer term economic (and social) consequences of having a 'rich world' and a 'poor world' and of having extremes of affluence and poverty within a nation. A purist might argue that this approach again introduces value judgements into economics but, when we stop to think about it, the existing distribution exudes value judgements about the rightness of inherited ownership and the entitlement to higher incomes attached to certain work. It is not as if the existing economic system were anywhere near the perfect competition model so beloved of some economists; it is not, so we might as well try to correct its most obvious imperfections by stating different distributional targets.

1.3   How Can Society Tackle the Economic Problem?

The mixed economy approach is the one most usually adopted. This means that most of the economy is left to work under a free enterprise system with markets determining the price of a wide range of goods and services and the price of factors, wages, rent and interest rates. The state, however, plays a larger role than simply acting as 'referee' or provider of basic legal, defence, law and order and foreign policy frameworks. It may own certain key parts of the economic structure; it may actively intervene to supervise and regulate some markets; it may decree that all its citizens shall perform certain economic duties or receive 'merit goods' such as education and basic health services; it may work to reduce consumption of 'demerit goods' such as alcohol, tobacco, pornography or, optimistically, party political broadcasts. The degree of such intervention varies from country to country and from decade to decade within one state. The United Kingdom's rapid progress away from nationalisation as a solution to the problems created by the existence of natural monopolies and low profit, low productivity industries towards privatisation with supervision is a case in point. The nature of the role of the state in the United Kingdom and the way it has changed is dealt with in Chapter 4. The mixed economy can take several forms and the boundary between the private and public sectors continually shifts. It is possible to draw up a spectrum to show degrees of state intervention and, broadly speaking, the post-war years to 1970 saw most states extending their powers and degree of intervention; the years since then have seen, in many countries, a shift back towards markets deciding what shall be produced and how.

The markets increasingly determine the question of distribution of what is produced in answer to the 'for whom' question. Various states respond to the needs of the disadvantaged in different ways. Some offer a flimsy 'safety net' to the very poor whereas some insist on either or both of private provision via insurance and compulsory state provision. It was once regarded as normal and desirable that the tax and expenditure systems should be used to ensure a more equitable distribution of income and wealth but there has been a revival of what may be called the social Darwinism school of economics which argues in favour of the survival of the fittest, economically speaking. The proponents of this view are, in effect, choosing to spend their private wealth upon security and burglar alarm systems rather than allowing it to be redistributed by the state into housing, education, training and employment creation projects. They argue in favour of choice but create a straitjacket for themselves and the rest of society by tolerating and even encouraging the growth of a large underclass of poor and unemployed. This is another instance of where the economist needs to beware of short-run and long-run effects and of value judgements.

The free market economy is another possible solution although no-one has achieved a complete one since before the first urban civilisations grew up, with the possible exception of societies in complete dissolution at the end of catastrophic wars. Realistically, a free market economy refers to a situation where there is the absolute minimum of state intervention beyond the provision of a basic legal, law and order, defence and foreign policy structure. Within such a minimalist framework the price mechanism would act to solve the three traditional economic problems. Prices would act as signals to buyers and sellers indicating whether they could afford to buy, or buy more, or whether to suppliers there was more profit in expanding or contracting production. Income would be derived from the sale or lease of the factors of production, that is people's labour, their land and their capital. The factors would flow between uses in pursuit of the highest price, wages, rent or interest. Risk takers, or entrepreneurs, would organise the factors to maximise their profits. They would enter high profit industries and in so doing would increase competition and reduce profit levels. They would leave low profit industries and thus cut competition and long-run profits would tend to rise. In the process resources would be used at their optimum and consumers would receive the maximum possible output at the lowest possible long-run price.

This is explained in the chapters on competition. Goods and services would be allocated according to people's willingness and ability to pay and according to their individual preferences. When the economy's resources and output are allocated in a manner where no reallocation can make anyone better off without making at least one other person worse off we have what is called a Pareto optimum after the famous Italian economist Vilfredo Pareto (1848–1923) whose work founded modern welfare economics.

The snag about the free market mechanism is that it does not fully possess the characteristics required for it to work in the perfect manner ascribed by the theory. The factors of production are not perfectly mobile between uses; there is not perfect knowledge of the market and of prices and conditions in it; entrepreneurs often prefer to collude rather than to compete; there are significant time lags between events and responses to them. It is also possible to dispute the underlying concept of the so-called 'economic man or woman' who behaves so as to maximise personal satisfaction and who is completely rational. The price mechanism also fails to deal with what are called external costs and benefits. For example, the price of a unit of electricity usually fails to incorporate the costs imposed on other people by the pollution created in its generation. External costs and benefits are discussed in Chapter 2.

The command economy is another extreme solution to the economic problem. Once again such extremes have never fully existed although Albania came close. Usually some remnant of a price mechanism remains to deal with, for example, the produce of people's private vegetable plots or privately owned animals. There is nearly always some sort of 'black market' as well in scarce commodities.

The usual picture of a command economy is that of the old Soviet bloc although the extent of state control varied greatly. China, Cuba, Vietnam and North Korea are remaining examples of the centralised state command structure. In its extreme form the state would decide what to produce, usually through a five-year plan system. It would also decide pay and rewards, usually within a limited banding system. It would decide on the price of goods and services. The price of what were regarded as essentials, basic foods, work clothing, housing and public transport would be kept exceptionally low and stable for many years. Health and education services would be free and pensions would be provided. The state planning authority would decide what would be produced and in what quantities. It would communicate this overall plan to the productive enterprises that actually supplied the goods and services and they would put in a request for the inputs of labour and capital and materials required to meet the output targets they had been given. After some modification of targets and input requirements the final output targets would be given, usually a percentage increase on the year before, and resources allocated.

The problems associated with this system are immediately obvious. If there are 20 000 separate parts in a modern motor car and 200 000 in an aeroplane someone has to get their figures for output targets right. There were, therefore, ministries engaged in what is called aggregating and disaggregating the requests for final products and inputs. The system did, however, lend itself to serious bottlenecks caused by the shortage of components or inputs or their over abundant supply elsewhere. The planning process was strongly biased against changes of design and many Soviet designs of, for example, tractors, trucks and cars went unaltered for decades. (This might not be altogether a bad thing because it avoids the waste inherent in cosmetic engineering and superficial redesign that is something of a plague in market economies.)

MARKET FAILURE

Market failure is often used to justify government intervention. It may take several forms:

- The price mechanism may not work properly and the market may fail to 'clear', that is the price may not change until the desire of sellers to sell is exactly matched by the desire of consumers to buy.
- The market may clear but in an imperfect manner because of the existence and activities of firms or others who are not competing in the perfect competition sense, that is there is some degree of oligopoly or monopoly.
- The market may not produce what is wanted particularly in respect of *public goods* which are goods or services such as street lighting and the police which have to be provided by the state because no-one can be excluded from using them and their consumption by one person does not prevent someone else consuming them.
- The market probably does not account for external costs and benefits, that is externalities, so the market price does not reflect the full cost to society of providing goods and services. This is especially true where environmental costs and benefits are involved.

Consider the oil industry:
1. Is the market for oil products competitive?
2. Is the degree of competition reflected in the movements of price at the petrol pump?
3. Does the market price of oil products reflect externalities?
4. Is there a case for government intervention in the oil industry?

The system was very slow to acknowledge changes in consumer tastes and preferences. A planner decided how many shoes of a certain type and size were to be produced. The result was that there were queues of keen buyers when new shipments were available in the shops. They snapped up the popular styles and left huge quantities of unwanted shoes without buyers.

People were uncertain of supplies and tended to buy up large quantities for storage in case the product became unavailable. This applied to all sorts of goods such as toothpaste as well as more 'luxury' type articles. Queuing was endemic in the system and rationing also became a feature for some products.

There were no real monetary incentives built into the system because wage levels were fixed. Rewards tended to be non-monetary and were expressed in terms of the sense of well being from working for one's fellows, or in terms of better accommodation or holidays. Enterprises tended to avoid over performing against their output targets because to do so simply invited a higher target next year. Outside observers alleged that the system was only about 80 per cent efficient compared with the typical Western economy and that it only continued to work because enterprises fudged and 'fiddled' to get inputs. There was alleged to be a great deal of hidden unemployment in the sense that people were employed doing jobs that in the West had been phased out or replaced by machines. The system also required isolation from external economies so foreign exchange and trade was centrally controlled as well.

The Soviet system in eastern and central Europe broke down for a variety of reasons. Among them was the fact that the ordinary people became aware that their economies were not catching up as promised with those of the USA and Germany. More travel and more tourism into their countries highlighted these facts as did television. They saw their generations of sacrifice of 'jam today for more jam tomorrow' as unfulfilled. Another factor was the inability of the Soviet-style economies to isolate themselves from the inflation following the oil price rises of the 1970s. A final clinching burden was that of defence spending when it became impossible to match the technological progress of the USA without further crippling sacrifice of consumer goods.

Exercise 3

The command system is usually heavily criticised. Why do you think it lasted so long in the Soviet Union (1921–1990)?

There is a tendency to write off the command economy as if it were already consigned to the dustbin of history but, human nature being what it is, do not be surprised if it is being strongly advocated again in twenty or thirty years time as a solution to the problems of grossly overpopulated countries where demand has outstripped resources.

1.4 Economic Jargon

Some students are put off by what they call economic jargon. If you have problems you should consult a dictionary of economics or look terms up in the index or the glossary that some books have. Alternatively you could build yourself a small dictionary of terms as you read. The charge which is often levied against economics, that it is jargon ridden, is generally unjustified; it simply takes time, as with all subjects, to become familiar with terminology that saves lengthy exposition and qualifications. No-one expects a car mechanic to discuss engines without reference to cylinder capacity, valves, fuel lines and injection systems. Why do they expect economists to discuss inflation without reference to real and money values, or unemployment without any classification of its types or causes? Having said that, this book does try to minimise the use of jargon without explanation, but it may not always succeed.

There is one phrase that all students of economics must be aware of even though it is frequently omitted. It is *other things being equal* or to give its Latin original *ceteris paribus*. This phrase means that there are several or many variables at work in the background of an economic happening and that we conclude that there will be a certain outcome if all the other variables do not change. For example, take the statement that 'a rise in the price of butter caused by a rise in its cost of production will, other things being equal, result in an increase in the demand for a substitute such as margarine'. The other things remaining equal are, for example, the incomes and tastes and preferences of consumers. The real problem for the economist is not the working out of what these unstated other variables are but the usual assumption that they do not change when we know full well that they may, particularly over time.

Exercise 4

Why do economists keep saying 'other things being equal'?

Figures and diagrams are the bane of some student's lives but are generally useful in explaining some relationships quickly. Part of the secret with diagrams is to study them very carefully and follow each curve individually in relation to what is on the axes of the graph before attempting to put the curves all together. Most people skip over diagrams without a detailed study. Ideally we should be able to reproduce them immediately from our own understanding.

1.5 ˙ The Distinction Between Normative and Positive Economics

This is a very important distinction because we need to be aware of the basis of our and other people's statements.

A normative statement contains a value judgement whether explicitly or implicitly. A value judgement usually includes words such as 'best', 'better,' 'most worthwhile', 'most beautiful' and 'fairest'. These are terms that are most associated with the study of the visual arts or poetry and literature. Although attempts have been made to reduce the study of literature to a non-subjective, non-emotional set of responses they have always failed because ultimately your view of what is the better poem is just as valid as mine because both views are based on our subjective feelings or assessment. Other people might trust your view more because of your experience and qualifications but there is no way in which my view can be rejected as invalid.

A positive statement has an objective basis, that is it refers to a quality that can be measured. We are able to make uncontrovertible statements about height, length, breadth, weight, mass, speed, temperature and so on because we have standards by which to measure them. Much of the study of economics is a quest for relationships between economic variables that can be measured against historic performance. If data is carefully assembled it should be possible, for example, to make positive statements about the relationship between the level of interest rates and the level of private sector investment expenditure. The list of such possibilities is endless but it throws into the forefront the need to keep saying 'other things being equal'. Without this qualification our conclusions may appear to be positive or objective but it does not mean they are of any use.

If we can do enough research it is possible to assemble what is called a model of the economy such as that employed by HM Treasury. The Chancellor of the Exchequer can use it to fill in certain possible tax and expenditure changes and predict the range of possible outcomes. The Chancellor may or may not act upon the predictions. Economists like creating economic models but the model of the economy used by the Treasury is of the whole or macro-economy, and purports to reflect the objective relationships between the variables such as interest rates, the quantity of money, employment, incomes and so on and their rates of change. The weight to be placed upon the model can be kept in proportion by realising that some economists do not like some of the assumptions behind sections of the model and have constructed their own versions to give greater or less emphasis to certain relationships. If they fed the Chancellor's figures into their own models they will get different answers. It is all a bit like a prize bull competition. We can be told objective things like the weight, height, number of progeny and age of the contenders but the winner depends on whether the judges prefer the bone structure or the haunches of one over the others.

Economics was defined earlier as a 'science' and that implies that a positive approach should be taken. We should attempt to be objective and to measure rather than to utter value judgements. Many people, however, find the subject very tedious if it fails to address questions that are essentially moral, such as those connected with the environment or world development. They ask what is the point of studying the subject if it is not to help provide solutions to society's economic problems. The answer to this is do this by all means but you should be fully aware of what you are doing and not pretend to be objective when you are not. There is also a case to be made for studying economics as an intellectual exercise whose precepts will help you understand what is happening around you for the rest of your life.

2 Key Concepts

Aims of the chapter

To explain:

- opportunity cost;
- external costs and benefits (externalities);
- national income;
- the concept of economic growth;
- index numbers;
- short run, long run and time lags.

2.1   Opportunity Cost

The concept of opportunity cost is central to the study of economics. Individuals, enterprises and nations are continually making choices. If resources are scarce, as they almost always are, and we make one choice, we almost certainly forgo the opportunity of doing something else or of buying other things. If there is no scarcity there is no opportunity forgone and so no opportunity cost. The economist calls the value of the next best alternative that is forgone 'the opportunity cost'. This may be called a *private opportunity cost* if it is the individual who makes the choice, or *social opportunity cost* if society in general is involved in the consequences of the choice.

Private opportunity cost manifests itself in many forms. For example, if I choose to keep a wallet full of cash I am sacrificing the interest which the money could earn in a building society or elsewhere. Instead of sitting here writing this chapter I could be adding to my collection of Lakeland peaks over 2000 feet altitude. One of the major choices for the individual that involves considerable short-term (we hope) sacrifice of money is the decision to undertake higher education courses. Once a person could be reasonably certain of obtaining employment straight from school and could expect to earn many thousands of pounds before any friends who had decided to study for a degree earned a penny from full-time employment. They, of course, expected to have higher aggregate life time earnings and their hopes were, and are, usually realised.

Society, in the form of governments, is also confronted by the need to make choices. Indeed much political argument is about the allocation of scarce resources and social opportunity cost. These choices are highlighted in the persistent battle over the last fifty years for resources between defence, education, health and welfare. When the cold war was at its chilliest the defence lobby put up a case that convinced successive governments to allocate 3 per cent of GNP in real terms to defence. (You might like to consider how 'defence' is defined.) One consequence of this policy has been the neglect of the transport system infrastructure, a steady deterioration in the quality and maintenance of school buildings and a failure of National Health Service programmes to keep up with the changing age-related needs of the population. More has been spent in these areas but not sufficient extra to cope with increased demand. The so-called 'peace dividend' of lower defence related spending has, somehow, been dissipated while attention has been focused on growing unemployment in defence industries.

Another clear case of social opportunity cost has been evident in the decision to develop a nuclear power industry. Critics of this policy argue that billions of pounds were spent unnecessarily on these developments in the sense that electricity could have been generated more cheaply by existing, traditional technology. The money saved by not developing nuclear power could have been spent on the alternatives forgone – health, education, defence and so on. The decision to create a nuclear power industry raises the issue of short-term versus long-term policy approaches. The supporters of nuclear industry would argue that the long-term requirement for renewable energy makes it sensible to establish the industry although the short run might involve a high opportunity cost. It is possible to argue that the current vogue of the privatised electricity companies for Combined Cycle Gas Turbine power stations, while possible to justify in terms of short-term opportunity cost, is extremely short sighted because of its profligate burning of a finite resource, natural gas, that has many other beneficial uses.

2.2 Opportunity Cost Applications

Most economic textbooks contain diagrams to show the principle of opportunity cost and the principal relationships between fully employed resources, production possibility and technological change. Such diagrams may or may not help your understanding but because examiners seem to enjoy setting questions on this topic, especially as the diagrams lend themselves to multiple-choice questions, it will probably be worth the sacrifice of your time to study the following points in some detail. You may decide the opportunity cost is too high and choose to indulge in some other intellectual exercise such as watching *Baywatch* on TV with the sound turned off.

2.3   The Production Possibility Curve (PPC)

The PPC may also be called the 'production frontier' or 'transformation curve'. The PPC is drawn up to show the maximum amount of two products that can be produced with the existing resources and technology if all resources were devoted to producing them exclusively. You can choose what to put on the axes; textbooks tend to favour hospitals/warships, capital goods/consumer goods or food/durable goods. See Figure 2.1 for an example of the PPC.

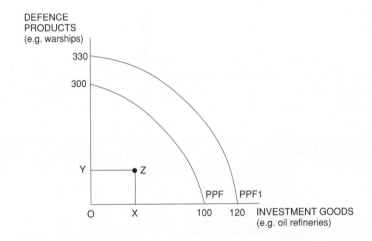

The curve represents possible combinations of output, when resources are fully employed, of defence products and investment goods. The increased output of one involves a sacrifice (opportunity cost) of units of the other.

PPF1 represents a new PPF when resources increase or are better combined or new technology raises efficiency.

Point Z is an inefficient level of combination and would result in underemployment of factors.

Figure 2.1   The production possibility curve

- The PPC is usually drawn, as in Figure 2.1, as concave to the origin because it is assumed that resources are not equally efficient at producing both types of goods. For example, warship builders may not be good construction workers. The curve need not be concave. It would be a straight line if there were constant returns to scale; it would be convex to the origin if there were increasing returns to scale.

- The curve, or frontier, shows a trade-off between the two products. Any point of combination on the curve is achievable but the production of one product involves a sacrifice of output of the other. Any point outside the curve is not attainable with the present, given, technology and resources.

- Any point inside the curve, such as Z, represents an inefficient use of resources and indicates the existence of unemployed resources, labour, capital and land. The indication is that the United Kingdom, with between 2 and 3 million unemployed people and unused factories and offices and land, could enjoy a higher standard of living if unemployment were removed.

- It is usually considered a desirable goal for the PPC to shift to the right as economic growth is achieved. Such a shift requires higher levels of investment expenditure, the development of new technologies, the better and more efficient combination of the factors of production and possibly the discovery of new resources such as North Sea oil and gas. Diagrams usually show this future curve parallel to the original but it need not be.

Exercise I

Consider the possible opportunity cost of the proposed Eurofighter project that may cost the UK taxpayer over £9 billion excluding future maintenance costs and replacements. Compare the potential benefits against the possible opportunity costs.

2.4   Opportunity Cost and International Trade

The theory which is usually used to explain the potential gains from trade between countries is called 'the theory of comparative cost advantage' and is based on the premise that, if two countries have different domestic opportunity costs of producing goods, specialisation and trade will benefit both. This is explained more fully in Chapter 17.

2.5   Money and Opportunity Cost

The principle of opportunity cost can be clearly seen if we choose to hold cash in our pocket where it earns no interest rather than in some form that does yield interest. There is also an opportunity cost if we leave our money in an account paying a low rate of interest when it could be in a different account earning more, assuming that the security and liquidity of the deposits are similar.

2.6   Labour, Land and Opportunity Cost

Each of us in employment has an opportunity cost which is measured in terms of what we could earn in our next best paid alternative occupation. In theory we would transfer to this other employment if the earnings in our present job fell to the level of this next best alternative. From this we derive the idea of 'transfer earnings', that is the opportunity cost of a factor, the level at which the factor ceases its present use and shifts to its next best alternative use. In the case of land any amount (surplus) above the opportunity cost is called, for some ancient reason, 'economic rent'. In theory land will remain in its present use as long as its return (revenue) exceeds its opportunity cost (transfer earnings).

Note: Any economic choice involves dozens of other lost opportunities but the opportunity cost is the value of the next best alternative forgone, not all of the alternatives.

2.7   External Costs and Benefits

A key concept of modern economics is that of external costs and benefits which are often lumped together under the word externalities. When a firm calculates its costs of production it takes no account of any additional costs it may have imposed on the rest of society. The airline operators at my nearby airport neither know nor care that I have to buy double glazing in order to get a good night's sleep when they start operating summer charter flights in the middle of the night. The firm is measuring its **private costs** only but I am bearing what are called **external costs**. The airlines count their revenues, their **private benefits** but I also benefit from the existence of the airport because of the excellent network of roads built to serve it and the time savings I enjoy when I fly from there. My benefits, and those of others, are called **external benefits**. Books differ in their terminology but the usual version is that:

Private Costs + External Costs   = Social Costs;
Private Benefits + External Benefits = Social Benefits.

The social costs are the opportunity cost to society of producing a good.

The point behind this is that the price we pay in a shop rarely represents the full cost to society of producing the product. The usual textbook reference here is to a chemical works which discharges effluent into the nearby river. This places costs on fishermen and water treatment plants downstream. It may provide benefits for those employed on cleaning up the mess. Society has to pay costs that in a better regulated society would be placed on the polluter. It is fairly easy to think of external costs because negative forces such as noise, pollution and congestion are usually obvious but it is less easy to detect external benefits. They do exist, however, in for example the building of a bypass where the external costs of building in terms of noise, congestion and destruction of wildlife habitats is matched, for a short term at least, by reduced delays, less congestion and possibly less urban pollution.

Exercise 2

Compare the external costs and benefits of disposing of North Sea oil platforms by deep sea dumping as opposed to dismantling them inshore.

2.8 Cost-benefit Analysis

When a proposed investment programme such as the Channel Tunnel High Speed Rail Link is analysed a technique called cost-benefit analysis (CBA) is applied. This calculates the private and external costs and benefits. Intrinsic in these calculations is the idea of opportunity cost because 'cost' to an economist, as opposed to an accountant, includes opportunity cost. The economist considers the benefits forgone by undertaking one project rather than another.

All significant public works schemes have a cost-benefit analysis study applied and an environmental impact study. One celebrated study on a proposal to build the Victoria Line on London's underground showed clearly that, if only private costs and private benefits were considered, the line would run at a commercial loss but, if external costs and benefits were also considered, society as a whole would show a net gain. CBA is, therefore, often used as a basis to justify public works programmes that are known to be loss making when judged by private, commercial standards. It may also be the basis of attempts to make industry pay the full cost of measures to protect the environment. The concept of externalities is used to justify state intervention in markets because the private costs and benefits do not reflect the true cost or benefit to society of a course of action. That is, price does not fully reflect social cost or social benefit.

Note: You will see references to *marginal social cost* and *marginal social benefit*. Marginal simply refers to the costs or benefits of producing an additional unit of the item referred to. Figure 2.2 illustrates marginal social costs and benefits. In the figure the private firm would produce at point A where MPC = MPB whereas, if externalities are taken into account, output would be at point B where MSC = MSB.

Exercise 3

Draw up a cost benefit list of possible benefits against possible costs of the Channel Tunnel High Speed Rail Link from Kent to Kings Cross/St Pancras in central London.

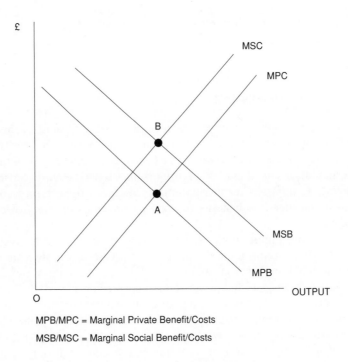

MPB/MPC = Marginal Private Benefit/Costs
MSB/MSC = Marginal Social Benefit/Costs

Figure 2.2   Price and output where externalities are incorporated

2.9   National Income

It is important early on in one's study of economics to have a broad idea of terms used in calculating the national income. The national income of the UK is calculated in three ways that, after an adjustment for statistical imbalance called the 'residual error', produce the same figure. National Income is a measure of the net value of all the goods and services produced in one year (national product). It can also be viewed as the incomes derived by households from providing the factors of production, land, labour and capital. A third approach is to regard national income as equal to the private and public expenditure on goods and services and fixed capital formation.

The three methods are called the Income Method, the Expenditure Method and the Output (or Value Added) Method.

It is very important to avoid double counting when calculating the national income.

Net National Product at factor cost = National Income = National Expenditure

The terms used are:

- **Gross National Product** (GNP). This is the largest figure because it includes capital consumption, that is the output of goods and services to replace depreciated or consumed capital assets. It also includes incomes derived from foreign trade or ownership of property.

- **Net National Product** (NNP). This is GNP minus capital consumption. It is a frequently used measure and NNP at factor cost is equal to (Net) National Income. The calculation for capital consumption is subject to the largest margin of error in national income measurement.

- **Gross Domestic Product** (GDP). This is the figure arrived at in the income and output methods of measurement before 'net property incomes from abroad' is added or subtracted. (The expenditure method calculates Total Domestic Expenditure at Market Prices before adjustments for exports/imports expenditure and net property income from abroad.)

- **Market Prices and Factor Cost**. Many market prices include expenditure such as VAT or excise duties. A few prices, such as some railway fares, are subsidised. The 'market price' calculation of national income does not adjust for these taxes and subsidies but the 'Factor Cost' adjustment deducts expenditure taxes and adds subsidies. It is used in the expenditure method.

2.10   The Growth of National Income

A frequently used measure of economic growth is the change in Gross Domestic Product per head of population over a time period, usually a year. The United Nations publishes figures which are based upon a standardised method of measuring National Income. The OECD also publishes detailed growth figures for its member countries.

There is a long running debate about the relative importance of the factors that affect economic growth but the main ones are the levels of expenditure on:

- investment;
- education and training;

- research and development;
- technological change, capital widening and deepening;
- population growth;
- the shift of workers from low to high productivity jobs;
- in a given period the growth is also related to the business cycle;
- mature economies tend to settle to a low rate of annual growth compared with developing economies.

Economic growth is important because it represents a rising output of goods and services and presumably a rising standard of living. National income is not the same thing as economic welfare. We must look very carefully to see how growth, and the national income itself, is distributed and at its constituents (the growth might be weapons) and at the costs to society of the growth. We have progressed from the view that all growth is good towards wanting to analyse the costs of growth in all their manifestations – civil liberties, pollution, family life, crime and so on. The questions 'growth for whom?' and 'at what cost?' should always be asked.

2.11 **Money Income and Real Income**

'Money' income is a simple concept. It is income received in all forms from selling one's labour and the services of land and capital at current price levels. Thus 'money' national income is the national income of a year measured at current prices.

'Real' income is a comparative concept because it takes current incomes and compares them with price changes (inflation) and expresses them in real terms. For example, my money income may have risen by 5 per cent in 1996 but because inflation was at 2.8 per cent, my 'real' income rose by only 2.2 per cent. Consequently, if prices were falling (deflation), the change in real incomes could be higher than the change in money incomes. A *deflator* in the form of a general price index is used to convert money to real national income.

The concept of real and money is applied to wages, to national income and to interest rates. The interest rate application is important because if we are receiving 5 per cent on our savings and the RPI is 3 per cent, our 'real' interest rate is only 2 per cent. It is possible, and has happened, that real interest rates are negative when the inflation rate is higher than nominal interest rates. There is then a strong disincentive to save and an incentive to spend.

In principle, real national income is measuring the output of real goods and services and real wages are measuring what the wages will buy over time.

Exercise 4

Why do economists usually state that national income is not the same thing as national welfare?

2.12 Index Numbers – A Useful Tool

Index numbers are frequently used in economics and it is important to learn their attributes and snares. Some index numbers such as the Retail Prices Index (RPI) are used to make comparisons over time usually on a monthly or annual basis. A date is chosen, arbitrarily, and the output or level of whatever is being measured on that date is called 100, the 'base year.' Thus the United Kingdom RPI takes as its base year January 1987. In constructing the RPI a 'basket' of goods and services is assembled which reflects the spending habits of an average family unit. The contents of the 'basket' are subject to regular review and each type of good or service is given a **weight** to reflect its relative importance. The weights are given in Table 2.1. The 'basket' is then priced and the total price is said to be equal to 100, the base year. At regular intervals the 'basket' is again priced and the new total price is related to the base year. For example, if in the base year the basket cost £200 (index = 100) and cost £220 in the second year, the index would now be 110. Prices have risen by 10 per cent. The usual formula for measuring the percentage change in prices is:

$$\frac{\text{Index in year 1} - \text{Index in year 2}}{\text{Index in year 1}} \times \frac{100}{1}$$

or

$$\frac{\text{The change in the Index}}{\text{Index in year 1}} \times \frac{100}{1}$$

Application of index numbers

1. Price indices – for example RPI, RPIX, RPIY, or indices for social groups such as pensioners are used to measure inflation. RPIX is RPI excluding mortgage interest payments. RPIY is RPIX excluding VAT, local authority taxes and excise duties.

2. Price indices for specific goods or services – for example house prices, import and export prices.

Table 2.1 Weights in the Retail Price Index

	All items	Food and catering	Alcohol and tobacco	Housing and household expenditure	Personal expenditure leisure	Travel and seasonal food[1]	All items except food	All items except	Seasonal food[1] food	Non-seasonal housing	All items except	Consumer durables
13 January 1987 = 100												
Weights 1992	1000	199	116	344	99	242	978	848	22	130	828	127
Weights 1993	1000	189	113	336	97	265	979	856	21	123	836	127
Weights 1994	1000	187	111	326	95	281	980	858	20	122	842	127

[1] Seasonal food is defined as: items of food the prices of which show significant seasonal variations. These are: fresh fruit and vegetables, fresh fish, eggs and home-killed lamb.

Source: Central Statistical Office.

3. Indices for wages, earnings, building costs (for insurance purposes). Some pensions are indexed-linked to the RPI and some pension contributions are linked to the annual average rise in earnings.

4. Output indices are used to measure changes in volumes of output of individual or groups of products.

5. Changes in the foreign exchange value of a currency can be measured using an 'effective exchange rate' index – for example £1 = 100 in 1987 against a weighted basket of currencies; in March 1996 £1 = 83.5 on the effective index and in February 1997 £1 = 97.2. The £ might have risen in value against the US dollar but have fallen against the DM and other currencies.

6. The Terms of Trade are measured using Index Numbers using the following:

$$\text{Terms of Trade} = \frac{\text{percentage change in export prices}}{\text{percentage change in import prices}} \times \frac{100}{1}$$

If the index is rising compared with the previous year the terms of trade are improving; if they are falling the terms of trade are deteriorating. The measurement relates to a base year, 100, so the terms can be improving against the base year but not against the previous year and vice versa.

Be careful with index numbers!

- The further away an index year is from its base year the more inaccurate it is likely to be. For example, the RPI 'basket' is regularly re-weighted to reflect changes in patterns of consumption but it is very hard to adjust for products and services which are completely new or a radical change on previous ones.

- There may be serious omissions in the range of goods and services included in the index. This explains why there is an RPI, an RPIX and a RPIY.

- We have to assume that the collecting of data and sampling techniques are reliable. This may be a leap of faith because all sorts of arbitrary decisions are made about the construction and administration of the index.

- Beware any politician who is quoting statistics, especially those derived from indices. They have a nasty habit, which we may charitably say is probably derived from ignorance, of finding one month's figure and multiplying it by 12 to give a projected annual figure. It will be a high or low figure depending on what they are trying to prove. A reliable annual figure, of course, adds a month's figures to the previous 11 to give a historically valid figure.

- Indices are all very well in their place but we often need to combine them with figures of real output, wages, pensions, and so on.

Seasonal adjustments

There is a seasonal cycle in output, employment, trade and prices. Their cycles are not always synchronised because they are differently affected by weather, holidays, leap years and administrative factors such as the change of car registration numbers in August. The effect of seasonal changes is usually discounted (or accounted for) in statistics which 'smooth' out changes which can be attributed to seasonal factors. Seasonally adjusted figures can produce some curious anomalies of which more people should be aware. To use a crude example, it is possible in a given month for the total of real human beings registered as unemployed to rise from 2 240 000 to 2 260 000 while the seasonally adjusted figure for unemployment falls from 2 220 000 to 2 200 000. The seasonal figure is saying that 'normally' they would have risen by 40 000, but in fact they have only risen by 20 000 so the seasonally adjusted figure has fallen by 20 000. Have a guess which one the government publicises.

2.13 Short Run and Long Run

Economists frequently use the terms 'short run' and 'long run' and generally use them with the meaning applied by Alfred Marshall (1842–1924) to whom we owe much economic terminology. (Efforts to modernise some of it have not been very successful.)

- The short run, in the context of the theory of supply is the time period in which output can be expanded using the existing variable factors (usually labour and raw materials) but the fixed factors (usually plant and machinery) cannot be changed. The time period will vary from industry to industry – it may be a second or so for packets of cornflakes off a production line but may be many years for a power station.

- The long run is the time period when all the factors of production can be altered within the existing technological framework.

- In the very long run, according to Marshall's terminology, the type of technology can also be completely altered. An example of this might be the shift from valves to transistors for most applications. A historical example was the sudden replacement of the guano trade from South America where bird droppings were loaded into (very smelly) ships and sent as nitrate fertiliser to European countries, by the new technology of fixing nitrogen from the atmosphere. As an interesting quirk of economics the price of nitrates has risen so much that guano shipping has began again in earnest.

Note: The distinction between long run and very long run has become increasingly academic as technology alters so quickly. Much depends on your definition of 'existing technological framework'.

2.14 Time Lags

Much simple economic analysis assumes an almost instantaneous series of reactions, rather like the Newton's cradle beloved of physicists where the suspended ball bearings, when one is swung, react instantly along the line hitting one another with immediate effect until the last one moves the same amount as the first. The results of this experiment are immediate and predictable. Economics is not capable of such prediction because so many things change between one economic event and subsequent happenings. It is sometimes very hard to pin down cause and effect. One reason for this is the existence of time lags between, for example, changes in demand and the consequent changes in supply, if any. In the government sector there are often very long intervals between tax changes and any impact on the economy. Most economic textbooks, including this one, say little about the implications of time lags, partly because it is not easy to convey the effects without a distinctively mathematical approach, but the reader should be constantly on the watch for situations in which they are important.

3 Underlying Economic Forces

Aims of the chapter

To explain:

● the forces which underlie the **demand** for goods, services and productive resources, land, labour and capital;

● the forces which underlie the **supply** of goods, services and productive resources.

3.1 Population

It is a truism that if there were no people there would be no economic problem. Human beings create a demand for goods, services and resources. The nature of this demand depends on the size, age, sex and geographical distribution of the population as well as upon its income, propensity to consume and its tastes and preferences. Many of the economic developments of history have been driven by population changes in terms of its absolute size and its rate of growth. Most of the early shifts of peoples were caused by population growth exceeding the capacity of existing indigenous resources to feed the extra numbers. Land hunger, assisted by political and religious persecution, augmented by the feeling 'the grass is greener on the other side of the hedge' has contributed to all major migrations. Some of these migrations have been spectacular in extent and distance travelled; others have been a simple nibbling away at the fringes of the existing cultivated area – a movement into forests, mountains and dry lands.

Thus, at its simplest level, a given population represents a given demand for food, shelter, clothing and energy. Dynamic effects arise as the population changes, particularly if its rate of growth alters. At a deeper level in modern society a population, depending on its level of income, represents a demand for a vast range of goods and services both home produced and imported.

Modern society is organised to make it possible to store production and to delay consumption. Time lags may develop between population movements, alterations of income and output and changes in final consumption. The best examples lie in the postponement of current consumption in order to enjoy a pension at a later date. In this context a rise in the birth rate may create an increased burden on society sixty or more years later. Figure 3.1 illustrates the effects of an ageing population on government budgets.

Exercise I

Explain why birth rate changes are regarded as the dynamic element in population growth?

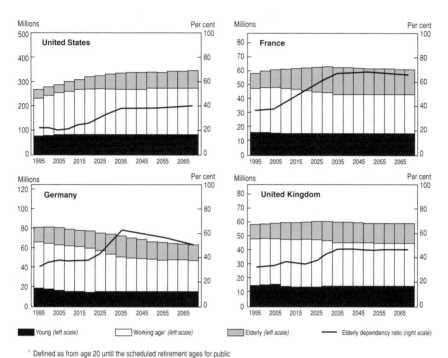

¹ Defined as from age 20 until the scheduled retirement ages for public pensions in each country

Source: The OECD Observer No. 200, June/July 1996, Paris, OECD.

Figure 3.1   Population projections and elderly dependency ratios, 1995–2070

3.2   Factors Underlying Population Change

There are three principal factors but, of course, there are many reasons why each of these may change:

- **Birth rate** – number of live births per thousand of total population, usually per year.
- **Death rate** – number of deaths per thousand of total population, usually per year.

- **Balance of migration** – number of emigrants minus number of immigrants. The number may be positive or negative.
  Figure 3.2 gives figures for the United Kingdom for births and deaths.

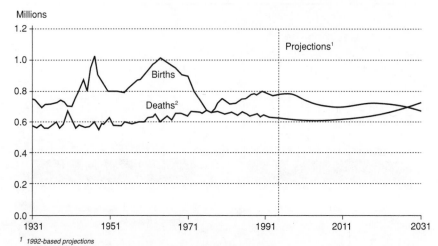

Millions

Source: CSO, *Social Trends*, London, HMSO, 1996.

Figure 3.2   Births and deaths, United Kingdom

Changes in birth rates

Birth rate changes are the most dynamic element in population growth and decline. For example, in Great Britain in 1956 there were 796 000 live births; by 1966 this had risen to 946 000, an increase of 18.8 per cent. On this basis experts were predicting a total population for the UK of 72 million by the year 2000. After 1966 the birth rate fell steadily until 1982 when it was 12.8 per thousand. In 1996 the total UK population is, in fact, just over 58 million, far short of the predictions. An upsurge of the birth rate is like a tidal bore moving up a river over time, creating increased demand on resources, providing extra labour, extra births and finally more demand for elderly care services.

The causes of changes in the birth rate are many and no-one knows for certain what particular mixture is working at a given time. If we acknowledge that human beings seem to have known how to limit their reproduction since ancient Egyptian and Biblical times, the following are possible reasons:

- Increased optimism and pessimism for the future. These are affected by economic and political events and climates such as the onset or end of war and recessions.

- The arrival at child-bearing age of a smaller/larger cohort of women.

- Altered costs/burdens of having children. For example, the introduction of compulsory education in the UK after 1870 made children a financial burden rather than a benefit.

- Changed attitudes to, or availability of, contraception and abortion.

- The age of marriage. When this falls women tend to have more children over their child-bearing life.

- Changes in income. The poor and disadvantaged tend to have more children, a fact that tends to keep them poorer. A few of the better off indulge themselves by having large families but traditionally the very rich avoided having too many children because of the system of primogeniture which left the children other than the first-born male potentially unprovided for. Moreover, having too many female children was a burden in terms of the provision of dowries.

- 'Fashion' which is a shorthand way of saying that we do not really know but there may be mixed reasons for a change in attitude to family size. Did the Queen having four children affect the UK birth rate? One sincerely hopes not.

Changes in death rates

Death rates in the United Kingdom fell rapidly after 1870 until the 1920s. Since then there have been only marginal declines accompanying the sharp fluctuations caused by bad winters. Infant mortality rates have continued to decline overall although not on a uniform basis for every region or social class. Life expectancy has continued to rise for both males and females. One of the less desirable features of the recessions since 1980 has been the rise in death rates in some regions among the poor, especially among young males. Raised suicide rates have contributed to this. As a generalisation, the rich have got richer and healthier and the poor have become poorer and less healthy. This reflects different diets and smoking habits as well as housing conditions. A study of patterns and causes of death in the UK shows that death rates are much less significant than birth rates in affecting rates of change of total population.

Factors underlying declining death rates include:

- Improved diet and living conditions, including housing;
- Better antenatal and maternity care;
- Higher quality public health provision – clean water supplies and good sanitation. This is probably the most important factor;
- Better medical care, especially preventative medicine such as vaccination;
- Better health and safety regulations which affect accident rates;
- Absence of war. Participation in wars raises death rates, especially among young males.

There tends to be an excessive concentration on improvements in medicine and in medical technology when discussing death rates. Although such improvements have extended life expectancy the main contributor was the late Victorian obsession with clean water, sanitation and disinfectants.

Changes in the balance of migration

Emigration. There are two main economic elements affecting emigration, first the 'pull' and secondly the 'push'. People are 'pulled' by the hope of better conditions abroad and 'pushed' by poor conditions such as unemployment at home. In general the pull factor is considered to be more important because times need to have been fairly good for people to save enough to afford to migrate. However the memory of the last recession may persuade people to go once they have saved enough in the following growth period.

The days of unimpeded migration have disappeared, beginning with the USA imposing immigration quotas in 1924. Many countries followed suit. Since 1989 the European Union has been establishing a common visa policy to control both economic and political migration.

Immigration. Until the late 1950s most immigrants into the UK were from Ireland or were refugees from various persecutions in Central and Eastern Europe. In the mid-1950s the United Kingdom's relatively relaxed controls permitted employers to recruit from the West Indies and the Indian subcontinent. Since 1970 various pieces of legislation have severely restricted immigration into the UK. Some emigrants are people who were immigrants and who are now re-emigrating, for example to Canada or back to the West Indies. Most of the evidence, contrary to the popular saloon bar wisdom, indicated that immigrants contribute more to the economy than they take.

3.3   The Labour Force

It is obvious that changes in the structure of population affect the size and make-up of the potential working population but there are many other influences as well:

- Retirement ages;
- The trend to earlier retirement;
- The age levels for compulsory education;
- The percentage remaining in higher education;
- The percentage of women working.

Not everyone who is in the potential labour force, that is who is not a dependent (retired, in education or a child), is willing to work because certain influences make work an irrational option to choose. These are:

- The 'poverty trap' where it is possible to receive a lower net income from employment than was obtained while unemployed. This situation arises, though less in 1996 than in the past, because of the existence of means tested benefits and rebates and because of the low income tax threshold;

- The nature and structure of the social security system which may delay or even deter the effort to seek work;

- The extremely low rates of pay available in many jobs, especially those requiring little training;

- The poor job security of many low paid jobs. There is also competition from school students who are willing to work on a part-time basis in these jobs. The supply of workers is very elastic into such occupations;

- Many of the jobs available are only part time and are not a sensible proposition for a person attempting to bring up a family, especially given the existence of the poverty trap.

As the economy develops, employment patterns change. Some of the trends are shown in Table 3.1 and Table 3.2.

Exercise 2

Is the trend towards early retirement beneficial to the economy? Draw up a list of points for and against.

Table 3.1   Labour force by age: Great Britain (thousands)

	16–24	25–44	45–59	60–64	65 and over	All aged 16 and over
Estimates						
1984	6214	12 201	7077	1252	429	27 172
1986	6326	12 788	6968	1083	402	27 566
1991	5684	14 256	7311	1102	462	28 815
1992	5224	14 192	7596	1069	501	28 582
1993	4941	14 258	7742	1070	443	28 454
1994	4710	14 301	7922	1051	437	28 421
Projections						
1996	4404	14 609	8227	1049	429	28 717
2001	4313	14 893	8748	1105	409	29 469
2006	4519	14 609	9252	1295	416	30 092

Source: Labour Force Survey, CSO: *Social Trends,* **26,** London, HMSO, 1996.

Table 3.2a   Employment by sector of activity in 1983[1] and 1992

		EUR 12		USA		Japan	
		1000	%	1000	%	1000	%
Total	1983	122 000	100	100 834	100	57 330	100
	1992	140 241	100	117 598	100	64 360	100
Agriculture	1983	11 230	9.2	3541	3.5	5310	9.3
	1992	8128	5.8	3383	2.9	4110	6.4
Industry	1983	43 352	35.5	28 253	28.0	19 930	34.8
	1992	45 743	32.7	28 950	24.6	22 270	34.6
Services	1983	67 418	55.3	69 037	68.5	32 080	56.0
	1992	85 852	61.4	85 249	72.5	37 980	59.0

[1]1983: Germany: Länder of the former Federal Republic

Table 3.2b   Share of the economic sectors in employment in 1992

	Agriculture		Industry		Services		Total	
	1000	%	1000	%	1000	%	1000	%
Europe15	8705	5.8	48 718	32.6	92 205	61.6	149 628	100
Belgium	109	2.9	1164	30.9	2498	66.2	3770	100
Denmark	136	5.2	715	27.2	1780	67.7	2637	100
Germany	1368	3.7	14 273	39.1	20 887	57.2	36 528	100
Greece	804	21.9	933	25.4	1942	52.8	3680	100
Spain	1257	10.1	4075	32.7	7126	57.2	12 458	100
France	1301	5.9	6497	29.6	14 187	64.5	22 021	100
Ireland	157	13.7	322	28.1	667	58.2	1149	100
Italy	1657	7.9	6962	33.1	12 396	59.0	21 015	100
Luxembourg	5	3.3	47	29.5	107	67.1	165	100
Netherlands	247	3.9	1571	24.9	4503	71.2	6614	100
Austria[1]	250	7.1	1261	35.5	2036	57.4	3547	100
Portugal	517	11.5	1468	32.6	2523	56.0	4509	100
Finland	187	8.6	602	27.7	1382	63.7	2171	100
Sweden	140	3.3	1112	26.5	2935	69.9	4195	100
United Kingdom	569	2.2	7715	30.2	17 237	67.5	25 630	100

[1] The data cover only persons who normally work at least 12 hours per week

Source: Eurostat, *Europe in Figures*, Luxembourg, Office for Official Statistics of the European Communities, 1995.

3.4   The Quality of the Labour Force

In modern economies the quality of the labour force is of greater importance than sheer numbers. It is essential, therefore, to maintain the levels of education, training and skill of the workforce and to ensure that they are appropriate to the needs of the time and of the future in so far as that can be forecast. Most people since 1870 in the United Kingdom have accepted the role of the state in providing, through taxation, minimum levels of education. There used to be, until 1979, a similar consensus about the state financing most of higher education but there has been a shift of government emphasis towards student loans and to private funding.

In the field of training it is natural that the greatest burden should be on employers but that is not fairly shared if only a few firms in an industry (usually the large ones) have full training programmes while the other firms rely on 'poaching' for their own recruitment. That represents an unfair subsidy from the virtuous to the bad. There have been various government attempts, such as the Industrial Training Boards (ITB) to attack this problem and they were reasonably effective until the 1980s' passion for deregulation of labour markets swept many of them away. It is very hard to follow the twists and turns of UK Government policy towards training because it has changed so often. The general allegation, however, is that in the United Kingdom training is inferior to that of its major competitors. Indeed, in 1996, German and Japanese firms with plants in the UK were discreetly saying that the level of skills of their workers here, derived from their basic education, was not high enough. It is argued that in the UK, when a recession begins to bite, the first saving to be made is in the training budget and the second is in R&D. Other countries are credited with increasing both so that they are prepared for the emergence from the recession.

The total supply of labour is also affected by the hours of work that are provided. The United Kingdom work force has the dubious distinction of working longer hours than any of those in the European Union; indeed UK hours of work have risen while those of other nations have been falling.

Tables 3.3 and 3.4 indicate the degree of training of the United Kingdom and other countries' workforce.

Exercise 3

The UK has had lower growth than most of its main competitors in recent decades. Consult Table 23.2. How, in the light of this information, do you explain the fact that the UK workforce works significantly longer hours than its competitors?

Table 3.3 **Proportion of employees receiving job related training: by gender and age, UK**

	1986 %	1991 %	1992 %	1993 %	1994 %	1995 %
Males						
16–29	18.1	20.3	19.5	19.2	19.5	18.1
30–64	8.0	11.8	11.9	12.0	12.8	11.6
All males aged 16 to 64	11.4	14.7	14.3	14.3	14.9	13.6
Females						
16–29	14.6	17.9	18.2	18.6	21.1	18.0
30–64	7.2	13.3	13.1	13.4	14.1	13.6
All females aged 16 to 64	9.9	14.9	14.9	15.1	16.3	15.0

[1] At spring each year

Source: CSO, *Social Trends,* **26**, London, HMSO, 1996.

Table 3.4 **Average hours usually worked[1] per week, EC comparison, 1994**

	Males			Females		
	Full time	Part time	All	Full time	Part time	All
United Kingdom	45.4	16.0	43.5	40.4	17.9	30.6
Portugal	42.7	26.3	42.4	39.3	20.2	37.9
Greece	41.4	25.6	41.0	39.0	21.5	38.0
Irish Republic	41.6	21.2	40.6	37.8	18.0	33.9
Spain	41.0	19.6	40.6	39.5	17.5	36.3
Luxembourg	40.6	26.7	40.5	37.9	19.7	34.3
France	40.6	22.5	39.8	38.8	22.4	34.2
Italy	39.7	30.1	39.5	36.3	23.0	34.7
Germany	39.9	18.9	39.3	39.2	20.2	33.0
Belgium	38.8	21.1	38.3	36.9	20.9	31.9
Denmark	39.8	14.2	37.1	38.0	21.2	32.0
Netherlands	39.6	18.6	36.3	39.1	17.9	25.2
EC average	41.1	19.5	40.2	38.9	19.7	32.8

[1] Employees only. Excludes meal breaks but includes paid and unpaid overtime.

Source: CSO, *Social Trends,* **26,** London, HMSO, 1996.

3.5   **Land and Natural Resources**

The traditional classification of land as a factor of production extends its meaning beyond that of land in its everyday sense to include natural resources such as mineral deposits, natural forests, rivers, lakes and products of the sea. Almost all land in the developed world has been improved or altered by the addition of capital, such as drainage, fencing, landscaping, building or exploitation. As population pressure has grown there has been a constant modification of land in order to maximise its potential. International trade can, to a large extent, compensate a country for deficiencies in its natural resources provided that it exploits a comparative advantage in other spheres such as financial services or manufacturing. Japan, for example, has relatively poor natural resources and is short of utilisable land but compensates by importing raw materials and energy. It pays for these imports by exporting a great variety of goods and services produced by exploiting its greatest resources, the skill and energy of its workforce. Other countries sell their natural resources in order to buy foreign consumer durable and capital goods. Some, like the USA, are very well endowed with natural resources and have appeared to be extremely profligate in their use. The growth of the environmental movement is partly the result of this extravagance.

If we simply look at the use and availability of land it is obvious that there is a big difference between the area of land in a country and the amount available for use. Table 3.5 shows statistics for Utilisable Agricultural Land (UAL) in the European Union.

Table 3.5   **Breakdown of the territory of the European Union (million hectares)**

	EUR 12 12 237
Utilized agriculture area (UAA)	128
Forest	61
UAA	
Arable land	70
Permanent pasture	46
Permanent crops	12
Other purposes	48

Source: Eurostat, *Europe in Figures*, 4th edn, Luxembourg, Office for Official Statistics of the European Communities, 1995.

3.6   **Capital**

Capital is another of the words that have a specific meaning in economics different from that in everyday speech. In economics, capital means the stock of goods which is used to produce other goods and services, so it is a collection of physical assets. There may be **fixed capital** such as buildings, machinery and plant, or **circulating capital** which is such things as raw materials in the process of being manufactured, semi-manufactured goods and components. In everyday speech capital usually means money capital. There are two important aspects of capital that should be borne in mind:

1. Capital is created by abstaining from consumption, that is we have to save so that productive resources are available to build, for example, an oil refinery rather than produce personal stereos. The creation of capital goods, therefore, involves an opportunity cost. In Soviet-style command economies the state decided on the balance of output between capital and consumption goods.

2. Capital goods deteriorate, or depreciate over time and may have to be replaced. This process of depreciation or 'capital consumption' gives the opportunity to either destroy, replace or upgrade existing plants with new technology.

The process of creating capital goods is called *investment expenditure*. This helps to increase the productivity of the other factors, land and labour. There is another concept, that of *human capital* which is improved by investment in education and training.

3.7   **Capital Widening and Deepening**

Capital widening occurs when the input of capital is increased at the same rate as the increase in the input of labour so that the proportion of capital to labour remains constant.

Capital deepening occurs when the increase in the input of capital is at a higher rate than that of labour so that the ratio of capital to labour rises. Capital deepening is needed if higher rates of economic growth are to be achieved.

3.8   **General Points about Capital**

- The money (savings) for capital creation comes from the retained profits of companies, from individuals' savings and from government surpluses (if any).

- The level of investment in new physical assets is heavily influenced by expectations of future profits and levels of current and expected interest rates.

- Entrepreneurs may shift their expenditure (investment) on new physical assets from country to country in pursuit of the highest returns, given the constraints of security. The so-called globalisation of the world economy has seen huge sums of money transferred around the world for investment in factories, plant and buildings.

- While investment in economics means expenditure on physical assets for the production of goods and services, in everyday use it may also mean the purchase of financial assets such as stocks and shares. This different usage is a source of confusion to students who do not make the distinction clearly.

- Government policy on taxation of capital gains and inheritance may have a significant influence on the growth of capital and on investment expenditure.

Exercise 4

Analyse the effects that the discovery and development of North Sea oil and gas may have had upon the capital widening and deepening of the United Kingdom's economy?

3.9   Enterprise

- A country with few natural resources may still be rich if its inhabitants show a high degree of enterprise or organisational skill, for example Switzerland and Singapore. Economists refer to the entrepreneur as the person who bears the risk of the enterprise and who organises the combination of the other factors of production in order to maximise their efficient use. The reward of the entrepreneur is profit.

- In a one-person business it is obvious who the entrepreneur is. In public companies the risk takers, entrepreneurs, are the shareholders who stand to lose their money if the company collapses.

- In most public companies the owners (shareholders) do not in practice control the company. There is what is called a 'divorce of ownership from control' because the managers/directors usually have relatively few shares but do control the company subject to what is usually ineffective shareholder control at company annual general meetings. Institutional investors such as pension funds who hold large numbers of shares have tended to avoid involvement in controlling boards of directors.

● Enterprise has become something of a buzzword since 1980 and features prominently in government pronouncements and policies. A whole set of beliefs has grown up around the idea of small and medium-sized enterprises (SME) both in the United Kingdom and the European Union. It has become fashionable to believe that the UK should try to emulate the so-called enterprise economies of South East Asia, Singapore, Malaysia, Taiwan and South Korea. Such a transplantation of methods from such different economies and cultures is unlikely to be successful.

3.10 **Summary**

● A major long-term determinant of economic change is population movement, geographically, in size, in proportion of males to females, in age distribution and in rates of growth or decline. In addition, there are changes in real income and its distribution, in preferences, fashion and in relative prices of substitutes and complements that shift demand patterns.

● On the supply side, the population changes referred to above have an important impact on the make-up of the labour force. In addition, technological change, movements of investment in real physical assets and progress in education and training, alter patterns of production and the location of industry and commerce. Government policies, which are dealt with in the next chapter, help to set the framework within which these forces of demand and supply operate.

● Changes in the allocation of resources from one use to another reflect these shifting patterns of demand, supply, expected profits and government policy.

4 The Role of Governments

Aims of the chapter

To:

- outline universally accepted functions of the state;
- indicate how the perception of the role of the state may change;
- show what tools or instruments a state may use to reach its policy objectives;
- show that policies are often unsuccessful or have unforeseen effects.

4.1   The Role of the State 1914–18

The First World War saw an enormous expansion of the role of the state. Huge sums were borrowed, steep rises in taxation were levied, property was requisitioned, conscription became the norm, labour was directed and businesses were controlled. The end of the war saw a return to normality in many areas but there had been created in the public mind the idea that the state could and should intervene in certain areas. Thus, in the United Kingdom, the state began in the 1920s to provide housing. The main pressure for increased state intervention came, however, from the Great Depression from 1929–1933 when unemployment reached unprecedented levels. The governing classes began to fear that conditions were ripe for Bolshevik revolution. Governments acted to try to resolve the financial crisis of 1931 and retreated into fierce trade protectionism – 'beggar my neighbour' policies. Despite the cries for the state to do something about unemployment successive governments steadfastly denied that it was their responsibility, or within their capability, to raise levels of employment. They expected the trade cycle to swing back up and resolve the problem. Others believed that free market capitalism had a fatal flaw and their view was backed by the theoretical work of J. M. Keynes who published his *General Theory of Employment, Money and Interest* in 1937. He established that the economy could reach an equilibrium with high levels of unemployment which would persist unless the government took counter cyclical action.

The United Kingdom government did very little to combat unemployment in the 1930s and some of its policies probably aggravated it. Rearmament and the war proved the better solution. Other countries tried national socialism and varieties of authoritarianism. The USA applied Roosevelt's New Deal after 1934 but its effects are debatable.

4.2   **The State Since 1945**

The broad consensus of opinion after 1945 until, say, 1970, was that the state had a more extensive role than pre-1939. In most European non-communist states, there was a great extension of state ownership of industry, transport and commerce. Most governments created welfare systems to provide free or cheap health, pension and social security for its citizens. Taxation and government borrowing tended to rise and the state accounted for a growing percentage of Gross Domestic Product. In 1910, UK Government spending as a proportion of GNP at factor cost was about 12 per cent. It rose to about 30 per cent in the early 1930s and to 40 per cent in the early 1950s. By the mid-1970s it had risen to over 51 per cent. In the 1980s, as a percentage of GDP at market prices it gradually fell from 47.4 per cent in 1982–93 to a low point of 39 per cent in 1988–89 but has again risen to about 44 per cent in 1994–95.

The prevailing economic philosophy was Keynesian in approach. In the United Kingdom the government had, in 1944, accepted responsibility for the maintenance of full employment. In the USA the federal government and budget expanded dramatically. Most governments regulated their financial sector stringently and subscribed to the new world organisations, the United Nations, the International Monetary Fund and the International Bank for Reconstruction and Development (IBRD). They, as a matter of course, fixed their foreign exchange rates and pursued domestic policies to maintain the fixed parities.

It may be said fairly that the post-war Keynesian consensus worked well, with some local problems, until the late 1960s. The fluctuations of the trade cycle were minor; most developed states had near full employment and moderate inflation.

Exercise 1

How would you try, objectively, to decide if the role of the State was too great in the United Kingdom? What measures would you use?

4.3   **Post-1945 Challenges to the Role of the State**

Full employment generated a degree of complacency among politicians and Keynesian techniques of demand management began to be used in some countries such as the United Kingdom to manipulate the economy for electoral purposes. Unreal expectations began to develop concerning the power of the state to control growth, prosperity and inflation. Gradually,

GOVERNMENT FAILURE

Market failure is used to justify some types of government intervention in markets but such actions may actually make things worse or throw up a different set of problems. Government intervention may not improve the allocative efficiency of the economy. Examples of government failure include:

- labour market policies that reduce the mobility of workers, for example the poverty trap whereby workers are deterred from accepting low paid work because they will lose more in means tested benefits than they gain in wages.
- taxation policies which encourage the wasteful use of resources or divert investment from one use to another in an arbitrary manner or which discourage work and saving.
- market interventions to control price such as the Common Agricultural Policy, rent controls and the regulation of privatised utilities. These may all make matters worse rather than better.
- subsidies may initially improve allocative efficiency but may degenerate into market distortions.
- macroeconomic policies may be so badly planned, timed and executed as to exaggerate undesirable trends in the economy rather than to counteract them.

Consider the UK housing market:
1. Does the existence of tax relief on some mortgage interest payments distort the market?
2. Does a system of rent control constitute government failure or is it necessary because of market failure?
3. Is the provision of 'social housing' by local authorities and others contributing to government failure or effectively redressing market failure?
4. In which area in recent times do you consider there has been the greatest evidence of government failure in the UK?

criticisms developed of some of the inefficiencies of centralised control and public ownership. Uncertainty developed as world problems arose and were not tackled effectively. Population rose rapidly; trade expanded; there was a shortage of international liquidity (money); wars such as that in Vietnam placed great strains on the world economies; the IMF system of managed exchange rates began to fail. Some responded by advocating greater co-ordination of national policies and more controls. Others began to advocate the adoption of free market approaches and a reversion to earlier, pre-Keynesian economic principles. By the mid-1970s there were strong voices in the USA, the UK and some continental European countries supporting a re-emphasis upon monetary controls and the abandonment of budget deficit policies. They advocated balanced government budgets, reduced levels of personal taxation and a pushing back of the boundaries of state intervention. In the United Kingdom this was eventually translated into campaigns to sell off state-owned assets (privatisation) and to deregulate certain areas of industry such as transport. Attempts were also made to liberalise financial markets and to decontrol labour markets. There developed an emphasis on 'competition' as a solution to economic problems. But by 1985 full-blooded monetarism was an intellectual dead duck.

By 1996 United Kingdom government policy had become a single-minded concentration on maintaining a level of inflation between a target range. In pursuit of this aim, public expenditure was curtailed, borrowing was to be reduced and more publicly owned assets were to be sold. In the background attempts were made to keep the pressure on interest rates downwards although alterations in interest rates was one of the few weapons left to the Government.

It is ironic that these attempts at deregulation and increased competition have been accompanied by the creation of an extensive range of regulatory bodies to control the newly privatised industries – OFWAT, OFTEL, OFGAS and so on. The government can use these as a buffer to shelter behind and as a means of distancing itself from public criticism but it has found it very hard to resist the persistent public pressure that 'the government should do something' whenever criticism emerges.

4.4   The Retreat from the Welfare State

The post-1945 consensus accepted that the state had a major role in providing for the welfare needs of its citizens in education, housing, health care, social security and pensions. To begin with the idealists thought that these should be free and universally available but some, such as pensions were always partly paid for by contributions. Others became means tested. Some services such as health and education were provided by private suppliers for those who could afford them. By 1996 the dominating Government philosophy was that of providing a social security safety net for those most disadvantaged. More and more people were excluded from its coverage. The state had also largely withdrawn from the provision of new housing for all but a small minority of elderly and special needs cases. There had also been a significant shift towards private pension provision. The state provision of health had been transformed into what is called a 'quasi-market'. Attempts were being made to introduce market forces and customer/provider relationships into education by the introduction of vouchers for nursery places. Almost all central and local government services were affected by Compulsory Competitive Tendering and many central government functions were hived off into agencies. In many ways it appeared as if the state had withdrawn from direct involvement in many functions but in practice indirect control remained via ministers and quangos. Democratic control and supervision suffered.

Exercise 2

(a) Why were early post-war Labour governments so keen on nationalisation?
(b) Why were post-1979 Conservative governments so keen on privatisation?

4.5   Instruments which the State May Use

Direct controls

1. The legal framework for civil and criminal law, plus the system of courts and tribunals.

2. Regulations – health and safety, supervision, minimum standards, procedures. Most of these may be changed by ministers using delegated powers. The regulations pervade our lives, for example regulations to control who can install and maintain gas appliances.

3. Licensing and prohibitions – many of these are exercised via local authorities but some, such as arms export licences, are directly controlled by government departments. Examples are pubs, clubs, taxis, abattoirs.

4. Financial and banking regulations – these control many operations in financial markets. They included strict controls over foreign exchange transactions in the United Kingdom until 1979.

5. Many customer protection laws and regulations.

6. Regulatory bodies such as OFGAS, OFWAT, OFTEL, and so on. They attempt to expand competition and control price structures.

7. Approval of schemes and inspection. Central and local government have a great apparatus to control buildings and development. They also inspect and approve a wide range of commercial activities.

8. European Union legislation may impose similar controls on some areas of business, for example, in agriculture, the labour market, trade.

9. International Agreements often fix standards, for example, in airline and maritime operations.

Fiscal policy

'Fiscal' technically means relating to taxes but it has come loosely to mean 'relating to government taxing *and* spending'. It is possible to try and make the tax structure neutral in its effects – that is, no-one buys, sells or behaves differently because of the existence of a tax. This is an impossible dream and fails to utilise taxes to achieve desirable goals. At the other extreme some people wish to use taxation to deter the consumption of demerit goods such as tobacco or private cars and to encourage, through tax relief, the consumption of merit goods such as education and whatever else they choose to define as a merit good, for example, mortgages on private housing, private pensions and unleaded petrol. Activists in the field of taxation would like to use taxes to redistribute income, to encourage investment, to stimulate savings, to help the aged and disadvantaged. The list is endless and we could all draw up our own favourites. Unfortunately for these enthusiasts such policies tend to produce additional bureaucracy and anomalies. The main beneficiaries are often the accountants who specialise in tax advice.

Politicians often give the impression that tax changes can be immediately effective but the truth is that most changes are implemented very slowly and with considerable time lags. New taxes in particular require a long lead-in time in order to educate the public and businesses. A few taxes may be changed with effect from 6 pm on the day of a budget but even some of these such as changed VAT will only apply as retailers purchase new stocks.

Since 1979, in the United Kingdom, there has been a significant shift of emphasis away from taxes on income towards taxes on expenditure. Taxes on income and capital have been reduced on the assumption that lower taxes will encourage work and enterprise. Taxes on expenditure have been raised and extended on the flimsy reasoning that we can choose whether or not to spend our money and on what. The overall effect of these changes has been to make the top decile of income receivers much better off after tax and the bottom decile much worse off. Everyone else has much the same average tax burden as before. The advocates of these changes assume that the rich will work harder if their taxes are cut but that low income recipients work harder if their pay rates are cut.

Many taxes need to be adjusted annually in order to compensate for inflation. This applied to such income tax allowances as still exist. The married allowance, for example, must be raised regularly to maintain its benefit in relation to incomes. Taxes on goods such as alcohol and tobacco have to be raised if it is desired to prevent them becoming cheaper in real terms. A government can adopt a more relaxed approach to taxation if the economy is expanding and unemployment is low. In contrast it suffers severe constraints if unemployment is rising or high because its tax revenues stagnate and its expenditure on social security benefits rise. One would normally expect a government to follow a full employment policy out of a measure of self-preservation.

Exercise 3

Attempt an *economic* judgement on whether redistribution of income and wealth is likely to be beneficial to the United Kingdom.

There are other constraints on the UK Government's powers in that it has agreed to European Union policies on VAT approximation and on import duties. The EU single market also restricts the likelihood of United Kingdom taxes, especially on companies, becoming too out of step with the European average, because capital and enterprise would tend to locate where taxes are lowest.

The phrase 'budgetary policy' used to incorporate both government revenue (taxation) and expenditure but many people now use 'fiscal' instead of 'budgetary'. On the expenditure side of government policy there are again polarised views. The trend of the 1980s in the USA on the Republican side and in the UK on the Conservative side was to view public expenditure as something that should be minimised. This trend has continued within both groups into the late 1990s. They argue that it should be reduced in order to help achieve a balanced budget but many take the view, with echoes from George Orwell, that 'state spending is bad; private spending is good'. They seem keen to reduce public spending on defence and security and even there some seem keen on private security firms running prisons and providing police services. They also advocate the armed forces using private contractors to, for example, service vehicles and aircraft. Rather reluctantly they are willing to put in place a 'safety net ' for the disadvantaged.

Against this extreme, but fairly popular, view there remain many who favour a version of the Keynesian version of public expenditure and taxation. This is that governments should deliberately unbalance budgets in order to influence macro-economic levels of demand, investment, saving and consumption. In practice many governments, for example Japan from 1990 to 1996, have used policies of increased expenditure to raise demand and employment. This concept of counter-cyclical policy is dealt with in Chapters 22 and 23. Government spending is a very powerful tool in influencing the economy. If used wisely, and not for party benefit in the electoral cycle, it can help maintain and improve the country's infrastructure, its regional balance and specific industries. Its greatest benefit, however, would be to maintain high levels of employment and prosperity.

Exercise 4

On what basis could you try to judge if the shift in the 1980s from direct taxes on income to indirect taxes on spending is economically justifiable?

Monetary policy

Monetary policy has two main elements.

The first is the attempt to influence the demand for money by altering its price, that is the level of interest rates. Modern experience shows that with the liberalisation of international capital movements and the globalisation of financial markets, an individual country cannot prevail for long against international market forces in its level of interest rates. Some countries, notably Germany and Japan, can exercise a powerful influence over their internal rates because of their strong economies. The USA has considerable influence because of the sheer size of its economy and financial sector and its international importance. Other countries such as the United Kingdom have some degree of control over the timing of interest rate changes but tend to be swept along by the international tide. United Kingdom interest rates tend to be about 2 per cent above Germany's because of the greater degree of fluctuation of the value of the pound on international markets compared with the Deutschmark which benefits from greater stability because it is in the Exchange Rate Mechanism of the European Union. There is, of course, a wide range of interest rates in a country. The differences reflect levels of perceived risk in lending, the loss of liquidity, the length of the loan and the credit rating of the borrower. Another important influence is the existing level of inflation and expectations of future inflation.

The second main element of monetary policy may consist of an attempt to control the quantity of money. The quantity of money is subject to many practical measurements, usually with quaint names that make them sound like motorways – M0, M1, M2, M3 £M3, M4, PSLR2. Each measurement, as it was adopted, reflected the view that the monetary authorities could control what they could measure. They discovered, to our cost, that once they named one measure as a target figure in order to control it, banks, financial dealers and ordinary people switched their funds or developed new methods of creating credit. Latterly the monetary authorities simply 'monitor', that is observe, the range of selected indicators such as M0 and M4, that is narrow money and broad money. This subject is dealt with in Chapter 20.

At this stage you will be making considerable progress if you realise that 'money' is far more than the notes and coins in circulation. It includes also what are in effect, computer records of bank and building society and other institutional deposits. If we all went to our banks and building societies and other savings institutions to draw out all our deposits in cash ('a run on the banks') they would quickly be unable to pay and would shut their doors. If, however, they are well managed institutions they would be able to pay eventually as they realised their assets. This might take twenty years depending on their liquidity.

In practice, efforts to control the quantity of money have usually consisted of attempts to control the expansion of bank deposits. Incidentally, the monetary authorities have frequently had to extend the net of institutions included in the definition of 'bank'.

The methods which *may* be applied constitute a sort of 'elephants graveyard'. Some worked well for a limited period in the circumstances of the time. Some were slow to work and had unforeseen effects. Others were regarded with great hostility because they applied to only a few institutions. Most came and went with the economic and electoral cycle and most reflected what was, at that time, fashionable views of monetary policy. The following is a rough classification of the methods. A full list is given in Chapter 20.

The monetary authorities (Treasury and Bank of England) **fixed certain ratios** that banks had to stick to – for example cash and liquidity ratios and a minimum reserve assets ratio. The most recent one, which is not a form of control ratio, is a requirement to keep a small, 0.35, minimum percentage of total deposits in an account at the Bank of England. Some countries still use versions of these ratios effectively. Some methods qualify for the title 'monetary base control'.

Operations in the markets

The existence of these ratios, some of which prudent banks would have kept to in any case, gave the monetary authorities leverage over the institutions. The Bank of England could, up to a point, depending on circumstances, increase or decrease the supply of liquid assets such as Treasury Bills and short-dated and long-dated bonds to influence the ability of banks to create deposits by lending to customers. The methods are usually called Open Market Operations, that is buying and selling bills in the money markets and bonds on the stock exchange and bond markets. One version was called 'Funding' which involved large purchases of short-dated bills and bonds to remove them from the market and their replacement by the sale of long-dated bonds. The process was intended to alter the volume of liquid assets in the markets.

Physical restraints

The Bank of England had the power to control the expansion of bank deposits. Two main methods were used. They were called Special Deposits and Supplementary Deposits (called 'the corset' by the media) which were techniques for 'freezing' a percentage of bank deposits at the Bank of England so that they were not available for lending to customers.

The old chums act

The Bank of England, under the act nationalising it in 1946, can send Letters of Request or Directives to banks. In practice it has always relied on sending ordinary letters to banks asking them to observe certain policies. The banks would do so in the knowledge that if they failed then the Bank of England could send an official Letter of Request. The 'old chums' process is also followed in periods of crisis when a bank is in difficulties and the Bank of England wants to launch a 'lifeboat'.

Points to think about

The power of the monetary authorities to regulate have been greatly reduced because of:

1. The deregulation of the financial markets, the abolition of foreign exchange controls and the partial deregulation of the banking sector;

2. The influx into the United Kingdom of a large number of foreign banks, many of which have enormous deposits;

3. The existence of the so-called Maastricht criteria for Economic and Monetary Union (EMU). These lay down targets for government debt, government borrowing, inflation, and interest rates. The United Kingdom, despite its opt out from Stage 3 of monetary union which is due to start in January 1999, has been adjusting its finances to policies to meet these criteria. The line taken by Her Majesty's Treasury in 1996 is that any prudent government would follow the principles of the criteria but, in practice, the United Kingdom appears to be toeing an externally imposed line. Its power of independent decision making is limited. If Economic and Monetary Union comes about, even without the United Kingdom participating in the single currency, this constraint will be stronger. If the United Kingdom joins a single currency after 1999 its monetary policy will be determined by a European Central Bank on whose board the Bank of England will be represented as one among several others.

Conclusion

Be very wary of those who try to persuade you that monetary controls are the answer to economic problems at the macroeconomic level. Fashions in monetary theory and practice come and go and there have been bitter divisions of opinion in the United Kingdom on monetary issues since before the Bank Charter Act of 1844. At the moment the Bank of England has the ability to make limited short-term changes to interest rates and the government has some influence via its control of the public sector borrowing requirement and the issue of bills and stock. But, overall, its influence is fairly feeble when seen against the backdrop of the European Union and the global financial markets.

You should expect to see a continual reassessment over time of the role of governments as political and economic attitudes and fashions change.

5 The Business Framework

Aims of the chapter

To outline commonly used ideas and terms relating to the framework of business, especially in the United Kingdom, and to place them in a theoretical background. Specific aims are to:

● explain and describe the manufacturing base, particularly in the UK;
● explain and describe the commercial base;
● explain and describe the financial base;
● discuss the relationship between the ownership and control of firms;
● outline the economist's approach to the business framework in economic 'models'.

5.1 The Basic Structure of Industry

The term industry was once reserved for manufacturing but is now extended to any commercial activity such as the 'leisure industry', or 'service industries'. This expression of the term derives from the usual classification of economic activity into:

1. Primary industry, that is agriculture, forestry, fishing and extractive industries such as coal mining.
2. Secondary which is manufacturing, energy industries and construction.
3. Tertiary which are all forms of services – financial, personal and distributive.

Some authors, as is always the way with economics, add a fourth but this is the result of attempts to overdefine and classify tertiary into distinctive types.

As economies grow they typically move from a preponderance of primary activity, especially in agriculture, to a dominance of manufacturing and finally to a concentration on the tertiary sector. The changes are marked by alterations in employment patterns, investment expenditure and by the percentage of Gross Domestic Product derived from each sector. If we take UK GDP at factor cost:

	Primary	Secondary	Tertiary
1964	5.8	40.8	53.8
1993	3.9	28.4	67.7

There is an active debate in progress about the degree to which an economy like the UK's should run down its primary and secondary sectors and rely on services. The decline of the UK's manufacturing base in the early 1980s (often referred to as 'de-industrialisation') is unparalleled in developed economies. The decline of manufacturing was caused by a mixture of factors such as an overvalued pound, inadequate research and development, insufficient investment expenditure and a shift of UK investment abroad, and a culture which favours making money over making goods. As a result employment in manufacturing fell and output took some years to recover.

As labour was shed and new technology was adopted, labour productivity rose and wage costs often fell. The industries that survived became more competitive but their contribution to the GNP was lower. Initially it appeared as if the expanding tertiary sector would absorb the surplus labour but many manufacturing workers left employment for good and tertiary employment also stopped growing. In late 1995 and early 1996 we have the phenomenon of unemployment and employment both falling because more people have been leaving the labour force than have been registering as unemployed and claiming benefit.

Exercise 1

How do you explain the fact that in certain time periods in the UK both the number employed and the number unemployed have been falling?

Many people instinctively feel that a job in manufacturing is superior to a job in services but the economist does not take this view. What matters is the contribution to supplying demand and to the national output of goods and services. Many economists do, however, express concern at the low percentage of national income now derived from manufacturing in the UK. It can be argued, fairly convincingly, that a strong manufacturing base is the rock on which service industries depend. If it becomes too small, the tertiary sector also stagnates even if some of it expands its international market.

5.2   The Primary Sector in the United Kingdom

Agriculture – output and productivity have risen steadily since 1940 largely in response to the UK government's policies until the early 1970s when the dominant factor became the Common Agricultural Policy (CAP) of the European Union. Not all sectors of agriculture have been subject to government policies, notably poultry and pig meat, and not all sectors have grown uniformly or consistently. The numbers employed in agriculture, both full time and part time have steadily decreased as investment in new technology and techniques has enabled less labour to be used or has made up for a shortage of labour. It is not always clear which comes first, the labour scarcity or the new methods that enable labour to be substituted. As the number employed has decreased the percentage of total employment attributable to agriculture has also declined.

Agriculture remains an extremely important market for service industries, banking, leasing, contracting and for machinery, plant and construction. A stable and prosperous agricultural sector is an important basis for a healthy economy, particularly in the context of regional development and the social fabric of rural areas.

Forestry is an industry that requires a long-term approach to viability and investment. United Kingdom government policy towards forestry has vacillated since the First World War when the excessive reliance on imported timber was discovered and again after 1945 when the housing shortage highlighted the heavy dependence and high balance of payments cost of imports. More recently, environmental issues have stimulated a renewed interest in forestry. The main plank of the original policy was to operate through a publicly owned body, the Forestry Commission and to encourage the private sector with tax concessions. More recent policy since the 1980s has been to sell off Forestry Commission assets and to encourage the private sector to invest in forestry by various subsidies in the form of tax and depreciation concessions. Straightforward commercial forestry where returns need to be made as quickly as possible tends to conflict with the views of the environment lobby who would like a longer term approach that would take account of external costs and benefits. The Forestry Commission is a commercial institution but, because it is publicly owned, had been able to take a longer, more socially aware view of its own activities.

Fishing – employment in the industry has steadily declined as the number of deep sea boats has fallen. The stocks of certain types of fish have diminished, mainly because of overfishing. New technology, larger boats and the Common Fishing Policy have transformed the industry. The advent of very large 'factory' fishing vessels from Central and Eastern European countries has magnified the industry's problems. Even the protected inshore fishing vessels have suffered a severe decline in numbers, income and employment. The decline has had a significant effect on the local economies of many coastal ports and their hinterlands. These effects have been echoed throughout Europe and the east coast of Canada and the United States.

5.3   The Secondary Sector

By 1914 the main industries of the United Kingdom on which its prosperity had been based were in relative decline compared with the most efficient foreign competitors, that is coal, iron and steel, shipbuilding and cotton textiles. The years 1919–39 saw a structural decline (permanent loss of demand) for coal, cotton goods and ships. New industries developed but they were insufficient to absorb the workers displaced by structural changes. The new energy industries, electricity and the electric motor, freed industry from the tie of the coal fields and steam power and enabled it to locate in new areas, usually close to the largest markets. The new consumption goods industries, radios, vacuum cleaners, refrigerators, electric irons and so on, became relatively 'footloose' with no obvious locational imperatives. The market pull of London and the Home Counties usually dominated their decisions on location. The new energy industry, oil, was capital intensive compared with the labour intensive coal industry. The new road transport industry quickly eroded the profitability of the railways and released firms from the locational grip of proximity to the rail freight yard. In the background, throughout all the changes from 1750 was a burgeoning civil engineering and construction industry which responded flexibly to demands for housing, factories, warehouses, docks, railways, bridges, roads, water systems, gas mains, and civic buildings.

The inter-war depression, the revival of protectionism in 1931 and the policy of industrial dispersal adopted during the Second World War all had a profound effect on employment patterns and location of industry. After 1945, until the early 1980s, the State intervened in industrial location using 'carrots' and 'sticks' to persuade industry to move to where the workers were. This 'work to the workers' policy was based on sensible intentions but came in for increasing criticism. Some objected to any interference with free market forces and argued that industry was being forced away from its least cost locations. Other critics alleged that the intervention was 'too little, too late' a criticism of government policy that is nearly always correct. The policy was also seen as being under-financed and too subject to alteration. The general prosperity and low levels of unemployment until 1970 make it very hard to tell if the policy was actually working in terms of the aim of reducing regional disparities.

In the 1980s, central government funding for regional employment policies was steadily reduced and the collapse of the manufacturing sector with its rapid rise in unemployment in all regions including those previously cushioned from industrial decline, led to an effective abandonment of the 'work to the workers' approach. Restrictions on commercial and industrial development in the south and southeast and Birmingham were largely removed. Reliance was placed on general tax concessions and subsidies for new investment in certain restricted areas. The main aim became a desire to attract foreign investment, preferably in the high-tech industries. In the background is the European Union Regional Policy with which United Kingdom policy sometimes conflicts.

The current state of the United Kingdom secondary sector

It is possible to look at the United Kingdom manufacturing sector, the construction industry and the energy industries and reach the conclusion that they are now, in comparison with the late 1980s, 'fit and lean' and internationally competitive. You could choose your base carefully and detect very encouraging signs of strength and growth. It is more likely, however, that the conclusion would be reached that the secondary sector, with notable exceptions, has suffered from under-investment, too little spending on R&D, too little investment in skills and training and a damaging emphasis on short-term profits at the expense of long-term growth. Most of these observations are based on comparisons with the United Kingdom's major competitors and the judgements are founded on the assumption that the United Kingdom's manufacturing base has shrunk too much.

Exercise 2

Does the 1980s decline of UK manufacturing industry matter? If so, why? If not, why not?

5.4   The Tertiary Sector

The tertiary sector can be subdivided along the lines adopted in government statistics.

1. The first group consists of distribution, transport, communications, hotels and catering and repairs.
2. The second is banking, financial services, business services and leasing.
3. The third covers public sector administration, defence, social security, education and health and the usual statistical dustbin 'other' which employed about 2.1 million people in 1993.

The tertiary sector as a whole employed 15.7 million people in 1993 in the United Kingdom, or 73 per cent of the total of 21.6 million. Nineteen years earlier, in 1964, only 11.1 million or 48 per cent of the total of 23.4 million were in the service sector. In the same period, employment in the secondary sector fell from 47 to 25 per cent of the total and from 11 million to 5.4 million people.

The significant growth was in banking and financial services although that trend seems to be reversing in the late 1990s. Some service areas also show rapid growth, for example education and health and distribution, hotels, catering and repairs. Some showed a decline, for example, transport and communication, the latter being subject to rapid technological change that reduced the demand for labour. The various movements over the years are also symptomatic of the movements of the business cycle.

There is no intrinsic problem with the growth of the tertiary sector although some people persist in applying the old biblical judgement that people in the service sector do not produce anything, 'they toil not neither do they spin'. This is, of course, nonsense to the economist who regards the provision of services as equally important to the supply of goods. In the case of the United Kingdom, however, there is some legitimate anxiety about the decline of the relative importance of the manufacturing sector which is a base for the health of the other sectors. There is also anxiety about the extent to which the tertiary sector is dependent upon foreign income or, in the case of the public sector, on taxation to support it.

5.5   Ownership and Control

It is arguable whether it matters who owns and controls a firm. It is natural to believe that foreign owners will care less about indigenous work forces and plant and will tend to favour workers and plant in their home countries. This may not be the case, however, if the firm is genuinely multinational with locations in many countries. It may then be driven by the need to satisfy its owners, that is its shareholders, with not just adequate profits but continuously rising profits.

One feature of modern capitalism is that ownership and control often lies in different hands. The shareholders own the firm and bear the risk of the enterprise failing. Those who sit on the board of directors which makes decisions for the firm frequently own relatively few shares in the enterprise and rarely own above the 50 per cent plus one required to control the firm absolutely. The largest shareholders are often financial institutions such as pension funds or insurance companies. They have a vested interest in continuously rising profits in order to fulfil their promises to their members. It is argued that this encourages a short-term view of a company's objectives and militates against the sacrifice of short-term profit incurred by investment in R&D and training. So-called company doctors who are put in charge of an enterprise in order to turn it round from loss to profit often achieve quick results by suspending training and cutting R&D as well as sacking employees (downsizing is the modern euphemism). They also sell profitable subsidiaries in order to raise revenue and improve the books. They have usually moved on, taking their performance linked bonuses with them, before the long-term damage to the company is revealed.

Exercise 3

Look up a well-known company's annual report and consult the tables at the back which detail the Directors' share holdings in the company. Is there 'a divorce between ownership and control' in that company? (Company reports are available by telephoning the *Financial Times* at a number given on the share prices page.)

5.6   Globalisation

This is a term that has recently come to prominence. It refers mainly to financial markets where modern communications and deregulation of capital and foreign exchange movements have fostered the growth of highly interconnected and interdependent markets. Movements in economic and financial indices and interest rates in New York have an impact in Tokyo, Singapore, and other markets and in European centres such as Frankfurt, Paris or London. World time zones place London in a very favourable position in relation to New York and the Far East and partly explain its pre-eminence in some financial markets and its attractiveness for international banks.

Globalisation is a term that is also being extended to some international corporations or activities which are effectively abandoning their original national roots and becoming 'global' rather than simply multi- or transnational. The phrase 'transnational corporation' (TNC) is applied to some of these. It is argued, by writers such as Dicken, that globalisation is different qualitatively from internationalisation in that it 'implies a degree of functional integration between internationally dispersed economic activities' (Peter Dicken, *Global Shift,* 2nd edn, 1992, London, PCP). These corporations are from industries such as petroleum, telecommunications, motors, chemicals, pharmaceuticals and civil engineering. It is possible to argue about the distinction between a transnational corporation and a global one and it is probably a fruitless argument. By definition a global corporation is transnational but a TNC may not be global because it may simply operate in two countries only. A corporation such as General Motors is obviously anchored in its original national base, the USA, but has production plants and subsidiaries in dozens of countries. It is also diversified into other global activities such as electronic data services and telecommunications. It might, however, legitimately be called a 'global' corporation because it now designs and produces cars for a universal market rather than for regional markets.

5.7   Terminology

- **Integrated processes**. As an industry develops various processes that began as separate processes may be incorporated into a single plant. Examples of this are found in the iron and steel industry where the process of iron making was once separated from the finishing stages and pig iron was sold to others who produced the final goods. The enormous economies involved in keeping metal hot instead of having to reheat it, quickly forced an integration of processes. The modern steel works is a completely integrated plant that uses heat and recycled heat with great efficiency to turn ore and scrap into products that are ready for their final use or, like car body steel, with one more stage to completion. In some industries the integration of processes was restricted by the financial benefits of spreading risks among various sources of supply. In modern times some industries have integrated processes in pursuit of economies of scale. These yield benefits from technical economies, as in the case of oil refineries where processes are continuous, and from an assortment of financial, risk-bearing, marketing and managerial economies. Over time the advantages of such integration may fade and the company may disintegrate processes.

- **Horizontal integration**. This is an economic term that means the merging together of two or more firms who are at the same stage of production of a good or service. Older examples include the frequent mergers of motor manufacturing companies. More recent examples tend to be in the financial sector with banks, building societies and insurance companies. Many of our modern high street retailers are the result of horizontal integration although the original firms may keep their names in order to simulate competition. There are examples of this in shoe shops and electrical goods. Horizontal integration tends to produce economies of scale in marketing and finance but may also yield considerable technical economies. On the whole a major motive behind such mergers or take-overs is the hope of increased market share together with an extension of customer base and brand names. Some companies' brand names are extremely valuable, as was revealed by the Nestlé take-over of Rowntree and its brand of chocolate bar, Kit Kat. Horizontal integration is rarely a simple merger of like with like. There is almost always some element of diversification involved because few large firms are single product or single service institutions. One economy of horizontal integration arises from possible reductions from shared research and development and the combining of head office and computing facilities. Such economies are clearly seen with the spate of mergers in the privatised energy industries.

- **Lateral integration**. Economists love to multiply classifications so many books contain references to lateral integration. This was originally simply a synonym for horizontal integration but became slightly differentiated from it by the argument that lateral involved the merger of companies at the same stage of production or selling but of different goods or services, for example the merger of a chain of shoe shops and a chain of clothes shops, or a car manufacturer and a heavy goods vehicle manufacturer. These are, of course, forms of diversification.

- **Vertical integration**. This arises when a firm merges with or takes over another which is at a different stage of production of the same good or service. For example, a steel manufacturer might gain control of a coke company or an iron ore supplier. This is called backwards vertical integration because it is back to suppliers. Such integration tends to take place when raw material or component supplies are scarce, uncertain or expensive. Eventually such supplies may become uncompetitive compared with alternative suppliers. Vertical integration may be 'forward' to the firms who buy or market the product. A shoe manufacturer may often own the chain of retail shops that sells the product. In the days before nation-alisation a steel company would often own shipyards or arms manufac-turers. Such integration tends to occur when markets are difficult and the manufacturer wants a guaranteed demand and a certainty that the product will be sold vigorously.

- **Diversification**. As firms grow they naturally look for new profit opportunities as tastes and preferences of consumers change. They also look for new products to balance any seasonal demand there might be for their main product line. When new technology is developed they often switch into new lines of production. A turntable manufacturer will eventually also produce cassette decks and CD players. A building society may also sell insurance, deal in shares and provide estate agency services. These are all forms of diversification. Some arise by accident as a result of mergers but some are embarked on deliberately in order to exploit new markets. In principle such diversification should improve the profitability of the business or create greater certainty of steady profit growth. In practice, some diversification is so far removed from the core business that management becomes inefficient and cumbersome. Take-overs are often accompanied by diversification but, increasingly, the new subsidiaries are sold off at the first opportunity and the proceeds used to reduce the burden of debt arising from the merger. An example is the way in which Kvaerner which took over Trafalgar House announced in advance that it would sell off the subsidiary Cunard because it had no interest in running cruises.

- **Core business**. A fashion developed in the 1990s for large corporations, mainly conglomerates, to sell off their so-called fringe or peripheral subsidiaries and to concentrate on what the top executives chose to call their core business. In some cases this process involved selling off a very large chunk of the company that had yielded good profits over the years.

The reasons given are usually that a narrow focus enables a business to be run more effectively and that too wide a dispersal of interests reduces overall efficiency of control. Another reason was that this can be a strategy to deter predatory take-over bidders who hope to sell off newly purchased subsidiaries to realise some short-run financial gain from the merger. It is obvious that this policy of retreat to the core business is a flat contradiction of the fashionable strategy of the last one hundred years of expansion via diversification. In one sense all that this new fashion for the core business indicates is that there are diseconomies of scale as well as economies, especially in the managerial sphere.

- **Conglomerates**. As the little old lady in the advertisement says 'I want to be in conglomerates'. The implication is that they are likely to be very profitable because of the large and diversified nature of their activities. They also tend to be the vehicles of well-known, thrusting entrepreneurs who make large capital gains for shareholders by their unexpected and aggressive take-overs. They may be tarred with the brush of 'asset stripper' but that simply adds to their attractiveness for some people. It is difficult to keep track of the company structure and subsidiaries of most conglomerates because they buy and sell companies so often. At any one time the juxtaposition of ownership appears rather bizarre. What connection is there between making bricks and batteries, between shoes and ships, between cola and airlines? The answer is usually 'not one of any significance' except that they are manufactured, run or sold by companies owned by the same holding company. We can liken the modern conglomerate to an ocean shark that feeds on other, smaller sharks until it, in turn, is consumed by an even larger shark. It is apparent that many conglomerates fall into decline when their original creator dies.

- **Holding Companies**. These are a legal device by which a company can hold shares in other companies. If 50 per cent plus one of the (ordinary) voting shares are owned by the holding company it can exert complete control over the company which is then treated as a subsidiary. Such holding companies may be dominated by a single person or a family or a family trust and control may be further strengthened by the use of interlocking directorships whereby individual members of the board of the holding company also sit on the boards of subsidiaries.

Exercise 4

Why has the earlier fashion for building conglomerates given way to selling off peripheral businesses and to 'concentrating on the core business'?

5.8   The Main Problem – Where to Obtain Capital

All businesses have one thing in common whether they are sole traders, partnerships, private companies or public companies. They all need capital both to start and to continue their business. Cash flow becomes all important for firms that are undercapitalised. A little hiccup in payment by a creditor, which is all too common, may put a business at risk of foreclosure as creditors, often banks, become uncertain about the security of their loans. Small firms, which predominate in number if not in value of sales or market share, are particularly vulnerable to a shortage of capital or to its intermittent availability. The very high proportion of small business failures in their first two years of operation is a testament to this. Even very large corporations may fall victim to overextended borrowing if markets take a turn for the worse. The collapse of the Mirror Group is a testament to this and even vast organisations such as General Motors and IBM go through phases of massive loss making that can only be covered by complaisant banks and creditors.

The most significant invention of modern capitalism was probably the idea of limited liability whereby the owner of shares has a liability for the debts of the company restricted to the shares themselves. Those with non-limited liability, such as Lloyds' underwriters, may have to sacrifice all of their assets in order to meet the debts of the enterprise. The development of limited liability gives savers the confidence to transfer their money into areas of risk and explains the rapid growth of corporate enterprise since the early nineteenth century. The basic framework of the capitalist economy provides systems for savings, from whatever source, to be channelled into enterprise. Figure 5.1 illustrates the process.

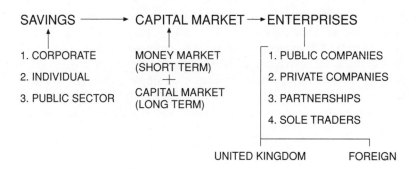

Figure 5.1   The flow of savings to enterprises

Economists regard savings as income which is not spent on current consumption. Households, firms and the government all abstain from current consumption in order to save, although governments more frequently exceed their income and borrow via the Public Sector Borrowing Requirement (PSBR). Household savings are channelled via building societies, pension funds and other savings media to the capital market. Some of their savings go to the government via national savings, premium bonds and savings certificates and new issues of government stock. Enterprises normally retain part of their profits and keep them in reserve, lend them to other people, or spend them on further investment in the future. Some large enterprises never borrow and rely entirely upon retained profits for expansion. The transfer of money via the short-term money markets and long-term capital markets employs very large numbers of people and makes up a significant part of tertiary sector employment. The financial markets have a wide range of instruments into which money can be transferred and held and there is a complex structure of interest rates which reflect the degrees of risk, uncertainty, loss of liquidity and the period to maturity.

The structure of the markets and the participants reflect the ever changing types of assets, bonds, bills, securities that are available. Over recent years the markets have expanded to include Eurodollars, ECUs, Certificates of Deposit (CDs), Options and Derivatives. As controls over the movement of foreign exchange and capital have been removed, a vast international market has sprung up with trillions of dollars of assets changing hands each day. This area tends to be regarded as glamorous by the media and receives a great deal of attention but has relatively little relevance to the small business that is seeking finance for a minor expansion of business. In these cases it is still a question of convincing a local bank that the proposal is sound. The small business still resorts to the traditional areas for new finance, to the family, to cashed in life insurance policies, to mortgages and to extensions of trade credit, or uses leasing to obtain assets such as office furniture and vehicles that in previous eras had to be bought. Having stated that the small business is largely divorced from the world of international finance it should be realised that in one important respect its main framework for operation is set by the world picture. That is in the area of interest rate determination where international flows of money have a strong influence on world and national interest rates.

5.9　Regulatory Bodies

A discussion of the financial framework is not complete without some reference to the regulatory bodies that exist. Some of these are of the institutional variety, that is they regulate their own members in an attempt to keep out crooks and to maintain the confidence of investors and depositors. Their effectiveness appears to be variable and there is always the suspicion that their main purpose is to look after their own interests. Such self-regulatory bodies are common in all sorts of enterprise areas, for example travel and leisure, insurance, air travel, the law, medicine and building. In some cases there are impartial arbitrators to settle disputes or an Ombudsman system. Other regulatory bodies are imposed by the state and their powers vary from country to country. There may exist what is called 'regulatory capture' where the regulator becomes the tool of the industry and facilitates its work rather than protecting the national interest or that of users. Some regulatory bodies are set up or modified as a result of specific events and after public enquiries. Such 'fire brigade' responses rarely produce satisfactory results and some sectors become over regulated and inflexible. Excessive regulation is a spur to innovation in order to avoid the rules. In the last resort the market may simply transfer to another country that has fewer controls. The international financial markets have several havens in which relatively unregulated activities can be centred. The United Kingdom has the Isle of Man and the Channel Islands and there are other places such as the Cayman Islands available for other transactions. Germans have tended to use Luxembourg for less regulated business and many people use Switzerland because of its strict confidentiality rules. The United Kingdom financial regulatory regime is discussed in more detail in Chapter 20.

5.10   Economists' Models

A few students come to love economic models. Most of us come to tolerate them as a useful way of looking at the real world when some simplifying assumptions are made. Do not, however, fall into the trap that some extreme right-wing economists appear to of believing that simply because a model seems to indicate a certain range of predictions about competition that all common sense should be thrown out of the window in pursuit of something like the model of 'perfect competition'. We should remember that many of the people who run companies are in pursuit of something more like monopoly and oligopoly and that many workers prefer to organise themselves into trade unions because experience dictates that 'in unity is strength' in relation to the typical capitalist employer. The following are models that economists frequently use to analyse the business framework:

● **Perfect competition**. This was an early model dating from the late nineteenth century and has not changed a great deal since the 1920s, although it has had a renewed impact since the 1970s as part of the obsessions of supply-side economists. The model creates an unreal world where there are a very large number of buyers and sellers of a homogeneous good (that is, identical, perfect substitutes) and there is perfect knowledge of market conditions such as price and where firms are free to enter or leave the industry. There is a tendency to skate over the necessary corollary of these assumptions that the factors of production must also exist in perfect markets and be perfectly mobile. The idea of perfect knowledge has been demonstrated not to be valid because of what is called asymmetric information in the market, that is some people know more than others. If this model existed, there would be an optimum allocation of resources and prices would be at the level of the lowest point of the long-run average cost curve. The individual firm is a 'price taker' with no market power to determine price because its output is a tiny fraction of the industry's total output.

- **Monopolistic competition**. This used to be a slightly more realistic model in the days when there were sometimes large numbers of producers of a similar product that the sellers differentiated by means of brand names, packaging and advertising. An important assumption of this model is that there are no barriers to new firms entering the market and there is no longer perfect knowledge of the market. The United Kingdom motor industry was like this in the early 1920s until merger mania struck. Today it is possible for a consumer to be unaware that two products are identical apart from the price and the brand name on the front. In some industries there may appear to be monopolistic competition because of the large number of brand names for similar products such as toothpaste but closer examination shows that many are produced by the same firm. The word monopolistic here means that the firm is the only seller of brand X and therefore has a monopoly of it. It is a very weak 'monopoly' but is sufficient to give the firm some slight control over its price and a separate demand curve for its product. The general outcome if such a model is applied is that prices are higher and output less than under conditions of perfect competition, and resources are not allocated in an optimum manner.

- **Oligopoly**. This model is closer to reality as is shown by the fact that there is no generally accepted set of conclusions from the model. It assumes that there are a few sellers of a similar good or service. The number qualifying as 'few' is debatable but is probably less than ten. Economists try to make the measure more objective by applying an index of concentration. Such an index measures, for example, the percentage of total output of a good that is produced by a certain number of the largest firms, such as five or seven. A five firm index in 1991 revealed that, in the tobacco industry, 99 per cent of net output came from the five largest firms whereas in the footwear industry only 46 per cent did. Oligopolists tend to compete by product differentiation so there is usually heavy advertising to create and maintain brand loyalty. There is often fairly bogus competition to develop new products with amazing characteristics. They will even invent problems we did not know we had in order to sell us cures or they endow products with almost miraculous qualities that make us rush to buy them. They may compete in any way except through genuine price competition. Sometimes, if the law is not effective or the watchdogs are asleep, they collude and share out markets and fix prices.

They may even form official bodies through which to collude; they are called cartels. Occasionally such cartels are sponsored by governments. Another feature of oligopoly is that there may be significant barriers against new firms entering. These may be high capital costs, the need for expensive advertising campaigns, legal problems with patents and licences, or simply that the existing firms in the market have a stranglehold over it. Needless to say, the oligopoly tends to use resources in an economically inefficient way and charge the consumer more than would our perfect competition model. On the other hand, they may enjoy great economies of scale and be able to spend large sums on research and development. They tend to have happy shareholders!

- **Duopoly**. Sometimes in an industry there are only two sellers so they can obviously have some impact on the market price. They may tacitly collude to share out the market and avoid price competition or they may genuinely compete.

- **Duopsony**. Sometimes there may be only two buyers of a good or service in a market.

- **Monopsony**. Occasionally there is only one buyer in a market and this gives that buyer considerable market power. It is frequently the government. In extreme cases there may be one buyer and one seller.

- **Monopoly**. This is a model where there is a single seller of a good or service that has no close substitute. The monopolist may control either the price or the output but not both at once because the demand is not completely inelastic. A pure monopolist exploits the consumer by charging a higher price and producing less than would be the case in perfect competition. In some instances the monopolist uses price discrimination to charge different consumers different prices. In practice a single seller is an unusual occurrence and the government defines monopoly for legal purposes in the United Kingdom as where one firm is responsible for at least 25 per cent of the sales of a good. The model can be interpreted very superficially because, in reality, many monopolists enjoy enormous economies of scale and are much more efficient than would be a collection of many smaller firms. The issue then becomes one of whether the benefits of these economies are passed on to the consumer or not.

Exercise 5

What industries or markets do you consider to be competitive? How do you judge?

Some of these models will be discussed in more detail later in Chapters 7 and 8 but you can expect to see references to them throughout this book and in your other reading. Remember that they are useful tools or approaches and do not rely too heavily on them. The real world is too complex and shifting to be encapsulated in textbook models. Attempts have been made to jettison the old model approach and to replace them with a new orthodoxy called **contestable markets**. Unfortunately, as is often the case in economics, the student ends up having to learn about this as well as the older ideas.

6 Price Theory

Aims of the chapter

To explain:

- the orthodox theory of how the prices of goods and services are determined in the absence of state intervention;
- demand;
- the elasticity of demand;
- supply;
- the elasticity of supply;
- the interaction of demand and supply;
- short-run and long-run considerations;
- the flaws in the theory;
- applications of the theory in the contexts of:
  - substitutes,
  - complements or joint demand,
  - joint supply,
  - intervention by the state or other bodies in setting market prices.

6.1 The Orthodox Theory of Price

Economists once thought that price was determined by supply factors, mainly the costs of production. One extreme version of this is the Marxist labour theory of value. They also toyed with the idea that it was demand that was the main element in price determination. Eventually, around the turn of the nineteenth century, the current orthodoxy emerged. In the United Kingdom the version that has most influenced our approach and terminology was expressed by Alfred Marshall (1842–1924).

The equilibrium price of a good is determined by the intersection of demand and supply. If, on the one hand in a given time period, supply exceeds demand, there will be a tendency for price to fall until the excess supply is absorbed. If, on the other hand, demand exceeds supply, there will be a tendency for price to rise until the excess is eliminated. Thus, for a typical good, price fluctuates around an equilibrium. Some students interpret supply and demand analysis to mean that price is always at an equilibrium but it is more likely that it is moving towards it. The general principle to remember is that if there is excess supply at any price there will be a tendency for price to fall; if there is excess demand there will be a tendency for price to rise. There may be time lags in this process of adjustment of demand and supply.

6.2 Demand

Demand has a particular meaning in economics and should not be confused with a simple longing to possess something. Demand means what is called 'effective demand', that is a want backed by the willingness and ability to pay for the good or service in question. An understanding of the difference between simply wanting something *and* being able and willing to pay for it helps to explain why a large proportion of the world's population is undernourished at the same time as there are surpluses of grain stored in the richer countries. Somebody, usually the US Government or aid agencies, has to create the effective part of the demand and pay farmers for their product.

The effective demand for a good is based on several factors that are usually called the determinants of demand:

1. The tastes and preferences of consumers. These change over time and are influenced by advertising, fashion and overall standards of living. At any particular time they are relatively fixed. Any demand curve that you see is drawn on the assumption that they are constant.

2. The incomes of consumers. Our individual income helps to determine the pattern of our demand and the amount we are willing to buy of a particular good at a given price. Again the demand curve is drawn on the assumption that incomes are fixed for the time period in question. If income changes the whole demand curve shifts to another position.

3. The distribution of income of consumers is assumed to be given when a demand curve is drawn. If it changes, for example because of an alteration in taxation or government expenditure, our demand is also likely to alter and the demand curve shifts to a new position.

4. The prices of related goods and services influence our demand for the one under consideration. If the price of a substitute or complement alters, the demand will change for any related good. For example, the price of lamb responds to a change in the price of pork or chicken. The price of cars has an influence upon the demand for their complements, petrol and tyres.

5. Some economists refer to other underlying factors such as population structure which has a profound long-term impact. Some refer to the availability of credit but it can be argued that this is simply an income factor and should be incorporated under point 2 above as all it does is to shift the time of consumption rather than its overall volume.

Marshall chose to draw his supply and demand diagrams with the variable quantity on the x axis and price on the y axis. If this convention is adopted in defiance of the usual mathematical practice, a good usually has a demand curve that slopes downwards from the left as in Figure 6.1. This figure refers to a particular time period, the short run, and assumes that the underlying determinants of demand are fixed.

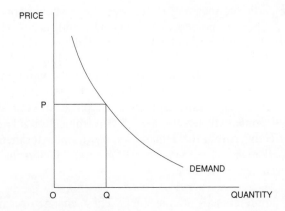

Figure 6.1   A typical demand curve

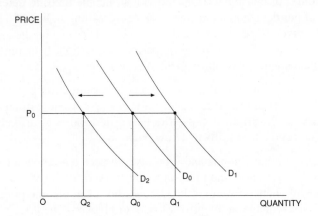

Figure 6.2   Increases and decreases of demand

If the underlying conditions of demand change, the whole demand curve shifts to a new position. These shifts are called increases and decreases in demand and are shown in Figure 6.2. An advertising campaign, a rise in incomes, a rise in the price of a substitute or the fall in the price of a complement would all tend to increase demand and shift the curve to the right. The end of an advertising campaign, a fall in incomes, the fall in the price of a substitute or the rise in the price of a complement would all tend to cause a shift to the left, a decrease in demand.

There is another piece of conventional terminology that sometimes causes problems for students. If there is no change in the underlying conditions of demand so the demand curve remains in the same position but there is a change in price caused by a shift of the supply curve to right or left because supply conditions have changed, there is a movement along the demand curve. These movements *along* the demand curve are called extensions and contractions of demand. The term may cause confusion because the quantity change is measured on the x axis and it is usual to refer to 'an increase in the quantity demanded' or to 'a decrease in the quantity demanded'. The words 'in the quantity' give the clue to whether shifts of the whole curve (increases or decreases) or movements along (extensions or contractions) are meant. Some writers avoid the problem by always talking about shifts of demand to mean increases or decreases. Figure 6.3 shows extensions and contractions of demand in response to prior movements in price caused by shifts in supply.

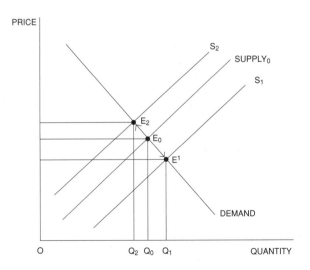

Figure 6.3   Extensions and contractions of demand

Exercise I

Why is the economist's definition of demand as 'effective demand' important?

Economics contains a great deal of discussion of the behaviour of demand in the form of marginal utility analysis or indifference curve analysis. Examiners tend to favour these topics because, broadly speaking, there are right and wrong answers which is rather unusual in economics. If you make certain assumptions and argue logically within them you are either right or wrong in your conclusions:

1. The typical demand curve slopes downwards to the right for two reasons, the income effect and the substitution effect. Marginal utility analysis can be used to explain these effects but you can do much more, and use lots of diagrams, if you use indifference curves. The latter enable you to see quickly the effects of changes in income and of price. They do, however, tend to lead people off in search of atypical types of demand to the detriment of studying the typical. The result is that generations of students become obsessed by what are called Giffen goods or Veblen goods. If you wish to fill your mind with this body of arcane knowledge, or if your examination syllabus demands it, you should read another book and allocate a few hours to practising the relevant diagrams.

2. The income effect of a change in price means that, if the price of something you buy falls, it is the equivalent of receiving an increase in income. You can choose to buy more of the same good or a little more plus a unit of something else. When (if?) petrol falls in price do you buy more petrol or spend the weekly savings on something else? It all depends on the individual but the cumulative effect for a typical good is to produce a larger demand at lower prices. The argument is reversed for a rise in price.

3. The substitution effect of a change in price refers to the effects of an alteration in price of an alternative good. We tend to buy more of something whose price has not changed in place of a substitute whose price has risen, and vice versa. With some products of course we have a limited physical capacity to consume them in a given time period so a fall in their price may not persuade us to consume more.

6.3   Elasticity of Demand

Price elasticity of demand (PED) is a mathematical measure of the responsiveness of the quantity demanded to a small percentage change in price. A simple formula for its calculation is:

$$PED = \frac{\% \text{ change in quantity demanded}}{\% \text{ change in price}}$$

If PED exceeds 1 demand is said to be elastic.

If it equals 1 elasticity is said to be unitary;
If it is less than 1 demand is said to be inelastic.

Note: the mathematical measure from this formula is always negative assuming that demand and price are inversely related; we ignore the minus sign when drawing conclusions. Thus minus 1.5 is assumed to be greater than 1 so demand is 'elastic.'

Price elasticity is mainly determined by:

1. The existence or otherwise of substitutes at the prevailing market price. If there are no close substitutes the PED will tend to be inelastic whereas if there are close alternatives demand will probably be elastic.

2. Another influence is whether the purchase of the good or service tends to be habitual or if a conscious decision has to be made before purchase. Habitually purchased items such as salt, newspapers, tobacco, toilet paper and so on tend to have low price elasticity. If a conscious decision is needed as in the purchase of a new car or books or many consumer goods the elasticity is likely to be higher.

3. If the price of the good is relatively low in comparison to the average income then demand tends to be inelastic whereas if it is high the demand tends to be more elastic. This links with the habitual purchase point above. Salt is very low in price relative to income and is a habitual purchase so its demand is relatively inelastic. A car, however, has a high price in relation to the average income and much thought is expended before choosing a particular model so the demand elasticity tends to be high.

Sometimes reference is made to 'rich' people's goods having an inelastic demand because they can easily absorb price rises but this brings in a new set of assumptions about the nature of their demand.

Applications of price elasticity of demand

● Businesses apply the concept whether they know it or not when considering price changes:

If demand is elastic a price rise would cut revenue from sales.
If demand is inelastic a price rise would raise revenue from sales.
If demand is elastic a price fall would raise revenue from sales.
If demand is inelastic a price fall would reduce revenue from sales.

The extent of the changes in revenue (price x sales) depends on the degree of elasticity or inelasticity. The higher the nominal value of elasticity the greater the change in revenue after a price change.

- PED is applied to the factors of production, land, labour and capital, that is to the prices called wages, rent and interest. For example, the demand for very skilled labour might be very inelastic in relation to the wage rate (price of labour), and the demand for capital may be inelastic in relation to changes in the rate of interest.

- PED is also applied when discussing exchange rate alterations. As the pound depreciates, other things being equal, imports become more expensive and exports fall in price. If the sum of the elasticities of demand for imports and exports exceeds 1 then the depreciation or devaluation of the pound is likely to improve the balance of payments on current account. This is called the Marshall-Lerner condition. In other words, the gain in revenue from the extra exports exceeds the additional cost of the higher priced imports, or the fall in revenue from exports is exceeded by a greater fall in expenditure on imports. This effect on improving the balance of payments is a delayed one, that is there are time lags, and when shown in a diagram is called the 'J' curve effect (see Chapter 17).

- Cross elasticity is another application of PED where the effects of a change in price of one good on another's demand is measured. The formula for measuring cross elasticity is:

Cross elasticity of demand = $\dfrac{\%\ \text{change in quantity demanded of good X}}{\%\ \text{change in price of good Y}}$

Substitutes will have positive cross elasticities;
Complements will have negative cross elasticities.

Exercise 2

How would you categorise the following in terms of price elasticity at prevailing market prices? a. salt; b. new cars in the 1300 to 1600 cc range; c. skiing holidays with one particular company; d. air travel to the USA?

Note on elasticity of demand

Price elasticity of demand is important when considering the gradient of the demand curve. There is a temptation to draw very steep curves and say demand is inelastic and shallow curves and say that demand is elastic but it is obvious that the apparent gradient reflects the scales that you have chosen to have on the two axes of the graph. Price elasticity is a measure of the proportionate change in the quantity demanded in response to a small proportionate change in price so, except where the price elasticity equals 0, 1, or infinity, the price elasticity will vary along the length of the curve even if it is a straight line. You will have noticed that straight lines are a particular type of curve to the mathematician so most economics textbooks use straight line demand and supply curves.

The elasticity of demand, as well as that of supply, determines the extent of quantity changes as price alters so the changes on the x axis in Figure 6.3 reflect the relative gradients of the two curves. In principle:

- the greater the inelasticity of demand in relation to supply, the larger the price change and the smaller the quantity change if the supply curve shifts.

- the more elastic the demand in relation to supply, the smaller the price change and the greater the quantity change if the supply curve shifts.

Income elasticity of demand

Income elasticity of demand (IED) is a very important concept and is of great practical significance because it helps to explain why some enterprises are growing and others are shrinking. IED measures the change in the quantity demanded of a good or service as incomes change in a time period. The formula is:

$$\text{Income elasticity of demand} = \frac{\%\text{ change in quantity demanded}}{\%\text{ change in income}}$$

- Normal goods have positive income elasticity because as income rises so does demand. Rapidly expanding sectors will have IEDs above 1; for example, a 5 per cent rise in income over a time period might produce a 10 per cent rise in demand. The leisure industries may be a case in point.

- Inferior goods are defined as having a negative income elasticity because the demand for them actually falls as income rises; examples may include some forms of public transport as people switch to private cars. Certain foodstuffs are inferior goods on this definition because as incomes rise people can afford better quality products. The evidence for this is seen in the decline in demand for potatoes and standard white loaves over the last thirty years although diet fads may also be an influence.

- There are probably a few products where, for some time periods, there is no change in demand as income alters so IED is zero.

- In general we would expect the IED to change over time as fashions, tastes and preferences alter. Last century's top holiday resort may now be regarded as passé. Brighton and Weymouth have given way to Bangkok and the Seychelles. These changes are reflected in the weighting (relative importance) given to goods and services in calculating the Retail Prices Index. For example, the RPI now takes account of 'meals consumed outside the home'. The weighting given to food has fallen steadily over the years because smaller proportions of our incomes are spent on food.

6.4   Supply

The supply of a good depends on the time period being considered and the textbook references to it are usually an oversimplification of the real world. The supply shown in the typical supply schedule which is a set of prices and quantities from which a supply curve is drawn, refers to entrepreneurs' willingness and ability to supply certain quantities at the prices listed. Obviously some are able to supply at low prices but others require higher prices to induce them to produce. This is seen clearly in agriculture where farmers working on marginal land enter and leave a market according to prevailing prices or last year's price. In practice, the supply of a good is a mixture of goods currently in shops, warehouses, and the distribution chain generally or which are in the process of being produced. Many modern durable goods such as cars are assembled to order and are part of the current supply. One nation's industry may be working to full capacity but imports may quickly boost the supply by, for example, the use of air freight. Marshall tried to simplify the matter by distinguishing three time periods and then added a fourth for good measure. His distinctions are simply a means of defining a set of assumptions so that logical reasoning can take place, so do not expect a complete match with reality. Marshall's time periods are:

1. When supply is fixed, for example in the immediate market for fish that follows the re-entry of the fishing boats to port. At such auctions the supply is fixed until the next landings and demand tends to dictate the price in the market. Writers give this time period different names, the momentary time period or the market equilibrium. Another example which is quoted is an auction for, for example, the works of a famous artist such as Vermeer, where the world supply is fixed and known (forgers excepted!).

2. When supply is alterable using existing capital stock by varying the inputs of labour and materials. This is the time period that produces the typical short-run supply curve which slopes upwards from left to right if quantity is on the x axis and price on the y. The clock time involved is different for every type of production. This period is called the short run.

3. When the existing capital stock can be changed as well as the inputs of labour and materials we have the long-run time period. The assumption here is that the technology remains the same which makes this a not very useful concept nowadays because it is rare for capital equipment to be

replaced without some degree of upgrading. You may have discovered this elementary fact if you have replaced a video, a CD player, a washing machine, a computer or car. The more recent models have enough gizmos on board to run the Star Ship Enterprise.

4. The last time period is the very long run when technology can change as well.

The long run and very long run may have been useful for Marshall in his analysis but they do not make a lot of sense in the fluid world of the late twentieth century so do not feel too guilty if you use the long run to include the very long run. Figures 6.4, 6.5 and 6.6 illustrate the first three time periods.

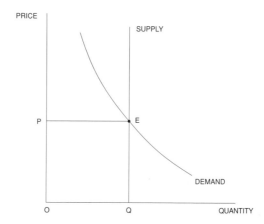

Figure 6.4   Market equilibrium

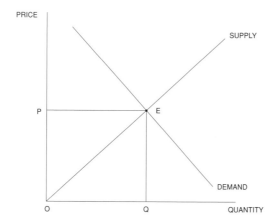

Figure 6.5   Short-run equilibrium

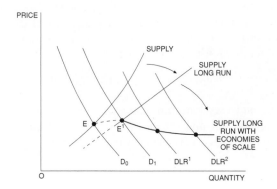

Figure 6.6   Long-run equilibrium

The factors underlying supply are costs of production. It is conventional to distinguish the short run from the long run in this context.

1. The short-run costs of production are related to the operation of the Law of Diminishing Marginal Returns which dictate the slope of the individual firm's short-run cost curve, that is its marginal cost curve above its average variable cost curve. Marginal costs are the costs of producing an additional unit. As output is expanded in the short run the marginal costs at first fall but then begin to rise. This is because of the definition of short run to mean the time period in which the firm has fixed capital equipment. Thus any expansion of output is achieved by using extra units of the variable factors. After a point these yield diminishing returns, that is the growth of output begins to fall. No-one in their right mind would go to the point where adding additional factors would cause total output to fall but many gardeners achieve this accidentally by putting on too much fertiliser. If they disobey the manufacturer's instruction which have been carefully worked out after field trials, they add extra fertiliser 'for luck'. They might as well tear up their five pound notes or compost them. The extra that they use is wasted or may even produce root growth when they want top growth or top growth when they want root growth or leaf growth when they want flowers. Their final output of crops or flowers may actually fall. All drivers quickly discover the law of diminishing marginal returns although they may not recognise it. As they depress the accelerator the car speeds up but after a point, as they add extra units of fuel into their engine of fixed capacity, the rate of increase of speed declines until no further increase in speed can be achieved.

2. The long-run costs of production are determined by the existence, or otherwise, of economies of scale. With some types of production, an

expansion of the scale of output enables the average cost of production per unit (unit costs) to fall. This is typical of mass produced consumer durable goods. The classic examples are calculators, computers, videos, personal stereos but the principle also applies to bulk produce such as steel. The various types of economy are classified as:

- Internal where the increase in scale of the individual firm's output gives it reduced unit costs, via technical, managerial, commercial, financial and risk-bearing economies.

- External where the growth of the industry as a whole may or may not provide the individual firm with lower unit costs via what are sometimes classified as economies of concentration, information and disintegration.

6.5   Elasticity of Supply

Elasticity of supply is an important concept but it tends to receive much less attention than the elasticity of demand. It measures the responsiveness of supply to a small percentage change in price using the basic formula:

Elasticity of supply = % change in quantity supplied
                        ───────────────────────────
                           % change in price

If elasticity of supply exceeds 1, supply is said to be elastic.
If elasticity of supply is less than 1, supply is said to be inelastic.
If elasticity of supply is equal to 1, supply is said to have unitary elasticity.

- Time is an important factor in determining the elasticity of supply. In the short run it is largely determined by the extent to which costs rise as output is raised in a situation in which, by definition, most of the factors are fixed in supply, particularly land and capital. The responsiveness of supply relates to the so-called law of diminishing marginal returns. In the long run the most important influence on the elasticity of supply is the extent of the economies of large-scale production which become available as all the factors of production become variable. Some industries such as those manufacturing consumer durable goods have considerable economies of scale while others, such as extractive industries may, in some cases suffer diseconomies of scale.

- Another influence on the elasticity of supply is the availability of stocks, the extent of over capacity in the industry and the response of foreign suppliers to price changes.

- Underlying the elasticity of supply are the elasticities of supply of the individual factors of production and the ease with which they can be substituted for each other (the elasticity of substitution).

Note on elasticity of supply

Elasticity of supply will vary according to the time period being considered, the nature of the product or service, the elasticity of supply of factors of production and the technology used. The same general warnings apply here as with demand. The usual assumption is that the more shallow the curve's gradient the more elastic it is but again this depends on the scales adopted on the graph. Elasticity of supply measures the response of the quantity supplied to a small proportionate change in price. The elasticity will normally vary with price apart from the limiting cases where it equals 0, 1 or infinity. There is a tendency to regard elasticity of supply as a measure of how easily and quickly supply responds to market changes but it should be considered as a response to price changes. In general, elasticity of supply increases over time.

6.6   **Market Price**

The interaction of supply and demand is supposed to produce an equilibrium price where the intentions of consumers and suppliers match but, as stated earlier, it is better to think of an equilibrium price as one to which the market tends not one at which it is. Figure 6.7 shows the traditional short-run market equilibrium price. To recap:

- If there is an excess demand at any price there will be a tendency for price to rise.
- If there is an excess supply at any price there will be a tendency for price to fall.

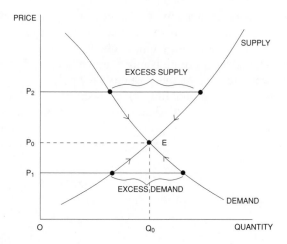

Figure 6.7   Equilibrium price

Flaws in the simple theory

- Markets are not perfect. Consumers are often very ignorant or misinformed about goods, services and prices. Sometimes sellers deliberately mislead them. They cannot, therefore, respond rationally to price signals. Sellers too may be ignorant of market conditions and not respond to changes in demand and supply conditions.

- There are time lags in the responses of buyers and sellers and the simple equilibrium diagrams do not lend themselves to representing time lags effectively. One effect of time lags is to produce different prices in the various parts of a market for short periods. This even happens on the most sophisticated of electronic markets.

- Markets are dominated by firms that do not compete in the traditional sense. Many are oligopolists who avoid price competition. Many firms have so few competitors that they have considerable market power to influence both supply and price. Some firms, especially large multiple retailers, use a system of offering 'loss leaders' to their customers. These are usually the regularly purchased items such as standard loaves, baked beans and sugar. They are, in effect, cross subsidising the loss leaders by charging more for other goods even if the volume of their overall sales is boosted by this sales technique.

- Some markets show destabilising effects which produce unstable equilibria. These can be seen in some agricultural markets where producers react to the previous year's prices and may create surpluses and shortages and extremely large price fluctuations. The price may actually diverge from an equilibrium rather than move towards it. These are sometimes called 'cobweb' effects.

- What are called 'price shocks' may occur which destabilise markets for varying periods. They are most evident in financial markets but are also seen in commodity markets. They may be caused by wars, political crises, droughts, floods, frosts and new discoveries. A recent example is the response of the beef market to BSE scares.

- There may be state intervention in markets. You can argue about the justification for such actions but they sometimes occur because of market imperfections and to protect consumers from exploitation by oligopolists and monopolists. Intervention may be on the grounds of national security or on public health grounds.

- The market price rarely takes account of external costs and benefits or externalities as they are called. These were discussed in Chapter 2 on key concepts. The market price usually only takes account of private costs and benefits. Some economists use the divergence between private costs and benefits and social costs and benefits to justify state intervention in the market by, for example, taxing firms who pollute so that revenue is available for cleaning up.

6.7   Some Applications of Price Theory

Most of the applications are in subsequent chapters on individual industries but a few of the more common, generalised ones are best dealt with here:

1. **Substitutes**. The degree to which two or more goods are substitutes for one another is measured by cross elasticity of demand. Substitutes have positive cross elasticity of demand when the formula is applied:

$$\textbf{cross elasticity} = \frac{\%\ \text{change in quantity demanded of good X}}{\%\ \text{change in price of good Y}}$$

If good Y, say butter, rises in price we would expect the demand for good X, say margarine, to increase because it is now relatively cheaper. Both top and bottom of the equation, therefore, have a plus sign. If Y falls in price we would expect, other things being equal, that the demand for X will decrease and both signs are negative so the result is positive.

If an examiner asks you to analyse the consequences of a change in price of one good in relation to what you consider to be a substitute, you should work out why the price of the first (call it Y) has altered. It may be caused by a change in demand which shifts the demand curve to a new position as in Figure 6.2, or by a change in costs of production as in Figure 6.3. The extent of any price/quantity change is related to the relative price elasticities of demand and supply of Y and X a relationship that is measured by the cross elasticity of demand. In general, if they are close substitutes they will have a high positive cross elasticity. Figures 6.8 and 6.9 are a simple application of the above argument. Let us assume that the price of butter (Y) rises because the Government has decided to kill thousands of cows because of the BSE scare. Milk becomes scarce relative to demand and less is available for butter manufacture. Some people will shift their demand to margarine (X) and its price will rise in the short run. We may reasonably assume that the supply of margarine is more elastic than that of butter because it is produced by an industrial, chemical process so the diagrams attempt to show that by having different supply curves. The elasticity of demand of the two is assumed to be similar. There is no need to make your life miserable by thinking about the long run unless the examiner insists, so do not go on to argue that margarine is now more expensive than it was so people switch to butter and so on in an endless loop. In the two diagrams you have to assume that the short run represented here stops with the rise in demand for margarine because its underlying conditions of demand have changed (a substitute has altered in price). Any long run analysis would be about the effect of such a change in demand on the quantity supplied and long run costs of production. These might rise or fall according to whether or not there are economies of scale to be had.

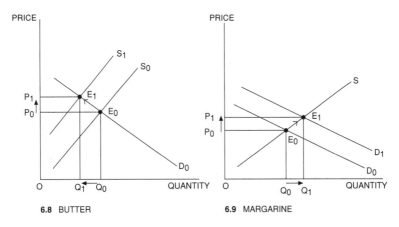

6.8 BUTTER   6.9 MARGARINE

Figures 6.8 and 6.9   The price of substitutes

2. **Complements**. There are many products where two or more goods are frequently bought together, occasionally in reasonably fixed ratios. Many of these are alcohol and mixers, gin and tonic, whisky and soda. Some are less fixed in their relationship, for example holidays and holiday insurance. On the whole, such pairings have what we might call a dominant partner; cars, for example, are more significant than tyres when it comes to examining changes in demand and supply. Not many of us are put off buying a car by the thought of the price of replacement tyres but we might switch the model we buy if a new set were likely to cost over a thousand pounds. We would, however, think twice if cars in general rose in price by say 20 per cent and our demand for tyres would suffer considerably. The cross elasticity of demand for complements is negative. If the price of cars rises because of an increase in the costs of production, we would expect the demand for cars and for, say petrol, to decrease. If we apply our cross elasticity formula we would have a positive sign on the bottom and a negative on the top. Figures 6.10 and 6.11 illustrate a simple case of complementary demand.

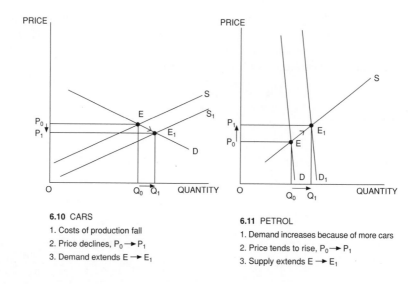

6.10 CARS
1. Costs of production fall
2. Price declines, $P_0 \rightarrow P_1$
3. Demand extends $E \rightarrow E_1$

6.11 PETROL
1. Demand increases because of more cars
2. Price tends to rise, $P_0 \rightarrow P_1$
3. Supply extends $E \rightarrow E_1$

Figures 6.10 and 6.11   The price of complements

3. **Joint supply**. Some of the most interesting applications of price theory are in the area of joint supply because they have important ramifications for producers and consumers. Joint supply occurs when the production of one good inevitably leads to the production of another or several others. The best examples lie in the processing of crude oil where, as you will know from your study of chemistry, the desire to produce petrol inevitably leads to the output of bitumen, fuel oil of different grades and a host of other products. You will probably have studied the distillation processes and the application of catalytic crackers and also other chemical processes that yield by-products. Older readers may have studied the process of manufacture of town gas with its accompaniments of tar, coke, ammonium, sulphur, producer gas and water gas. You may have thought that this was all a bit academic at the time but such study will now prove useful. In the 1960s the mass rush to car ownership and petrol buying brought about an inevitable upsurge in supplies of fuel oil. The oil companies were desperate to get rid of this fuel oil and went to great lengths to persuade private individuals and public bodies to switch to oil burning central heating and electricity generation. The change over, which was accompanied by what were, in effect, subsidies to people to switch to oil burning boilers, helped to sound the death knell of the coal industry. A few years later, the change had to be partially reversed during the massive oil price rises of the 1970s.

There are many examples of joint supply in agriculture, in for instance beef, veal, milk, milk products such as cream, cheese, yoghurt, whey and skimmed milk powder. One reason that the European Union ended up with a large mountain of skimmed milk powder was that the demand for beef and veal reached very high levels and cows produced milk when they had calves to satisfy the demand. The BSE scare will have the opposite effect; the decreased demand for beef and veal will reduce the number of calf births and the supply of milk may fall. The decline will be aggravated by the enforced cull of cows before their normal reproducing span is completed. In one case the joint supply element in farming creates a cost to the farmer. Under stringent new regulations farmers have been spending very large sums of money to deal with the effluent created by their cattle. The joint supply aspect of the straw that is produced with wheat may be an asset if it can be sold or used but becomes a burdensome cost if it cannot. Figures 6.12 and 6.13 illustrate elements of joint supply.

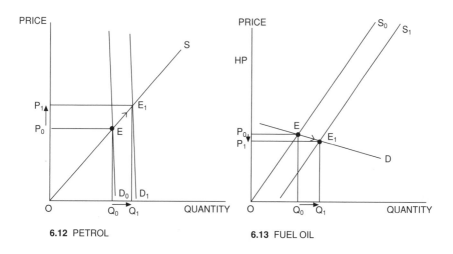

6.12 PETROL   **6.13** FUEL OIL

The demand for petrol increases as car ownership rises, despite more fuel efficient engines. This results in an extension of supply of petrol, assuming the costs of production stay the same in the short run. There is, inevitably, an increased output of fuel oil because of the conditions of joint supply. If the conditions of demand remain the same there will be a price fall and an extension of demand. This actually happened in the boom years of car ownership in the 1960s when oil companies were desperate to get rid of their fuel oil and persuaded people to shift to oil burning with cheap loans and low-priced contracts.

Figures 6.12 and 6.13   Joint supply

4. **The intervention of the state and others in the price mechanism.** There are many examples of various bodies intervening in the operation of markets. Indeed, one of the functions of the rulers of the early Mesopotamian city states was to regulate markets and prices, mainly for

their own benefit but also to control prices in the interests of all. Joseph advised Pharaoh to intervene and store grain during the seven fat years ready for the seven lean years. His actions must have influenced market prices. His was an early version of the Common Agricultural Policy. There are various examples of such intervention in modern times:

- The European Union intervenes on a large scale in agricultural pricing and production, a topic that is dealt with in detail in Chapter 16.

- Various cartels around the world try to maintain certain price bands with an emphasis on controlling supply in order to achieve a minimum price for their participants. OPEC (Organisation of Petroleum Exporting Countries) is the best known example but there have been others in cement, iron and steel, heavy chemicals and cross border telecommunications.

- Many governments intervene in foreign exchange markets to control the price fluctuations or levels of their currency. This is dealt with in detail in Chapter 15.

- A favourite area for state intervention is in housing markets where many countries try to control rents or to allocate dwellings on a basis other than a willingness and ability to pay. In the United Kingdom house prices are heavily influenced by tax concessions on mortgage interest payments, though less so than in the past.

- During crises governments often impose price controls on what they regard as essentials such as some foods and fuel. They may also do this in order to keep inflation under control although the policy may simply postpone the problem because the controls act like a dam on a reservoir which is broken when the price restraints are removed. The most stringent of these price controls occur in war time and are usually accompanied by rationing of essentials and harsh penalties for anyone who breaks the regulations.

- One particular example of price controls is the system called **Resale Price Maintenance (RPM)** which has now almost disappeared in the United Kingdom except for some branded pharmaceuticals. RPM on books withered away in 1995 when the Net Book Agreement was ended. The RPM system on branded pharmaceuticals was referred in late 1996 to the Monopolies and Mergers Commission for study and may be abolished as well. RPM was introduced gradually into the United Kingdom in the early part of the twentieth century in response to demands from small retailers to manufacturers that they be protected against the price cutting activities of the new breed of large scale multiple retailer. Eventually, by the time legislation was passed in 1956 and 1964, almost all branded, packaged, non-perishable products had a fixed price which was often printed on them. Many people obtained discounts on some goods by belonging to groups such as Trade Unions or clubs. In 1956 the practice of manufacturers applying collective 'punishments' to any retailer who broke the price code by discounting was made illegal. The other practice of individual manufacturers applying their own sanctions against a price cutting retailer (Tesco was a chief culprit who probably wanted the publicity rather than the increased sale of the products concerned) was actually strengthened by the law in 1956 but was almost completely abolished in 1964 by the Resale Prices Act. A few remnants persisted because manufacturers such as book publishers, map makers and pharmaceutical producers managed to persuade The Restrictive Trade Practices Court (RTPC) that what they were doing was in the public interest. They argued that they helped to keep small shops open. It is interesting to note that in France, where RPM on books was abolished many small shops did close and the system was reinstated.

- One area where we are all affected by price fixing is in the sale of tickets for events where there is a fixed capacity, such as Wimbledon finals, cup finals, concerts. The organisers have to make difficult decisions on pricing so that they combine high revenues with what the public perceive as a fair distribution of tickets for lower income, loyal supporters. They almost always create a situation where effective demand exceeds supply at the official prices and a 'black market' develops. Some people are able and willing to pay very high prices for the limited supply and tickets that were originally available at the official low price are quickly transferred by touts to those with effective demand, that is fat wallets.

Figures 6.14–6.17 show the application of two of the main types of official price controls. The first is where maximum prices are fixed (see Figures 6.14 and 6.15) and the second is where minimum prices are aimed at (see Figures 6.16 and 6.17).

Exercise 3

How does OPEC try to influence the world crude oil price? What determines its degree of success?

Maximum prices are usually fixed by governments in response to expected shortages, often in war time but they may exist in peace time. For example, the maximum price of milk sold on the doorstep is still controlled by the

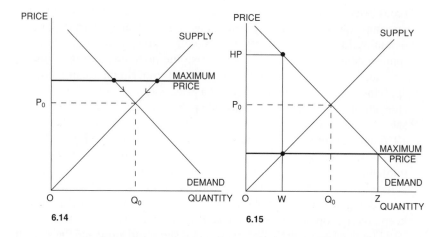

In the left-hand diagram there is no immediate effect from the imposition of a maximum price because the excess supply depresses the price back to E. There might, however, be a psychological effect. If the supply and demand shifted over time the maximum price might become effective.
In the right-hand diagram problems are created because the maximum price is set below the market equilibrium. There is an excess demand of WZ at the maximum price. Some people are willing to pay the price HP for the supply OW so some supply shifts out of the official market onto the 'black' market. Rationing may be introduced resulting in people paying the cash price equal to the maximum price plus coupons. The coupons represent the volume of supply available per time period

Figures 6.14 and 6.15   Maximum prices

United Kingdom Government and the maximum price of the standard white loaf was controlled until the late 1980s. Many multiple retailers sold it as a loss leader and made their profits from diversifying into other sorts of bread such as the granary types with little pieces of grit on top that give extra trade to dentists. Currently the system of regulation of the privatised utilities such as BT, Gas and Electricity through OFTEL, OFGAS and OFFER contains what amounts to a maximum price because the sellers are only allowed to raise their prices in a given time period by the RPI minus X, a formula that usually means that prices must fall below the previous year's level.

The maximum price is originally set somewhere near the market equilibrium price or slightly above it to allow scope for changes in supply and demand but, over time, it may become an unrealistic price in terms of the actual market conditions. In war time, for example, the 1939 price that was usually taken as a basis quickly became outmoded as supplies diminished and demand increased as war time incomes rose when overtime became the norm and unemployment disappeared.

If the maximum price is set above the normal market equilibrium it will have no effect on price until supply and demand conditions change to raise the market price. But, if the maximum price is set below the market equilibrium or becomes below it as a result of shifts in supply and demand, problems will develop that may have to be solved by rationing and strong anti-black market laws (see Figures 6.16 and 6.17).

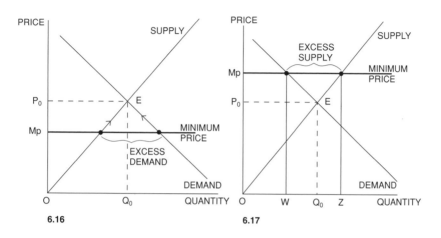

6.16   **6.17**

In the left-hand diagram where the minimum price is set below the market equilibrium there is no effect because there is excess demand at that price which would keep the price at E. In the right-hand diagram where the minimum price is set above the market equilibrium trouble will develop because there is excess supply at that price. Someone has to be prepared to buy the excess if the price is to be kept above E. It will cost them the rectangle WZ x Minimum Price. The buyers are likely to be governments or commodity agreement buying agents or Common Agricultural Policy intervention buyers.

Figures 6.16 and 6.17   Minimum prices

Minimum prices. These create no problems if set below the normal market equilibrium price because the excess of demand at the minimum price will raise price towards the equilibrium. If, however, the minimum price is set above the market equilibrium there will be problems because excess supply is generated at that price. This has been the perennial problem of the Common Agricultural Policy (CAP) although the reforms of 1992 have gone some way to reducing the difficulties. Minimum prices are also applied in some international commodity agreements when they exist. In practice, the minimum price can only be maintained if some body, government or commodity agreement authority, is willing and able to buy up and store any surpluses generated by a minimum price that is set above the market equilibrium. Many governments, for example, buy and store in their currency reserves a variety of currencies, especially their own, in order to prevent their currency value falling below either pre-announced levels, as in the ERM (Exchange Rate Mechanism) or below a level that they have secretly decided upon, as when

Nigel Lawson shadowed the Deutschmark and kept the price of the pound near to a particular rate.

Exercise 4

Why is it hard for the UK to maintain a maximum and a minimum value for the pound on foreign exchange markets, as in the period to 1971 and between 1990 and 1992?

---

7 Degrees of Competition (1)

Aims of the chapter

To:

- explain the basic concepts relating to types of costs and revenues;
- explain the concept of normal and supernormal profit;
- put the above into the context of the real economy;
- explain in more detail, using the usual diagrams, the economist's models of the various types of competition, perfect competition, monopolistic competition and monopoly.

7.1   Basic Concepts

Costs of production in the short run are usually classified into fixed costs and variable costs. Total Fixed Costs (TFC) are the costs to which the entrepreneur is committed before anything is produced. Total Variable Costs (TVC) are those costs which the firm incurs as it starts production and which change as output alters. If the fixed costs and variable costs are added together we have Total Costs (TC). It is assumed that all costs are variable in the long run because all the factors can be altered and their combination changed. Most of us find these totals easy to understand but the economist finds them too cumbersome and usually uses average figures for all three: average fixed costs (AFC), average variable costs (AVC) and average costs (AC) in the short run and average total costs (ATC) in the long run. Average costs are sometimes called unit costs. The average figures are obtained by dividing the totals by the level of output. Economists also place great store by marginal costs (MC) which are defined as the change in total costs as output is altered by one unit. There are a few points worth remembering about these costs and the curves that are drawn to represent them.

- Marginal costs are assumed to fall up to a point and then to rise because of the operation of the law of diminishing returns. It is the rising section of the curve that is important.
- The marginal cost curve always cuts both the average cost and the average variable cost curves at their lowest points.
- The average fixed cost curve is a rectangular hyperbola, that is it has the same area rectangle under the curve at every point of the curve. This is

because the total fixed costs are constant and we are simply dividing the same quantity of costs by an increasing number.

- The total fixed cost curve is a horizontal straight line parallel to the x axis.
- The total variable cost curve starts at zero because there are no variable costs if nothing is produced.
- The total cost curve is parallel to the total variable cost curve and starts at the same place as the total fixed cost curve. This is because the only costs at zero output are fixed.

Figures 7.1, 7.2 and 7.3 illustrate these points and are drawn from the data in Table 7.1.

Table 7.1   Costs of production

Output	Total Fixed Cost	Total Variable Cost	Total Cost	Average Fixed Cost	Average Variable Cost	Average Total Cost	Marginal Cost
0	25	0	25	0	0	0	
1	25	25	50	25	25	50	25
2	25	45	70	12.5	22.5	35	20
3	25	63	88	8.3	21	29.3	18
4	25	88	113	6.25	22	28.25	25
5	25	120	145	5	24	29	32
6	25	156	181	4.16	26	30.16	36

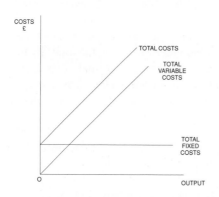

Figure 7.1   Total fixed and total variable costs of production

Figure 7.2   Average fixed, variable and total costs

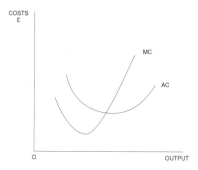

Figure 7.3   Average and marginal costs

Revenues. The simplest form of revenue is Total Revenue (TR) which is calculated by multiplying the selling price by the number sold or the output. The other forms which the economist usually prefers are Average Revenue (AR) and Marginal Revenue (MR). Average revenue per unit is the total revenue divided by the output. Marginal revenue is the change in total revenue when output is altered by one unit. Points to remember about the curves drawn to represent these are:

- Under conditions of perfect competition the total revenue curve is a straight line from the origin. This is because the selling price is assumed to be constant because each firm is a price taker. Nobody bothers to draw the TR curve except in perfect competition presumably because it is an unpredictable curve in other forms of competition.

- Under conditions of perfect competition, the average and the marginal revenue curves are the same because all units sell for the same price so the average price is the same as the selling price of each unit, the marginal revenue. The AR = MR and also = the firm's demand curve, d. See Figure 7.4.

- Under all other forms of competition, monopoly, monopolistic competition, and oligopoly it is assumed that the selling price declines as output expands and therefore that the average and marginal revenue curves both slope downwards to the right.

- The average revenue curve is the demand curve for the firm's products and slopes like a normal demand curve. There are some further technical points about the AR curve and its relationship to the MR curve which are marked on Figure 7.5.

- The less competition that exists in an industry, the less elastic the demand curve for the firm's product so the demand (AR) curves drawn to represent monopoly are usually steeper than those drawn for monopolistic competition.

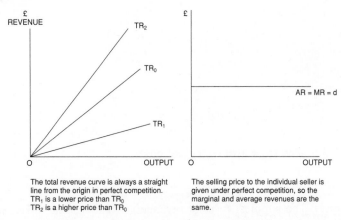

The total revenue curve is always a straight line from the origin in perfect competition. TR$_1$ is a lower price than TR$_0$ TR$_2$ is a higher price than TR$_0$

The selling price to the individual seller is given under perfect competition, so the marginal and average revenues are the same.

Figure 7.4   Perfect competition, total, average and marginal revenues

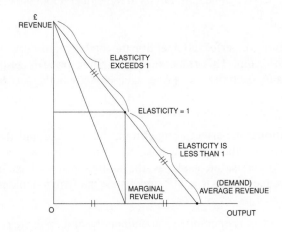

Figure 7.5   Elasticity and revenue

Normal and supernormal profit. These are concepts that reveal the quirkiness of the orthodox manner of looking at things in economics. They are another example of how economists' definitions differ from the ordinary person's daily use of terms. It may explain why some economists can only talk to other economists. The economist usually regards the minimum reward expected by the entrepreneur for undertaking the risk of a business as '**normal**

profit'. As this minimum reward is seen as an opportunity cost, that is the return on capital that the entrepreneur could expect in the next best alternative use for the capital, this normal profit is included in the average cost curve because it constitutes part of the fixed costs of production. In considering the opportunity cost, the entrepreneur must study what return could be obtained if the capital were placed on deposit earning an interest rate or what yield could be obtained by putting the money into other enterprises. The particular enterprise being studied might be more risky than normal, gold mining for example, so a higher return for the greater risk might be expected. There will also come a point when the capital will need to be replaced so, in the short run, the entrepreneur will expect to earn enough to replace the fixed equipment. The conclusion is that the minimum return required to retain the entrepreneur in the current enterprise is 'normal profit.' Thus, when we draw a diagram where Average Cost = Average Revenue, normal profits are being earned because we have incorporated the normal profit in the cost curve.

Supernormal profit is any level of profit above the 'normal.' It is sometimes called 'abnormal profit'. Therefore, if we draw a diagram where Average Revenue exceeds Average Cost at the profit maximising level of output, the entrepreneur is earning supernormal profit. The concept is important because the existence of supernormal profit attracts new enterprises into the industry and this should, over time, reduce or eradicate the excess together, probably, with some of the firms in the industry who are less efficient. You may have seen this process at work over the years in all sorts of enterprises and its effects can easily be seen in a typical high street where shops earning low profits have been replaced by those earning higher, or supernormal profits. It can be seen in the small building industry where it is relatively easy to enter and leave. Over the years there have been successive phases of expansion and short-run supernormal profit, such as central heating installation, showers, kitchen improvements, bathroom replacements, secondary double glazing, replacement windows, conservatories and block paving. The early entrants into these fields tend to make high profits until competition forces lower prices and bankruptcies.

Exercise I

Why is 'normal profit' incorporated in the average cost curve? Can you think of enterprises, apart from those mentioned, where supernormal profit has been earned in recent years?

7.2   **Perfect Competition**

Some economists still find something useful in this ancient model and some use the conclusions that stem from its artificial assumptions to advocate extreme forms of competition in the belief that they will produce the best of all possible worlds. It is better to avoid such extremism and adopt a sceptical approach to this model because it is so far away from reality that it is mainly an intellectual exercise. The assumptions of the model are that there is a very large number of buyers and sellers of a homogeneous product which means that they are selling an identical good that is not differentiated from their competitors' goods in any way. The firms are, therefore, selling perfect substitutes so that each firm has a perfectly elastic, horizontal, demand curve for its good. The firm produces such a small part of the total supply of the industry that it cannot affect the market price by adding its output to or withholding it from the market. If the USA Government did not intervene in grain markets, an excellent example would be the 400 000 mid-West wheat producers who, individually, have no effect on the Chicago market price. They are, effectively, price takers which is one of the requirements of the perfect competition model. Another assumption is that the participants in the market have perfect information or knowledge of market conditions such as prices. This is an extreme assumption that almost takes the model into the realms of fantasy especially when you consider the percentage of the population who do not know who is prime minister at any particular time let alone the price of basic items in their local supermarket. Yet another assumption is that there is complete freedom for firms to enter or leave the industry. This is an important starting point for a competitive model because, in the real world, there are sometimes formidable barriers to the entry of new firms. Indeed, many new entrants are subsidiaries of very large corporations who can afford to bear the loss of a new venture for a few years. There is a variety of barriers, such as patents, economies of scale of existing firms, advertising costs and the restrictive size of the market where there may only be room for one or two firms who have carved out a share of the market by virtue of low cost production. There are other assumptions in the model such as the state of technology being the same for the firms in the short run and that for the process to work there should be perfect mobility of the factors of production. This latter is not often stated but the rest of the perfect market would not work if labour, land and capital could not move between uses without obstruction or delay. It is, of course, another extreme assumption that is divorced from the real world.

The conclusions of the perfect competition model are divided into short-run and long-run applications. Fancy diagrams can be drawn to illustrate most of these points but, as many students develop a certain glazed look as the diagrams pass before their eyes and end up unable to distinguish between them, they will be kept to a minimum.

The short run:

1. Firms can be earning normal profits where they are maximising profits so that MC = MR; and AR = AC. See Figure 7.6. These firms can continue into the long run because the normal profit enables them to replace their fixed equipment and there is no incentive for the entrepreneur to leave the industry.

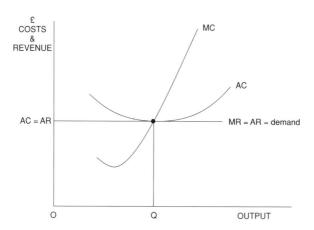

Figure 7.6   Perfect competition and normal profit

2. Firms can be earning supernormal profit where their AR exceeds their AC at their profit maximising output where MC = MR. The existence of these abnormal profits attracts new firms into the industry and the extra competition erodes the excess as prices tend to fall and costs of production may rise as there is extra competition for factors of production. By the time the long run is reached every firm is earning normal profit. See Figure 7.7 and try to visualise the AR line gradually falling and the AC curve slowly rising until there is no shaded rectangle. The output will change as well.

3. Firms may have a decision to make when their selling price is above the average variable cost of production but is not sufficient to cover all the fixed costs as well. In this situation they are minimising their losses if they produce where MC = MR in the sense that the losses would be larger if they stopped producing. The losses would then be the whole of their fixed costs. If the AVC = AR (the selling price), the firm is making as much loss, the extent of the fixed costs, as if it closed down. In brief, the firm must at least be selling at a price that covers its variable costs in order to remain in production. (See Figure 7.8)

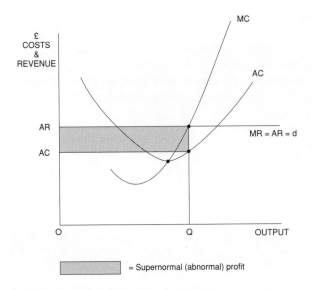

Figure 7.7   **Perfect competition and supernormal profit**

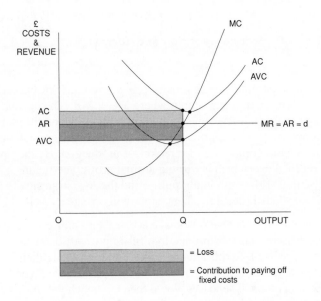

Figure 7.8   **Perfect competition, covering average variable costs**

4. Firms could be in a situation where they might as well leave the industry because their selling price, AR, is less than their AVC. Next time you see an almost empty offpeak bus passing, stop and wonder if the number of passengers is sufficient for it to cover its variable costs of fuel and wages. If it is less than about half full it almost certainly is not and must be receiving a subsidy from a local authority, from a profitable route elsewhere or from its own route where profits are made in peak hours.

The long run is defined by Marshall as the time period when all the factors of production can be varied but there is insufficient time to change the basic technology of the processes. In the very long run the technology can also change. This distinction is far divorced from reality because almost no-one replaces their existing technology with an exact replica. Indeed, it is often difficult to get replacement parts after a few years let alone a replacement system. How often have we heard the immortal phrase, 'Sorry Gov., we don't keep spares for that anymore'. There is some sense in the distinction if the basic technology does not alter but what is 'basic?' Many writers nowadays do not distinguish between the two time periods. The main conclusions of the theory in respect of the long run are:

- All firms will be earning normal profits and producing where $MR = MC$.

- All firms will be maximising profit and producing an output where the selling price = the average total cost of production: $AR = ATC$

- The industry will be in equilibrium in the sense that no firm will enter or leave the industry, (because only normal profits are available).

- Firms will be producing an output at the lowest point of their long-run average total cost curves, that is the most efficient, low cost point and will have no further economies of scale available to them. This maximises society's use of resources since they are being used most efficiently.

- The market price will be equal to the lowest level of long-run average costs so that consumers are obtaining the greatest possible benefit.

Some of these conclusions are apparent in Figure 7.9.

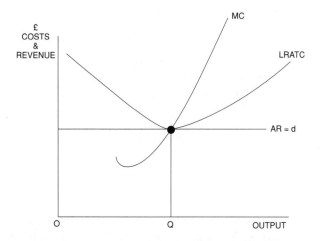

Figure 7.9   Perfect competition, long-run equilibrium

Why do some economists regard perfect competition as a desirable objective?

Some economists are so overcome by the conclusions of the perfect competition model that they see it as justifying any policy that, in their view, increases competition. These views have supported the fashion since the early 1980s for privatisation, deregulation and most policies that come under the general heading of supply-side policies. There are two main planks on which this belief in competition is based:

1. **Productive efficiency.** The theory concludes, based on the analysis above, that productive efficiency is maximised in an economy when all industries are producing at the lowest possible average total cost. In this situation, no greater benefit could be achieved by transferring resources from one industry to another. The concept of opportunity cost can be applied here.

2. **Allocative efficiency.** The theory also concludes that, if price equals the marginal cost of production in the whole economy, allocative efficiency is also maximised. The concept of allocative efficiency relates the extent to which consumers benefit from the consumption of a good to the use of resources required in its production. The so-called neo-classical theory in this respect applies the idea of utility here and concludes that where marginal cost = price, the value to consumers of the last unit consumed is equal to the cost of utilising the factors of production. If MC does not equal price the consumers can obtain greater economic welfare if output is altered until MC does equal price. If price is less than MC output should be reduced and if price exceeds MC output should be raised. There are some serious objections to these ideas in that they take no account in the usual

statements of external costs and benefits. Despite the criticism of the analysis there is strong support in some quarters for policies that aim at achieving prices equal to either short-run or long-run marginal costs. Some stick out for price, including marginal *social* benefits to equal marginal *social* cost which does take account of external costs.

The supporters of competition usually bolster their analysis with the argument that any departure from perfect competition involves what is called a 'welfare loss'. This idea is most easily applied to monopoly where there is only one seller. It is argued, in defiance of what happens in the real world, that the monopolist is protected from competition by barriers to the entry of competitors and therefore has no incentives to maximise technical efficiency and achieve allocative efficiency. In practice some near monopolists are at the forefront of technological change. It is argued that consumers suffer a welfare loss in terms of what is called the consumer surplus (another piece of economic jargon) but that some of this loss is transferred to the producers. We end up with what is called a 'dead-weight welfare loss'. Consumer surplus is the area under the demand curve and above the price line, the shaded triangle in Figure 7.10. It exists because we pay the market price as determined by supply and demand but some of us were willing, as shown by the effective demand curve, to have paid a higher price. We are, therefore, left with a 'surplus' which we did not have to pay because the market price is lower than that price we were prepared to pay. There is also a 'producer's surplus' below the price line as shown in Figure 7.10. This arises because some sellers receive a higher market price than they were willing to accept. Figure 7.11 shows the dead-weight welfare loss when a perfectly competitive industry is monopolised.

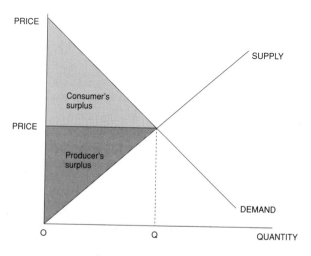

Figure 7.10   Consumer and producer surplus

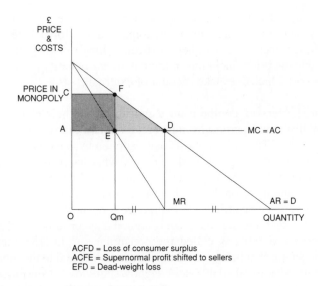

ACFD = Loss of consumer surplus
ACFE = Supernormal profit shifted to sellers
EFD = Dead-weight loss

Figure 7.11   Dead-weight welfare loss

Exercise 2

Count up the number of building societies in your nearest main urban centre. Do they constitute a competitive market? How can you judge?

7.3   Monopolistic Competition

When this area of economic theory was first mooted there were examples of industries where there were large numbers of firms in an industry producing very similar products and where it was easy for new firms to enter. The motor industry was like that until the late 1920s and it was also the case in financial sectors and pharmaceuticals. In all cases we may have an oligopoly situation if national producers only are counted but something closer to monopolistic competition if foreign competition is counted. It is extremely difficult to find realistic examples of monopolistic competition nowadays because of the merger and take-over mania of recent decades. The distinctive feature of the model is the idea that this large number of sellers of a product try to persuade buyers that their product is unique and superior to that of their competitors. They do this by the use of advertising, brand names, packaging, design, patents and so on. There is no longer perfect knowledge of the market on the part of buyers and sellers. It is still assumed that sellers are trying to maximise profits. As a result, all sellers have a separate, downward sloping demand curve for their product although it will be very elastic because of the close substitutes available. The conclusions of the model are shown in Figures 7.12 and 7.13, which illustrate the short-run and long-run equilibrium.

The short-run analysis concludes that the firm may be earning supernormal profits or normal profits. Figure 7.12 shows the short-run supernormal profits in the shaded rectangle. Their existence encourages new entrants into the industry and the extra competition erodes the supernormal profit until, by the long run, they no longer exist. The normal profit diagram for the short run looks like the long-run diagram, Figure 7.13, except that the AR and MR curves would be less elastic.

The long-run analysis shows that all firms are earning normal profits and that the demand curve is more elastic because of the extra competition. The main difference, however, between this and the prefect competition model is that long-run output is no longer at the minimum point of the firm's average total cost curve. The implication is, therefore, that consumer welfare is not maximised and productive and allocative efficiency are not being achieved. Figure 7.13 shows the long-run equilibrium.

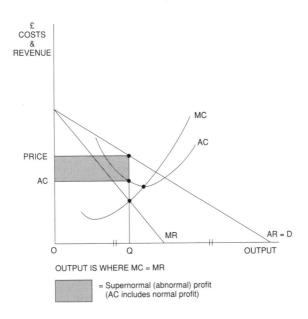

Figure 7.12   **Monopolistic competition, short-run**

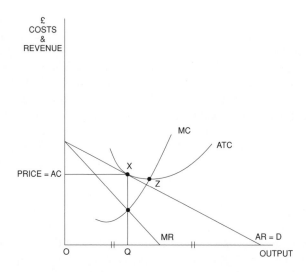

ATC is at X when output is at Q, where MC = MR.
This is not the minimum level of ATC which is at Z.
Therefore allocative and productive efficiency are not maximised.

Figure 7.13   Monopolistic competition, long-run

Exercise 3

Are there any potential problems arising from the competitive drive to cut costs of production? What might they be?

7.4   Monopoly

The economic model of monopoly is less unrealistic than the previous models but it does assume that there is a single firm, which is therefore by definition the industry as well, selling a good or service for which there is no close substitute. Such monopolies may be created by state decisions or may be a publicly owned institution. They may also grow up from some natural deposit of minerals which are owned by one firm or from physical geography which gives a particular location such as a river crossing an effective monopoly of ferries or bridges. Another type of monopoly that may arise is called a 'natural' monopoly although there is some dispute about the exact application of this term. Modern technology and state intervention may enable competition to be enforced. An example of this type of natural monopoly is in the gas pipeline grid in the United Kingdom where it would obviously be uneconomic to have two or more pipelines to each town or house. The pipes might be duplicated in some instances for security of supply reasons to large consuming areas or firms. Modern computer technology enables the natural monopolist's power to be broken. Natural gas is a homogeneous product and any company can put its gas into the system because British Gas, the owner of most of the grid, is legally obliged to give them wayleave. The inputs from different sellers can be measured and the individual consumer can be billed and British Gas paid for its pipeline services. A similar system now operates with the electricity grid and telephones. The method adopted to privatise the railways via Railtrack which owns the track, signalling system and most stations and via franchise operators who run trains after payment to Railtrack, is an attempt to break a natural monopoly.

There are several conclusions from the model and some technical points to be borne in mind. These are:

- The monopolist maximises profit where MC = MR.

- The monopolist earns supernormal profit and there is no reason why this should be eroded because new entrants will be kept out as long as the monopoly is effective.

- The monopolist will not be producing at a level of output yielding the minimum level of average cost and price will not be equal to minimum average costs so there will not be productive or allocative efficiency. The monopolist is exploiting the consumer by charging a higher price and producing less than would be the case under perfect competition, unless there are very large economies of scale.

- The monopolist produces an output where the price is in the elastic sector, the top left, of the AR curve before the marginal revenue (MR) reaches zero. Otherwise the additional units would be sold at a negative price.

- The monopolist cannot fix both the price and the output unless the demand is perfectly inelastic but most monopolists will develop an understanding of their market so that they can judge accurately the effect of price changes. The theory tends to assume that they fix output, that is where MC = MR.

- There may be economies of scale available to the monopolist that are not available to the large number of small firms working in competitive conditions. The monopolist may, therefore, produce more at a lower price than a perfectly competitive industry. There are still supernormal profits being earned, however, and the full benefits of the low price and greater output will not all be handed over to the consumer. In some people's opinion this is a good reason for the state to control or own such a monopoly so that the benefits could be passed on to the consumer or taxpayer rather than to the shareholder. This was one of the motives behind the nationalisation of the old natural monopolies, gas, electricity, railways and telecommunications.

- A monopoly is only strong as long as it can keep out competitors and it will be relatively weak if competitive products or substitutes become available. One of the more pervasive and persistent myths of modern times is that monopolists have bought up and shelved new technologies or inventions that would have ruined their business. One such myth concerns the 'everlasting light bulb'.

- The United Kingdom Government defines a monopoly situation as one where 25 per cent of the sales of a good or service originate with one supplier. Such market situations may be investigated by the Monopolies and Mergers Commission and ordered to change their prices or methods of marketing.

Figure 7.14 is the usual diagram to show a monopoly. It applies to both the short and the long run.

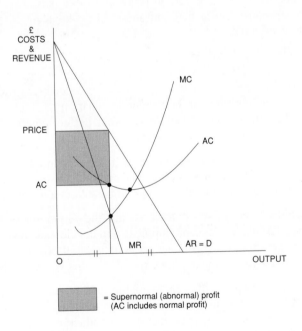

Figure 7.14   **Monopoly**

Exercise 4

Why cannot a monopolist fix both price and output at the same time? What limits the power of a monopolist?

Oligopoly and contestable markets are dealt with in the next chapter, 'Degrees of Competition (2)'.

8 Degrees of Competition (2)

Aims of the chapter

To extend the analysis of competition to oligopoly and to outline the newer theory of contestable markets. In particular to:

- explain the nature of oligopolistic markets;
- consider collusion in oligopolistic markets;
- consider non-collusive behaviour;
- explain the operation of cartels;
- consider degrees of price stability and price competition;
- outline the role of advertising in oligopolistic conditions;
- examine the nature of barriers to the entry of new competitors;
- outline the theory of contestable markets;
- examine UK and European Union competition policy.

8.1 Oligopolistic Markets

We can say that a market is an oligopoly if a few firms dominate the sales or production of the industry. There is, of course, a need to define *few* and this is usually done by using what is called an index of concentration or concentration ratio. The researcher chooses a number such as four, five, six or seven and calculates the share that this number of the largest firms in the industry has of its total output or employment. One of the most concentrated industries is shown, by this measure, to be the tobacco industry where, in 1991, a five firm concentration ratio of net output worked out at 99 per cent. In contrast, printing and publishing had a ratio of only 17 per cent. This ratio is quite a good guide but more information is needed to make a full analysis. The five firms in the example above might be completely dominated by one or two companies and the industry might, in practice, be a duopoly rather than an oligopoly. The existence of a number of very small firms in an industry may create a smokescreen and hide the real market power of the few dominant companies. An alternative method of measuring market concentration is called the Hirschman–Herfindahl Index (HHI) which produces a figure close to zero if the industry consists of a large number of firms of equal size whereas the closer the figure is to one the more concentrated is the industry in a few hands. The HHI is calculated by obtaining the values of each firm's market

106

share and squaring them and then summing them across all the firms in that market. Both of these methods have defects but they do put some objective foundation on to what is usually apparent from a subjective cursory glance at the market shares of one or two firms in an industry. For example, you only have to look in your local newspaper to find out what films are on for it to be obvious that film distribution in the United Kingdom is mainly in the hands of two chains of multiscreen cinema operators.

Characteristics of oligopolistic markets

Heavy expenditure on advertising is a typical feature in oligopoly. Its purpose is complex but tends to be dominated by the need to maintain market share against rival producers' products. It may be used in the classic manner to inform the consumer about a new or revamped product. Relaunches in 1996 of Pepsi in blue livery and of Persil in blue packaging are examples. Advertising may also be used to counteract the launch of a rival's new or improved product. In other words it is used as a spoiler. It is also apparent that much advertising takes place because sellers are frightened of the consequences if they stop and their rivals persist. In this circumstance the firm might lose market share irrevocably, especially in certain luxury goods markets such as cosmetics.

Competition by any means except genuine price cutting is also a feature of oligopoly. Most of us have half completed sets of wine glasses or unredeemed 'money off next purchase' coupons in our houses. Some people desperately seek points with their credit card purchases or air miles or go by roundabout routes to get the right sort of petrol points. These are all results of the attempts by sellers to maintain consumer loyalty without the pain of price cutting. Such schemes are accompanied by persistent advertising campaigns which have the same sort of effects upon the firm's costs of production as normal advertising. Any increased customer loyalty that results makes the demand for the individual firm's products less elastic and gives it more market power. It may raise demand and enable more economies of scale to be obtained with the possibility that the price to the buyer might be lower than would otherwise be the case. Alternatively, the firm might keep the price high and reap larger profits. Some non-price competition is a simple matter of copycat activity, for example the rush of insurance companies and banks to provide emergency services telephone lines and assistance to their customers. One pioneers the idea and the others follow suit.

Strong brand differentiation is usually a characteristic of oligopolistic markets. Product design and packaging, corporate logos, corporate store design and décor and the skilled placing of advertisements are largely twentieth-century phenomena. In some cases a large company such as a multiple retailer derives considerable economies of scale from building all its stores to the same corporate design and décor and from having a corporate identity for its own brands but the regular revamps that occur, often at fairly short intervals, must be exceptionally expensive. Who pays the cost when a large retailer or building society revamps several hundred outlets in new livery? The suspicion is that it is the customer rather than the shareholder in oligopolistic markets. We know that the designers and shop fitters benefit through the extra work and so do the paint manufacturers but do sales rise sufficiently to justify the expense? Some brand differentiation is based on the creation of fears in the consumer's mind or on the invention of supposed problems. A classic example of this nature is the identification of split ends in human hair and a 'cure'. Did anyone know such defects existed until it was pointed out in advertisements? Many cosmetics and patent medicines are sold on the basis of 'problems' and so are washing powders. Did you lose much sleep over the 'bobbles' on your clothes until an advertiser who had developed a product to prevent them told you about the problem? Probably not.

Exercise I

Which brands can you identify from the shape and colour of a bottle, can or package without being able to read the label? Would you know which retailer's shop you were in if you were taken in blindfolded and then had the blindfold removed? How would you know (without reading signs and labels)?

Barriers to the entry of new competitors are commonplace in oligopoly. These barriers take many forms. Some arise from the nature of the product and from the technology required to manufacture it. If it is a good that lends itself to large economies of scale as output is expanded there is likely to be an obstacle to the entry of new firms because of the huge capital, fixed cost of building plant to manufacture it and to train a workforce to assemble it. Some recent Japanese investments in new car plants in the United Kingdom have cost over £500 million.

There may be an extremely large investment into the research and development of a new product, for example new airliners which can cost $3–8 billion (US) before an aircraft is granted approval by the aviation authorities. Few firms can afford, or are able to borrow such sums, and the market is left to established players. These existing firms have enormous advantages in terms of customer goodwill, knowledge of the market, possession of skilled work forces, lower fixed costs and service and dealer networks. Pharmaceuticals which can cost millions of pounds to develop are another example. Some types of barriers may be strengthened if the existing firms think that a new entrant is about to appear. For example, the proposed launch of a new newspaper is always accompanied by special offers from existing papers and even by fierce price cuts. The opening of the Channel Tunnel was met by the ferry companies introducing more frequent ferry crossings and strong price competition. The existence of a high risk of failure to cover the fixed cost of entry is a serious deterrent to new entrants and not many can afford to take a very long view of the market and wait for profits to come. The ones that can afford to finance heavy short-term losses may be foreign entrants and it is noticeable that many national oligopolies are diluted by new foreign firms entering the market. Occasionally new technology creates a market where the initial capital investment is so large that only a few firms can afford to enter and bear the risks. Eventually, as the market matures, or the technology becomes cheaper or more commonplace, more firms may enter. Satellite television broadcasting is an example, as are cellular mobile phones.

Exercise 2

What has been the long-run effect on ferry prices and the ferry companies' share of the market of the opening of the Channel Tunnel?

The State may create barriers to entry in the form of laws about patents, trade marks, copyright and licensing. It may also perpetuate an oligopoly when it introduces regulation of previously nationalised industries. In the United Kingdom in 1996, the privatised utilities are all oligopolistic and the state, via the official regulator who is largely independent, has set a legal framework that ensures the continuance of the few firms and prevents the emergence of any successor to the old natural monopoly of the nationalisation era. The regulatory system is supposed to stimulate and maintain competition but there is still a long way to go before all consumers can choose their gas and electricity suppliers or before they can choose from more than two or three telecommunication providers. It is also very unlikely that consumers will ever be able to choose between water suppliers so regulation will probably be permanent.

Some markets are limited in size by a variety of factors and there may be room for a very restricted number of suppliers, occasionally only one if there are geographical and income factors involved. At one time the United Kingdom market could only support one manufacturer of industrial gases, BOC, until an American company, Air Products, entered the field. At one time local newspapers were produced with a technology that required a circulation of about 30 000 copies per week for them to be viable so a town or district usually had only one. New web offset and computerised technology changed that.

Some writers follow the work of an American economist, Joe Bain who, in 1956, classified barriers to entry into three types, product differentiation, absolute cost advantages and scale economies of existing firms.

Collusion between suppliers has often been an accompaniment of oligopoly. Such co-operative behaviour takes many forms. At one extreme it materialises as the cartel with a formal organisation. Cartels are discussed separately, below. At the other extreme, collusion takes a loose form with tacit, unspoken or unwritten agreements not to compete in certain ways. Some industries have a dominant firm which provides leadership in price and product changes. Others have what the economist calls a 'barometric' leader, that is one firm, which is not necessarily the largest, that pioneers new approaches to products, pricing and marketing. Newcomers can have a similar effect on an established industry; examples include the impact of the then Midland Bank subsidiary 'First Direct' which has caused an enormous shift towards telephone banking, and Direct Line Insurance which, through its irritating but highly effective advertising campaign featuring a musical red telephone, has changed the face of United Kingdom insurance for ever.

Between the two extremes there is a wide range of collusive behaviour which, it should be emphasised, is in a continual state of flux. In the United Kingdom most collusive behaviour is illegal unless the Restrictive Trade Practices Court specifically permits it. That was the case with the now defunct Net Book Agreement that allowed publishers to fix the resale price of books designated as 'net books'. Firms have had a legal obligation since the 1956 Restrictive Trade Practices Act to register any agreement that restricts prices or conditions of trade. Subsequent legislation has extended prohibition to what are called 'information agreements' where various methods can be used to appraise collusive competitors of proposed price and product changes. Several firms have been prosecuted and fined for failing to register agreements. Their practices have usually been revealed by so-called 'whistle blowers' who have a grudge against their employer or who are publicly spirited, or by new entrants to the market who find it difficult to compete. On the practical level it is probably impossible to eradicate all collusive behaviour that is not registered. In any case, the prosecution system is extremely cumbersome and the penalties are usually weak. Full details of collusive activities that have been investigated are to be found in the reports of the Monopolies and Mergers Commission and of the Restrictive Practices Court.

Cartels are also usually illegal unless they have received legal dispensation. Some are national but many are, or become, international. A cartel has a formal organisation, usually in the form of a central administrative structure. A number of firms in an industry agree to set up such an organisation that then supervises the execution of their collusive agreement to control prices in different markets for various products and to allocate market shares in different regions, sectors or countries. They tend to form when business is bad and to collapse when trade picks up but this is not the inevitable rule.

Cartels have a very ancient history but came to prominence in the late nineteenth century, particularly in Germany in the coal, iron and steel and heavy chemical industries. They were important in developing the industrial strength of the new German empire behind a protective barrier of tariffs. They were particularly important in 1930s Germany under Hitler. Cartels became a normal part of international business life and formed and collapsed with movements of the trade cycle. Most industrialised countries had them and in some cases they were sponsored by governments, for example the 1931 British Iron and Steel Federation (BISF) was formed with Government agreement, ostensibly to modernise the industry, behind a protective tariff of 33.3 per cent.

Cartels may sometimes affect everyone's lives. It can be argued that the actions of the most famous cartel, the Organisation of Petroleum Exporting Countries (OPEC) have shifted the balance of economic power in the world. OPEC was formed, as were many cartels, in response to poor market conditions in a period of falling prices. In 1960 a number of oil producing nations joined together to try and increase their bargaining power against the international oil companies who, in the 1950s, had used the excess supplies then prevailing to keep down the price they paid for crude oil. In 1996 there were 12 members with Saudi Arabia as the dominant member. OPEC is mainly a Middle Eastern cartel with Iraq, Iran, the United Arab Emirates, Kuwait, Qatar, Libya and Algeria as leading members but also includes states such as Venezuela, Gabon, Nigeria, Indonesia. Ecuador was a member from 1973 to 1992. The organisation was most effective and came to prominence in the 1970s when it forced up crude oil prices on several occasions by strict controls of the output of its members. The consequences were far reaching. They included an enormous shift of money from the industrialised countries to the OPEC members which then achieved greater economic power by reinvesting the money in the USA and Europe and in building up their own economies and military machines. There were time lags between the payment for the oil and the reinvestment of the proceeds and the delays had a disruptive effect on the world economy. The effects of the oil price rise, usually called an 'economic shock,' were very inflationary and contributed to the depression in the world economy in the mid and late 1970s. There were other effects such as the accelerated search for oil and gas elsewhere and the reopening of United States' oil fields. There was also added impetus to developments in designing fuel efficient vehicles and energy conservation.

OPEC's power declined as alternative supplies became available from Mexico, the North Sea, Russia, Alaska and so on. The world economic slump in the 1980s also weakened the cartel's influence. The cartel began to become undisciplined as some members tried to 'cheat' on the other members by producing more than their agreed quotas of output. Their cheating helped to create an oversupply and the world price fell below the cartel's target range. There were often political motives behind their attempts, for example those by Iran to finance its war with Iraq, by Nigeria which needed more money for development and to meet its debts, and by Libya to finance its political stance at home and abroad. Iraq broke from the cartel's policy prior to its invasion of Kuwait. OPEC in the 1990s is torn between those who wish to cut prices and those who want quotas to be reduced and more strictly applied.

There are, or have been, other cartels that affect our lives. One of the most prominent is IATA, the International Air Transport Association which is an organisation of airlines that has tried, with varying degrees of success since the 1970s, to fix prices. It has proved vulnerable to price cutting from new entrants and in periods of an overall fall in demand. Sometimes the aggressive new price cutters are eliminated by counter action, as was the case with Laker Airways in the 1970s or are absorbed into the structure once they are established and realise the benefits of co-operation as opposed to competition. Another cartel that works quietly in the background controls competition and pricing between the major international telephone companies in respect of international calls. It is called the International Telegraph and Telephone Consultative Committee which is known by its French initials as CCITT. Yet another modern cartel that is well documented is the United Kingdom cement cartel operated legally by the Cement Makers' Federation until its dissolution in 1987. The Restrictive Practices Court allowed it to exist on the grounds that a system of fixing common prices meant that the capacity of the industry could be controlled in a manner beneficial to the public as well as to the industry. The three dominant producers with 60, 22 and 18 per cent respectively of the market met regularly and discussed price, market shares and supplies. The cartel ceased operating in the face of possible investigation from the Monopolies and Mergers Commission and against the background of fierce price cutting from imports from Greece and Turkey. The United Kingdom cement industry appears to have 'won' the price war against the cheap foreign imports but the cartel has not been resurrected. The European Union has strong policies against cartels but one that is permitted controls the pricing of shipping cargoes. It came under investigation in 1996 when it tried to extend the price fixing to inland transport to the ports.

Exercise 3

Why might the government allow a cartel or even support it?

Price stickiness is a phrase that often appears when oligopoly is discussed because some economists think that they have observed a tendency for prices in oligopolistic markets to be more stable than in other types of market. Their findings have been disputed by other researchers. This debate began as far back as 1939 when two British and one American economist proposed an explanation of these 'sticky' prices. They suggested that there was a kinked demand curve in some oligopoly situations. A simplified version is shown in Figure 8.1 but you will find extremely complicated drawings of the kinked demand curve in some text books. You should be warned that some economists argue that there is little or no evidence in the real world for the kinked demand curve and you should avoid regarding it, as some books used to, as the *only* explanation of oligopoly behaviour. If price stickiness does exist, there are other explanations for it, for example the sheer administrative cost of altering prices at frequent intervals in response to competitors' actions. Another is that, in a given industry such as petrol, all the firms have roughly the same costs for their raw materials on the open market and their prices are almost bound to move in line over time. There is also the practical consideration that the consumer becomes accustomed to a certain price range for a product and there is a psychological barrier to change at certain levels. In these cases the seller may simply adjust the quantity in the packet or container rather than raise price. It is also inconvenient to shopkeepers to start charging prices that do not easily fit the coinage available.

GAME THEORY AND FIRMS' BEHAVIOUR

The theory of games (game theory) applies mathematics to a game, a business situation or military problem in order to maximise gain or minimise loss.

The French mathematician Emile Borel proposed game theory in a series of papers between 1921 and 1927 and was the first to define games of strategy. John von Neumann, a mathematician and physicist, collaborated with an economist, Oskar Morgenstern, to apply game theory to competitive economic behaviour. Von Neumann put forward his 'minimax' theorem in 1928 and elaborated it in his joint work with Morgenstern published in 1944, *Theory of Games and Economic Behaviour*. An important early contribution to game theory was by Philip Morse who analysed its application to submarine warfare and convoy protection in the Second World War.

Game theory distinguishes three situations: a. singular games such as solitaire where there is no conflict and the player simply selects the best course of action. A pure monopolist can be analysed in this way; b. dual games such as chess or bridge where there are two pairs. These dual games exhibit direct conflict where what one player gains the other loses (zero sum games); c. plural games where one player's gain does not necessarily imply loss by another player.

1. Games can be described as zero sum where one person's gain is another player's loss.
2. Non-zero sum games are where all players can gain from an individual's decision.
3. Games may be co-operative where collusion is possible or non-co-operative where the participants do not collude.

In 1994, three economists, John Harsanyi, John Nash and Reinhard Selten, won the Nobel prize for economics for their work on game theory and its applications to monopoly, oligopoly, cartels and bond markets. However, despite all the interest in game theory in modern economics, there are still few real life applications.

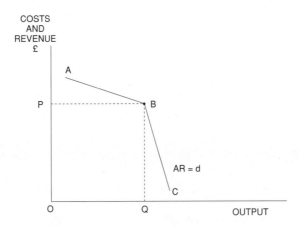

Section AB exhibits greater price elasticity than BC because, if one firm in the oligopoly raises its price, the competitors delay following suit or do not do so in the expectation of obtaining a greater market share. If the firm cuts its price the others would follow suit to maintain their market shares.

Figure 8.1   The kinked demand curve in oligopoly

Interdependence is another characteristic of oligopolistic markets and **Game theory** can be applied to oligopoly because it is essentially a set of situations where there are several 'players' of a 'game' and each firm's decisions may be taken in relation to perceptions of how the rivals may behave if a certain course of action is taken. Firm A can behave as if the responses of its rivals are able to be ignored completely. It may be arrogant or simply not be able to work out all the permutations of the various possible reactions, although it would learn from experience over the years. Alternatively, it can behave in a manner that assumes certain reactions by its rivals and plan accordingly. It may even plan subsequent reactions to their reactions. The modern mathematical application of game theory began when it became imperative in the Second World War to calculate the best method of using escort ships to protect convoys against submarine attack. It expanded into war games and is now applied to oligopoly and is used to try to predict whether collusion or competitive behaviour is better and in what circumstances it is better. You will find references to *zero sum* games where the winner takes all and the loser has nothing and to the *prisoners' dilemma* where criminals are arrested and must decide in the light of promises of remitted sentences and threats of longer punishments and in the lack of full knowledge of how their fellow criminals are behaving, whether to confess or not (see boxes). These theoretical activities are a source of enjoyment to economists but the conclusions of all this cerebral activity are inconclusive. It appears that oligopolists may benefit from collusion and from competition and that oligopoly may result in stable and non-stable prices and that there may be price competition and non-price competition.

THE PRISONER'S DILEMMA

The 'prisoner's dilemma' is a famous example of a non-zero sum game where all the players may gain from an individual decision. The conclusion is that the individual pursuit of private self-interest produces a solution which is less satisfactory than a possible alternative.

Criminals are arrested, kept separate, and interrogated. All know that if no-one confesses and informs on the others they will get off completely or with a low sentence. But, if one of them confesses and the others do not, he will go free and the rest will be given stiff sentences. If all of them confess they will receive sentences less severe than if only one confesses. If self-interest dominates, it is rational for the individual to confess and leave the fellow criminals in deep trouble. If they all behave in this way, however, out of rational self-interest, they will all, collectively, end up worse off. Ideally they need a prior agreement that no-one will confess.

The lesson of the prisoner's dilemma is that rational decisions at the micro-level may lead to an outcome that is not rational at a macro-level. This conclusion can be applied to firms competing in an oligopolistic market.

8.2 Conclusions on Oligopoly

There are so many varieties of competition within what is called oligopoly and each example seems to change its behaviour over time that a case can be made that we should stop trying to make generalised statements about it and instead study individual industries in their own right. We would then say that a particular industry was an oligopoly and that it had behaved for a certain time period in a manner that ensured price stability and non-price competition and that, between certain dates, it had for this or that reason begun to compete via price, and so on.

The idea that oligopolists simply aim to maximise short-run profits or even long-run profits has to be strongly modified. There are, inevitably, in the light of the previous paragraph, some firms who do appear to maximise short-run profits. These are companies that indulge in aggressive take-overs using borrowed money who then sell off assets or run their new subsidiaries in a way that replaces a long-run strategy with a short-run aim. They do things such as strip out research and development, sell physical assets and 'downsize' their labour forces. They maximise shareholder values in order to keep their institutional investors quiet and to make their own share options more valuable. After a period of time the subsidiary is sold, usually with a significant paper gain. It is a moot point whether society as a whole has benefited.

In practice, firms have several different objectives and these may change over time:

- They may aim at steady growth of profits over time, with allowances for alterations in the economic climate. This aim usually keeps the City analysts reasonably happy and institutional investors make no trouble. The ordinary small shareholder can be ignored. This general strategy works well until there is a fall in profits or, possibly, a failure of profits to match the rest of the sector. At that point there is considerable fuss made and suggestions in the media that chief executives be replaced. If the company is a household name, as was the case with J. Sainsbury in early 1996, any fall in profits after years of steady growth are regarded with the same degree of shock and horror as the England football team being knocked out of the World Cup in the early rounds by Ascension Island. The modern United Kingdom media is not renowned for its sense of proportion.

- Another possible aim of firms is to maintain their market share against their main competitors, given the constraint that profit levels need to be considered as well. This partly explains the obsession of certain sectors, such as the car industry, with the monthly publication of market shares of different models and the cunning devices adopted to keep or raise market share. It also partly explains the endless advertising of brands and products that are already well known to the public. The assumption must be that these captains of industry must think they are spending their money wisely on advertising otherwise they would not do so. An effective campaign may raise market share and give a critical advantage to a firm, especially when new products or developments are introduced. An example of this has been the initially very effective advertising campaign for Orange digital mobile phones in 1995 and 1996 against the established analogue networks and other digital systems introduced by One-2-One, Cellnet and Vodaphone. A side effect of these attempts to maintain market share is to raise barriers to the entry of new competitors because the power of established brands is very great and the advertising costs of a new product may be huge, as has been the case with new newspapers. Presumably the existing firms in the industry like it that way although they may also resent having to increase their spending in the face of threatening new entrants. There are some interesting case studies in this area with newly introduced newspapers such as Robert Maxwell's short-lived London evening paper and the *Sunday Correspondent*.

- Some firms in oligopolistic markets are apparently driven by the desire to maintain their reputations for quality and technological excellence. There must also be a profit constraint in the background and it could be argued that such a reputation does one's profits no harm at all. It is argued that this principle applies to some German companies such as Daimler Benz and BMW and to, for example, Rolls Royce in both its car making form and aircraft engine manufacturing form. It used to be alleged that some United Kingdom companies were so obsessed by technological excellence that they underplayed the marketing side and failed as a result.

- We must also recognise that some firms are driven by obsessives who are satisfying personal ambitions for power as well as economic objectives. There are many twentieth-century examples such as Howard Hughes and Henry Ford. Some of the modern pioneers of the computer industry appear to have accumulated their wealth as a fortuitous by-product of their technical obsessions.

- Occasionally a successful firm will spring up that appears to sacrifice short-run profit potential for the welfare of its workers. Some of these are properly constituted co-operatives but others are run at the whim of a benevolent entrepreneur. It can of course be argued that a happy, well cared for work force will actually be more productive than one which is exploited and cowed so there may be a long-run profit benefit. A recent example in this category might be the John Lewis Partnership.

Exercise 4

Is the United Kingdom new car market oligopolistic? Is the United Kingdom daily newspaper market oligopolistic?

8.3   **Contestable Markets**

Some economists and students come to love the traditional models of the firm. They admire the beauty of the logical progression from assumptions to conclusions; some even come to revel in the multiplicity of diagrams; fewer, however, come to a complete mastery of the different figures – indeed a number of students are heard to wail that the diagrams all appear the same. The reader is advised to treat most of it as an intellectual exercise and not to become too serious about it. If you are ever in a position to influence the real economy of the country, say as a mandarin at The Treasury, or Chancellor of the Exchequer, please do not behave as if the theory of the firm is a collection of unassailable truths that must be applied. The overall trend of the conclusions is that competition is preferable to collusion from the consumer's point of view and probably from the national viewpoint as well in terms of the efficient use of resources but a study of firms in action, particularly in the dominant market form, oligopoly, indicates that entrepreneurs, if left to themselves, often try to avoid competition. Much of what appears to be competition in the 'real world' is not. Thus there is a need for state intervention and supervision whose very existence undermines the case of those who argue that markets are best left to themselves.

Economists are usually aware that there are few if any industries which approximate to the model of perfect competition and few which are pure monopolies in the sense that they are free from the threat of new entrants to their industry. They realise that most industry and commerce manifests degrees of imperfect competition. One result is that there is a different approach which is called the theory of **contestable markets** that uses as its main approach the question of whether new firms can enter and leave the industry and under what conditions. If a market is to qualify for the title *contestable* there must be free entry and exit for firms. That is, there must be no effective barriers to the entry of new firms who have access to the same technology and the same cost curves as existing firms and who might be attracted by the existence of what they see as supernormal profits. This is a continuation of ideas in the traditional theory of perfect competition and oligopoly. The real difference contained in the contestable markets theory is that there should also be free or cost-less exit from the industry. Initially this is a hard concept to grasp, that a firm can leave an industry without having any of the costs that economists call *sunk costs* but, on closer examination there may be instances where this is the case. The phrase sunk costs means irrecoverable costs so if these are zero it means that the firm can recover all its initial investment costs, minus depreciation, and money spent on establishing goodwill and market knowledge. There have, for example, been instances of small airlines setting themselves up with leased aircraft to operate on selected routes. Their set-up costs are very small. They make inroads on existing firms' profits and exit the industry after being bought out with no losses and possibly significant profits. The same sort of process has happened since deregulation of the bus industry.

One of the features of contestable markets is the presumed existence of what are called *hit and run* competitors who spot supernormal profits, enter the industry without hindrance, and exit without loss having taken market share and profits by undercutting the incumbent firms. The conclusion of the theory here is that, if the market is perfectly contestable, the firms in the industry will behave as if they are in a perfectly competitive situation even if there are very few of them. Thus oligopolistic markets can be contestable. They will produce an output where their selling price equals their marginal cost of production and where their average costs are at a minimum. It is apparent that the idea of contestable markets requires a shift of emphasis towards a study of the degree of effectiveness of any barriers to entry to the industry on the part of potential entrants and of the possible costs of leaving it.

The theory is fully explained in *Contestable Markets and the Theory of Industrial Structure* (Baumol *et al.*, London, Harcourt Brace Jovanovich, 1982). It is a refreshing alternative to the traditional theory but does not replace it as some optimists once hoped and it is, inevitably, not beyond criticism itself. The main difficulty is that there are many situations where sunk costs are not zero or where they can only partially be recovered. It is also not common for new entrants to be immediately on the same footing as existing firms because there is a great deal of practical and embedded expertise in any particular industry. New entrants would expect, in most situations, to be at a disadvantage compared with incumbent firms. It is rare, in any industry that uses advanced technology or has great economies of scale, for there to be no barriers to entry such as the classic trio of product differentiation, economies of scale and absolute cost advantages of existing firms. It is also unlikely that the firms already in the industry will not alter their behaviour when threatened with new competitors. In this context is should be remembered that ease of entry to an industry depends partly on the availability of venture capital and that some economic environments such as the USA are apparently better suited to its provision than the United Kingdom.

8.4   Competition policy

Competition policy covers several strands:

- mergers;
- restrictive trade practices;
- monopolies;
- regulation of privatised utilities;
- consumer protection.

This section deals with the first three; regulation is discussed in Chapter 4.

The main bodies concerned are:

1. The Secretary of State for Trade and Industry who is responsible overall and takes the final decisions;

2. The Director General of Fair Trading (DGFT) who is in charge of the Office of Fair Trading and who keeps an eye on the business world and advises the Secretary of State;

3. The Monopolies and Mergers Commission (MMC) which investigates and reports on matters referred to it by the Secretary of State or DGFT;

4. The European Commission.

Mergers

Any merger has potentially anti-competitive implications and may damage the consumers' interest. Since the Monopolies and Mergers Act of 1965 it has been possible to prevent or modify most mergers. The Fair Trading Act of 1973 added to previous law and provides for the DGFT to be informed about merger proposals and for the firms to be consulted about the implications. The DGFT then advises the Secretary of State on whether the merger should be referred to the MMC for investigation. The advice may be ignored but if the merger is referred to the MMC a detailed study is conducted and a report given to the Secretary of State. These reports are a gold mine for the economist. There are limitations on what mergers can be referred to the MMC. The assets taken over must be more than £30 million or the market share of the firms concerned would reach 25 per cent or would be raised from an existing 25 per cent. (Special conditions apply to newspaper mergers and the Secretary of State's permission is needed if the proposed merger involves papers with a combined paid for circulation of more than 500 000.)

A proposed merger can be stopped if it is judged to be against the public interest or it can be allowed with certain conditions attached. The firms concerned may be asked to provide undertakings concerning these conditions. The Secretary of State may make an Order to impose conditions but this is rare. The weakness of the system lies in this gentleman's agreement approach; many critics favour a more robust system of legally enforced behaviour with very effective monitoring. Some mergers may be subject to European intervention. See the section below on European responsibility.

Restrictive Trade Practices

Restrictive Trade Practices (RTPs) are sometimes called anti-competitive practices and can be loosely defined as any practice which distorts the market.

When they first had to be registered after the 1956 Restrictive Trade Practices Act over 7000 were notified to the Registrar. He referred them to the Restrictive Practices Court unless they were withdrawn and those remaining could be defended in the Court and apply for exemption from the Act via what were called 'gateways' to exemption. The DGFT currently performs the functions of registrar and can refer agreements to the Court but may seek changes by discussions with the firms concerned rather than resort to the law. The effectiveness of the system is partly dependent on firms registering their agreements and practices and there have been some cases of failure to do this which were punished by heavy fines. There may be many more that no-one knows about. In general RTPs are an attempt to restrict competition and to give existing firms an unfair advantage. The Court occasionally permits an agreement to continue. The crackdown on RTPs in the late 1950s and early 1960s was one of the factors leading to an increase in mergers. Resale Price Maintenance (RPM), where the manufacturers could insist on fixing the retail price of their products, is treated as a restrictive trade practice but is subject to slightly different 'gateways' to exemption by the Court. The Net Book Agreement ended in late 1995 and was finally dissolved by the Court in March 1997. The DGFT referred the remaining example of RPM, the price fixing of branded, non-prescription medicines, to the Court in late 1996. Both forms of RPM were originally allowed on the grounds that they helped maintain the numbers of small retailers, book shops and chemists.

Monopolies

The DGFT may observe what appears to be a monopoly situation where the market is being distorted and may refer firms or groups of firms who supply the product or service to the MMC for investigation and report. The monopoly is defined as where a firm or group of firms have more than 25 per cent of a particular market. The procedures are basically the same as for RTPs with the Secretary of State having the final say and an attempt being made to reach agreements with firms rather than applying the weight of the law against them. Once again Orders are rare and critics argue that there is insufficient monitoring of agreements. The critics also argue that the Secretary of State has often made irrational and inconsistent interventions and ignored the recommendations of the MMC and DGFT.

European Union Competition policy

The Single European Act of 1986 aimed at a genuine single market for goods, services and capital and the free movement of workers from the beginning of 1993. The process was still not fully completed at the end of 1996 but remarkable progress has been made. At the heart of the concept of the single market is free competition, or a level playing field if you prefer sporting metaphors.

The European Commission is central to the maintenance or establishment of this free competition.

The current EU law is largely based on Articles 85 and 86 of the Treaty of Rome and on a 1989 Regulation. The Treaty fixes the general application of competition and there have been many important cases at the European Court of Justice that have established the right to trade on equal terms in another member state. An important one is the *Cassis de Dijon* in 1979 which applied to the sale of the French drink cassis in Germany. The Court ruled that there was a basic right of free movement of goods and that, in principle, goods legally manufactured in one member state could be sold in another. This decision removed a fundamental barrier and members were forced to resort to technical or health or administrative barriers if they wished to keep out another member's products. Since the Single European Act establishing the single market there has been a stream of Directives and Regulations to implement the free movement of both goods and services. The free movement of persons is still not fully established, partly because of the United Kingdom's xenophobic obduracy over passports and customs inspections and because of its concerns about immigration and a common visa.

An important part of the current policy is the liberalisation of competition in many fields, for example in road transport which has almost been completed. Another is in financial services such as banking and insurance. This has been slower to achieve. Others that have proved difficult are telecommunications and air transport but the next five years should see a major change in those markets. The change has been delayed, up to a point, by the need to achieve international co-operation and the USA has not been easily persuaded of the benefits of some of the proposals.

The specific rules under the Treaties include a general prohibition of agreements to restrict competition and of all abuses by enterprises that have a dominant market position. These abuses include limiting production, imposing unfair prices or restricting technical developments. The policy also bans state subsidies to industries, either to individual firms or to whole sectors, unless they have been approved by the Commission which subjects them to the test of whether an unfair competitive advantage can be gained by the recipient. The Commission can order the reduction or repayment of any subsidies that have been paid already.

Exercise 5

Why is there a European Union competition policy? Would not national policies be enough?

European Union Merger Policy

The Commission published a Green Paper in January 1996 'On the Review of the Merger Regulation' and responses were due in by March 1996 so we can expect some changes soon to the existing system which dates from a Regulation formulated in December 1989 and which came into operation in September 1990. Before this Merger Control Regulation of 1989 the Commission had used the two Articles 85 and 86 of the Treaty of Rome, referred to above, as a means of preventing dominant companies exploiting their market share. Under Article 85 there was only voluntary notification to the Commission of agreements between firms that resulted in restricted competition but Article 86 banned firms from 'abuse of a dominant position'.

The 1989 Regulation gave the Commission specific powers to assess all concentrations of enterprises such as mergers, acquisitions or joint ventures that had a European Community dimension subject to three conditions:

1. The world wide turnover of all the companies involved had to exceed ECU 5 billion.

2. The Community turnover of at least two of the companies involved had to exceed ECU 250 million (that is a minimum of ECU 500 million combined Community turnover).

3. All companies involved do not realise more than two-thirds of their Community turnover in one and the same member state.

The measurement of some of these figures is complex and banking figures are calculated differently. In principle the Regulation was intended to create a 'one stop shop' system so that a concentration would be investigated either by the European Community or by the member state's system, if any. This has not proved completely straightforward in practice. The new Regulation introduced a system of mandatory prior notification for all concentration with a Community dimension. The basic concept is that of 'creation or strengthening of a dominant position'.

Between September 1990 and the end of October 1995 there were 376 concentrations notified to the Community under the Regulation and 357 decisions on them had been adopted. Of these:

- 31 said the Regulation did not apply to the operation;
- 303 said the concentration was compatible with the common market at the end of the first phase of the investigation;
- 19 decisions said the concentration was compatible with the common market at the end of the phase two in-depth investigation;
- 4 decisions prohibited a concentration;
- of the above, 24 cases were cleared subject to conditions and/or obligations being placed on the concentration.

When the Green Paper was published there were 11 national merger policies of which eight were mandatory and one of the four remaining countries, The Netherlands, was about to adopt a mandatory pre-merger control. The Paper contains a detailed analysis of the national variations of control. They are very extensive in regard to notification requirements, the procedures adopted and the legal processes. The Green Paper addresses the problem of the liaison or demarcation between the European Union merger policy and that of the member states. In general the Green Paper makes three main proposals:

1. The thresholds should be lowered and have a combined world wide total of ECU 2 billion and a Community threshold of ECU 100 million for each of at least two companies involved. This reduction is recommended because of the large number of operations with cross border effects that fall outside the present Regulation.

2. The second conclusion dealt with the problem of multiple national notifications of concentrations, that is the need to register in all or many of the member states. Such multiple notification increases uncertainty and imposes costs on businesses. The reduction of the thresholds in Proposal 1 would help remove the problem and a 'second best' alternative solution would consist of bringing cases of multiple notification below the current thresholds under the control of the Commission only.

3. The third group of proposals is to improve methods of dealing with the treatment of co-operative joint venture operations under Article 85 of the Treaty of Rome. The Commission has been happy with the working of the 1989 Regulation and regarded it as an adequate instrument of control so these proposals are essentially a tidying up measure. The proposed changes were rejected by the Council in late 1996 and are being reviewed. If they occur, they will be backed by a streamlining of the Directive on Take-overs (13th Company Law Directive) after 1996.

9 Markets: Distribution

Aims of the chapter

To use the economic theory and concepts of previous chapters to analyse the markets for the distribution of goods and services, particularly in the United Kingdom. Specific aims are to:

● outline the main recent trends;
● speculate about future trends.

Introduction

The distribution of goods and services is among the most interesting areas of daily economic study because new ideas and techniques are always being adopted. There is continuous pleasure in seeing economic principles at work and frequent puzzlement when economic experience seems to be ignored. A high proportion of students have worked in retailing and can bring their own experience to bear. Retailing shows many splendid successes as well as heroic and humiliating failures. There are always plenty of examples to be had of applications of many economic principles and you can see most of them in your own shopping area or read about them in your own newspapers. You can even have an excuse for developing an obsessive interest in advertising, particularly on television.

Background

Distribution is an extremely important industry in terms of the employment, income and investment it generates and in terms of its contribution to the efficiency of the economy. Table 9.1 shows the contribution to GDP of various types of services.

Table 9.1   Services contribution to GDP: selected countries, 1984 and 1994 (value added, % of GDP)

	Wholesale and retail trade, restaurants and hotels		Transport, storage and communication		Finance, insurance, real estate and business services		Community, social, and personal services		Producers of government services	
	1994	1984	1994	1984	1994	1984	1994	1984	1994	1984
Belgium	18.50	15.40	7.90	7.80	5.10	5.60	21.50	19.00	12.60	13.67
France	15.00	14.60	5.80	5.90	23.10	17.90	6.00	4.90	17.20	17.20
Germany	10.30	10.10	5.50	5.80	12.50	12.80	20.50	14.90	10.30	11.40
Italy	18.40	18.90	6.30	5.30	26.30	21.30	1.00	0.80	12.30	11.90
Japan	12.50	14.00	6.30	6.60	16.20	15.20	18.40	15.50	7.90	8.40
Spain	21.30	20.20	5.30	5.60	17.80	17.70	5.90	5.70	12.50	11.60
Switzerland	17.20	18.30	6.10	6.40	16.50	16.00	15.50	11.60	12.10	11.40
United Kingdom	12.50	11.30	7.40	6.80	21.30	16.30	8.70	4.90	11.60	13.30
United States	16.80	17.10	6.10	6.30	27.10	22.80	11.40	8.90	12.30	11.90

Note: Not all of the figures are for the dates given, but are for a year or so earlier so they should be used for purposes of general comparison only. German figures are for the ex FRG only.

Source: OECD in Figures. Supplement to the OECD *Observer,* **200**, Paris, OECD, 1996.

Distribution covers a wide range of activities in the service or tertiary sector:

- It includes buying, collecting, transporting, selling, and delivering raw materials and components to their users, perhaps via a series of markets which may be physical markets or controlled by electronic dealing.

- It also includes the extensive range of markets that operate throughout the world to fix the prices of agricultural produce including commodities such as coffee, metals, raw materials such as rubber and items such as shipping space and aircraft cargo space.

- In addition there are the large number of firms engaged in work that permits the distribution system to operate effectively – shipping agents, insurance and financial service providers. These are now heavily reliant on electronic data processing and transfers of funds.

- Finally there is the great network of wholesalers, transport companies, retailers and delivery companies who put the goods into the hands of the final consumers.

Some of the groups mentioned above require large amounts of capital investment to operate, for example cold storage firms or shipping companies, but others require little apart from expert knowledge and a good reputation.

At the core of an analysis of distribution of goods lies the question of transport costs. In the distribution or provision of services the existence of a core of expertise may be more significant and, in some cases, a location where time zones favour communications. This latter point helps to explain the pre-eminence of the City of London in foreign exchange markets.

Historically, the development of some markets has been assisted or thwarted by the legal climate established over time. The growth of financial markets in The Netherlands and the United Kingdom owed much to the legal acceptance of new instruments such as bills of exchange and letters of credit. Later in the United Kingdom, the growth of commerce and industry was accelerated by the legal framework of limited liability. The attempt to establish a genuine single European market after 1992 is already having an effect on the growth and development of financial markets and is leading to major changes in transport networks and organisation. The presence of lax tax regimes may encourage the growth of certain types of financial markets. Another example is the flag of convenience system which is largely based in Liberia. In the early 1990s about 94 million dead-weight tons of oil tankers were registered in Monrovia, the capital of Liberia. In this context we should also remember Switzerland which has benefited from its confidential banking system and Luxembourg which has attracted large amounts of German funds because of subtle differences in its banking regulations. In some cases it is trust, speed and simplicity of operation that stimulates a particular market. The London Stock Exchange and Lloyds insurance grew on this basis.

9.1   The Trend Towards Direct Selling

Direct selling has always occurred where the product is very specialised or expensive or where the client has specialised requirements. In such circumstances there is usually a formal or informal tendering process whereby the buyer chooses on the basis of design, price, delivery dates, back-up, servicing and other factors. Large firms employ specialist purchasing managers in order to get the best deals on all of their inputs and one consequence is the trend to source supplies from overseas, particularly from the Pacific rim countries. This process of importing supplies is partly responsible for the growth of unemployment in United Kingdom manufacturing industry since 1979.

There is, however, also a trend towards individual consumers buying direct from manufacturers. The term manufacturer is used loosely here because some of the firms concerned are assemblers of other people's components. There have always been 'factory shops' which sell 'seconds' or remainder lines to local people and some of these advertise nationally as well. Examples are common in textiles and footwear or in ceramics and glassware, as well as the ubiquitous farm shops. Some of these factory shops also sell products produced elsewhere in the country and even imported goods.

A trend has developed towards the selling of computer equipment direct from the manufacturer or assembler to the consumer. This has always tended to be the case when the customer is a firm which is buying a significant quantity of equipment but is now common for personal computers. Some of the fastest growing companies in the USA, Dell and Gateway 2000 for example, sell personal computers by mail order and there are several British examples who pursue a similar policy. Amstrad, for example, now sells all its personal computers by mail order rather than through the high street retailers on the grounds that it was not being given a fair competitive deal and that its margins were too small because of the buying power of the multiple retailers. The main reason for the adoption of the direct sales technique is that, if it works properly, the seller has enormous benefits from the bulk purchase of components and only sells to order. There need be no manufacture for stock except as a precautionary measure to reduce delays in supplying customers. The orders are often received over the telephone from customers using credit cards. Many will be of standard products, which can be stockpiled up to a point, and which can be priced and advertised very competitively. Many orders, however, will be non-standard and made to the specific requirements of the customers. It is this flexibility to meet non-standard orders that gives the mail or telephone order company its edge over the high street retailer. There is also the opportunity to sell peripheral items where the profit margins may be higher. The scale of the successful businesses of this type enables them to advertise widely and to keep ahead of the pack technologically and to provide good servicing and back-up systems. In the background, however, lurks the danger of economic recessions where the volume of sales fails to continue to rise to support the company's operations. One recent variation on the direct selling theme in the market for personal computers is in the approach taken by the large German firm Escom which opened a large number of retail outlets in the United Kingdom in 1995 to sell its products direct. The shops were mainly in city and town centres and were once the Rumbelows electrical goods chain. The UK company went into receivership in mid-1996 so the approach was obviously not a good one.

Exercise I

Consider the range of shops in your nearest shopping centre. What changes have you seen in the types of retailer there in the last five to ten years? What types have opened/closed?

Another version of direct selling from 'manufacturer' to consumer is in services such as banking and insurance. The Midland Bank introduced First Direct as a telephone banking system aimed initially at the younger age group whose main requirements from a bank could be met from an automatic teller machine or 'hole in a wall'. It was a brave, innovative venture and succeeded far beyond the expectations of the critics partly because it advertised itself and its lower charges very effectively and partly because it struck a chord with people who were slightly intimidated by atmosphere of the traditional bank. Another new entrant has been Direct Insurance which marketed itself mainly through television and stressed its low premiums. It became successful and was taken over by The Royal Bank of Scotland. It diversified into other types of insurance such as household contents and buildings. The success of such direct selling and the quick appropriation of a large market share attracted considerable competition from the existing firms, some of whom have also set up direct selling arms. As a result, the market share of Direct Insurance has fallen and it is now questionable whether the take-over was wise. It is worth considering the reasons for the initial success of direct selling of insurance. The sellers gave the impression, and it is partly true, that they were able to cut the premiums on offer because they were cutting out the middleman or insurance broker and because their telephone systems enabled them to cut administrative costs. In practice, a major reason for their success was that they, to use economists' jargon, cherry picked or cream skimmed. These terms mean, in this context, that they only accepted proposals for insurance from people who were good risks and were less likely to cause them grief and expense from accidents and claims. Almost any company could offer low premiums in these selective conditions. One of the important impacts of the intervention of the direct selling companies has been to force insurance companies into much more discriminatory setting of premiums to allow for the age, sex, claims record, abode (using post codes), and factors such as the type of vehicle and property of the proposer.

Most of the points made above suggest that direct selling is always beneficial but there will always be a place for the seller who provides a variety of products from a wide range of sources and who gives that most valuable of all services, personal advice and human contact. Experience also dictates that they are not always more expensive than the large direct selling firms.

Exercise 2

How do you explain the popularity of direct insurance and banking services? Have they any drawbacks?

9.2   Modern Trends in Distribution

The growth of the multiple retailer has been the most obvious trend over the last 50 years. They have outlets in almost every major shopping centre throughout Britain. This movement began in the late nineteenth century with stores such as Liptons and Home and Colonial. The twentieth-century success stories have been Sainsbury, Tesco, Marks and Spencer and a host of others, some of the department store type and others of the specialist sort such as shoe shops. A fairly recent innovation has been for some of them to be based on a franchising operation where the 'parent' provides the products, the design, the logos and often the advertising and the individual supplies the operating capital and takes most of the risk. Many of these multiple retailers are under the same ownership because of mergers and take-overs. It is very difficult for the ordinary consumer to keep track of these common ownerships and many falsely believe that there is genuine competition when there is not. The main reason for the expansion and market penetration of the multiple retailer is the enormous economies of scale available, particularly in buying and selling.

There are fewer and larger shops in most sectors in the United Kingdom. This is the consequence of the trend towards multiples as explained above and partly the result of a number of other factors such as the shift of retailers to urban peripheries in response to the growth of car ownership. In out-of-town retail parks the firm has the benefits of planning from scratch and can maximise the efficiency of the unit's layout in terms of display, presentation, flow of goods and customers and parking. The modern retail 'shed' is purpose built and has a limited 'shelf-life' until fashions in shopping behaviour change. The other attraction to the retailer is that land is cheaper on urban fringes than in city centres and developments are less expensive and disruptive. Until 1995 it was easier to obtain planning permission for retail parks than for rebuilding in town centres, especially in urban conservation areas. The government began making noises, and it may be no more than that, that out-of-town shopping precincts and developments should be curtailed. In France, in 1996, President Chirac announced a new policy to prevent out-of-town hypermarket development. The number of shops in certain sectors such as food retailing has reduced steadily over recent years and there are far fewer of the so-called 'corner shops'. Many of these disappeared as urban areas were redeveloped; many, for example greengrocers, bakers and butchers, have been absorbed into supermarkets. The growth of the petrol station as a shop has also helped to push many small shops out of existence. Seven-day trading has not favoured most small shops and scares such as BSE have helped to destroy many small butchers shops.

There are some sectors in which the small shop has expanded, especially where there is a high income elasticity of demand, such as for antiques, restaurants, leisure goods, leisure activities including garden centres and nurseries and in certain niche markets where personal service and variety of product is important.

Perceived rather than real competition is a feature of modern retailing. Chains of shops with different names that are selling similar products such as shoes, clothes, electrical goods, DIY goods or books may be under the same ownership. For example, Dixons and Currys are under the same ownership although there is not a complete overlap in what they sell because Dixons specialises in home entertainment, photography and computers while Currys specialises in white goods such as refrigerators, cookers and other home appliances. The group also owns a 60 per cent share in shops called The Link which deal in mobile communications and whose business overlaps to some extent that of the other two. BT bought the other 40 per cent in early 1997. Another example is Sainsbury whose Homebase subsidiary now owns the Texas chain of DIY stores although it is in the process of 'rebadging' them. In some towns both stores are still trading in close proximity to each other. Perhaps the most frequent example is in shoe shops where, in 1996, until half of it was put into receivership, the Facia group owned Freeman Hardy and Willis, Trueform, Manfield, Saxone and Curtess as well as Bata in Germany. Consumers are usually ignorant of these common ownerships and behave as if there is full unfettered competition. There may be a management policy to encourage genuine competition and the individual store types may fit slightly different markets but there must be a strong drive to avoid unnecessary competition particularly of the price variety.

There is another type of perceived competition that merits close examination. It is clearly apparent in electrical goods retailing where it is very difficult to find stores that stock exactly the same product or model so that genuine price comparison becomes impossible. Manufacturers must connive at this system because they produce so many similar but slightly differentiated models and change them so often. The stores aggravate the problem by selling their own brands of most items. If a consumer magazine such as *Which?*, the journal of the Consumers' Association, is consulted it is clear that an identical model may be sold under more than one brand name. It is obviously hard for the average consumer to make properly informed decisions before purchase.

Most consumers are convinced that the large multiple food retailers have been heavily engaged in fierce price competition for some years. When the actual prices of a standard basket of goods sold by each of these major retailers are compared it is clear that there is little genuine price competition on most goods. There is a great deal of hype about the price cutting on items such as baked beans or the standard white loaf, or milk but this is to a large extent a smokescreen. The overall level of prices is maintained and the price of some items may be raised in order to finance the selling of loss leaders elsewhere in the store. Some observers have placed great emphasis on the impact of foreign chains of discount stores such as Netto and Aldi, or in the case of household goods, Ikea, but their significance has probably been overrated because they are still relatively few in number and have not made the rapid inroads into the market that were predicted. They have, however, provoked responses in their immediate localities in much the same way that big petrol companies respond to price cutting by supermarket filling stations.

COMPETITION IN THE GAMES CONSOLE MARKET

In March 1997 Nintendo launched their latest games console, the Nintendo 64, on to the United Kingdom market. The console was available in limited numbers to begin with but the Nintendo was able to command a high initial price because of its technological lead with 64-bit processing, cartridge loading and with brilliant graphics and 3D effects. Four games were available at the launch – Super Mario 64, Pilot Wings 64, Shadow of the Empire and Turok-Dinosaur Hunter – with more promised. On 5 April 1997, the multiple retail chain Comet were quoting a price of £309.98 for a package of Nintendo 64 and Super Mario 64; Currys, their main competitor, were asking £249.99 for the console on its own. At both stores purchasers can expect to have to buy accessories such as extra control pads and an N64 memory card if they wish to save games.

Sony, whose bestselling Playstation had been on the market for nearly two years, responded to the new competition with a complex mixture of offers and price cuts. On 5 April 1997, Comet were offering the Sony Playstation plus four 'top title' games as a package for £244.95 ('separate selling price £314.95'). The games were Formula 1, Actua Soccer, Mortal Kombat 3 and Ridge Racer Revolution. On the same date, Currys were

cont'd

offering the Sony Playstation with a different four-game pack at £199.95 ('separate selling price £299.95). The games were Alien Trilogy, Pandemonium, Hardcore 4 x 4 and Outside Soccer. Currys were also offering the console on its own for £129.99 ('was £197').

The third competitor, Sega Saturn was being sold by Comet as a package with four 'top rated' games at £229.99 ('separate selling price £344.95'). The four games were Worldwide Soccer, Virtua Fighter 2, Sega Rally and Daytona USA. The business media were predicting the eventual demise of Sega which had sold 1.6 million units in the UK compared with the Sony Playstation which had sold 3.2 million. Currys was not advertising Sega Saturns on 5 April 1997 in its newspaper advertisements.

Note. The various offers from the major retailers are hard to compare because of different credit terms, guarantees and combinations of games and accessories.

1. Assess the current situation in the market of these three competitors. How has it changed since 5 April 1997? Suggest reasons why it has changed.
2. Has Nintendo's technological advantage been maintained and did it benefit from being first with a 64-bit console?

Own brands are another expanding phenomenon. The seller adopts own brands (or own labels) as part of the attempt to persuade the buyer that the shop is providing value for money and a guarantee of quality. The impression is given that the store buyers devote their lives to seeking out and maintaining the quality of the own brand. The own brand is sold at a marginally lower price than the manufacturer's brand, usually in packaging that mimics the original within the boundaries allowed by the law. The impression is given, and this does occur in practice, that the own brand and the manufacturer's brand come off the same production line and are simply put into differently labelled containers. The consumer has no effective or foolproof way of detecting whether this is the case or not although the date stamping codes on the container may give the game away if the print style is identical. The seller obtains the own brands at a lower price per unit because of the power of bulk purchase. The manufacturer gains from the certainty of the large order that can guarantee continuous and more economical production runs. Some manufacturers advertise the fact that they do not manufacture own brands for anyone. This is part of their effort to maintain their own brand differentiation.

Kelloggs cornflakes is probably the best example of this. Although some sellers rely very heavily on the promotion of their own brands and these account for a very high proportion of their total sales, many consumers are wary of them and persist in demanding nationally advertised products. They know from experience that some own brands are cheaper because the contents of the packets and cans are inferior and do not represent genuine value for money. Cans of fruit for example often contain different ratios of solid fruit to juice or syrup; washing-up liquid is of different strengths; own brand electrical goods may be thought to be less reliable, and so on. The perception of consumers is all important and their reactions are reflected in the price elasticity of demand for the own brand in relation to that for the manufacturers' brands.

Not all sellers are permanently committed to the own brand system. Own brands or own labels have a tendency to become 'tired' and need refreshing if they are to continue to have an impact on the buyer. They can develop an image of cheapness and lower quality or a sense of overfamiliarity. It is expensive to maintain parallel stocks of different versions of the same goods although some of the more successful food retailers benefit from selling a very wide variety of similar products in order to satisfy as many customers as possible. The individual who can no longer buy his or her favourite marmalade or whatever at a particular store may begin to shop elsewhere and the whole of their weekly food expenditure is lost to a rival. Even a dominant retailer such as Marks and Spencer has considered the gradual withdrawal of its famous St Michael label.

Exercise 3

What is the economic rationale behind own brands when they take up valuable shelf space and sell at a lower price than named manufacturers' brands?

Niche marketing is a contemporary phrase that describes the ancient policy of identifying a clearly separate market or group of customers and specialising in it. Whatever it is called there has been a great expansion of attempts to meet niche markets and many have been highly successful. Some have been temporarily successful and have then suffered from the mistake of over rapid expansion or have fallen foul of recession. Many so-called niche marketing successes have resulted from identifying products or services with a high positive income elasticity of demand. Some of these are in the leisure industries and supply specialised equipment or services to feed the insatiable demand for new experiences or locations for holidays. Some provide specialised food products to meet the understandable desire to find alternatives to the blandness of mass provision. The nostalgia market is heavily tapped in order to supply those who remember when potatoes, tomatoes, fruit and cheese had distinctive tastes or who, from the security of their modern suburban villas, want to sample vicariously the living conditions of their youth or of their parents' generation in the various industrial hamlets around the country. The original niche market may become something like a traditional mass market; the successful Sock Shop or Tie Rack becomes a multiple retailer in the grip of a holding company. The growth of specialist sellers, some of whom operate from workshops or via mail order rather than from traditional shops, has been accelerated by rising incomes and leisure time and has also been helped by the availability of shops in older town and city centres as other retailers have moved to out-of-town locations. On a note of caution it should be noted that there is a very high rate of business failure among would be niche marketeers.

The growth of 'out-of-town' shopping is another important modern trend. The phrase 'out-of-town' needs some clarification. If a typical small town of up to say 30 000 people is being considered, then an out-of-town development is almost certainly exactly what it says, a set of buildings on a greenfield site on a main road out of the town with a number of well-known multiple retailers centred around a major food retailer such as Tesco or Sainbury or Morrison. These constitute the typical retail park with its 'Essex barn' architecture or the occasional foray into the steel shed style. A major feature is a large car park and vestigial public transport access. Such developments now usually sport a petrol station and sometimes fast food outlets. If, however, a larger town or city is considered, the so-called 'out-of-town' retail park may be well within the city boundaries and may simply be a redevelopment of a disused or under-utilised industrial area. An example is Meadowhall in Sheffield. Many companies have made more profit from the retail development of their industrial sites than they have from manufacturing. In many cases there will also be commercial development with 'science parks' or 'industrial parks' close by. In these contexts the phrase 'out-of-town' simply means not in the traditional retailing centre of the city. There are signs that the out-of-town retail park development is becoming a saturated market although many are still in the process of creation. The government has begun to accept the arguments of those who state that out-of-town shopping development is usually undesirable on environmental and social grounds in that it generates traffic, pollution, noise, uses good agricultural land and leads to the decline of the inner urban areas.

Franchising is of increasing importance in modern distribution of goods and services. It is not always apparent to the consumer that a particular outlet is a franchise because one of the essentials of franchising is that each outlet is almost indistinguishable from the others in its shop fitting, décor, products, uniforms of staff and so on. The individual who places his or her capital at risk receives training, supplies, advice and marketing assistance in return for a commitment to maintain the standards of the franchiser. A franchise principal such as Wimpy needs to ensure that everyone who takes on a franchise does not let the side down by lowering standards or breaching the franchise's code of operation. The individual expects the franchise principal to restrict the issue of franchises so that there is no local competition and to operate in such a way that the individual benefits. Benetton came under fire from some of its franchisees over the nature of some parts of its controversial advertising. Franchising is not limited to the traditional retail outlet for clothes, hardware or fast food but also extends to services such as car tuning, plumbing and copy shops. Some versions of franchising operate by working within existing stores such as department stores to sell specific ranges of goods such as perfumes and cosmetics.

9.3   **Future Trends**

Future trends depend on many factors such as the growth of incomes, the changing population structure, levels of inflation, leisure patterns and govern-ment policies to tackle the problems posed by the private car and urban congestion:

- There may be a return to the old urban centres by major multiple retailers, especially if the problem of urban congestion and pollution is tackled by restrictions on private car use and/or the stimulation of public transport. Boots, for example, has expressed an intention to return to some of its smaller shops in small town centres despite its recent tendency to move in alongside shops such as Sainsbury in retail park developments. There will almost certainly be a resurrection of many decayed urban shopping centres when the economy is fully recovered and investment funds become available and entrepreneurs are again willing to take risks.

- Large numbers of small filling stations will close as the supermarkets continue their loss leader approach to petrol retailing and push their share of the total market up towards the levels of Europe. Rural petrol stations will either disappear or survive by becoming diversified retailers of food and newspapers. The effect of this increased market concentration may appear to be beneficial at first but, in the long run, there may be detrimental effects on the consumer arising from restricted choice and elements of oligopolistic control if a world shortage of petrol develops.

- Supermarkets will attempt various forms of diversification of services and products in an attempt to maintain and increase market share and profits. This will be a continuation of the trend since the 1960s where, for example, a clothes retailer such as Marks and Spencer diversified into food selling, into plants and books, into shoes and into some household goods. It has also benefited from its adoption of its own store card and from the credit transactions attached to the card. Tesco is in the process of becoming a savings bank via the extension of the use of its Clubcard which was launched in February 1995 as a shopper's loyalty card. We can expect other retailers to follow this pattern towards credit provision and banking services in the same way that they adopted the loyalty card or similar systems. In October 1996 Sainsbury announced its intention of starting a bank in conjunction with The Bank of Scotland. It will be a telephone bank with cash machines at branches rather than a conventional bank.

Exercise 4

Why has J Sainsbury, a multiple food and DIY retailer, decided to start a bank?

- Mail order and telephone ordering are likely to increase either through catalogues or from direct response to television advertising or from the use of home computers. The use of computers for direct purchase from the home has long been heralded as the shopping method of the future but it has been a long time reaching a significant level. The growth of home banking has been slower than predicted and many people prefer the human contact of 'real' shopping where goods can be seen and touched. There will, however, undoubtedly be a rise in the direct purchasing of holidays, travel facilities and other services via computer links rather than by the traditional methods of telephone or personal contact.

- It is probable that the trend to a smaller number of shops will continue. Transport economics and the adoption of the new European Union 40 tonne heavy goods vehicle standard will accelerate the trend to more centralised distribution systems and the elimination of the wholesaler stage in distribution.

- As the European market expands and technical and other standards become more homogeneous there will be a faster trend towards the globalisation of firms and products. The mass of consumers will endure less genuine variety but more advertising of similar goods while the rich will seek solace in more custom-made or conspicuous consumption goods. There may be an emphasis on false differentiation of the old badge engineering type whereby two or more models are sold which are identical except for their badges and minor styling variations.

- The power, revenue and influence of the advertising industry will increase as commerce becomes increasingly a battle between oligopolists intent on maintaining market share.

- Methods of payment will continue to show a shift away from cash and cheques to credit transactions and to EFTPOS, electronic funds transfer at the point of sale or the use of switch cards. Some shops may reduce the number of checkouts and allow shoppers to tally up the contents of their trolleys with specially issued hand-held computers. If interest rates remain low, there is likely to be a continuation and increase in 'interest free credit'. The car market is likely to expand the offer of leasing and other alternatives to full purchase.

10 Markets: Services

Aims of the chapter

To:

- analyse the different categories of services;
- explain the factors leading to expansion and contraction;
- discuss the ramifications of changes in the service sector for employment and growth;
- speculate about the future.

10.1 Categories of Services

There are several possible ways in which services can be classified and it is largely a matter of personal choice that dictates any particular listing. The main classes of services are:

- Personal services such as hairdressing, cleaning, the provision of meals or 'food eaten outside the home' as the statistician tends to call it, public houses, hotels and guest-houses, bed and breakfast, repairs to all sorts of goods, and building and maintenance services. The last can be separately classified because it is so important in terms of money spent and employment.

- Advisory services which consist of such things as legal advice, management consultancy, educational and training services, estate agency, surveying, holidays, travel, architectural services and interior design and landscape design.

- Transport services which include all forms of transport for goods and people from airlines and trains, buses, coaches, boats and ferries to taxis and minicabs. We could include garage services and maintenance in this category but they may be classified as personal services by some people.

- Office and factory services may be classified separately but could be subsumed in other categories if we chose. They consist of servicing of machines, cleaning, maintenance, security, recruitment, provision of temporary workers, and the supply of office equipment. We can add telecommunications, computing and other information services into this category or we could categorise them separately on the grounds that they are so important that they can stand alone.

- Leisure services can be listed separately although some parts of them have been mentioned as examples under other headings. Is a public house a leisure service or a personal service? Leisure includes sports and social clubs, the multitude of health clinics, cinemas, theatres, other clubs and the mixed array of stately homes, safari parks, leisure parks such as Alton Towers. Large numbers of people obtain their incomes from providing for other people's leisure. One notable aspect of the United Kingdom economy since 1960 has been the rapid growth of the gambling industry. Another is the growth of the corporate entertainment sector.

- Financial services are almost always kept as a separate category because they employ so many people and have grown so fast in recent years. This is not to say that they are necessarily easy to list comprehensively because new services are constantly being introduced. Most spring easily to mind, banking, insurance of goods, property and risks, life assurance, mortgages and savings institutions such as building societies. There are, however, many others which provide the money and advice for the conduct of trade and commercial operations through various commodity and financial exchanges such as the Baltic Exchange and the Stock Market. Large numbers are employed as brokers, advisers and clerical and administrative staff in these areas.

- Advertising and promotion can be treated separately because they generate large flows of money and employment throughout what is usually called 'the media'. Some economists use the advertising industry as a leading indicator of the health of the economy. A downturn usually presages a decline of the rest of the national economy.

Exercise I

Why does a fall in advertising expenditure indicate that a recession may be coming and an upturn indicate that a recovery may be on the way?

It may be helpful on occasion to further subdivide services into those provided by public bodies and those supplied by the private sector.

- Education services can be provided by both private and public sectors but, in the United Kingdom, the public sector dominates despite the modern growth of private education. The provision of nursery education in most areas is a mix of both sectors. Primary education is largely provided by the state or by day attendance at private schools. Preparatory school boarding is another form of private education at this level. Secondary school provision is also largely provided by the state, mainly through local authorities although some schools are now supervised and financed directly by the central government in the grant maintained sector. Many schools are partly financed through charitable organisations or religious bodies. Higher education still receives most of its money from the state despite attempts to substitute private funds but there is a trend towards asking students to contribute to their tuition fees as well as their maintenance following the LSE's lead in 1996. There are privately funded institutions of higher education, notably the University of Buckingham but they are relatively insignificant. Employment in the educational sector has rapidly expanded since 1960.

- Health services have also grown in terms of employment and expenditure since 1947. They too can be provided by both the state and the private sectors. Private provision is normally made on the basis of insurance taken out by individuals or companies on behalf of their employees. The private health insurance industry is one of the fastest growing of all service industries. Allied to the medical services are the caring services, especially for the elderly and another rapid growth industry has been in running homes for the elderly. There is an enormous range of different jobs in health care ranging from highly skilled medical specialists and scientific researchers to relatively unskilled manual jobs. A large modern hospital is like a small town.

- Administration is a generalised term for much of the work of local and central government. Employment in this sector has expanded overall since 1914 but there have been contractions in some parts of the administration as departments have been reshuffled or functions have been discontinued. There is often a gap between what governments say they are doing to contract public service employment and what actually happens. Since 1979 there has been a trend to hand over central government functions to agencies who operate at arm's length from the government but there has been little overall change in total civil service employment.

- Law and order services are one of the remarkable growth areas of the last twenty years. Most of these are public sector services, courts, probation and social services, detention centres, prisons and the police. Traffic wardens could be included here. There has also been a remarkable expansion of private sector security services, not only the well-known Securicor and Group 4 but also a wide range of companies provide guards for venues ranging from shopping malls to weddings and night clubs. In the United States cynics reckon that, if their present sentencing policies and prison building programmes continue, by the year 2010, half the adult population will be inmates of prisons and the other half will be employed looking after them. The expansion of employment in the police forces has been remarkable. The number of police officers authorised by the Home Office for each police authority's establishment has steadily risen as has the employment of 'civilians' by the police forces to do clerical and administrative work.

● Defence work can be included under the heading of law and order but it is better to classify it separately. Again, the numbers employed are a mixture of serving members of the armed forces and civilians who are employed in a wide range of tasks. Much defence work is now contracted out to civilian firms, for example vehicle, ship and aircraft maintenance. The numbers have fluctuated over the years in accordance with defence and foreign policy and the state of the cold war. The end of the east–west confrontation should yield a 'peace dividend' in terms of the ability to reallocate resources but an inevitable accompaniment will be the reduction of employment at defence installations.

10.2   Trends in Services – Expansion and Contraction

There have been conflicting trends over recent years as entrepreneurs have tried different solutions to what they have seen as problems or opportunities. Such conflicts are normal but there are a few distinctive trends that enable us to generalise despite examples of contrary developments.

The growth of diversification in the provision of services is one obvious trend although some companies have retreated back to their core business. This trend is most apparent in financial services such as banking, insurance, building societies and travel and tourism. Sometimes it is done with a form of horizontal integration by merger or take-over and sometimes it is done by setting up wholly owned subsidiaries. The high street banks diversified early on when they set up finance companies that lent money for hire purchase. They were also quick to provide investment and unit trust services through subsidiaries. More recently they have expanded into many forms of financial services such as life insurance, household insurance, personal mortgage provision, personal equity plans (PEPs), travel insurance, pensions, payroll administration, credit and charge card protection insurance and unemployment insurance. Some deal in estate agency services through subsidiaries. In addition they have expanded and heavily advertised developments of their traditional roles as providers of finance and advice to new businesses. Insurance companies have also spread their wings into investment and unit trusts and PEPs as well as expanding their private and company pensions schemes. Building societies have branched out into banking, investment and unit trusts, PEPs, insurance and estate agency. Some, like the Abbey National have become plcs and are now classified as banks but some, such as the Nationwide have decided to remain as mutual societies owned by their members. Some building societies and insurance companies made disastrous moves into estate agency at the end of the 1980s and made enormous losses when the housing market collapsed. They had bought out large numbers of small local estate agencies and spent huge sums creating chains with their own corporate logos and images that were suitable for national advertising. They also tried to sell packages of a wide range of services so that they could be one-stop house purchase shops. Unfortunately for them the volume of business was insufficient to cover their enlarged overheads. Many of their branches have been closed and some have reverted to their original owners or to new individual entrepreneurs.

Exercise 2

Can you think of examples where services industries exploit complementary demands to sell more than one product to their customers?

New entrants into traditional markets is another trend. Some of the points made above could also be classified in this manner, for example the bank that begins to sell insurance or the building society that deals in foreign currency or stocks and shares. There are, however, some clear examples of leaps into new areas. Examples include Virgin which has moved into life insurance after its successful diversification into cola drinks and airlines. Retailers such as Tesco and Sainsbury have diversified into banking by offering interest on savings accumulated via its Clubcard. Marks and Spencer makes considerable sums from its credit operations. The impression is given sometimes that these new activities are stumbled upon by accident as a result of the attempt to satisfy and retain customers. The world of modern communications is full of examples of new entrants moving into new areas, presumably because of the expected profits growth obtainable. It was inevitable that newspaper owners would diversify into television broadcasting and then into satellite broadcasting but it was not so obvious that a telecommunications company such as BT would want to supply video on demand down its wires nor that cable TV companies would be so keen on supplying telephone services. Sometimes a company starts off by providing a service for itself and sells offpeak capacity or surplus capacity to others. An example of this is the sale of surplus satellite channels by TV companies. Another is the telecommunications company Energis which was set up to utilise the communications network of the old Central Electricity Generating Board and the National Grid.

The integration of service provision with other activities is now common. Many of the old distinctions between manufacturing and services are fading as firms try to create 'value added chains'. An example is the supply of services by the manufacturers of copying machines where the hardware is sold or leased at a near loss and any profit is made from the servicing contract and supplies of consumables. Another simple example is the modern car selling system whereby one buys a car, borrows the money and has the car repaired at one dealer. Once these three functions were provided by separate people and, of course, still can be if the customer chooses. There are also examples in the supply of computer equipment and software where there is an integrated approach rather than the use of separate providers. If software is regarded as a service it is significant that since the 1970s there has been a complete reversal of the situation where hardware used to represent 80 per cent of the cost of an IBM system and the software 20 per cent. Hardware's share of the total cost continues to decline from the 20 per cent figure of the mid-1990s. There are also many examples within the leisure industry of the integration of services. The original Thomas Cook provided a complete service of tickets, reservations and hotel accommodation but the modern company supplies insurance, foreign exchange, and has part ownership of other companies in the sector in a vertically integrated manner as well as providing modern updates, such as fly-drive, of old services.

The share of services in world trade has expanded from one-quarter in 1975 to more than one-third in 1995. The trade has become globalised and is dominated by a few countries, the United States, Japan, Germany, France and the United Kingdom. Trade in services brings with it an increasing amount of foreign direct investment (FDI). This is shown in Figure 10.1. Such FDI is subject to strong cyclical tendencies as is revealed by experience in the recessions and recoveries of the late 1980s and early 1990s.

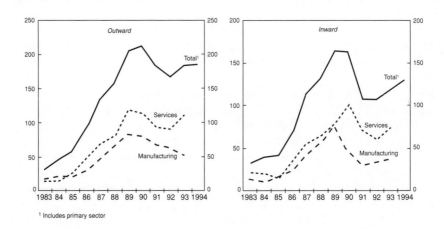

Source: The OECD Observer, **200**, Paris, OECD, 1996.

Figure 10.1   Trends in OECD foreign direct investment, 1983–94 ($billion)

Research and development in services is of increasing importance. R&D is normally associated with manufacturing industry but recent work has collected and analysed data in respect of services. It shows that services are not simply users of technology and innovation but also generators of them. In some countries it appears that a up to a third of all R&D expenditure by business is on services. Much of this may be on the development of software and new applications of information technology. A great deal depends on the classifications adopted but if the definition is used to include telecommunications, transport and pipelines then expenditure on R&D is obviously high but more R&D and capital investment is now carried out by the financial services and administrative sectors. Statistics in this area have to be treated with great caution because of the lack of international comparability.

10.3 Future Trends

Services and manufacturing will converge at an accelerating rate because of the development of information and communication technologies. These have the effect of what is called 'codifying knowledge' which means that services can be traded internationally via computer programmes as in the case of financial dealings. The term also applies to the use of expert systems in, for example, law and medicine to give advice or perform simple tasks.

Information technologies will be used to create new service products. This process is sometimes called the 'reverse product cycle' which has three stages. The first occurs when information technology is used to improve an existing process. The second happens when the improved process produces a substantial improvement in the quality of the process or product and the third emerges when it is apparent that there is a foundation for a completely new product in the improvement. The textbook example is the American Airlines seat reservation system called 'Sabre'. It was originally used to improve ticket booking procedures but was adapted for the use of other airlines. American Airlines obtained a better return from this than from actually flying aeroplanes. The third stage came when Sabre was extended to other booking applications for hotels and car rentals and, more recently, into dealing with insurance claims and managing airports.

Services will be more important in affecting the economic or business cycle because they represent growing levels of employment, income and investment. Some people used to think that services were immune to the cyclical movements of the world economy but that was never the case and experience in the late 1980s and early 1990s shows that as economies such as the USA, Japan, France and the United Kingdom began to shrink the service sector showed negative growth.

The service sector will become more capital intensive. Some parts of it always have been, for example, telecommunications, transport and pipelines but financial and community and social services are also progressing towards being capital intensive. In the USA about 80 per cent of information technology investment comes from services. In the United Kingdom about three-quarters of computer systems are bought by service industries. It is estimated that about half of all IT expenditure by industry is spent by six services, air transport, telecommunications, retail and wholesale traders, banking and insurance and health.

Any further predictions about the future normally assume that present trends will continue even if the rate of change becomes variable or ceases to accelerate, but a great deal depends on when, if ever, the long predicted information revolution actually occurs. People have been predicting it for some time and paint pictures of workers beavering away at their computer terminals in remote locations, They predict the end of the office block as we know it and of most commuting. The prophets tend to be the same people who anticipated the 'paper-less office'. We may get there one day but all progress is slower than the pundits predict. The same argument applies to the information superhighway. No doubt it has reached some of the elites of our world and is beginning to creep into affluent homes but we have not yet reached the critical mass required in order to announce that the future is here.

Exercise 3

Assuming that they do, how do direct sellers (by phone) of car and house insurance manage to charge lower prices?

11 Markets: Labour (1)

Aims of the chapter

To:
- explain the theoretical background to wage determination;
- examine the imperfections of labour markets;
- discuss supply and demand factors;
- discuss the mobility of labour.

Background

- Economists try to create models of labour markets that fit in with the different types of goods and services markets, so there is analysis of competitive as well as monopolistic markets. One specific instance that can also be analysed is where there is only one buyer of a particular type of labour, that is a monopsonist.

- The analysis is normally in terms of supply and demand factors because it is variations of these that cause wage levels to differ. In this context it is important to remember that no-one wants labour for its own sake. The entrepreneur wants workers for what they contribute to output and to the value of that output. This is called a **derived demand** and the concept applies to all the factors of production, land, capital and labour. The value of what an additional worker adds to total revenue is usually called **the marginal revenue product (MRP)** which is measured by multiplying the marginal product of the extra unit of the factor, say the additional worker, by the selling price of the extra output produced by the worker. In practice the MRP is extremely difficult to measure and in some cases, where the product is not actually sold, impossible. One example of the impossibility of measurement of MRP used to be in the National Health Service because most of its services were not priced but the introduction of the so-called 'internal market' into the NHS presumably makes it possible to calculate the MRP of an extra nurse, surgeon or cleaner.

- On the demand side it is important to remember that in some markets the employers combine into what are usually called trade associations in order to negotiate wage levels and conditions of employment such as working hours and holidays with the representatives of trade unions. This is the employers' side of the collective bargaining process.

- There has been a great deal of analysis of the supply of labour both in general and into particular occupations or groups of occupations. There has also been much study of the attitude of the individual to work and the response to wage levels, incentives and taxation. The factors influencing the overall numbers of workers available are very clear – population size and its structure in terms of age and sex distribution. Those influencing the numbers able and willing to work at a particular job, or in a specific district or for certain wage levels are much less clear. Obviously educational levels are important, as are levels of skill and training, but there are more imponderable factors such as the so-called net advantages of jobs or the impact of the social security system. We have, in the United Kingdom, what is called the 'poverty trap' where people who would like to work find that working for the low wages in the only employment that they can obtain gives them less disposable income than remaining within the social security system with its multitude of means tested benefits. When the individual's attitude to the supply of labour is studied it becomes apparent that most of us reach a point, some sooner than others, after which we prefer extra leisure to the additional income offered from working longer hours. This fact give rise to what is called the **backward bending supply curve of labour**.

Exercise I

If you have had a job paid by the hour, have you ever refused to work overtime at a higher rate, say at weekends? If so, could you draw for yourself a supply curve of your own labour with hours on the x axis and pay rates on the y axis? Is it a backward bending curve?

- Another important aspect of the supply side is the impact of organised labour, that is of trade union activity. The economic power of trade unions varies from industry to industry or occupation to occupation and over time. The effective union must be able to control the supply of labour to a firm or industry and be able to persuade it to act in a collective and disciplined manner. Ideally it requires a good financial buffer to maintain its members' unity in periods of industrial disputes. In recent years most emphasis has been on the mass, manual unions such as the coal miners or on the more skilled craft unions such as printers but the most effective 'unions' have been the professional associations of doctors, the BMA, the solicitors, the Law Society and similar groups.

- Entrepreneurs combine the factors of production in order to produce and they have a choice in how they mix the amounts of land, labour and capital. Labour and capital in particular are often good substitutes, especially over a long period of time. If labour becomes too scarce or expensive there will be extra incentives to replace it with machines or new technology or by redesigning and de-skilling the work. If spot welders in a car factory become too expensive and unreliable they will be replaced with robot welders. Expensive dock workers are forced out of jobs by containerisation; skilled and expensive plumbers are replaced by unskilled general workers using new push-fit assembly plastic plumbing systems. Deep-sea divers in the oil industry take a long time to train and have short working lives so the work is partially redesigned so that undersea robot tools can do the job. Agricultural workers become relatively scarce and are replaced by larger, more efficient machines for arable farming and for milking. One of the interesting areas of study here is the contrasting combinations of workers, capital and land in different firms and countries. What matters is the final average cost per unit of output but there is a tendency in Western economies to emphasise the importance of labour productivity.

- It may be useful to see labour markets as a series of separate compartments or segments with little or no movement of workers between them. There may, for example, be over 2 or even 3 million unemployed in the United Kingdom at any one time but there may still be a great shortage of a particular type of skilled or experienced worker and there may be no effective institutional mechanism for any of the unemployed to be retrained to take up the available work. Some economic commentators talk a lot about flexible labour markets and imply that the unemployed can, with relative ease, move between occupations. This may be a very long-run tendency and does apply to the general run of unskilled service jobs for young people but the short and medium term may be very different with little take up of the unemployed into occupations displaying shortages of qualified workers.

11.1 Supply Factors

The supply of labour in general, or the total labour force, is dependent on the size of the nation's population, particularly on the number of those between the normal school leaving age and the normal retirement ages. It is also reliant on the willingness of the people in this pool of potential workers to engage in paid employment and on how much work they do when working. There is, therefore, a mix of quantity and quality. Many in this pool of potential workers may not, in practice, work. Many of them are women who choose to withdraw temporarily or even permanently from the labour market in order to rear children. A few men do the same. Others retire early, either voluntarily or as a result of pressure. Some choose to work part time and nowadays many can find no other sort of employment. There is also a group within this age range who are unable for physical or mental reasons to work or who work sporadically. Some countries, although the number is falling, have conscription into their armed forces and thereby reduce their available labour force. A very important reduction in the pool of workers is caused by large numbers entering higher education and thus withdrawing from the mainstream workforce although many students do work intermittently and an increasing number are compelled to work regularly to finance their studies. There are a few factors that increase the supply of labour in general, for example immigration although that may be matched or exceeded by emigration in any given time period. Some countries have large seasonal flows of foreign workers and some attract workers in particular trades for varying periods, for example in the construction industry. Another factor raising the labour supply is the fact that some workers have more than one job and thereby swell the labour force. The overall supply may be augmented by the use of children within the family unit as workers or illegally by other employers. Some countries, especially developing economies, have large, active child labour forces even though it may be against their laws.

The supply of labour into one occupation is based on what may be called a winnowing process where, like an ear of wheat, the various non-useful parts are separated and discarded until only the desired material is left. We start from the point where all of the general supply of labour is theoretically available for a specified job. As we examine the qualities required for the efficient performance of the work many of these potential workers become non-qualifiers. The more skill, training, experience and educational qualifications that are needed for a particular job the more people who are disqualified. If we take a manual job as an example, even one that requires no literacy skills, some people will be excluded for reasons of physical disability. If the job requires physical strength and stamina far more will be excluded. The moment a literacy hurdle is introduced about 10 per cent of the adult population will fail to qualify although a high proportion of these will be elderly. As soon as a paper qualification is demanded such as GCSEs, A levels, GNVQs and so on, the numbers are further whittled down. The moment that specific subjects or grades are required the numbers begin to dwindle rapidly. Large numbers of people in the United Kingdom have excluded themselves from a wide range of occupations by their choice of optional subjects at the age of 14 and later at 16. There are a few limited schemes to overcome this premature specialisation but they are of marginal importance. If we delve into the sociology of educational opportunity we find that some people start with 'a silver spoon in their mouths' because their families can afford to provide them with all sorts of advantages beginning with nursery care, pre-school teaching, the arguable benefits of private education and family entrée into college or business. At the other end of the social scale there is often a cycle of deprivation and poor education passed from parents to children.

Exercise 2

Try creating a breakdown of the people who were in your class at school in terms of their educational and training records after the age of 16. Can you identify points of decision which have affected their life time earnings? Are you expecting higher life time earnings to reward you for the opportunity cost of your studies?

There remains another set of hurdles for the aspiring worker to clear. The law sometimes forbids anyone without a specific qualification performing certain tasks. The objective is, of course, to protect the public against charlatans or ill-qualified operatives, especially in the medical spheres and on transport such as ships, aircraft and public passenger vehicles. While some of these prohibitions are in the professions there are also several in skilled maintenance areas such as gas fitting and electrical installations. All of these restrictions have the effect of reducing the available supply of workers into an occupation and of making the supply more inelastic. In terms of the theory, the supply curve shifts to the left and has a steeper gradient. Some of these hurdles related to qualifications seem to be the result of effective pressure group activity and produce demarcation areas allocated to different types of worker. One of the best examples is in the legal field where we have the demarcation between the work of solicitors and barristers. The boundaries are slowly being eroded but both professions are extremely active in trying to perpetuate their privileges and to prevent non-members practising, in the case of solicitors for example, in the field of property conveyancing. Such distinctions are not restricted to the professions. In train driving, for example, the driver has to be qualified to drive a particular class of locomotive as well as the road (route) over which the train is to go. This need for multiple qualifications explains why some trains are cancelled for lack of a driver.

Individuals are attracted into an occupation by many factors, the most obvious of which is the wage rate or the prospect of future earnings and pension provision. Some workers are able to think in terms of the 'remuneration package' offered – that is pay, bonuses, commissions, share options, expenses, pensions, private health insurance, discounts, paid leave and cars. Workers also take account of non-monetary influences such a job security, working hours and conditions, travelling costs and time, the danger and pleasantness of the task or its repugnance. We each have different subjective views on these matters and there is a large body of academic research on people's motivation for work. The unsurprising conclusion is that for many people, especially in the more skilled and demanding jobs, the financial rewards, although important in signalling society's approval, are less important than in unskilled jobs. Most workers want job satisfaction and the ability to satisfy personal achievement goals as well as money. This approach to what are called the 'net advantages' of a job helps to explain the persistence of wage differentials. It also helps to explain why people in the state sector caring professions such as nursing, teaching and social work seem willing to accept lower remuneration than similarly qualified people in the private sector. It also partially explains why civil servants are paid less than comparable occupations. The difficulty of effective comparisons of earnings in different jobs should not be ignored. Civil service pay was, for a period, measured against the non-state sector and changes there were used to justify pay increases in the civil service but Mrs Thatcher abandoned the comparability element because it was proving too expensive to maintain.

There are some anomalies in the labour market which need explaining in the light of the paragraph above. You would expect, in view of what has been said about net advantages, that the dangerous, risky, dirty and unpleasant jobs would carry the highest rates of overall remuneration but the harsh fact is that the opposite is generally the case. It is true that dangerous jobs such as deep-sea divers and coal miners normally earn quite high premiums above comparably skilled jobs with lower risks and longer working life expectations but the best paid jobs usually have the best working conditions, the highest levels of non-financial benefits and the lowest levels of personal danger. The most interesting, creative and challenging jobs tend to be among the highest paid. This is partly a reflection of social factors and attitudes and partly the result of the clever and able reaching positions of authority from which they determine their own pay or that of their contemporary high fliers. Boards of directors usually have a remuneration committee composed mainly of non-executive directors who are supposed to be impartial but, of course, these non-executive directors' pay also comes up for consideration by the people whose remuneration they have decided. It is human nature in these circumstances to adopt an attitude of 'if you scratch my back, I'll scratch yours'. The only people who might be able to restrain the high earnings of company directors are the institutional shareholders but, again, they are run by people with the same business philosophy who also want high earnings so they are unlikely to challenge the high pay of directors in the companies in which they have large shareholdings.

A special case of restricted supply gives rise to the application of the concept of economic rent to the labour market. Rent in this context does not mean the usual commercial rent paid for property or land but a surplus in excess of the factor's transfer earnings as defined by Ricardo. Transfer earnings are the opportunity cost of a factor, that is the minimum reward needed to keep the factor in its present employment. If a piece of land can earn £1000 from growing wheat and £800 from its next best alternative use of growing barley then it is earning a surplus (economic rent) of £200 above the level at which it will transfer to the alternative of barley growing. The idea is applied to types of worker when they have very scarce talents or skills that are in high demand. Thus a world class tenor, of whom there appear to be only three in the public's imagination, will command a huge 'rent of ability' over and above what he could earn in his next best occupation which might be in an opera chorus. An example might be someone like Elton John who was, for a brief interlude, a lowly paid insurance clerk. His subsequent multi-million pound earnings give him a colossal economic rent of ability. It should be emphasised that the economist is not concerned with whether the quality of the performance or work is desirable but whether there is demand for it. It is quite salutary to look back over the popular hits of the past and wonder 'why did anyone ever buy that?' There is an element of rent, often very large, in the payments of all top-class performers in the world of entertainment and sport. The application of the idea has its limitations because we cannot imagine people like Elton John ever going back to being an insurance clerk even if his earnings from performing shrank to nothing. In the past, when they were paid £10 or £15 a week as players, a few world-class England footballers retired to keep pubs but we cannot imagine most current members of the team doing that, although a few might finance nightclubs with their accumulated earnings. The idea also has a weakness in that some performers live for their art and would carry on working for very much less than they might be currently receiving.

It is possible for this element of economic rent to be temporary, in which case it is called 'quasi-rent.' A good example is deep-sea divers in the North Sea. When the oil fields were first being developed there were few people trained to work at the required depths so the available workers were in extremely high demand relative to the supply and could command very high payments for their dangerous job. They also had a very short working life because of the physical conditions of deep-sea diving. Over time the oil companies responded to the shortage of divers by creating training establishments which increased the available supply and reduced the individual diver's market power. In the longer term they established working techniques that enabled the divers to remain beneath the sea longer and changed the technology so that some work could be done by remotely controlled underwater robots. Eventually the divers were paid a premium related to the risk and danger and anti-social hours of their job and the brevity of their working lives rather than to an overall scarcity of skilled workers. The short-run quasi-rent arose because of a relatively fixed, inelastic supply. Similar shortages have occurred in other spheres. It should be said that the concept of quasi-rent is usually more applicable to units of capital, such as oil tankers, where short-run scarcity creates a short-run rent.

Exercise 3

How do you explain in economic terms the £15 million paid as a transfer fee for the footballer Alan Shearer?

11.2   The Mobility of Labour

There are three types of mobility of labour and each has a different bearing on wage levels and differentials. Wage theory tends to assume a high degree of mobility but, in practice, labour may show a distinct tendency towards immobility for reasons that are often not economic but sentimental. Some modern economists are extremely keen to have what they call flexible labour markets and the mobility of labour is a cornerstone of such a policy. The three types may be intermingled in any specific case:

1. **Occupational mobility** refers to the movement between occupations as when a redundant coal miner becomes a minicab driver or retrains as a hairdresser. Many workers retrain and shift occupations over their lifetime and the level of training and re-education provided by the state and companies is very important. The United Kingdom has been strongly criticised for its record in this respect.

2. **Industrial mobility** is the second type and refers to a worker keeping the same occupation but changing the industry in which the work is performed. Many clerical workers shift industry and so do some skilled workers such as electricians and fitters. It is essential to have a degree of industrial mobility if the economy is to respond effectively to changing demand and profit opportunities.

3. **Geographical mobility** means the physical movement of the worker to another location. This may or may not be combined with occupational and industrial mobility. For example, an unemployed Scottish shipbuilder might shift location to Slough and work as a machine minder in a chocolate factory, an occupational, industrial and geographical shift. A scaffolder from Tyneside might work on a permanent basis in London, a simple geographical shift. Migration is, of course, an extreme version of geographical mobility.

The mobility of labour affects the elasticity of supply. The idea of elasticity of supply of labour deals with the relationship of changes in the quantity supplied to a change in the wage rate. As the wages offered in different jobs change we would expect, other things being equal, that workers would shift from the lower to the higher paid work. This does of course happen over time as school-leavers begin to decide what line of work they want to do. It explains why law courses and accountancy courses became so popular in the late 1970s and early 1980s. Lawyers and accountants were seen as receiving well above average earnings. There was a similar influx into financial jobs as the high earnings of some City workers were splashed across the media. It seemed as if every 16- to 18-year-old wanted to be a member of the bright braces and striped shirt brigade and drink champagne for breakfast, lunch and tea.

Obstacles to changing occupation

- The labour market appears to have segments and there is little movement between some of them even if they are apparently closely connected. One would think that a software engineer is a generic sort of job with programmers able and willing to shift easily between firms, industries and areas. Although the occupation is noted for the large number of self-employed, mobile, short contract workers who earn large sums on a short-term basis, many of them are experienced in some applications, hardware and programming languages but ignorant of others. They would need an expensive period of learning and readjustment before they became productive if they were employed on systems in which they had no experience. There may, therefore, be a much smaller pool of qualified labour for a particular vacancy than one would expect. Workers may become very specialised until they only fit one niche in the labour market. Employers often compound their problems by specifying ages in their recruitment adverts, a practice which is illegal in some sensible countries but not yet in the United Kingdom. To take another example, an industry may expand so quickly that the available qualified labour force becomes numerically inadequate to satisfy demand but if there is no established recruitment and training system the industry as a whole will continue to suffer labour shortages even if there is unemployment elsewhere in the economy. The British economy since 1975 has displayed evidence of this phenomenon because, despite the large numbers of unemployed as the economy comes out of recession, there are shortages of skilled labour and wage inflation becomes apparent in some sectors while large numbers remain unemployed. There is what is called a mismatch between the skills of the unemployed and those required in growth industries.

- Changing occupation or place of residence costs money. Some of the cost may be an opportunity cost in terms of lost earnings as the individual often needs to stop working in order to obtain new qualifications or to be retrained. Some new jobs have lower initial earnings than the previous work although the long-run prospects may be better. There may be a considerable reduction in other benefits when a job or employer is changed. Although most people would expect an improvement in such circumstances the threat of unemployment or forced and prolonged redundancy often propels people into lower paid employment. The other major cost which reduces geographical mobility is the cost of moving house. The average cost of selling one house and buying another is estimated at between £3000 and £4000 but the most important penalty is suffered by those who sell a 'good' house away from the southeast and then find that they can only afford an 'inferior' house in the south or Greater London. Since most moves in recent years have been in this direction the regional house price differential has constituted an important brake on the mobility of labour. Some organisations do, of course, attempt to overcome this particular problem with generous relocation packages.

Another cost of changing jobs lies in the actual search. Many unemployed workers find it extremely hard to look for jobs locally because of the delayed payment of expenses for interviews and travel. They find it even harder to apply for jobs at a distance where overnight stops may be needed. There have been various allowances paid for such job searching and they have had a marginally beneficial impact.

- The next group of reasons for the immobility of labour may be classified as sociological or sentimental depending on your taste. Despite all the rhetoric about the amazing modern mobility of the United Kingdom population the evidence is that the vast majority of people live and work near their family and where they were brought up. The chattering classes and the better educated are more mobile and tend to assume that everyone else is as well. Individuals, especially those in or near their families, are markedly reluctant to leave the warm bosom of their nearest and dearest and venture off into strange parts where the beer, pubs, social clubs, football teams, schools, shops and recreational facilities are unfamiliar. They would rather be unemployed near their friends and families where they are guaranteed some support rather than among strangers. This is less true of the young and unattached but older workers have to consider their children's schooling and the ties of ageing parents. When all these psychological bonds are taken into account, and we all have different ones, and when we add the money costs of moving, it is no surprise that labour is not as mobile as some economists think is necessary for their 'flexible' labour markets to work.

- It can be argued that an 'excessively' generous social welfare system which cushions the unemployed against the harsh economic realities of moving and adjusting to new employment reduces mobility. Since 1979 the United Kingdom government has gradually reduced the cushioning effect of unemployment benefits and of other social welfare payments. Their main motive has been to cut government spending but they also hoped to create greater incentives to mobility. These ideas have a superficial attraction but rely mainly on the idea that workers can price themselves into jobs by accepting lower wages and poorer conditions of employment. If the unemployment is caused by a world trade recession and by deficient demand and if there is a severe lack of investment it is unlikely that reducing the levels of welfare payments will have much impact. It may have a harmful effect in reducing effective demand and by lowering workers' morale and productivity.

Exercise 4

What impact might social security benefits have on the mobility of labour to increase it or decrease it?

11.3 **Demand Factors**

It was explained at the start of the chapter that the demand for labour, like that for all factors of production, is a derived demand, which is to say that entrepreneurs only want labour for what it contributes to production as measured by the additional revenue generated. This extra revenue is usually called the marginal revenue product (MRP) of the factor. In the short run it is assumed to rise at first and then reduce in accordance with the law of diminishing marginal returns. The MRP is determined by two things:

1. The selling price of the product of the labour. To some extent, of course, this selling price is influenced by the levels of wages paid to the workers but it is also related to the other costs of production arising from land and capital. The price is also influenced by the degree of competition in the market. The less competitive the market the more control the supplier exercises over the selling price.

2. The marginal productivity of the labour in combination with the selling price determines the MRP. The marginal production of the additional worker is assumes to rise in the short run and then, after a point, decline again in accordance with the law of diminishing returns. When and how fast it declines depends on the nature of the product and the production process, that is the ease and cost of stretching more output from the relatively fixed factors in the short run. In the long run, when all the factors are assumed to be variable, the decline of the MRP will be delayed and reduced because increased efficiency will bring improved productivity. It should, perhaps, be noted here that productivity is a measure of output in relation to the inputs; it is not simply a measure of output. Thus productivity might be expressed as tonnes of steel per worker shift or per unit of capital or sales per employees rather than as tonnes or sales. One characteristic of many mass-produced consumer durable goods industries is that they enjoy sufficient economies of scale to ensure that the price of the product falls over time. In this case the MRP over the long run may also fall unless the increased output per unit of marginal factor rises faster than the fall in selling price.

Another important point to remember on the demand side for labour is that the entrepreneur has a choice, within limits, of how much of each factor to use and that the combinations will be altered as their price changes. It is often said that labour can price itself out of the market by which is meant that the entrepreneur finds it cheaper to use capital instead or, in some rare cases in agriculture, land. The phrase may also mean that cheaper labour will be employed, that is less qualified, youthful and inexperienced or foreign. Many United Kingdom industries have shifted production to the Pacific rim or East Asian countries in the pursuit of cheaper and more amenable labour. Except in the case of China itself, and in a few pockets elsewhere, this policy is beginning to be counterproductive as, for example, some labour in Korea is now more expensive that in some regions of the United Kingdom. As a result Korean firms are opening plants in South Wales.

The demand for labour, therefore, is related to the elasticity of supply of alternative factors particularly that of capital. If capital equipment is elastic in supply the labour is in a less strong position to demand higher wages or even to insist on previous levels of remuneration. The main issue is the degree of substitutability of the labour by other factors and the time periods involved.

AN EXAMPLE OF FACTOR SUBSTITUTION

If we study modern economic history it is possible to see a major trend towards the replacement of labour. The motor industry is an excellent example. When Henry Ford began mass production of the Model T he combined flow line production with the interchangeable parts principle and used enormous numbers of workers. He also applied a doctrine of management that is called Taylorism which meant that each worker was trained on a 'need to know' basis, that is he was told only the bare minimum that enabled him to do the work efficiently. Over time there were enormous pressures to economise on labour which had become less tractable and more demanding of regular pay rises and better conditions. Gradually, therefore, the assembly process was reorganised and products were designed to cut manufacturing costs. Today the body panel pressings can be much larger and the parts are usually handled by automatic transfer machines between each hydraulic press and then by robot welding machines. Similarly, the once labour-intensive and skilled tasks of engine cylinder and piston manufacture have been superseded by lines of automatic machines supervised by computers and a few highly trained engineers with a few relatively unskilled manual workers who shift the raw materials and waste. This process of substitution for labour has been followed in almost all industries except some of the service industries. Even so, in the financial services industries, the initial trend towards rapid expansion of workforces has begun to give way to contraction as computerisation and information technology become more refined.

The elasticity of demand for labour is directly related to the elasticity of demand for the product of the labour. Usually, but not always, if the demand for the product is elastic so is the demand for the labour; and if the demand or the product is inelastic so is the demand for the labour. There are exceptions if the labour represents a very small fraction of the total costs of the production process such as the few workers who run a power station or oil refinery. They are mainly skilled, well-paid workers who have to be employed in certain numbers otherwise the huge investment in capital will not be operated efficiently. The demand for their services is, therefore, inelastic irrespective of the demand for their product. There may be a few workers without whom even the largest plant cannot operate, boiler operatives, plant maintenance operatives and security people. They have to be employed whatever the elasticity of demand for the product.

11.4 Putting Supply and Demand Together

It is argued that the free market price of labour is determined by the inter-action of the supply and demand. Wage levels or, if we take a more complex view, remuneration in general, act as signals to employers and workers to choose or shift occupations or to change the levels of wages offered. In theory workers will shift towards higher paid jobs from lower paid work and employers will offer higher pay to attract workers and not raise wages where workers can be easily replaced. Wage levels will also help to allocate resources between different uses and help entrepreneurs to balance the combinations of the factors, land, labour and capital in the optimum manner.

The optimum combination of the factors of production occurs where the ratios of the marginal product of the factors to their price are equal:

$$\frac{MP\ Land}{Price\ of\ Land} = \frac{MP\ Labour}{Price\ of\ Labour} = \frac{MP\ Capital}{Price\ of\ Capital}$$

If the price or marginal product of any of the factors changes then the quantity of each employed will also alter. For example, if labour becomes cheaper relative to land and capital, the ratio for labour rises and it will tend to lead to a reduction of the use of land and capital as labour is substituted for them.

We have already seen that the labour market is anything but perfect and there are many obstacles to the free movement of labour and the other factors which may be very specific to one use but the general trend is stated correctly.

Each occupation will have a separate supply and demand equilibrium with different elasticities of demand and supply in the short and long run. Unskilled jobs will tend to have more elastic supply and lower overall wage levels and larger numbers employed. Skilled occupations, or ones that require long training and scarce qualifications will tend to have a very inelastic supply, higher remuneration and much smaller numbers employed. These differences in supply and demand help to explain why wage differentials exist. The next chapter deals with wage differentials, with state intervention in labour markets and with the role of trade unions.

12 Markets: Labour (2)

Aims of the chapter

To:

- explain the basis of wage differentials;
- discuss discrimination in labour markets;
- examine the role of trade unions and their impact in the labour market;
- examine the role of the state in labour markets.

12.1 Wage Differentials

There are several types of wage differential. The phrase 'wage' here is used to mean earnings and encompasses all forms of payment to employed labour, the hourly, weekly or monthly pay, the bonuses and commissions, the value of payments in kind such as housing, services and discounts, low interest charges and the benefits of luncheon vouchers, train season tickets and company cars. In some jobs the pension contributions made by the employer are of major importance and some higher paid jobs carry significant share option benefits. Many firms give the majority of their workers some payment in company shares or an option to take shares but such annual awards are usually small. Where there has been a management buy-out the share ownership may be of much greater significance. The main differentials occur:

- **Between different occupations**. Doctors are usually paid more than nurses; landscape designers are paid more than most gardeners and so on. We take this situation to be part of our everyday life and most would find it odd that, in the old Soviet Union, a Leningrad tram driver was paid more than a doctor because the job was deemed to be harder and less rewarding.
- **Between different ages** in the same occupation. Many jobs carry automatic annual increments in pay and many more have one pay scale for the 16 to 18 age group, another for 18 to 21 and another for the over 21s.
- **Between the same job in different regions** of the country. The most obvious are those where a so-called 'London weighting' is given often under the guise of a 'cost of living' allowance (which it rarely is in practice).

- **Between men and women**. It is illegal in the United Kingdom to pay women less pay for the same job or comparable work but women as a whole earn only two-thirds of the average man's earnings.

- **Between different ethnic and racial groups**. There has been a great deal of analysis of this area since statistics became available.

In the following discussions it should be borne in mind that there have been many theories which attempt to explain differentials, that the points made are mainly tentative and that we can all find exceptions to some of the statements made.

Differentials between jobs

These are usually explained in terms of supply and demand conditions with an analysis of the main factors influencing them. We can take an example of contrasting occupations in order to highlight the issues, say hospital consultants and agricultural workers.

On the supply side the number of people able to work in agriculture far exceeds those able to be consultants. People start working on the land immediately after leaving school, or before if they are brought up on a farm, or spend a relatively short time at college. A smaller number take degrees related to agriculture and land management. Much of the basic work is learned on the job from experience and there is a system of extra payments for acquired skills such as machinery maintenance. In general the farm worker of today is much more skilled than those of 30 years ago. The opportunity cost of the training of a farm worker is comparatively low because of the short time between leaving school and becoming proficient and qualified. Less earnings are sacrificed in the pursuit of qualifications than is the case with consultants who undergo lengthy extra schooling and medical training and then some years as relatively lowly paid hospital doctors before becoming a consultant. Society expects that some reward will be offered to make up for the lost earnings of the training years and this opportunity cost is often put forward as a justification for higher earnings and differentials. It will be interesting to see what the impact of student loans will be on differentials in future years when the system is bedded down. One implication of the high educational standards required of consultants, beginning with high grades at GCSE and Advanced level, is that there is a wide range of highly paid jobs available to them at the age of 18. This means that the pay and career conditions offered to consultants must remain attractive enough to persuade potential doctors that the non-financial rewards of being a doctor outweigh those of the other highly paid careers that they might follow.

Another aspect of the supply side is that consultants are specialists and those who aspire to such positions direct their work experience towards certain areas of medicine. As a result there will be relatively few applicants who have the desired qualifications and experience for the available posts and the scarcity may be magnified because of variations in the popularity of certain regions. The majority of posts will tend to be in centres of large population. Within the range of specialisms some types of consultancy are more popular than others and the supply in relation to the demand for those posts will be greater. Agricultural workers are, in contrast, available throughout the country although there may be a relative scarcity near large towns and cities where better paid jobs are easier to obtain. In some areas there may be few alternatives to work in agriculture so there is an excess supply of available workers. The different supply conditions are reflected in the curves on Figure 12.1. The supply curve for consultants has been drawn with a steeper gradient to indicate a more inelastic supply than for agricultural workers.

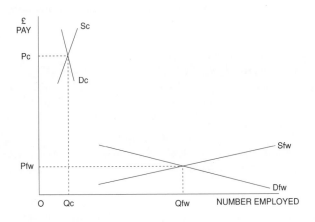

Sc/Dc = Supply/Demand for consultants;
Sfw/Dfw = Supply/Demand for farm workers

Figure 12.1   Wage differentials

The demand side for the two occupations indicates how markets are influenced by the state, even where there appears to be a free market. Agricultural workers will be demanded as long as there is a demand for the produce of the land, that is apparent from the idea of the demand for labour being a derived demand. If farms are profitable and demand for food is buoyant, other things being equal, there will be a persistent demand for farm workers. There will, however, be regional differences in farm profitability and, within a given area, differences in the levels of farm incomes according to the type of farming, milk, cattle, arable, sheep, or mixed. As farm workers are not homogeneous and are not very mobile because of the tied housing system and their lower than average incomes, there may be some variations in the strength of the demand for differently qualified workers. Shepherds may be scarce while experts with cows or pigs may be plentiful in relation to local demand. The more competitive the market the larger these differences are likely to be. If farm incomes are good and there is confidence for the future, there is likely to be a strong demand for agricultural workers. Having said this, much will depend on the price and benefits from using capital equipment or new techniques or even contractors instead of directly employed labour. The state enters the scene because farm incomes are heavily dependent on European Union agricultural policy and many farms find that most of their income comes from support payments; a few get all of their income from set-aside payments. The demand for labour, therefore, is ultimately dependent on these policies and the Common Agricultural Policy price and subsidy regime.

The demand for consultants is also affected by government policy. Most posts are created within the National Health Service but many NHS consultants also work in the private sector where their income comes mainly from health insurance schemes such as BUPA. Even with the new internal markets within the NHS it is difficult to measure the marginal revenue product of consultants because the pricing systems are not 'real' but based on notional prices. Some consultants work entirely in the private sector and their marginal revenue product could be measured because their work is priced to the patient. The government indirectly decides the numbers of consultant posts available in the NHS through the administrative apparatus of the NHS and through its decisions on overall funding. Behind their decisions on funding lie some population factors, especially age and sex distributions, but they also take into account the overall budget situation and political pressures. The demand for medical services is complex and there is often a choice about the nature of treatment, its length and variety. This has led some economists to argue that the NHS is driven by an ever increasing demand based in the growth of income and tastes and preferences rather than upon medical need. Many treatments, such as cosmetic surgery are completely optional and, at the other extreme, some such as emergency appendicitis operations are completely necessary. In between these extremes there are many treatments and procedures that may or may not be appropriate or desirable. Those who want a free market in health services tend to magnify their number and will refer to heart bypass operations, tonsillectomies, circumcision, ear grommets and such things as caesarean section births as driven by demand from the medical profession and articulate patients rather than by medical imperatives. Heart bypass operations are more frequent in rich countries such as the USA where medical insurance pays the bills. We might observe that these economists who regard such procedures as 'optional extras' probably change their tune when they or their nearest and dearest have medical problems.

If we were comparing two occupations that were entirely in the private sector, such as car assembly workers and bricklayers, we might place more emphasis on the net advantages of the jobs in terms of risk, job security, benefits in kind, pleasantness of working conditions and so on. In both cases the demand side would be easier to analyse than the example of consultants because there is an obvious and direct relationship between the number of cars sold and the demand for car assembly workers and between house building and construction and the demand for bricklayers. There might be an element of quasi-rent in the wages of bricklayers if a property boom were in full swing.

Wage differentials persist over long periods of time because there is a tendency for them to become institutionalised in the wage negotiating process between trade unions and employers' organisations. Several strikes have been caused by the long-term determination of certain groups to retain their place in the hierarchy of industrial earnings. The coal miners in particular were keen to maintain their traditional top ranking and skilled unions such as ASLEF, the locomotive drivers' union have always tried to keep their differentials over the other railway unions. Attempts to retain differentials have also been accompanied by a strong emphasis on demarcation of work, that is an insistence that certain work can only be done by workers in a particular trade and with the right qualifications. Demarcation disputes have also caused strikes because employers who ignore agreements are seen as diluting the labour force with less skilled workers. Sometimes the supply side of an occupation is heavily influenced by the insistence of a trade union, or professional body in the case of doctors, on entry qualifications. Going back to our example, the agricultural workers have a comparatively weak union because their workers, although numerous, are scattered throughout the country and rarely work together in sufficient numbers for one employer to exert much power. Shop workers are in a similar position. Consultants are in a much more powerful position because they are able, through their links with the government department which controls the medical services and regulations, to insist on specific qualifications for surgeons and doctors. They constitute a powerful pressure group that usually has the backing of the public. No-one wishes to be operated on by someone who has qualified via a do-it-yourself guide book, although we may end up employing plumbers who are trained by that method. Differentials persist despite the economic theory that suggests that workers will move from the lower paid to the higher paid jobs until the differentials are eroded. This is because the units of labour are by no means complete substitutes for each other.

Exercise I

Do you consider the differential in earnings between doctors and agricultural workers too large? What economic criteria would you apply to the question of 'too large'?

Age and pay differentials

Many firms which employ workers who can be trained in a very short time, for example food retailers or engineering assemblers, pay their workers according to their age and often use three ranges, 16 to 18, 18 to 21 and over 21. This sort of differential is frequently supported by trade unions. The justification for such age-related increments is not based on short-run marginal productivity because there is usually little variation between the MRP of young and old workers. The extra payments are given to reward loyalty to the firm and to save the increasing costs of recruitment and the training given even if it is of a minimum standard. There also seems to be a popular belief that older people with more responsibilities such as families to support should be paid more but there is little economic justification for this argument. In other sorts of occupation, such as teaching, the civil service and local government, the employee is paid annual increments for a number of years. The usual justification for such annual increments is that the employee becomes more productive, experienced and skilled over the years. In most professions covered by the annual pay rise system the number of years on the pay scale has been reduced, usually in response to trade union pressure or as way of giving better pay rises. The stepped pay scales according to age act as an incentive for the more unscrupulous employers to shed labour as it reaches the thresholds and to replace it with younger, cheaper labour. In the United Kingdom this tendency has been accelerated by the recession of the early 1990s and the abolition of Wage Council protection for younger workers some years before it was also abolished for older workers.

Some countries, such as the USA, have laws against what is called 'ageism', that is the discrimination against workers on the grounds of their age. This discrimination is usually done by specifying ages in advertisements but the application of an age range is often used as one of the criteria for weeding out job applicants if there is a big surplus of applicants. Attempts have been made in the United Kingdom to have the practice made illegal but the United Kingdom government favours deregulated markets and has opposed the moves. Some recruitment agencies have, however, introduced their own bans on age references in advertisements of vacancies. Some firms have begun to find that their over enthusiastic 'downsizing' in recent years has left them with a serious corporate knowledge and experience gap because they have got rid of too many of the age groups who would make the next generation of top managers. Ageism and the discrimination that follows from it are not, of course, based on rational application of the facts about labour which indicate that older workers are frequently more loyal and more productive than younger workers and are not any the less innovative. They are, moreover, able from their experience to reach conclusions quicker and avoid repeating previous errors.

Exercise 2

Are firms wise to 'downsize' by sacking or prematurely retiring their older workers? Give reasons for and against.

Regional pay differentials

There are wide variations in the pay of workers in the same occupation in different regions of the United Kingdom and even larger variations over the countries of the European Union. In theory, the pay differentials should persuade workers to move area in search of the higher pay but, as was explained earlier, there are strong influences, economic and sociological, that reduce the mobility of labour. We do see this process of movement in periods of recession, for example in the commuting of building workers from Merseyside and the northeast to the development sites of the southeast, or on a wider scale to Germany.

There are also regional pay differentials that are created by large national firms which choose to offer higher pay scales to those who work in the Greater London area and sometimes in Birmingham. Many of these firms are in the financial services sector, banking and insurance and some are in public administration. These employers are competing in a market where good, qualified workers are relatively scarce and they use the 'London allowance' as a way of raising their bid for labour. They also compete by providing other benefits such as luncheon vouchers and help with season tickets or motoring costs. The general public regard these extra payments and benefits as some sort of compensation for the higher cost of living in the London area but this is a mistaken view. The cost of living is only significantly higher in housing and is lower than many regions for a wide variety of goods and services such as durable goods because of the greater competition among sellers. The housing costs are, of course, higher mainly because of the larger average incomes of the southeast. It is the competition for labour that pushes up earnings in these areas and stimulated the shift of many head offices of companies to other regions.

The United Kingdom Conservative government has been keen to abolish national determination of pay scales for occupations such as nurses, hospital workers, teachers and so on, and is also keen to end national pay bargaining by trade unions and employers in the manufacturing and utilities sectors. It hopes that this will create a market for labour that is more sensitive to regional cost differentials and that cheaper labour in areas of higher unemployment would attract more inwards investment. There has been some movement of Korean firms into South Wales who say that it is because Welsh labour is now cheaper than some types of Korean labour. The government grants they are given are also an attraction. Trade unions are usually opposed to plant or local bargaining because it reduces the power of the worker *vis-à-vis* the employer.

Exercise 3

Why do regional pay differentials persist?

Male and female pay differentials

Background. In 1961, in the United Kingdom Civil Service, equal pay was achieved and this equality was quickly applied in local government and teaching. In 1970 the Equal Pay Act came into operation and provided for a five-year period of implementation so that gradually differences were ended between pay for the same or broadly similar work or work rated as equivalent under a job evaluation study. The pay of women had to be raised to that of men. This Act was bolstered by the Sex Discrimination Act of 1975 that made illegal any unequal treatment on the grounds of sex and marital status in the other areas of employment apart from pay. The European Economic Community rules under Article 119 of the Treaty of Rome were interpreted by the European Court in such a way that United Kingdom legislation had to be modified in 1983 in the Equal Pay (Amendment) Regulations. Men and women are now supposed to receive equal pay for equal work and 'equal' is defined as of equal value. This is a more practical definition because there are relatively few instances of men and women doing exactly the same work side by side. Where it did occur before 1970 it was quite common for trade unions to negotiate a wage for women that was two-thirds of the basic wage of the men doing exactly the same work.

The broad effects of the legislation appear to have been a raising of women's hourly earnings relative to men. For a very long period from 1886 to the 1970 Act women in the United Kingdom in manual jobs received around about 50 per cent of male hourly earnings, including overtime. Hourly earnings excluding overtime were about 60 per cent because women work less overtime. In the five years after 1970 these figures rose to over 6o per cent including overtime and to over 70 per cent excluding it. If all adult women, manual and non-manual, are studied there was a rise from 64 per cent in 1970 to nearly 74 per cent of male earnings six years later. These figures have remained remarkably consistent ever since. There are, therefore, several issues that need examining under the general question of why these differentials exist and persist.

Possible reasons for male/female pay differences

Different productivity may exist because there are variations between men and women in their marginal revenue products; in other words women may have lower value to an employer than men. (We are talking in generalities here.) It is conceivable that this may be the case in jobs requiring specific types of physical strength and stamina as can be borne out by comparing overall performances in athletics, although women may have greater outputs in certain occupations. If MRPs were different there would be a justification in economic terms for pay differences. In many cases, however, the use of capital equipment places men and women on the same footing in terms of marginal productivity.

Employers may, and often apparently do, regard women as having lower *long-run* productivity because they expect them to take time off work for child bearing and rearing and to miss opportunities for training and promotion. They may regard them as being more prone to absenteeism through sickness although the statistics do not fully bear this out. The attitudes expressed here are more likely to result in less recruitment of women rather than in paying them lower rates for a specific job.

Education may be an important factor explaining differentials. There is still a tendency for families in the United Kingdom to put more money into the education of boys than girls although the numbers of girls going on to higher education has risen steadily over the last 25 years and women outnumber men on many courses and approach 50-50 in law and medicine. In many developing countries there is a strong bias towards the education and health care of boys. If education levels are different, and the type of higher education is biased away from preparing women for a whole range of better paid jobs, then women are not being given the full range of opportunities in the job market. The tendency for girls to choose arts subjects rather than science and maths based subjects will handicap them in the market for higher paid jobs.

Training differences are also important where they exist. Women may choose to undertake less postgraduate training or to undergo shorter training. When they are employed their employers may take the view that investing in their training is less productive in the long term because of their child-bearing and rearing responsibilities even in this age of the alleged 'new man'. Certainly many women do take some years off work or become part time and do miss out on training and promotion chances. These missed chances lower their overall earnings relative to men's. There are some statistics to bear out the assertion that women overall used to receive less training than men before 1990. (See Table 3.3.) Men stated in a survey that their main reason for training was to gain promotion; women wanted to make their work more interesting.

Promotion opportunities differ between men and women and this results in women being under-represented in better paid, higher status positions. The reasons are partly historical or related to generations in that it is still rather early for women to have reached the stage in certain occupations, such as the law, where they are equally represented as, for example judges. If the pressure towards equal pay and treatment began in the 1960s and became accepted in the 1970s we would expect there to be a delay of some years before women reached the higher echelons of a profession in equal numbers. There has, however, been excessively slow progress and the term 'the glass ceiling' has been coined to explain the phenomenon of women reaching the middle and next to the top layers of responsibility but not getting to the very top. They can see the top, the board of directors, but there is an invisible barrier that prevents many of them reaching the top in proportionate numbers. With some notable exceptions, those who do make it on to the top board of directors are often employed on the personnel or related sides of the business. Several explanations are given for this phenomenon and the most plausible is that men choose men rather than women, probably for deep psychological reasons such as fear or lack of security. They may rationalise their choice in terms of experience and fitting in as one of the team but, deep down, it is discrimination. Attempts have been made to measure discrimination and over 10 per cent of the earnings differences might be attributable to sex discrimination rather than to other factors such as experience and education.

Part-time working, which is more prevalent among women is responsible for some of the earning differences. Men work more overtime on average and that boosts their weekly earnings. Working part time also reduces women's eligibility for promotion and training. It is also associated with gaps in working life for child rearing and frequently with lower paid occupations. Table 3.4 illustrates the variations of working patterns between men and women.

Crowding into a few occupations is sometimes seen as a feature of women's employment and a cause of their lower average earnings. Men, in contrast, work in almost all the occupations that are available although they are under-represented in some. There is a preponderance of women in certain lower paid occupations such as catering, retailing, contract cleaning, light assembly work, textile and clothing manufacturing and clerical jobs. Women also 'crowd' into the caring professions such as nursing, social services and teaching all of which are not exceptionally well paid. They are beginning to be better represented in the legal and medical professions but are under-represented in science, engineering, computing and highly paid financial services jobs. Women are grossly under-represented in the House of Commons although they are not quite as much so in the number of candidates who stand for parliament. The indication is that they find it harder to obtain 'safe' seats for which to stand. There is some debate as to whether women select these occupations into which they allegedly crowd or are 'forced' by economic and social pressures into them. They may expect from observation not to achieve promotion in certain male dominated professions and therefore do not train or educate themselves to enter them. In terms of economic theory, if they do so crowd into relatively few occupations, they are raising the supply in relation to the demand and tending to lower the earnings of those occupations. An interesting case study may be made of teaching where women now outnumber men overall and completely dominate the primary sector. If pay rates are compared from say 1960 to 1996, the pay of male graduate secondary teachers has fallen compared with male graduate entrants to occupations such as the civil service. This may be due to the introduction of equal pay, to the teaching profession becoming all graduate or to the other sectors being better organised in the labour market. The crowding argument has some validity but there arises the question as to why do women not realise that if they adopted a wider range of occupations they would earn more. Perhaps it will take a much longer period of time for the earnings gap to be reduced by the entry of more women into what have been traditional male preserves.

Other discrimination and wage differentials

There is much evidence that ethnic and racial minority groups also suffer discrimination in labour markets and that their earnings are, therefore, lower than average although there are disparities between groups and in different regions. Many of the reasons given are similar to those given about women, that is less education, less training and a narrower range of occupations entered. The abolition of Wages Council protection in 1989 and 1994 may also be a contributory factor. There may be language problems. Many members of ethnic minorities may be recent immigrants and enter a limited range of low paid jobs. Usually, the next and third generations are almost completely integrated into the workforce and are distributed fairly normally throughout it. A worrying aspect of some United Kingdom minorities is that this process does not seem to be operating with the speed that it once did especially among young males of Afro-Caribbean origin. There is a large amount of research in the area of discrimination but most of it in the United Kingdom is in the field of male/female distinctions and the analysis of ethnic and racial discrimination has been concentrated in the USA. The inclusion of questions on ethnic origins in the Population Census and Labour Force Surveys has, however, given a statistical base for more research in the United Kingdom.

12.2 Trade Unions and the Labour Market

A trade union is 'a combination of employees whose principal activity is the regulation of relations between employees and employers' (Donovan Commission, 1968). It is often forgotten that there are also employers' associations which go under a variety of names which also try to regulate their labour relations. Collective bargaining is the interaction between the two sides, trade unions and employers' associations. The role of trade unions became a political football in the 1970s and 80s because of the widespread perception, fostered by a right-wing dominated press, that they were too powerful and were the cause of inflation and the United Kingdom's relative economic decline. Historically there are four types of union.

The craft unions which were the first to be formed, mainly in the early and middle nineteenth century, were composed of very skilled workers who paid relatively high membership fees. They remained small in membership numbers and, depending on the state of the general economy, were quite effective, powerful and influential. They placed considerable emphasis on the welfare of their members and the maintenance of entry requirements for their job so apprenticeship was often the way in to the occupation. A typical example was ASLEF, the Associated Society of Locomotive Engineers and Firemen. Such craft unions were effective in maintaining and raising the relative wages of their members because of their control over an inelastic supply of the skill and because of their strike funds.

Mass unions or the 'new unions' developed after bitter strikes in the late 1880s. These new unions were mainly unskilled workers who were poorly paid and had little job security. There were a large number of amalgamations of trade unions in the United Kingdom in the 1920s and well-known unions emerged such as the Amalgamated Engineering Union (AEU) and the Transport and General Workers Union (TGWU). The AEU extended its membership to less skilled workers. Until the period after 1945 they were generally ineffective in raising their members wages because of the plentiful supply of unemployed unskilled labour available. Some of these unions metamorphosed by amalgamation and redirection into industrial unions.

Industrial unions developed in the United States in the 1920s and sought to organise workers in an industry, for example automobile workers irrespective of their individual skills. The United Kingdom amalgamated unions such as the AEW were not industrial unions in the American sense but a few developed such as the National Union of Mineworkers, (NUM) although certain groups of colliery workers such as pit deputies and winding engine men kept their separate unions. Industrial unions were more popular in Europe. The result of the British failure to adopt industrial unions is that, in many plants or firms, several unions are involved in negotiations with the employer and this leads to disputes over demarcation and differentials and a tendency to try and leapfrog in pay negotiations. Some newly established foreign firms will only recognise one union and insist that they represent all workers in each plant.

White-collar unions have developed among clerical, scientific, managerial and professional workers. The term white collar is an Americanism used as a contrast with 'blue-collar' workers who are supervisory workers such as foremen in industrial plants. The term blue collar has not caught on in the United Kingdom. Some professional unions have become very large, for example those in education, local government and health services. Many white-collar unions use the word professional or association in their titles but they behave as trade unions and are registered as such under the law. They differ from other unions in their emphasis on legal, financial and educational services to members and in their closer contact with government departments in a consultative role.

Summary

Table 12.1   Trade union membership[1] as a percentage of the civilian workforce in employment: by gender and occupation, Autumn 1994

United Kingdom			*Percentages*
	Males	*Females*	*All persons*
Managers and administrators	20	21	21
Professional	39	59	47
Associate professional and technical	33	53	43
Clerical and secretarial	35	24	27
Craft and related	29	27	29
Personal and protective service	38	24	29
Sales	13	10	11
Plant and machine operatives	44	32	41
Other	30	23	26
All in employment[2]	31	29	30

[1] includes organisations described as staff associations.
[2] includes those who did not state their occupation.

Source: CSO *Social Trends*, **26**, London, HMSO, 1996.

Table 12.1 shows union membership in the United Kingdom in 1994. The number of trade unions has fallen drastically as a result of mergers, and the number of members fell steadily from 1979 until a new rise began in 1995.

The fall in membership reflected the decline of manufacturing employment, the recessions and the growth of part-time working. If other things are equal, part-time workers and women workers are less likely to become trade union members.

Some commentators are not happy with the classification of trade unions into the four types listed above, craft, mass or general, industrial and white collar because some unions do not easily fit the criteria so they have adopted the idea of **open, closed** and **intermediate** unions. Closed unions restrict entry and control the qualifications for entry to the occupation in much the same ways as the old craft unions. Open unions try to maximise their membership and intermediate unions have sections which show both open and closed characteristics, usually resulting from amalgamations.

12.3   The Effects of Trade Unions on Wage Levels

One of the issues in the study of unions is whether their members benefit financially. In other words, do trade unions manage to get higher wages for their members than would be the case if the union did not exist? Unions can be seen as protective organisations that attempt to shield their members against the abuse of economic power by monopsonist (single) purchasers of their members' services or against the power of governments. They can also be seen as trying to maximise their members' incomes from employment or the total wage bill. In some cases it appears that they may be aiming to maximise employment. Cynics suggest that some of them have been dominated by the idea of maximising their membership in order to retain political clout at Labour Party and Trades Union Congress meetings. Although this may once have been a factor it is less likely to be since the reforms of the Labour Party from 1992 and onwards. Common sense tells us that trade union motives and aims must change over time and in accordance with economic circumstances such as recessions, new technology and foreign competition. They must also trim their policies to meet the political climate. There are times when they must trade employment for pay increases or sacrifice pay rises for employment.

Many theories of the wage bargaining process have developed over the years and none is completely satisfactory. A very full discussion of them can be found in D. Sapsford and Z. Tzannatos, *The Economics of the Labour Market* (Macmillan, 1993). In practice, a great deal depends on the nature of the market for a particular type of labour, whether it is dominated by a trade union which has a virtual monopoly of the supply of the labour and/or whether it has a monopsonist buyer of labour or many firms competing. In other words, the extent of competition in the market is extremely important. It is also significant that a trade union's power in the market is always limited, especially in the long run, by the potential availability of substitutes such as cheaper, unorganised labour, or capital equipment or the ability of the

employer to shift production abroad. These points can be summarised as the
elasticity of supply of the alternative factors. If we assume that the union is
concerned with its members' employment, it must also be affected by the
possibility that its members will become unemployed if it pushes its demands
too far. Some economists argue that there are *insiders* and *outsiders* where
unions are concerned. The insiders are currently members and the outsiders
are not. Many members leave when they become unemployed. If this idea is
accepted then the union operates for the benefit of the insiders and may ignore
the employment needs of the outsiders. To some extent the discussion of
whether trade union membership benefits unionists is confused by the fact
that non-unionists in a firm usually receive the same wage increases as the
union members. This circumstance often leads to conflict between members
and non-members with the argument that only those who conduct the struggle
for better pay and conditions should reap the rewards.

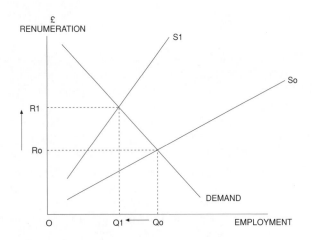

So/Ro = supply/renumeration before action to restrict entry
S1/R1 = supply/renumeration after action to restrict entry

**Figure 12.2   The effects on the supply curve of labour of
professional associations and trade unions**

Figure 12.2 shows the situation if we assume that a union or professional
association is trying to maintain entry requirements at a high level and to keep
out less qualified substitute workers. Examples of this might be chartered
accountants, solicitors or doctors who all have the law on their side in keeping
out competitors. Architects have a similar legal backing to prevent non-
members from calling themselves 'architect' even though they may, to all
intents and purposes, still practise the trade. In the diagram, So is the supply
curve for the labour before the union or professional association manages to

introduce effective entrance requirements such as membership of a professional institute. If the demand is Do, the level of employment would be OQo
and the level of remuneration would be ORo. After the setting up of entry
standards or their tightening, the supply shifts to the left and becomes more
inelastic and the number employed falls to OQ1 and the remuneration rises to
OR1. This process can be viewed as those who are better qualified keeping out
the others in order to maintain or boost their own incomes. They will, of
course, justify their actions in terms of protecting the public and maintaining
standards of service. Thus a partial answer to our question about the impact of
trade unions on the pay of their members is that, in some circumstances, they
may raise it but probably at the expense of employment.

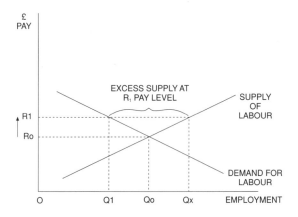

R1 = the new pay levels; OQ1 = the new level of employment;
Q1 - Qo = the increase in unemployed workers.

**Figure 12.3   The effect of pay demands without an increase in
productivity**

A trade union may use its power to threaten employers with strike action if
its demands on pay and conditions are not met. The employer or employers'
association must then decide whether to resist or how far to compromise or
whether to capitulate. If the union forces a capitulation and wages are raised
without any compensatory rise in productivity then some of its members may
subsequently become unemployed as a result of marginal firms being forced
out of the industry as their costs of production increase. If the industry is not a
competitive one, that is a monopoly or oligopoly with supernormal profits, the
pay rises could be met by a reduction in the employers' profits without a fall in
employment. Figure 12.3 shows a possible fall in employment in a competitive industry as a result of a union exercising its power and not giving a
commensurate increase in productivity. This may seem an irrational act by the

trade union but its leaders probably gain kudos from achieving the short-term gain and no-one notices the longer term loss of jobs. In a period of rapid inflation it may be that the firms can raise their prices to accommodate the pay increases. In this general instance we could note the power of the pilots employed by British Airways who threatened to strike in July 1996 unless their pay demands to protect the pay of pilots of a recently absorbed airline were met. BA blustered for a short time but the prospect of chaos in schedules and enormous loss of revenue and goodwill forced it to give in.

12.4 **Differentials Between Unionists and Non-unionists**

American economists began studying these differentials in the early 1960s and there have been many studies of American conditions since then. The first British study was published in 1974 by Pencavel based on an analysis of firms in 1964. He estimated that manual workers in unions had their hourly earnings raised by between 0 and 14 per cent compared with non-members. The higher figure was related to the degree of bargaining in the plant; the more plant bargaining the higher the differential. There have been many studies since and the work has been helped by the publication of the *New Earnings Survey* from 1973 onwards. The following is a summary of some of the broad conclusions of these studies, some of which will be no surprise:

- There are significant variations depending on the industry and unions. In 1973 the differential in favour of members ranged from 16 to 27 per cent in a study of male, female, manual and non-manual labour.

- There are significant variations depending on the level of skill. A 1983 study estimated that semi-skilled workers in unions had a differential of about 8 per cent whereas that of the skilled members was lower at 3 per cent.

- The employment sector, private or public, is very important. For example, a 1983 study showed that semi-skilled manual worker unionists in the public sector had a 25 per cent differential over non-public sector workers.

- The differentials vary over time in accordance with the economic climate.

- Earnings of members and non-members respond differently to recession and upswings. Trade union members' earnings do not fall as much during periods of falling demand but do not rise as quickly in the upswing. This is called 'wage-rigidity' and is based on the fact that most union collective agreements are for a year or more whereas non-union members' agreements are usually for shorter periods.

- It appears that, in both the USA and the United Kingdom, the differential between union and non-unionists grows as the unemployment rate increases so membership is beneficial.

The overall conclusion, therefore, is that union membership is usually beneficial depending on levels of skill, the degree of plant bargaining, whether it is the public or private sector and the stage of the business cycle. There are, however, some criticisms of the impact of trade unions in maintaining wages as demand falls in recessions, that is the wage rigidity hypothesis. There seems to be less concern about union earnings not rising as quickly once the upturn begins. There have been some media studies of whether strikes for more pay benefit the workers. A lengthy strike with the sacrifice of several weeks earnings for the reward of a few pence an hour or a few pounds a year may be foolish unless the lost wages can be made up by working overtime to catch up on the backlog of work. Many public sector workers such as teachers actually save their employers money when they strike because there is not a product to be sold.

Although trade unions appear to benefit their members, there is another question about whether they adversely affect the allocation of resources within the economy. This is another complex area of comparison but the conclusion about both the USA and the United Kingdom is that the effects of trade unions have been minimal on the allocation of resources measured in terms of output loss. There is another relevant point of discussion in this context and that is the view that unions actually increase the productivity of their members compared with that of non-members. As usual the conclusions differ but the general thrust is that union workers do have a higher productivity than non-unionists and that this benefit outweighs any of disadvantages arising from the wage differentials discussed earlier. The higher productivity can result from several conditions but an important one is that unions communicate directly with management and thus channel discontent and reduce labour turnover. They also encourage training and reduce friction between groups of workers. It is likely that the higher earnings create greater motivation and better morale, both of which tend to raise productivity.

12.5 State Intervention in Labour Markets

The state has at least three roles:

1. It sets the legal framework in which employers and employees operate. It sets standards and qualifications for certain sorts of worker such as doctors, vets and gas fitters. It also creates the laws within which organised labour and employers can act in the collective bargaining process as trade unions and employers' associations.

2. It is an important employer of labour although the process of privatisation has reduced the number significantly. In many cases it is virtually the only employer of certain types of worker especially in the defence and security fields. It may use this employer role to try and control inflation via public sector pay policies and to control levels of public expenditure.

3. It helps to create the social and economic policies under which the country operates. It does this increasingly in the context of the European Union despite the Conservative Government's objection to and opt out from the Social Charter. Its education, employment, industrial and regional policies all affect the labour market. Its expenditure policies and management of the macroeconomy are also influential.

In recent years an issue that has dominated and distorted the political debate in the United Kingdom has been trade union legislation. The Labour Governments of the late 1960s and 1970s failed to create a balanced, up-to-date, trade union legislative framework. The Thatcher Government from 1979 to 1990, and to a lesser extent the Major Government since, passed a series of laws and amendments to legislation that were aimed at two things.

1. The first was to place the blame for the United Kingdom's relative economic and industrial decline and poor economic performance generally at the door of the trade unions. The 'over mighty' trade unions were seen as holding the country to ransom in the 1970s in pursuit of their claims for improved pay and conditions. They were held to be responsible for 'wage inflation' despite the evidence that other factors such as rising crude oil prices, higher import prices and a depreciating pound contributed to rising costs of production. The sympathetic media accepted this simplified version of reality and plugged it. Many trade union leaders behaved and spoke in a manner that helped the critics of unions and successive election victories demonstrated the value of union bashing. The law reforms that occurred all reduced the powers of trade unions and forced them to behave in a more democratic and accountable manner. By 1996 it was apparent that many of them had come to terms with the new laws and were beginning to exploit the ballot for strikes and other action to their own advantage. They were now able to claim democratic legitimacy for their industrial actions.

2. The second was aimed at improving the 'supply side' of the economy, that is to reduce trade union power so that wages could be lowered as well as raised and that the unemployed would be ready to accept other jobs, even at lower wages, rather than stay in receipt of welfare payments. One part of this strategy was the removal of Wage Council protection from the poorly paid, firstly the young and then all workers except agricultural workers. Another part was to remove as many workers as possible from the public sector by privatisation and the creation of agencies attached to the civil service. This policy reached its zenith with the closure of many coal mines

and the sale of the remainder to the private sector with the accompaniment of mass unemployment of miners. An integral part of reform of government policies in health and education was to try to remove national pay bargaining and replace it with localised bargaining but this has been only partially successful. Not many commentators argue that these supply-side reforms have been successful. Figure 12.4 (below) lists the more important pieces of trade union legislation in recent years.

RECENT TRADE UNION LEGISLATION

1980 **The Employment Act** attacked secondary picketing, sympathetic strikes, the closed shop (only union members could be employed) and insisted on postal ballots as a basis for industrial action. It removed the obligation on employers to recognise the rights of trade unions in the workplace.

1982 **The Employment Act** further attacked the closed shop and gave employers the right to cite the union in legal actions rather than individual officers. It established the concept of a political strike which, if a dispute was so designated by the courts, enabled the employers to obtain legal redress from striking employees. It said that any contract which attempted to enforce the exclusive use of trade union members would be illegal.

1984 **The Trade Union Act** insisted on secret, unsually postal, ballots for a union's senior positions. It also said that if a union wished to continue with a political fund (usually to give money to the Labour Party) it had to have a ballot every ten years.

1988 **The Employment Act** established a Commission for Union Affairs to finance union members who wanted to take legal action against their union. It made it illegal to take industrial action to enforce closed shops and to take disciplinary action against a member who refused to join industrial action. It insisted on postal ballots, supervised by an independent organisation for the election of presidents and general secretaries of unions. Members could seek injunctions against their unions to prevent industrial action without ballots.

1989 **The Employment Act** amended the 1978 Employment Protection (Consolidation) Act to restrict the burdens on employers from giving time off with pay to union officials.

1990 **The Employment Act** removed various immunities that unions enjoyed for secondary picketing under an Act of 1974. It also made it illegal to refuse to employ someone because they were not a member of a union or would not agree to join one. Employers were given greater powers to sack workers who had joined unofficial actions. Unions were forced to repudiate trade union officials, such as shop stewards who called unofficial actions.

1992 **The Trade and Labour Relations (Consolidation) Act** consolidated most of the above Acts.

cont'd

1993   The Trade Union Reform and Employment Rights Act abolished
Wages Councils and with them the minimum wages and conditions
applicable. It also specified regulations on the daily running of unions; it
extended employees' rights and choice of union; it forced unions to give
seven days notice to employers of industrial actions. It gave employees
the right not to have the political levy to the Labour Party taken from their
wages without their written consent.

Figure 12.4   Recent trade union legislation

12.6   Minimum Wages

Another issue that is preoccupying many economic commentators and politicians is whether the United Kingdom should adopt a national minimum wage.
The USA has a minimum wage, which was raised in 1996, and so have the
others members of the European Union. The form of their regulations differs
enormously and there has been a discussion going on since the mid-1980s as
to whether the Union should try to adopt a common European Union
minimum wage policy. The United Kingdom refused to sign the Social
Charter in 1989 and forced the other members to allow it to have an opt out
from the Social Chapter of the Maastricht Treaty on European Union. There is
a great deal of misunderstanding about both the Social Charter and its treaty
version, the Social Chapter, but it is not the case, as the United Kingdom
xenophobic press and Eurosceptic MPs assert, that the United Kingdom
would be forced to accept a uniform European minimum wage and working
conditions. There is a similar argument, which generates more heat than light,
about the imposition of Works Councils in certain pan-European companies.
The economic argument about a national minimum wage is complex and, for
many commentators, inconclusive.

Arguments about a national minimum wage

The basic assertion of those who oppose a national minimum wage is that it
would raise the wages of some or many of the lower paid workers and thereby
price them out of the labour market. The opposition is, therefore, justified as
being in the interests of the low paid. It is stated that many small, marginal
firms are only kept in existence because they pay low wages. The waters are
muddied a little by combining these arguments with the belief that a minimum
wage would reduce labour market flexibility. Figure 12.5 shows how the
simple application of supply and demand can lead to the conclusion that a
national minimum wage could lead to unemployment.

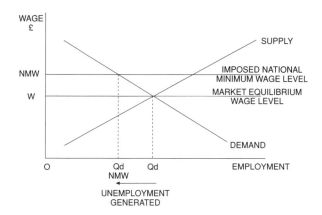

Figure 12.5   The impact of a national minimum wage, simplified

The extent of the unemployment that might result is the subject of much debate. The United Kingdom government between 1979 and 1996 was alleging that over 2 million might lose their jobs but other commentators were saying a few hundred thousand. If the demand for this type of labour is relatively inelastic it is likely that the fall in employment would be smaller than if it were elastic. It is acknowledged that the supply of the types of labour which would be affected by the national minimum wage is relatively elastic. A major influence on the effect on employment is the extent to which the employers are earning supernormal profit. The suspicion is, despite all the heart-rending stories about the marginal producers who would go bust if they raised wages, that many of them are 'exploiting' their workforces and could quite easily afford to pay their employees more if they themselves were willing to forgo some profit. A great deal depends on how competitive the industry is and the degree of imperfection in the particular labour market concerned. In many cases the work is in services where there is no foreign competition and where the labour is young, female, from ethnic minorities and not unionised.

It is possible to argue that a minimum wage would not reduce employment and might, in some instances, even raise it. If there is a single buyer of a particular type of labour, a monopsonist, there is no inevitability about an increase in unemployment because there is no competition with other firms for that labour. If the industry is earning supernormal profit it can also afford the higher wages without reducing employment. Many comparisons have been made with European countries and with the USA and there is an instance of employment in fast food catering rising in a state that raised its minimum wage for fast food employees whilst employment fell in a neighbouring state that did not raise the minimum wage for such workers. There is also a suggestion that higher paid workers become better motivated and have higher marginal revenue productivity and that demand for labour therefore rises. There is another factor to take into account and that is the rise in disposable incomes of the workers who are now paid more. Their higher incomes will generate more consumption spending, and they will have a high marginal propensity to save, so that further employment is created. Most commentators are agreed that there would be some change in the numbers employed in different occupations if the minimum wage were introduced, that is, there would be a change in the pattern of employment in low paid work. They cannot, however, agree on the figures.

Exercise 4

If national minimum wages are so bad why do they exist in other countries such as the USA?

13 Capital and Financial Markets

Aims of the chapter

To:

- outline the main features of money and capital markets;
- discuss the role of financial intermediaries between lenders and borrowers;
- explain the role of interest rates;
- discuss explanations of the determination of interest rates;

13.1 The Main Features of the Markets

There is still a useful distinction to be made between money markets and capital markets although there is an increasing overlap and blurring at the edges. Both markets link people who have money to lend with those who wish to borrow. The people and institutions in the middle through whom the links occur are called financial intermediaries.

Money markets are traditionally short term and this normally means up to 91 days (three months) and assets are normally regarded as liquid if they have less than 91 days to maturity. The definition can be stretched to six months. Liquidity is a very important concept and refers to the ease with which an asset can be changed into the most liquid of all assets, cash. Such markets may lend money for very short periods of time, such as overnight but their normal bread and butter is earned from the buying, selling and holding of financial instruments such as bills. Other short-term markets are discussed below.

There are many different types of bills which are financial instruments that are negotiable, that is they can be sold and bought in the period between their issue and their maturity. The original bills were called 'bills of exchange' and were a type of postdated cheque related to an exchange of goods (trade bills). The buyer of the goods, usually an importer, would wish to sell the goods or manufacture them for sale before paying for them and would give the supplier a bill promising to pay the amount of money agreed in say 91 days time. The supplier could keep the bill for the full term and collect the cash from the original issuer of the bill but would normally sell it at a discount to someone else. The bill might change hands several times before it reached maturity and its price would rise as it got closer to the date of redemption. The bill would be more acceptable and thus be more easily negotiable if the issuer had been vetted by a merchant bank who would sign it ('accept it') and guarantee to pay if the original issuer defaulted. A bill guaranteed by such an 'accepting house' became a first class bill of exchange or 'fine trade bill'.

The system gradually extended to financial loans where firms or individuals issued bills in exchange for money. Several Victorian novels, including *Middlemarch*, have subplots that relate to the failure of the issuer of the bill to meet his obligations and the problems created for the guarantor who became liable to meet the debt. These so-called 'finance bills' rapidly superseded trade bills which went into decline before the First World War. Both types of bills became less significant by the 1970s but were revived as a response to government attempts to restrict other forms of bank lending.

The Treasury Bill is a very important type of bill issued on behalf of the government by the Bank of England. They were first issued by Gladstone as a method of raising short-term loans to cover the occasional discrepancies between tax receipts and government expenditure. Such discrepancies are now the norm and Treasury bills are issued weekly, on a Friday. A typical issue might be of £300 million, although the totals rose to £600 million in the late 1970s and fell to £200 million in the late 1980s and early 1990s. The bills are bought by an assortment of institutions, at a discount. They may hold the bills to maturity or they may sell them. Most Treasury bills are 91-day but some are 63-day and more modern issues include 182-day bills.The most important aspect of the weekly sale is the tender issue to the discount houses. They used to offer a joint price but nowadays they make competitive offers. The price they pay, the so-called 'discount rate' is an extremely important factor in reflecting and determining short-term rates of interest in the money markets and, therefore, in other longer term markets. It may help to see how a simple discount rate is calculated.

A bill might have a value of £100 000 pounds at maturity in 91 days' time. The initial buyer might pay say £99 per £100, that is £99 000. From the buyer's point of view the discount rate is £1 for every £99 lent for 91 days, that is 1 over 99 x 100, equals 1.01 per cent but to obtain an annual rate we need to multiply this by 4 because the transaction could be done four times a year. The annual discount rate is, therefore 4 x 1.01 which is 4.04 approximately. This initial buyer, if the bill were kept to maturity would receive £1000 over £99 000 x 100 x 4 which is also 4.04 per cent per year. It is apparent, therefore, that if the price of bill is close to £100 the discount rate (the interest rate) is lower than if the price of the bill is some way below £100. When very large sums are being placed in bills the discount rate will be quoted to several places of decimals.

Bills are held by a variety of people and institutions who want very liquid assets combined with security. At the core of the United Kingdom market are the discount houses who borrow enormous sums of short-term money from the banks and use them to buy, hold and trade bills. Other institutions become very interested in holding bills as they get closer to maturity because the liquidity of the bills enables them to manage their assets in such a way as to expand their longer term lending in the knowledge that they can realise the short-term liquid assets if there is a sudden demand for cash or the withdrawal of deposits.

Although bills are the most important type of short-term instrument in the money markets there have been other additions over the years. These include certificates of deposit of different types and government gilt-edged securities that are close to maturity. The market is notable for its flexibility over the years in responding to change. The importance of the bill market can be seen from the following figures. In March 1996 banks in the United Kingdom held £7.5 billion in Treasury bills, £11.8 billion in eligible bank bills, £1.2 billion in other bills and £13.8 billion in bills in currencies other than sterling. There were liabilities of almost £80 billion in certificates of deposit and 'other paper issued'.

The main participants in the money markets are retail banks, that is mainly the UK clearing banks such as Lloyds, wholesale banks, which include overseas banks and merchant banks, the Bank of England and the discount houses. Merchant banks appear in the market as wholesale banks and some of them act as accepting houses for bills.

Exercise I

Calculate the approximate discount rate if the price of a 91-day Treasury bill bought at issue is £98.25 per £100.

The significance of the United Kingdom money market is that it reacts extremely quickly to changes in market conditions, that is to imbalances in the supply of and demand for funds. There are many institutions looking for temporary holding places for their surplus funds and many others whose financial practices force them to balance their assets and liabilities at the end of every day. A large oil company, for example, has a huge flow of cash each day and may wish to deposit some of it for a very short period, even overnight. A discount house must balance its books each day and may require some overnight lending to achieve this position. It will in any case be borrowing huge sums at 'short notice' or 'at call' from banks. For longer periods of time it may be more profitable to buy or sell bills or certificates of deposit because of the attraction of their liquidity and security.

The market is also significant as a haven for foreign short-term deposits as they move about the financial markets seeking marginal improvements in their return or to take advantage of changes in interest rates. When the UK pound was managed and kept within fixed limits on the foreign exchange markets it was important for the government to consider the effects of interest rate changes on the flow of such foreign money. It is sometimes referred to as 'hot money' because of the speed with which it moves across national boundaries in search of higher returns. Nowadays large volumes of money may shift in anticipation of interest rate changes.

The market also presents opportunities for the Bank of England to intervene and to manipulate the markets insofar as this is possible in the light of the vast amounts of money that flows through it. There is some temporary impact arising from the terms of the weekly Treasury bill issue, both through its quantity and via the terms of acceptance of the issue by the discount houses and others. There are also opportunities to adjust the daily shortages and surpluses of funds and bills in the market with a view to moving the discount rate in a particular direction. This is important on those occasions when the Bank of England wishes to change base interest rates. Any change in the discount rate is reflected in changes in other interest rates although there may be time lags before the effects are felt.

13.2 Secondary Markets

Over the years various secondary or parallel markets have grown up alongside the discount market to deal with new financial assets and securities. The most important of these is the Inter Bank market where banks borrow and lend between themselves on a wholesale scale. There are also separate markets for Sterling Commercial Paper and local authority issues. Other specialised markets are the Finance House Market and an Inter Company market. A recent growth has been in financial futures and options and a specialised market called LIFFE has developed using an open outcry method of dealing on the American pattern. There is also an extensive market in Eurocurrency. A Eurocurrency transaction relates to wholesale deals in a currency other than the country in which the transaction takes place. The 'Euro' in the title is misleading because it can be US dollars being traded under the name Eurodollars outside Europe and outside the USA. This market originated in the trading of Eurodollars outside the USA and expanded into other countries' currencies, so we now have Eurosterling, that is pounds traded outside the UK.

13.3 Capital Markets

A capital market connects lenders and borrowers. It is essentially a long-term market for periods of over six months but there is a blurred distinction between short-term money markets and capital markets. The lenders in the market take many forms and most operate through financial intermediaries. Private savers' money is channelled into the capital market whether by building societies, pension funds or insurance companies or banks. Some of their savings is given to unit and investment trusts who spend it on already existing stocks and shares but some finds its way into the creation of new physical assets in the form of investment expenditure. Pension funds behave in the same way. They have huge annual inflows of premium incomes to invest and choose to do so by buying a variety of stocks and shares both in the United Kingdom and abroad. Some of this inflow finds its way into new assets such as buildings, property development and research. Some is used to finance mergers and takeover bids. It is relatively rare to find clear examples where these institutional investors finance completely new enterprises but the £8 billion Channel Tunnel is one.

Firms also save and channel some of their savings or retained profits into new enterprise. Occasionally the firm will choose to keep its reserves as a 'cash mountain' earning interest in the money and capital markets rather than spend it on new capital equipment. This is a sensible thing to do if the return on the cash mountain is higher than could be earned from normal investment but it is not a popular tactic with the financial analysts. Generally, if a company reinvests its own profits or reserves it does not require any financial intermediary to help although it may call on specialist help for certain investments.

The following figures indicate the sources of finance for UK industrial and commercial investment in 1995:

	%
Internal sources	59.9
Bank borrowing	12.3
Ordinary shares	7.2
Debenture and preference shares	3.0
Other overseas investment	5.4
Other	12.2

Source: Bank of England, *Quarterly Bulletin*, May 1996, vol. 36, No. 2, p. 219.

Exercise 2

Comment on the figures given for sources of finance for United Kingdom industrial and commercial investment in 1995.

Classification of capital markets

It is helpful to distinguish between two types of market but, once again, the boundaries are sometimes blurred. The main types are as follows.

New issue markets. These are sometimes called primary markets. As their name indicates they are concerned with the raising of new capital, usually in the form of flotations of new share capital (equities) for companies or in the form of gilt-edged securities for governments. They may also issue bonds or stock on behalf of local authorities and others. In the United Kingdom there are several routes by which new issues can be made. Established companies with a good record and a long standing quotation on the London Stock Exchange (LSE) may make a public offer for sale although this method is expensive and is only really suitable if very large sums are to be raised. The nationalised industries were usually privatised by the use of the public offer for sale. Another method, if smaller sums are to be raised, is the public placing whereby an issuing house places up to three-quarters of the new issue directly with purchasers, usually institutional investors such as pension funds. Smaller companies may opt for a private placing where the shares are also taken up by directly contacted purchasers. Many companies, however, prefer to make 'rights issues' to their existing shareholders who may take up the newly issued shares. Rights issues are simpler and cheaper to implement.

Gilt-edged stock is issued by the Bank of England on behalf of the United Kingdom government. Old stock is constantly maturing and the repayment may require a new loan, that is an issue of new stock. Sometimes the holders of the maturing stock are offered a 'conversion' stock to replace their old stock. There will be some sort of financial incentive to take up the offer. When the Public Sector Borrowing Requirement (PSBR) is large or growing there will be additional pressure on the markets to accept the necessarily larger issues of gilts. The pressure may be in the form of favourable interest rates or discounts or maturity bonuses. In the late 1970s the pressure to sell large quantities of government stock to finance the PSBR was alleged to have raised interest rates and to have 'crowded out' private borrowers who could not afford the higher interest charges. Not all economists accept this allegation which is, in any case, very difficult to prove.

Secondary markets. These are markets where existing or second-hand securities are traded. Most of the business of the London Stock Exchange has always been in this type of security. Indeed it was the need to make stocks liquid that led to the creation of the stock market. People who had invested in voyages of exploration and trade by buying stock in a venture sometimes needed their money before their ship literally came home. They therefore offered their stock for sale in the local coffee houses and meeting rooms and the stock exchange was born. The great argument in favour of such exchanges is that they give liquidity to the purchasers of stocks and shares. Few people would buy shares if they could not sell them in times of need or emergency.

Stock exchanges have always been accused of embodying an element of gambling or speculation and have been likened to casinos but this accusation is usually deflected by the argument above about giving liquidity to investors. In recent years, however, there has been a rapid expansion of markets in options to buy and sell. These are highly speculative but potentially very profitable. Some also give their youthful participants the opportunity to shout a lot and wear brightly coloured blazers so they cannot be all bad. Such option markets are defended on the grounds that they enable hedging to take place and they thereby give business and enterprise certainty about the prices they will pay for currency, stocks and commodities. One might legitimately wonder how business coped before the spawning of these markets. They seemed to manage quite well with simple futures and forward markets without all the derivatives and options. Perhaps the real justification for markets such as LIFFE is that they create enormous daily turnovers and generate valuable commissions for their participants, and they add colour to an otherwise drab life in the City.

Exercise 3

What is the importance of liquidity in financial markets?

13.4 The Relationship Between Lenders and Borrowers

Financial intermediaries

Lenders and borrowers do not as a rule have direct contact with each other and their respective needs are met through intermediaries. (There is a process called disintermediation where lender and borrower are brought into direct contact and this is discussed later.)

Banks. Some intermediaries are able to create credit and are defined as banks whilst others cannot and are called non-bank financial intermediaries. In the United Kingdom the Bank of England decides what is and is not a bank according to legal definitions and the list is very long when foreign banks are included. The Bank published a list in the February 1996, *Quarterly Bulletin* (vol. 36, no. 1). The following is a summary:

UK retail banks	24
British merchant banks	22
Other British banks	95

American banks	32
Japanese banks	37
Other overseas banks	270

Discount houses. In addition to the above groups there is a separate category of discount houses which were seven in number. Most countries do not have separate discount houses and their function is exercised by ordinary banks.

Non-bank financial intermediaries. These include institutions that accept deposits such as building societies, finance houses (who provide, among other services, hire purchase finance) and the National Savings Bank. In addition there are the other institutions that channel savings and premium income – insurance companies, investment trusts, unit trusts and pension funds.

Exercise 4

Why have foreign banks moved into the City of London in recent years?

Disintermediation

This clumsy term is applied to the process where funds flow from lender to borrower by means other than via the intermediaries. Such disintermediation is often accompanied by the use of new types of financial asset rather than straightforward lending. Markets now use many forms of 'securities' such as swaps and Eurobonds. Companies may issue their own bonds which may be sold on many times so that the original issuer does not know who owns the security. This process involving the creation of new types of financial asset is sometimes called 'securitisation' and produces problems for the Bank of England when it tries to supervise the monetary system.

Globalisation

Modern technology and communications have had considerable impacts upon financial markets. They have removed the need for face-to-face communication and the London Stock Exchange is no longer a floor trading activity. The removal of controls on financial markets in the United Kingdom after 1979 and in the lead up to the Single European Market at the end of 1992 have stimulated electronic dealing and new markets on a global scale. There is now an even closer link, and 24-hour trading, between London, New York, Singapore, Tokyo, Frankfurt, Paris and so on. London is very favourably placed in a time zone that enables it to benefit most from global trading.

The new technology has also made it possible to cope with the vast increases in the volumes and value of daily trading and to speed up settlement of deals. The London Stock Exchange ended its traditional fortnightly account periods in 1996 and the paper share certificate will become a thing of the past except for some individual deals. Computer-based real time trading is the norm in most areas and in some markets the trading is done by computers although the automatic dealing is suspended if prices move too much. The new technology has also enabled new forms of trading to be introduced, for example the London Financial Futures Exchange (LIFFE) where computerised recording of open outcry dealing permits huge and growing volumes of business to be conducted. The problem of trust is overcome by video recording every part of the trading floor all day and recording every telephone call. The changes in the capital and financial markets are similar to those that have occurred in the international foreign exchange market. They are summed up in the word globalisation.

Interest rates

Lenders and borrowers are linked inextricably by interest rates which can be defined as the reward for lending or the price of borrowing. The word price is important because it implies that there is a market for funds in which a price, the interest rate, is determined by the interaction of supply and demand. There is also the implication that there will be similar shifts of supply and demand curves for funds and that these curves will embody different elasticities in respect of interest rate changes in the same way that curves for goods and services do. There will, however, be different underlying determinants of the demand and supply for money.

Interest rates reflect the following factors:

Risk
There are different degrees of risk and we all have our own perceptions of the risk to our money or of an enterprise we are about to embark on. Generally, interest rates are higher when the perceived risk is higher and lower when risks appear slight. There are agencies who make money out of classifying institutions and their bond issues against a scale of risk, hence the concept of a triple A risk, meaning that there is no real risk of default unless the Martians invade. Historically we can see that dodgy South American dictatorships had to offer a much higher rate of interest on their borrowings than sedate democracies such as the United Kingdom. People are still hopeful of receiving some return from the successors to various governments around the world who defaulted on their debts in 1914–18, Russia for example, and China in 1949. The same principle applies to investment in equities where we would expect a higher return from more risky enterprises such as gold mining than from food retailing. There is a complicating factor in risk assessment and that

is the added element of the possibility of capital gains. Many bonds are issued 'below par', that is at a price lower than the face value of the bond, for example a £100 bond might be sold for £98.50 with a capital gain of £1.50 when the bond matured. Most purchases of equities involve an assessment of the possibility of capital gains or growth. The risk involved in any loan may be offset by the borrower providing some sort of security or collateral. Companies, for example, may guarantee their debenture borrowing by securing it against a particular physical asset. Estimates of risk are also embodied in the next factor.

Liquidity
Money is perfectly liquid and other assets are judged in relation to the speed and ease with which they can be converted into money. Some costs may be involved in the conversion as well. This aspect is called the convertibility criterion and is easily applied to the assets that we each own. On the whole we expect to receive a higher interest rate for a greater sacrifice of liquidity, This is why building societies offer higher rates if we agree not to make withdrawals for 90 days or some other period of time. More recently economists have applied another view of liquidity, that is the extent to which an asset is free from fluctuation in its capital value. Some assets may be very liquid in terms of their convertibility in terms of money but illiquid in the sense that they are more prone to capital loss if their sale is not carefully timed.

Period of the loan or the term of the asset to maturity
It is usually believed that longer term loans require higher rates of interest to persuade lenders to sacrifice liquidity and to undertake the inevitably greater risk of long-term investment. This appears to be common sense and is but, in recent years, there has been a trend for longer term interest rates (yields) to be below those of short-term assets. There are long and involved explanations of this unexpected fact which revolve around the effects and anticipation of inflation and the prospect of capital gains. It is probably sensible to retain the belief in short-term loans having lower interest rates than longer term but to remember that it is not always the case.

Information problems
Economic theorists assume, as usual, that individuals are perfectly well informed about the markets for money, that is the conditions of loans and interest rates. The practice is, of course, different and many lenders are very ignorant of the rate they receive let alone the rates they might obtain elsewhere. On the borrowing side, they are also frequently ignorant of the rates they are paying for loans and the rates they could obtain elsewhere. Fewer than half the people of the United Kingdom know what APR means or how it is calculated. (The answer is in Table 13.1.) In the retail market there also seems to be a policy of deliberate obfuscation so that consumers do not understand fully what they are paying or receiving, despite the legal requirements on lenders to publicise certain facts.

The wholesale market is different and is peopled by highly trained experts with powerful computers and sophisticated software so that they can maximise returns and minimise risk. Even so, much of their time is spent anticipating changes in interest rates and predicting inflation rates so there is a great cloud of unknowing surrounding them. Markets tend to react to deviations from what was expected rather than to what has actually happened. A gross example of this is the tendency in the USA in early 1996 for their bond markets to fall sharply when unemployment fell more than anticipated. Instead of being happy and cheerful for those no longer in the dole queues they gloomily expected a future rise in interest rates to curtail any consumer boom arising from the rise in employment so they sold stock. They may appear mad from the outside but they do possess a certain internal logic. The United Kingdom markets behaved in a similar way in October 1996.

13.5 **Patterns of Interest Rates**

Economists tend to talk about 'the rate of interest' as if there were only one but there are, in practice, a large number both within a nation and internationally. There is, however, a structure or hierarchy of rates whose relationships are based on the factors discussed above, liquidity, risk, term of loan and status of borrower. In the United Kingdom the structure is related to a central rate, a discount rate, applied by the Bank of England to Treasury bills during its daily dealings in the bill market. This discount rate is normally set to enable the market to operate smoothly, ironing out surpluses and shortages of bills, but it may be used to indicate that a rise or fall is required by the monetary authorities. Once it has been changed the other rates in the short-term money market follow suit. The next day the main banks alter their base rates and other institutions such as building societies may follow later. There may be some delay in their response because of the individual society's position in terms of flows of funds and demand for mortgages. The banks' so-called 'base rate' is what it says, a basis from which their lending rates are calculated. No-one pays the base rate; everyone pays more – at least two per cent more and far more on borrowing on credit cards. Cynics observe that interest rates are quicker to rise than to fall in response to changes in the Bank of England's discount rate but such ratchet effects are fairly common in the economy.

It is worth examining the structure of interest rates. It is usually given, for borrowers and lenders, in the sections of weekend newspapers devoted to family finance (see Table 13.1).

An extremely important element in determining interest rates is the level of inflation and the expectations of future inflation. If the inflation rate exceeds the prevailing interest rate then there is a **negative real rate of interest** and people become reluctant to save once they are aware of the fact. Different rates of inflation between countries also have an effect on the rates of interest prevailing in each. Germany, for example, has had a lower rate of interest than the United Kingdom, often by about 2 per cent, because its inflation record has been much better. Market dealers build expectations of inflation into their decision making in the same way that they incorporate expectations of interest rate changes.

Table 13.1   Sample borrowing and lending rates: October 1996

Savings	Rate % pa	Borrowing	%APR[†]
National Savings	4.75 to 6.75	Overdrafts, authorised	9.5 to 11.9
TESSAS	7.0 to 7.45	Overdrafts, unauthorised	29.5 to 29.8
Cheque accounts	4.0 to 5.0	Personal loans, unsecured	13.9 to 14.9
Fixed rate bonds	6.6 to 7.1	Personal loans, secured	7.5 to 9.6
Notice accounts	5.5 to 6.0	Mortgages, fixed rate	0.2: 6.45: 7.49
			1yr: 3yrs: remainder
Rates depend on capital sum deposited and on notice period required for withdrawals. It is important to know if rates are net of tax or not when depositing.		Mortgages, variable rate	0.65: 3.50: 4.24 to 2001
		Credit cards	7.9 to 14.5
		Store cards	18.0 to 29.8

[†]APR = Annualised Percentage Rate assuming capital is repaid monthly. This figure is about 1.8 times the nominal rate on a one-year loan and 1.9 times on a two-year loan.

Exercise 5

Credit cards were charging the following APRs in November 1996. How do you explain their ability to maintain such different rates when the theory of competitive markets says that the rates should tend to equalise? Visa: Co-operative Bank* 7.9%; Midland Bank* 11.9%; Royal Bank of Scotland* 12.9%; English Heritage 13.9%; Hamilton Direct 14.5%. Mastercard: Midland Bank* 11.9%; Royal Bank of Scotland 14.5%. (* = an introductory offer.)

13.6   Theories of Interest Rate Determination

The pure rate of interest is defined as the rate of interest on a risk free loan used to buy capital. Economists have a simple theory to explain this 'pure' rate. They then add a number of factors, most of which are referred to above such as risk and liquidity, to explain the **market rate of interest**.

The pure rate theory assumes that the interest rate is determined in the context of entrepreneurs borrowing money for an enterprise without risk. The existing stock of capital is assumed to change only slowly and is described as *exogenous*, that is constant over the short run and slow to grow over time. The theory argues that, over the short period, the interest rate tends towards what is called the marginal efficiency of capital, that is the revenue earned by an additional unit of capital. As the stock of capital grows, the marginal efficiency of capital, the rate of return on the additional unit, declines. It is reasonable to accept that as the stock of capital rises the rate of interest will fall and so will the marginal efficiency of capital. When equilibrium is achieved the rate of interest will equal the marginal efficiency of capital. This 'pure' rate idea is based on the borrowing of money to finance new capital expenditure but there are many other reasons for borrowing especially by households so the idea is intellectually interesting but not a lot of use otherwise.

The market rate of interest is explained in terms of the supply of money (Sm) and the demand for money (Dm) and many other practical factors. There is a conflict among economists about the nature of the demand and supply of money. Classical economists and modern monetarists have argued that the rate of interest is a real phenomenon. That is to say, they say that the return on financial and physical assets will move towards equality over the long run. Keynes argued that the rate of interest was a monetary phenomenon. He argued that the supply of money is determined exogenously, that is by the monetary authorities, the Bank of England in the United Kingdom, and that the demand for money is based on three main elements or motives for holding money. These three refer to the reasons why people and firms choose to hold money balances or cash rather than deposit their funds in interest earning forms. Holding money implies an opportunity cost in terms of the interest forgone. The desire to hold money or not is called *liquidity preference*. The three motives are:

1. **The transactions motive**. We all have to hold some money as cash for daily transactions despite the advertisements that used to show a bikini-clad young woman going around the world with only a Barclaycard for company.

2. **The precautionary motive**. People vary in the extent to which they hold money against unforeseen circumstances, unexpected bills, sudden tax demands or unexpected expenditure.

3. **The speculative motive**. This is the most significant reason for holding or not holding money as opposed to having or not having interest earning assets such as bonds and bills or interest earning deposits. Keynes argued that bonds had the possibility of yielding capital gains or losses. If the possibility of capital loss exceeds the possible rate of interest a person would choose to hold money rather than bonds. As bond prices rise yields (interest rates) fall and vice versa. In other words, the price of bonds is

inversely related to the rate of interest. If people expect a rise in interest rates they will assume that the price of bonds will fall. If they expect a fall in interest rates they will expect a rise in the price of bonds. You can test this idea by studying United Kingdom government stock prices over the few days before a change in interest rates. The stock market nearly always anticipates a fall in interest rates by raising gilt-edged prices, and vice versa. It is occasionally taken by surprise.

The first two motives are based on people's incomes but the third is based on uncertainty. The three combined produce a *liquidity preference schedule* which is regarded as the demand curve for money. Economists argue about the degree of elasticity in this demand curve. Figure 13.1 shows how the rate of interest is determined where the supply of money, Sm, is equal to the demand for money Dm, or the liquidity preference curve. As the LP curve shifts to LP_1 and LP_2, assuming that the supply of money remains constant, the rate of interest changes to R_1 and R_2 from the original R_0.

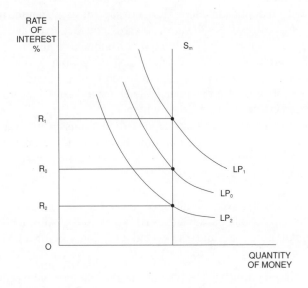

Figure 13.1   Interest rates and liquidity preference

There is some doubt about the ability of the monetary authorities to fix the supply of money in the circumstance of the modern world. The United Kingdom government signally failed to do so in the early 1980s despite its continual redefinition of what the money supply was. There is a tendency among the general public to believe that the government fixes interest rates and the Chancellor of the Exchequer seemed to encourage this view, especially when cutting them but, in practice, there are many international forces at work influencing the trend of a given nation's rates. The United Kingdom is heavily influenced by US and German rates and by what international financial markets expect and anticipate about future trends. The British government is very much in thrall to the globalisation of financial markets. Chapter 20 discusses in more detail the setting of interest rates in the United Kingdom and the role of the Bank of England.

14 Markets: Land and Housing

Aims of the chapter

To:

- explain the concepts of economic rent and transfer earnings;
- outline the structure of the housing market;
- discuss the main underlying demand and supply factors in the housing market;
- consider the importance of the housing sector in the United Kingdom economy.

14.1 Economic Rent and Transfer Earnings

In economics land is defined as a factor of production but the definition includes natural resources such as rivers, minerals, forests, the produce of the sea and soil fertility. It is sometimes difficult to distinguish some of these items from capital. A quarry, for example, is land in the sense that its stone is a natural resource but it would be largely useless without an investment in machinery and vehicles.

Economic rent is one of those concepts that many students dislike because it uses different terminology from the normal. In the nineteenth century, Ricardo, Mill and Marshall defined economic rent in one way but the usual modern definition is taken from Pareto. He defined economic rent as a *surplus* above the factor's *transfer earnings*. This is best explained with an example, remembering that any factor, not land alone, can earn economic rent. A piece of land might earn £20 000 in a year if used for growing wheat and £15 000 in its next best alternative use growing turnips. The revenue from the turnip growing is called the *transfer earnings* because if revenue from wheat fell to that level the farmer would transfer to turnip growing. The £5000 of extra revenue from wheat growing, the 'surplus,' is called *economic rent*. Thus economic rent is defined as a *surplus over the transfer earnings of a factor*. The transfer earnings are, of course, the opportunity cost of the factor when it is used for wheat, that is the revenue forgone from it next best alternative use. Textbooks usually illustrate three possible situations arising from different supply and demand conditions:

- If supply is absolutely inelastic all the earnings of the factor are economic rent as in Figure 14.1.
- If the supply is perfectly elastic all the earnings are transfer earnings as in Figure 14.2.

- If all supply is neither absolutely inelastic or perfectly elastic, the earnings are a mixture of economic rent and transfer earnings as in Figure 14.3.

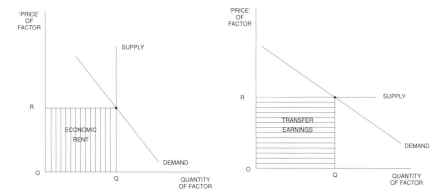

Figure 14.1   Economic rent   **Figure 14.2   Transfer earnings**

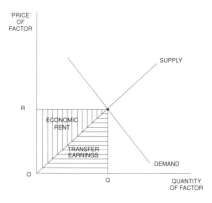

Figure 14.3   Economic rent and transfer earnings

The elasticity of supply of land is a topic that causes some debate. Early discussions tended to emphasise the inelasticity of supply of land. The total is fixed by nature except insofar as land can be reclaimed or erosion prevented. The supply can also be augmented within limits by high-rise building or by creating deep basements. But land is rarely restricted to one use so there may be an extremely elastic supply into a particular use. Land available for shops may be restricted, especially by planning controls, but most shops can be changed into other types of shops very easily, unless they sell take-away food where regulations may be prohibitive.

Another point that should be remembered is that the demand for land is a **derived demand**, that is no-one wants it for its own sake but for what it contributes to production. The entrepreneur, therefore, is only willing to pay a price, or rent in the everyday sense, that relates to the revenue and profit from the activities conducted with the land. There is a concept called the *rent gradient* which plots the tendency for rents to fall as distance from commercial centres increases. Land use changes over time as the profitability of different activities varies. Boutiques or other shops, for example, have tended to drive greengrocers out of most of our urban shopping centres. The central London squares that the nineteenth-century middle classes inhabited are now mainly offices.

The market price of land is subject to many influences. In the United Kingdom land is designated for certain uses under the town and country planning laws and such designation is not easily changed. It is possible to consult your local structure plan put forward by the planning authority in which you live, most often the county council. Land is designated for residential, commercial, industrial, mixed, recreational and open space purposes. Some parts around London are designated as green belt and should be protected, but are not completely, from building development. Agricultural land is classified into grades by quality and its price varies accordingly as well as in relation to geographical influences.

Land that has received outline planning permission for buildings and development commands a significant premium over similar land that has not. One of the persistent problems over the last century has been how to price land that has development potential and how to treat or tax the capital gains that may result. Farmers, for example, may believe that a piece of their land on the outskirts of a village is worth £4200 per hectare with vacant possession as agricultural land and be happy to receive that figure and sell it. They will, however, be very annoyed and feel cheated if, two years later, the buyer managed to obtain planning permission for a small housing estate on the land and obtained an enormous capital gain from the newly designated housing development land. The government has, periodically, attempted to tax the capital gains on development land and, under the Labour Government of the late 1970s, tried to tax developers who held on to housing development land for years without developing it. They chose to hold it unused because of the rapid capital gains created by inflation and because it could be used as a security against which to borrow money.

Inflation and expectations of inflation are also important in determining land prices. People prefer to hold real assets in times of inflation and some societies place very great emphasis on land as the ultimate protection against the fall in the value of money. In the case of tenanted buildings, the value of the building is related to the ability to raise rents as inflation rises and the purchase price tends to be a multiple of the annual rent income minus charges such as insurance and tax. An office block with an annual rental income can be used as a security on which to borrow more money for further development.

This use of such assets under pinned the property price booms and slumps of recent times.

The type of tenure may affect land and property prices. Vacant possession usually raises the price while the existence of tenants who have legal rights will usually lower it. Recent reforms of the laws relating to leasehold and freehold in England and Wales have altered the basis of ownership of leasehold property because the leaseholder may enjoy the right of enforced purchase of the freehold from the freeholder according to a statutory formula. Scotland has a different, some say feudal, pattern of landholding which may change in the next parliament.

14.2 The Housing Market

We talk about the housing market but there are several parallel markets for what the housing experts call 'dwellings'. The word dwelling is more appropriate than house because it encompasses flats, bungalows, cottages, multi-tenanted apartments and buildings as well as the conventional house. The market splits into the following sectors, some of which are closely interrelated and some of which stand alone and impinge little on the others.

The private market for purchase. Before 1914 only 10 per cent of UK households owned their own dwellings. By 1981 this figure had risen to 50 per cent and by 1994 to 67 per cent. Private ownership whether outright or via a mortgage has become regarded as a desirable norm by most British people although post 1990 events of falling house prices and negative equity did lead to a resurgence of the rented sector. The main initial stimulus to owner occupation was the First World War which caused the supply of rented dwellings to dry up and even fall. The inter-war period of cheap labour and falling building costs, the rapid expansion of speculative building, the transport revolution and rising real incomes for those in steady work, all led to an economic imperative to buy. The inter-war rented sector was partially satisfied by new local authority building of council housing. After the Second World War, private rented accommodation fell sharply, partly because of the inflexibility of the rent control laws and the premium put on property with vacant possession. It became economically sensible to sell property that had hitherto been rented to tenants, mainly because of the capital gains but also to avoid legal restrictions. After 1979, the Conservative Government cut back sharply on local authority housing expenditure and established the right of council tenants to buy their dwellings (with some exceptions) at a discount.

The major stimulus to home ownership, however, was inflation which created steady and persistent capital gains for home owners who were willing to 'trade up' the market at regular intervals. Building societies also altered their lending policies and became willing to lend higher multiples of people's earnings as a mortgage and a higher percentage of the dwelling's market price. The societies were assured that the continuously rising market price of most dwellings would guarantee them against loss if they were forced to foreclose on a mortgage because of non-payment by the borrowers. It was this cavalier and competitive flurry over twenty years that led to the massive shock of negative equity when the market collapsed in 1989–90.

The market for home ownership was also fuelled by the activities of the speculative building firms who made it appear easy and cheap for people to enter the market and to trade up. Their growth was accompanied by the expansion of a whole host of services connected to housing – lawyers, surveyors, estate agents, removers, valuers and small property improvement firms. There were elements that contributed to the ownership boom, for example the tax relief on mortgage interest payments and the constraints on the local authority sector which could not find sufficient financial help from central government for its building programmes. The rented sector, both public and private, could not have coped with the post-war demographic and social changes.

Exercise I

Explain in economic terms the shift towards ownership rather than renting of domestic property in the 1980s.

The private rented sector has declined since its high point in 1914 although there has been a slight upturn since the housing market crisis after 1989. People who have fallen into negative equity, that is their mortgage debt is higher than the market value of their property, have taken to renting out their dwelling rather than selling it, when they move. Before 1914 it was normal for the middle classes to put their savings into United Kingdom government gilt-edged securities and into buying a number of houses which they then rented out. In a period of negligible inflation or even of deflation the rental income was as good as a pension or annuity especially as the tenants had almost no security of tenure. The situation changed when rent controls were introduced in the First World War and were only slowly removed afterwards. Rent controls were imposed more extensively and more effectively in 1939 and tenants of unfurnished dwellings became known as statutory tenants who had complete security of tenure as long as they paid the rent. Their rents were fixed at 1939 levels, despite inflation, until 1957 in the case of properties with higher rateable values, and until 1965 for the rest. In some instances the statutory tenancy could be inherited. Since 1965 there have been many changes in the law but tenants still have some protection against summary eviction although there are important differences between furnished and unfurnished properties. Large numbers of properties that were once rented have been demolished as part of slum clearance and urban regeneration projects, or simply to build new roads in inner cities. It is generally believed that a healthy private rented sector is good for labour mobility and that the sector can be too heavily regulated. Unfortunately there are still sufficient numbers of bad landlords about to make it essential to maintain a system of rent arbitration and legal protection.

The Local Authority and New Town rented sector has undergone enormous change since 1980. Before 1914 local authorities provided accommodation for the destitute in the workhouses although many preferred to live rough rather than endure the humiliation of the typical workhouse regime. A number of authorities also provided better quality dwellings than the average jerry-built Victorian terrace under the Housing Act 1909. Previous permissive acts of 1868 and 1890 had been ineffective. The real beginning of the local authority rented sector as we know it was in the 1920s as they began to build properties to rent as an attempt to make up the deficiency of the private market. The central government lent the local authority most of the cost of building council houses for sixty years at a low rate of interest that was below normal market rates. The money came from the Public Works Loan Board, a subsection of the Treasury. Local authority housing became the dominant sector in the period from 1945 until 1951 and few private dwellings were built until after the new Conservative Government took office in 1951. Even then there was a strong bias towards local authority housing which persisted until 1979, although the bias was strongest under Labour governments. The first new towns, under the Act, were established after 1947 and a second wave followed after 1965. There were also a number of expanded small towns that took mainly London overspill population and enterprises such as the new city of Milton Keynes which was a Buckinghamshire County Council venture to divert development away from smaller towns such as High Wycombe, Amersham and Slough.

The local authority and new towns had the benefit of cheap money in the form of low interest loans and the right, within limits, of compulsory purchase. They also found it easier to obtain planning permission because they were often the judge and jury in their own case. The new towns also had sweeping powers and could attract industry and commerce with cheap rents. Local authorities did, however, develop a major disadvantage over the years. This was that new properties became exceptionally expensive to build, particularly in urban development areas where new infrastructure had to be built to replace decaying Victorian systems. It reached the point where an inner London council house could cost over £100 000 to build. There was no chance of this price being recouped by setting an economic rent that would repay maintenance and administrative costs as well as the loan. The probable tenants could not afford that level so a system grew up where rents were pooled. Older houses paid higher rents than were necessary to repay their costs and newer houses paid less. There was, therefore, a system of cross subsidisation of newer properties by the tenants of older properties. The problem was made worse by the fact that prospective council tenants did not want to live in the older houses. As a result there were quite large numbers of empty council houses in some areas, or houses that remained vacant for longer than was desirable at the same time as more and more people became homeless.

In 1980 the Conservative Government passed legislation to give council tenants the right to buy their homes at a graded discount dependent on the number of years they had been tenants and a scale of repayments of the discounts if the house was resold within five years. Labour controlled councils that were tardy in implementing the new law were leaned on to conform. Initially, some specialised properties such as flats, sheltered accommodation for the elderly and properties adapted for the disabled were exempt from compulsory sales. The politically naïve thought that the revenues from the sales would be left to the local authorities to invest in new housing, especially in areas of greatest need but, of course, the Treasury took most of it because they had lent most of the money in the first place. Local authorities were left with a percentage that was usually about 20 per cent but there were very strict constraints on how the money could be spent. Most of it stayed idle accumulating interest. This was and is part of the government's macroeconomic policies to control public spending. Local authorities' building programmes lapsed into constructing specialised dwellings for the elderly and into joint programmes with housing associations to build similar property or homes for single, low income people.

The statistics show a rapid decline in the numbers of council dwellings but this fall is not entirely due to the sale of council housing. Part of the fall is the result of what are called Large Scale Voluntary Transfers (LSVTs) where local authorities can transfer all or part of its stock to new landlords after a vote of the tenants and the approval of the Secretary of State. Between 1987–88 and 1993–94, 148 000 were transferred in England by 30 councils. The new landlords are usually non-profit making bodies such as housing associations.

Local authority housing has always raised many non-economic issues, mainly about cross subsidisation by tax payers of tenants although this is now non-existent and was always exaggerated when it was possible. The quality of the provision was always an issue because the decision was made in the early years to make council housing less desirable than private housing. Oddly, the quality of council housing was higher than most private building from the 1960s to the mid-1980s because local authority dwellings were constructed to the so-called Parker Morris standard which defined requirements for water, heating, insulation, electrical systems and so on. The location of many estates was also controversial with the usual British concern about property values if a council estate were placed near a private estate.

Housing associations have existed for many years in different forms and are a direct development from the charitable enterprises which provided alms houses and better housing for the artisan classes in nineteenth-century Britain (the Peabody Trust, for example). They have undergone considerable changes since the 1960s and became very popular with governments who wanted an injection of more cash to make up for their own inability to provide sufficient funds. Housing associations are non-profit making bodies that raise money for specialised types of housing provision and for joint projects with local authorities. They construct, allocate and manage housing for the retired, the elderly and the young, usually in small groups near town centres on redeveloped or infill sites. The local authority sometimes provides the land, helps with the planning permission and operates a joint waiting list of prospective tenants. Housing associations have become a very important supplier of what is called 'social housing'.

Other sectors that require mention include 'tied' dwellings, that is accommodation that goes with employment. The best known of these are probably the agricultural cottage, the prison officer's house and the police house. Others used to be the miner's house and the railway worker's cottage. An important group under this heading is the housing owned by the Ministry of Defence. In 1996 the Government announced controversial plans to sell its dwellings to a Japanese company and lease them back at an annual fee that also covered management of the dwellings. The finances of this deal appear to be most peculiar but many firms do similar things with their assets. Approximately 1 per cent of tenures in the United Kingdom are tied to a job or business.

Tenure, 1994–95, United Kingdom

Owner occupied	%
Owned outright	25
Owned with mortgage	41
Rented unfurnished	
LA/New town	20
Housing association	4
Privately	4
Rented furnished	3
Rented with job or business	1

Source: CSO, *Social Trends*, 1996, Table 10.16, London, HMSO, p.183.

Exercise 2

What role remains for local authorities in the provision of housing?

14.3 Supply and Demand in the Housing Market

The supply side

There is a tendency to assume that the supply of dwellings is homogeneous but the analysis above indicates that there are, in fact, several separate markets. Having said that, however, it is clear that there is considerable movement between some of the sectors, for example from rented to owner occupation and from tied housing into the council sector. In the immediate post war period there was a major shift of dwellings from the private rented sector into the owner occupied category and from 1980 a great shift from the council to the owner occupied sector. The existing supply is the accumulation of building over the centuries but most of the stock has been built since 1918.

The statistics of the change in supply are given in Table 14.1 and the generalised supply factors that change the stock of dwellings are as follows.

Table 14.1   Permanent dwellings completed

	UNITED KINGDOM			
	Total	For local housing authorities	For private owners	Housing associations and other
1970	362 226	176 926	174 342	10 958
1971	364 475	154 894	196 313	13 268
1972	330 936	120 431	200 755	9 750
1973	304 637	102 604	191 080	10 953
1974	279 582	121 017	145 777	13 388
1975	321 936	150 526	154 528	16 882
1976	324 769	151 824	155 229	17 716
1977	314 093	143 250	143 905	26 938
1978	288 603	112 340	152 166	24 097
1979	251 816	88 495	144 055	19 276
1980	241 986	87 974	131 974	22 038
1981	206 636	68 050	118 590	19 996
1982	182 863	39 960	129 022	13 881
1983	209 033	38 921	153 038	17 074
1984	220 494	37 408	165 574	17 512
1985	207 481	30 303	163 395	13 783
1986	216 594	25 070	178 017	13 507
1987	226 162	21 095	191 212	13 855
1988	242 334	21 129	207 387	13 818
1989	221 446	18 627	187 504	15 315
1990	201 887	17 653	166 655	17 579
1991	190 970	11 132	159 290	20 546
1992	178 733	5 453	147 094	26 186
1993	182 261	3 206	144 604	34 451

Source: CSO, *Annual Abstract of Statistics*, London, HMSO, 1995.

New construction is carried out by a multitude of small builders and by a small number of nationally known development companies such as Barrett, Wimpey and Laing. Much of their construction is speculative in the sense that they build without knowing who their customers are going to be. This technique can be modified by building new developments in phases and suspending later phases if the market is not healthy. The larger companies have large 'banks' of development land in their possession and the required planning permission. Much of their finance is with borrowed money so they are susceptible to interest rate levels. Smaller builders tend to be more sensitive to interest rate levels because they are usually less well funded and have greater problems with liquidity because the custom is to receive payment in three stages, when foundations, roofs and internal fittings are completed. The builder is often buying materials and paying for labour on credit and interest changes can cripple the firm. Housing market analysts are very interested in the number of 'starts' on new dwellings because they indicate the likely future growth of the economy although they are also a reflection of recent experience. Local authority building has reached very low levels and is no longer of much importance.

Slum clearance and demolition has been an important negative factor in the supply of housing. This can be seen from the fact that 90 000 dwellings were demolished for slum clearance in England and Wales between 1982 and 1992. Rates of clearance were higher in earlier decades.

Building costs are an important influence on builders and they are linked with rates of inflation as well as with the interest rates on borrowed money. Building remains labour intensive despite developments in technology and off-site assembly so wage costs are significant. A high proportion of building materials is imported, including the oil used in many processes, so the foreign exchange rate has an important role to play. Building materials show a different rate of price inflation from the ordinary retail index. There is, of course, great competition from other parts of the construction industry for the labour, capital and materials available so house building costs may rise simply because of a boom in office development.

The price of land is of fundamental importance in fixing the selling price of buildings. There is a controlled market for housing land in the sense that it is subject to planning constraints. This makes the supply very inelastic and price rises accordingly, especially in older urban areas in the southeast. Developers prefer to build on cheaper land on the peripheries of urban areas and villages rather that have to redevelop existing inner urban areas. There are government and European Union grants available in some parts of the country for urban renewal and local authorities still provide finance for some urban development. There are great regional differences in land prices which reflect the pressure of demand on the locality and there are also major variations within a region and in parts of a given city.

Renovation and subdivision affect the available supply. There was a fashion in the 1950s to the 1970s for wholesale clearance of older dwellings and their replacement but the trend more recently has been for renewal and refurbishment. This latter process often involves the subdivision of older, larger houses into apartments so the total stock increases. There is, of course, a trend in the opposite direction for smaller properties to be merged especially in commuter villages and inner London where the nineteenth-century artisan's cottage is not deemed large enough for the modern affluent family. The subdivision of property and therefore the total supply can be influenced by the attitude of building societies who may prevent people subletting and by the tax system which may deter or encourage similar processes.

Exercise 3

Draw up an outline of advantages and disadvantages of demolishing old housing in urban centres and starting from scratch on rebuilding compared with renovating and restoring it.

The demand side

Housing is an area where there is a wide divergence between many economists and other human beings. Most people consider that everyone has a need for shelter and probably a right to some form of adequate housing. Market economics stresses the concept of *effective demand* which means the ability as well as the willingness to pay for something. The logical outcome of this is that those with insufficient means to pay would be homeless or, perhaps, live in poor and overcrowded conditions. Most of us would probably regard housing as a merit good that should be provided in adequate measure even to those who cannot afford it. We can introduce all sorts of welfare arguments to bolster this view along the lines that our own quality of life suffers if the homeless impinge on us via begging, poor sanitation and possibly crime and disease. Suffice it to say that there is a fundamental ambiguity at the heart of United Kingdom housing policy because of the failure to address directly this question of housing need. For some years from the late 1960s to the late 1980s local authorities had the legal obligation to house the 'homeless' although those who made themselves homeless were excluded from this. It is very difficult, however, to persuade many of the British public to pay taxes to supply accommodation to people who are regarded as 'undeserving' and neither is it easy to persuade them to maintain a high standard for such accommodation. There seems to be a strong belief that the homeless are in that state because of their own failings and an element of punishment is introduced. There has been some modification of this approach because there have been over 500 000 repossessions of dwellings by mortgage lenders between 1982 and 1992 so the problem of homelessness has shifted to include far more people. The economic factors on the demand side are as follows.

Population structure

The growth of population inevitably exerts pressure for more dwellings or, at the very least, enlarged dwellings so the rise in the United Kingdom's population since 1900 from 36 million to 58 million has had a major impact. The growth in size is, however, only one influence. There are also important changes in the age structure which have created an enlarged demand for retirement homes and single person dwellings. There has been a rapid expansion in the number of young people who no longer wish to remain in their family home until they marry. They represent a significant demand for flats and small houses. There has also been a great increase in family break up through divorce and this has again created an expanded demand. The trend towards cohabitation rather than marriage has had a mixed effect because it enables two people to share the cost of a home rather than remain in their family homes but it may also reduce the demand compared with two people living separately away from the family home.

The average age of marriage, or cohabitation, and the number of children per household have changed over the century and have had an impact on the demand for different types of housing. There have been periodic shortages and surpluses of three bedroom houses and of single person dwellings. The current problem is the shortage of sheltered accommodation for the elderly.

Population movement within the country has led to surpluses of housing in some areas and scarcity elsewhere. Shortages in some areas are compounded by an inflow of second home owners who are able to outbid the local population; examples arise in the West Country and parts of Wales and the Yorkshire Dales.

Real incomes

House prices rose by more than three times between 1939 and 1991 in real terms with 1971 as the base year for comparison so we need to be able to explain how people have been able to afford to buy in increasing numbers because home ownership rose in the same period from 33 to 68 per cent of the total of the stock of dwellings.

Real incomes rose but there were also administrative changes that caused mortgage lenders to offer higher multiples of individual incomes and to accept joint incomes as a basis for lending. They also began to lend higher percentages of the purchase price, frequently over 90 per cent and even 100 per cent for council housing being sold to tenants at a discount. Loans were made for longer periods of time which enabled payments to be lower. All these developments are in contrast to countries such as Germany and France where only about 60 per cent of the valuation is normally lent as a mortgage.

A crucial factor in the United Kingdom in raising real incomes for house purchase has been the very large state subsidy in the form of tax relief on interest payments on mortgages. This relief amounted to about £9 billion per year at its peak in 1993 and was particularly favourable to those paying at higher rates of income tax, but there has been some reduction in the budgets since then. All political parties privately recognise the lack of logic in this huge transfer of money, much of it from non-house owners to house owners, but they have not been prepared to announce the abolition of the system. The relief greatly reduces the monthly repayments, but not as much as in the past, and enables people to bid a higher price for a property.

Another influence on real incomes has been the ability, until the collapse in the housing market, to sell and make capital gains that could be put forward as a bigger deposit on a larger and more expensive house. Some of these gains were spent on consumer durable goods and holidays but most seem to have been ploughed back into house purchase. Another source of gain in this context arose from the inheritance of houses on the death of relatives.

The overall effect of these trends can be seen in the very important charts showing the relationship between house prices and earnings. The normal relationship was a ratio of price to earnings of a round about 3:1, rising to 3.5:1 but there were three periods where the ratio rose well above this historic norm. The first was 1970–75 when it reached a peak of 5:1; the second was 1978–81 when it reached 4.1 per cent; and the last was in the period 1985–90 when a peak of 5.6:1 was attained in 1989. It seems very odd in retrospect that anybody thought that such a market was healthy, unless of course they were making money out of it from commissions and capital gains.

Easy credit
The early 1980s saw the introduction of greater competition in financial market. Banks entered the mortgage market on a much greater scale; some building societies became banks; many other lenders entered the mortgage market. Several different types of lending were popularised. Endowment mortgages were sold in large numbers (to the current regret of many people because they have failed to produce the gains predicted). There was fierce competition to reduce lending rates and to expand sales of complementary services such as life insurance cover, unemployment insurance and buildings and contents insurance. These elements combined with the government policy of subsidising home ownership fuelled the inflationary spiral of house prices.

Second homes
The Survey of English Housing showed that 1.2 per cent of households in England owned more than one dwelling for their own use in 1994–95 so there is only a marginal impact overall from the demand for second homes but its effects may be felt more heavily in specific areas where ownership by outcomers distorts local markets.

Homelessness
Most of the available statistics in this field refer to the homeless who are found accommodation by local authorities. In 1985 the Housing Act altered the obligations on local authorities to help the homeless who fitted certain categories although they may voluntarily help or advise others. Those who meet

the definition are said to be in 'priority need' and are mainly families with young children, pregnant women, and people who are vulnerable because of their age, mental or physical infirmity. In 1993–94 about one-third of new tenants of local authorities were classified as homeless so that sector is fulfilling its social housing role. In 1994 in Great Britain about 135 000 households were defined as homeless and found accommodation, a reduction from the previous year of 12 per cent. The causes of homelessness in these cases were varied. About one-third were people whose relatives were no longer able or willing to house them. About 21 per cent had undergone a break from their partner. Many cases arose from repossession of the family home. Charities who work with the homeless on the streets of big cities say that the problem of homelessness is understated by these statistics, especially of young males.

Table 14.2   Homeless households living in temporary accommodation[1]: GB 1982–94 (thousands)

	Bed and Breakfast	Hostels	Short-life leasing	All
1982	2.0	3.7	4.8	10.5
1983	3.0	3.6	4.5	11.1
1984	4.2	4.2	5.3	13.7
1985	5.7	5.0	6.7	17.3
1986	9.4	5.0	8.3	22.7
1987	10.6	5.7	10.5	26.8
1988	11.2	6.8	14.2	32.3
1989	12.0	8.6	19.9	40.5
1990	11.7	10.4	27.0	49.1
1991	12.9	11.7	39.7	64.3
1992	8.4	12.6	46.6	67.6
1993	5.4	11.9	40.7	58.0
1994	4.7	11.9	35.7	52.4

[1] Data are at end year and include households awating the outcome of homeless enquiries. Households made temporarily homeless through flooding in Wales in 1990 and 1993 are excluded.

Source: CSO, *Social Trends,* **26,** London, HMSO, 1996.

Exercise 4

Suggest some solutions, based on an economic assessment of costs and benefits, for the problem of homelessness in the United Kingdom.

15 Foreign Exchange Markets

Aims of the chapter

To:

- give a brief description of the market;
- explain forward and spot markets;
- explain how exchange rates are determined;
- refer to the theory of exchange rate determination;
- discuss government intervention in foreign exchange markets.

15.1   The Market

The market brings together, by telephone, telex and computer networks, buyers and sellers of different currencies. The most commonly traded pairs of currencies are sterling and US dollars, and US dollars and Deutschmarks.

There are three main types of participants in the market, customers, banks and brokers. The customers are, for example, multinational companies or pension funds who need currency for their trading activities or to finance their investment programmes. Banks play a variety of roles. Some are market makers and will continuously quote dealing rates for buying and selling currencies. They make their profit on the spread between their buying and selling rates. Other banks and institutions shop around them asking for rates before concluding deals. Brokers are intermediaries between the banks and have direct lines around the world so that they know where to obtain the best buying or selling rates. Brokers charge commission for their services.

The international foreign exchange market has grown enormously over the last decade. In April 1995 the global turnover per day in all currencies was calculated at about $1.2 trillion. London was the largest centre and dealt in US$464.5 billion. See Table 15.1 for details of dealings by the main international centres.

The London market is the most important single foreign exchange market because of the great volume of business generated by the presence of important commodity, insurance, shipping and banking markets. It also benefits from its position in international time zones because its normal business day from 8 am to 5 pm overlaps the Far Eastern markets in Tokyo, Singapore and Hong Kong, then New York and finally west coast USA in Los Angeles and San Francisco. The global foreign exchange market operates 24 hours a day.

212

Table 15.1   Average daily net foreign exchange market turnover in the main centres

April 1995	US$ Billions
United Kingdom	464.5
United States	244.4
Japan	161.3
Singapore	105.4
Hong Kong	90.2
Switzerland	86.5
Germany	76.2
France	58.0
Australia	39.5
Denmark	30.5
Canada	29.8
Sweden	28.1

Source: Bank of England fact sheet *The Foreign Exchange Market,* London, Bank of England, 1996.

Although it is the 'London' market most of the business is done by overseas banks, many of whom are in London to benefit from its time zone location. Of the total London business, 80 per cent is done by these overseas banks, particularly the North American banks. United Kingdom institutions account for 20 per cent of the business. It is an odd quirk of the markets that the London market trades more US dollars and more Deutschmarks than are traded in the USA and Germany respectively.

In the United Kingdom foreign exchange markets the banks are regulated or supervised by the Supervision and Surveillance Division of the Bank of England. The bank also supervises other institutions that operate in the wholesale money markets, including the foreign exchange markets.

Exercise 1

We read about the colossal sums traded on the foreign exchange markets every day. Whose money is it and where does it come from?

Spot and forward markets

Spot transactions are conducted with the aim of exchanging the currency (this is called delivery or settlement) two business days later (which is called the value date). Spot trading now accounts for less than half of total foreign exchange turnover on the London market.

Forward transactions set a delivery date which is some time ahead, perhaps even a year or more. The main purpose of forward trading is to protect the buyer or seller against exchange rate fluctuations. The forward rate is higher or lower than the spot price by an amount called a premium or a discount. These reflect the interest rate differentials between the two currencies at the time the deal is made rather than expectations of future exchange rates. The premium or discount is calculated using a formula.

There are also transactions in currency futures and options which have developed to facilitate hedging which is a method of protecting oneself against unexpected movements in exchange rates. Currency futures are traded on a formal exchange according to a set of rules that enables dealers to buy and sell smaller amounts than on the normal spot and forward markets and to operate on margin payments which produce greater leverage, that is a larger contract sum in relation to the initial outlay. Currency options are similar to share options. They give the buyer or seller the right but not the obligation to buy or sell a quantity of a specified currency at a rate and on a date agreed in advance.

15.2   The Determination of Foreign Exchange Rates

Short-term exchange rates are determined by what the markets decide is the correct general level given certain economic factors. In the very short run they are heavily influenced by the day's political and economic events and by the market's reaction to them. Many of these events, such as the announcement of economic statistics will already have been absorbed by the market so the reaction is in response to the degree to which the announcements match the already adjusted rates. If the figures, for example for inflation, are worse than anticipated, the market will probably adjust further downwards; if they are better it may adjust further upwards. However, it should be noted that the market's view of 'better' and 'worse' may not be the same as that of non-market participants. Modern markets are obsessed with what might happen to interest rates which is understandable when it is remembered that forward premiums and discounts are based upon them.

The real economic factors that are taken into account are rates of interest, rates of inflation, rates of economic growth, changes in unemployment levels, changes in trade and investment flows. The other underlying factors that affect the demand and supply of a currency are threefold: trade, capital flows and speculation. If we talk in terms of an example such as the pound and the US dollar, the demand for dollars in the UK arises from importers of US goods and services who need to be able to pay the Americans in dollars. Similarly, those who wish to move capital to the USA from the UK have to buy dollars with their pounds so they also create a demand for dollars. Speculators may have a variety of reasons for demanding dollars but they will sell pounds to obtain them if they think the pound will depreciate and/or the dollar will appreciate. Obviously, if enough speculators behave in this manner they have established a self-fulfilling prophecy and the pound will fall in value against the dollar. The supply of dollars arises from the opposing elements. UK exporters earn dollars from their sales to the USA but want to be paid in pounds; those who transfer capital into the UK have to sell their dollars to buy pounds and speculators who assume that the pound will appreciate will sell dollars to buy pounds.

The modern global currency market enables people to hold deposits around the world in different currencies and to transfer them easily and quickly but such transfers are not free. There will be commission charges but there may also be an opportunity cost in terms of interest forgone. It appears that at least 90 per cent of transactions on foreign exchange markets relate to 'speculation' rather than to trade or capital flows. Not everyone would call these deals in the 90 per cent 'speculation' but would insist that they are hedging or protective deals to avoid loss rather than attempts to make gains. As George Soros the American currency speculator might have said 'You could pull the other leg, it has bells on it!' This is not to say that speculation is necessarily bad because it can be argued that it irons out the peaks and troughs of price movements and reduces the extremes of price fluctuation. This is because some of those who are expecting prices to rise will sell before the market peaks in order to take their profits. If enough of them do so it will blunt the peak by causing prices to rise less fast or to turn downwards. Conversely, those who are anticipating price falls may buy before the bottom of the trough in order to take their profit and again, if enough of them do so the price will cease falling and begin to turn upwards. It is, of course, impossible to know what might have been the degree of price fluctuation if the speculators had not existed or if they had behaved differently.

It is usual to depict foreign exchange rates with supply and demand diagrams but you have to be very careful about reading the units on the axis of the graphs. The following diagrams have the quantity of US$ on the x axis and the price of US$ in £s on the y axis. An increase in demand for US$ shifts the demand curve to the right and a decrease shifts it to the left. An increase in the supply of US$ shifts the supply curve to the right and a decrease shifts it to the left (see Figure 15.1).

Exercise 2

Over a period of a week or two track the exchange rate of the pound against the US dollar, the Deutschmark and the yen. Also track the effective index of the pound. Use the financial pages of the daily newspapers or BBC 2 Ceefax, City Index page 200.

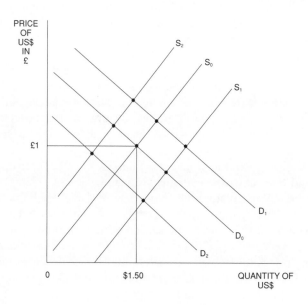

Figure 15.1   The determination of the foreign exchange rate

Theories of exchange rate determination

Economists try to explain the fundamental relationship of two currencies in terms of the 'purchasing power parity' theory (PPP). This formidable title disguises a fairly simple idea, although it can be expressed in a variety of ways and with different degrees of sophistication. At its simplest the theory says that a given collection or 'basket' of goods and services will have a certain price in each of two countries. This price will be expressed in the two currencies. The PPP says that the exchange rate between the two currencies will tend towards that existing in the prices of the basket of goods in the two countries. Thus, if our basket costs £100 in the United Kingdom and $150 in the USA, the foreign exchange rate will tend to be £1 = $1.50. The competition in markets will lead to shifts in demand and supply for goods and services if price differences become apparent.

The theory applies common sense and can be seen operating in border trade between developing countries. It does, however, become less applicable in the short and medium terms in developed economies. It is, however, applicable in the long run. The PPP theory is much harder to apply when capital as well as goods and services enter trade and when speculation is common. There are several monetarist models of exchange rate determination that do take into account these capital and speculative flows. The three main types are *flexible price*, *sticky price* and *real interest rate differential* models.

Another major problem which arises is the fact that certain important items of expenditure do not entail trade or international exchange. These are things such as power in the form of electricity (although its cost is incorporated into the price of exports), housing services, a wide range of personal services and local and central government services. More sophisticated versions of the theory try to take this into account and there is sound evidence that the PPP theory of the exchange rate between two countries is valid over time, albeit with short-term aberrations.

The effective exchange rate

The exchange rate of the pound alters at varying rates against each other currency; on a particular day, or over a year, it may rise against the dollar and yen but fall against the Deutschmark or some other combination. There is, therefore, an *index of the pound* against a 'basket' of foreign currencies, weighted according to their importance in dealings. The base year date is 1990 average = 100. In 1996 the second quarterly average of the effective sterling index was 84.8. In late March 1997 it had risen to 98.0. You can see this index daily on Ceefax on BBC2 page 201.

15.3 Government Intervention in Foreign Exchange Markets

It is rare for governments to leave their exchange rates to float freely at the whim of the market. Some have gone to the opposite extreme and tried to fix their foreign exchange rate absolutely against other currencies. An example of this is the old USSR where it was illegal to take roubles out of the country and where all foreign money had to be changed inside the USSR at a predetermined rate which stuck rigidly and completely unrealistically in the case of sterling at £1 = 1 rouble for years. Outside on the streets you could get several hundred roubles on the black market if you were prepared to risk prosecution. Most countries have compromised and allowed their currencies to float but with the occasional, or even frequent, hidden intervention in the markets to buy or sell according to whether they wanted the rate to rise or fall. This modest, irregular intervention is usually called 'dirty floating' and has been indulged in by the United Kingdom since 1992 and in the period 1971 to

1990. The two years 1990–92 were spent as a member of a more interventionist, managed system, the European Exchange Rate Mechanism or ERM as it is usually known. In the period 1947–70 the UK was a member of an almost universal system of exchange rate management known as the Bretton Woods system. It was named after the North American town where a conference was held that led to the creation of the International Monetary Fund (IMF) and the International Bank for Reconstruction and Development (IBRD) or the World Bank as it is generally known.

The Bretton Woods system of managing exchange rates

The 1944 Bretton Woods Conference agreement set up the IMF in December 1945 and it is still a very important institution. One of its aims was to assist members to correct balance of payments deficits and to promote exchange rate stability. The method of achieving this until the breakdown in 1970–71 was to have **fixed exchange rates** combined with the elimination of exchange restrictions, currency convertibility and a system of multilateral international payments. Currency convertibility meant the ability to change a currency into gold or, more relevantly, into US dollars although many restrictions applied to ordinary citizens and even to banks until 1979 in the United Kingdom.

Countries were required to fix their currencies at a level, a par value, that was notified to the IMF. The rate was set in relation to the price of gold but was, in effect, set against the US dollar because the USA had most of the world's gold buried in Fort Knox. The USA fixed the world price of gold in intergovernmental exchange. The price of gold remained stable until the USA decided to suspend the convertibility of gold in 1971 and later that year devalued the dollar by 10 per cent. The system was modified for a short time to what was called an **adjusted par value system** where the par value was replaced by a margin of wider fluctuation but the whole system finally ended in 1973 and most currencies were left to float.

Once a par value had been set the member state needed to keep the exchange rate within plus or minus one per cent of the par value. It normally did this by using its reserves of convertible currencies to enter the foreign exchange market and buy or sell its own and other currencies. The United Kingdom, for example, has kept its reserves in the Exchange Equalisation Account at the Bank of England since 1931 and used, and uses, them for this purpose. To begin with, the pound had a par value of £1 = $4.00 but it had to be devalued in 1949 to £1 = $2.80. Thus, from 1949 to 1967 when the pound was again devalued, the UK Government had to intervene to keep the pound between £1 = $2.82, the ceiling, and £1 = $2.78, the floor. Over the years to 1967 it kept closer and closer to the floor and balance of payments problems forced a new devaluation to a par value £1 = $2.40 in November 1967. It remained at this level until it was allowed to float in 1971. The pound has floated ever since with the exception of the period of 1990 to 1992 when the

United Kingdom became a member of the Exchange Rate Mechanism (ERM) of the European Union. There has been frequent intervention in the markets to nudge the pound in a particular direction and there was an attempt in the late 1980s by the Chancellor of the Exchequer, Nigel Lawson, to 'shadow' the German mark prior to entry to the ERM.

Exercise 3

Why did the United Kingdom find it hard to maintain its fixed rate for the pound against the dollar in 1967 (and was forced to devalue the pound)?

The Bretton Woods system broke down gradually. The main reasons were the development of a huge balance of payments deficit by the USA, especially as it financed wars in Korea and Vietnam and huge military spending programmes. The dollar became weaker. Another reason was the failure of countries to take effective preventative measures against inflation and their own balance of payments deficits. They tended to react too slowly and too late to taking the unpleasant medicine needed, that is tax increases, cuts in public expenditure, tighter credit and controls over incomes. Countries with persistent deficits were too slow to devalue, that is to reset the par value of their currency at a lower rate, and a few with surpluses, such as Germany, were reluctant to revalue, that is to raise the par value of their currency. The breakdown was also related to the failure of the system to create enough international liquidity, that is financial resources, to finance the expansion of world trade although this problem was eventually largely resolved by the creation of special drawing rights (SDR) by the IMF. These were the equivalent of creating gold, or 'paper gold'.

The origin of the Exchange Rate Mechanism

In theory floating rates relieve a government of the obligation to control the economy in pursuit of an exchange rate objective and remove the need to take either regular budgetary measures to control spending, investment and taxation or to impose monetary policies to manipulate interest rates. Thus floating rates appeared to be the answer for politicians who preferred popular policies. The theory implies that balance of payments problems are self-correcting because of the changes of the relative prices of imports and exports as the exchange rate moves. Unfortunately this effect is very slow and the large volumes of monetary movements may interfere with the process. In practice the governments end up controlling their economies by much the same means as before but with different stated objectives which are usually low inflation and lower government borrowing combined with pay restraint in the public sector.

The members of the European Community as it was then called decided to replace the Bretton Woods system with their own version. Their long-term aim was a closer monetary union, a state that may be realised after 1999 when a single European currency may be adopted by some members. The Community wanted exchange rate stability in the early 1970s for the reason just mentioned but also for the practical reason that the budget of the Community would become unworkable if exchange rates fluctuated too much. They tried to establish a joint float against the dollar in a system quaintly named 'the snake in the tunnel'. It had an upper and lower level within which the currencies jointly moved. It failed because the German mark appreciated too strongly, the French franc depreciated too fast and the system could not cope. France withdrew and the replacement devised was the ERM section of the European Monetary System (EMS).

15.4   **The EMS in Operation**

The EMS comprised four sections:

1. A European Monetary Co-operation Fund (EMCF) which was established in 1973 and whose functions are now exercised by the European Monetary Institute (EMI). It operates as a cross between the IMF and a European Central Bank holding reserves and supervising the issue of European Currency Units (ECUs)

2. The ECU, which was introduced in 1975 as a new version of the previous unit of account that was used as the medium for the conduct of the Community's finances. It is a 'basket' currency made up of fixed proportions of the currencies of the twelve members (currencies of the new members, Austria, Finland and Sweden, are not included) based upon weights. That is to say the German mark has the greatest weight. The ECU is revalued daily in relation to other currencies. The ECU is important in all the daily budgetary dealings of the European Union and will be the foundation for the new euro when it is introduced in 1998. On 22 August 1996 £1 = ECU 1.2216 or 1 ECU was worth almost 82 pence.

3. A Very Short Term Facility (VSTF) whereby each central bank could make credit facilities available in its own currency to other members.

4. The Exchange Rate Mechanism, which was introduced in March 1979.

The first three are dealt with more fully in Chapter 20 but the ERM requires more explanation in this context of exchange rates.

The Exchange Rate Mechanism 1979–93

As it was intended to be and was until August 1993
The mechanism was intended to help create a 'zone of monetary stability' and is a currency grid system. Each participant fixed a central rate for its currency which was expressed in ECU against the currency of each of the other participants. The rate had to be approved by all. From these central rates a grid can be constructed as in the sample in Table 15.2. Each currency was allowed to float around the central rate within limits which were ± 2.25 per cent above or below the central rate. New members entered a 'wide' band; for example, between 1990 and 1992 the United Kingdom was allowed a divergence from their central rates of ± 6 per cent.

Table 15.2   The currency grid (bilateral central rates and selling and buying rates in the EMS exchange rate mechanism for four countries from the nine in the system, from 6 March 1995)

		Belg/Lux 100 francs	Danish 100 krone	French 100 francs	German 100 DM
Belgium/	S	–	627.880	714.030	2395.20
Luxembourg	C	–	540.723	614.977	2062.55
B/L francs	B	–	465.665	529.660	1776.20
Denmark	S	21.4747	–	132.066	442.968
D. Krone	C	18.4938	–	113.732	381.443
	B	15.9266	–	97.943	328.461
France	S	18.8800	102.100	–	389.480
FF. francs	C	16.2608	87.9257	–	335.386
	B	14.0050	75.7200	–	288.810
Germany	S	5.63000	30.4450	34.6250	–
deutschmarks	C	4.84837	26.2162	29.8164	–
	B	4.17500	22.5750	25.6750	–

C   =   Bilateral central rate
S/B   =   Exchange rate at which the central bank of the country in the left-hand column will sell/buy the currency identified in the row at the top of the table

Source: Bank of England Fact Sheet, May 1994 updated.

Participants were expected to intervene in the market to buy their currency if it fell too close to the lower edge of their band, that is close to the 'floor' and to sell their currency if it rose too close to the 'ceiling', that is the upper part of their band. They would receive assistance from the other country or countries involved. They would use their reserves in order to intervene and/or borrow from the VSTF.

Although the so-called narrow bands of ± 2.25 per cent seem to imply that each currency could diverge by that amount, 4.5 per cent, around the central rate, the degree of divergence was restricted because of the grid. For example, the Belgian franc might reach its limit against the peseta before it could make full use of its range against the French franc. The practical effect of this was that the band was closer to 2 per cent than to 4.5 per cent.

It was intended from the start that the ERM would be flexible and allow for changes as the relative strengths of currencies altered. Between 1979 and 1995 there were 19 realignments within the ERM. For example, in March 1995 the peseta was realigned by –7 per cent and the escudo by –3.5 per cent. The German mark has been revalued several times. In 1992 the United Kingdom chose not to realign and was forced out of the ERM instead.

Exercise 4

How does the ERM differ from the old Bretton Woods system?

Changes in the ERM since August 1993

Great speculation was seen in 1992 against some of the currencies in the ERM. The pound had entered the mechanism in October 1990 at a central rate against the Deutschmark of £1 = DM 2.95. Almost everyone thought that this was too high a rate and the pound operated close to its floor of £1 = DM 2.78 for much of early 1992 (it was using the wide ± 6 per cent band). There was also speculation against the Italian lira and the French franc. In September 1992 both the lira and the pound were forced out of the ERM and their currencies floated. Since that date the pound has depreciated by over 20 per cent against the Deutschmark and fell to DM 2.18 at one time. In late 1996 it had risen back to £1 = DM 2.45 because of the weakness of the US dollar and to £1 = DM 2.77 in March 1997.

The speculation revived in 1993 and there was a major attack on the French franc and on the system as a whole. In early August 1993 the normal bands were suddenly widened to ± 15 per cent. This move effectively removed the target at which the speculators were aiming, that is the floors of certain currencies, where countries were forced to intervene and buy their currency. The speculators were hoping to force a downward realignment so that they could make large profits. For a short time some of the currencies fell well below their original central and floor rates but gradually almost all of them returned to within the normal ± 2.25 bands although there was a realignment of the peseta and escudo in 1995. In October 1996 Finland put its currency, the markka, into the ERM and Italy rejoined.

The proposed European Single Currency

This is dealt with more fully in Chapter 20 on 'Money' but when, or if, it happens, those countries that join in will irrevocably lock their currencies into a completely new currency to be called the euro. The euro will then have an exchange rate against the dollar, the yen and so on but also against the currencies of those members of the European Union who have not qualified to join the euro or who may not have wanted to join. It could happen, therefore, that the euro will have an exchange rate against the pound after 1999 if the United Kingdom government decides to exercise its Maastricht Treaty opt out and not join in Stage 3 of monetary union. The European Union is planning to organise a new version of the ERM for those members who are not in the euro zone because it will still need to run the Union's budget efficiently.

Conclusion

Supporters of the ERM look at its record and are reasonably happy that it has achieved the degree of monetary stability that could be expected in an ever changing world and that it has withstood most of the economic shocks of the last fifteen years. Others prefer the advantages of completely freely floating rates. There is, however, a trend towards attempting to resurrect some form of the Bretton Woods agreement as an effort to manage the world markets, The huge volumes of money flowing through the exchanges every day represent a powerful economic force that governments would prefer to be able to restrain, if not control.

16 Agriculture and Commodity Markets

Aims of the chapter

To:

- explain the special nature of agricultural markets in terms of demand and supply conditions;
- discuss methods of state intervention in agricultural markets with particular reference to the Common Agricultural Policy (CAP) of the European Union;
- discuss the nature of commodity markets, many of which are based on agricultural products.

16.1 Agricultural Markets

Introduction

People often ask why the agricultural industry is treated differently from ordinary manufacturing industry in most countries and receives a higher level of state intervention and support. The answer is partly political, partly social and largely economic. The economic influences are related to the peculiar supply and demand conditions in agricultural products and are dealt with in detail below.

The political influences are greater in some countries than in others depending on the proportion of the national population that derives its living from the land and from distribution of agricultural goods or from the supply of agricultural factors of production. In many countries the rural vote is extremely important. Even in the United Kingdom there are many marginal seats in mixed urban/rural areas. In countries such as France the farming vote is vital and farmers have a long history of active demonstration against unfavourable government actions. In some continental countries the rural areas have been strongholds of the Communist Party and in some developing countries the rural areas have been the seedbed of revolution.

The social factors relate to the desire in most countries to maintain a good balance between urban and rural areas in terms of prosperity and development. Not many people favour rural depopulation and all the problems that it creates and it is generally simpler and more economic to maintain rural areas than to foster the expansion of urban areas to absorb the displaced rural populations.

Exercise I

Is the government assistance given to agricultural industries compared with that given to other industries justifiable?

Demand in agricultural markets

There is an enormous variety of agricultural products and there are three main sources of demand:

1. From manufacturers and industrial users for leather, wool, cotton and other fibres such as flax, dyes, alcohol, starch, oils from seeds, timber, products for brewing and more recently biofuel as a petrol or diesel substitute. Even milk can be used to make certain types of plastic.

2. From manufacturers of processed and preserved food products. Humans have always sought new methods of preserving food in order to make the supply more certain and to avoid its seasonal element. We, therefore, dry, pickle, smoke, bottle, can, freeze, dehydrate and irradiate it.

3. From households who buy fresh food directly from shops and farms and through the normal distribution chain.

    -   The demand for many foods is both price and income inelastic although their degree varies enormously among the various products available. Price inelasticity means that there is a smaller proportionate change in demand in relation to the price change when price alters by a small percentage.

The formula, you may remember from Chapter 6, is:

Price elasticity = $\dfrac{\%\text{ change in quantity demanded}}{\%\text{ change in price}}$

Demand is said to be price elastic if the result is greater than 1 and inelastic if it is less than 1. The consequence of this is that if price falls because of, say, a good harvest, the producer will end up with less total revenue from sales and if price rises because of, say, a bad harvest the farmer ends up with a greater total revenue.

Demand is said to be income elastic if a given percentage increase in income leads to a greater percentage rise in demand. If it is income inelastic, as most food products are, a given percentage rise in income results in a smaller percentage rise in demand. The reason that most foods are income inelastic is that we have a limited physical capacity to eat and although we, as a society in the UK, waste an enormous amount of food, we do not increase consumption proportionately to our rises in income. We may buy more dairy produce or exotic imported fruits and vegetables but we do not buy proportionately more potatoes or cheap vegetables and cheap cuts of meat. Some products have a negative income elasticity of demand which means that we consume less of them as our incomes rise. These are called *inferior goods* and include cheap white bread, potatoes and delicacies such as tripe and black pudding and many types of offal:

- A major underlying influence on the demand for agricultural products is obviously the size and structure of population. The rate of change of population has a profound effect on demand and on the nature of the output of the agricultural industry. In the long run we face the Malthusian nightmare of demand outstripping the resources available. After decades of surpluses in grain production, the world since 1995 seems to be moving rapidly towards a situation where there is very little spare grain in the world's silos and grain prices have begun to rise rapidly. There has long been a mismatch between the availability of supplies and the ability of people to pay and this has given rise to widespread malnutrition but this has, in the past, been largely a matter of distribution. In the future it may be that the overall supply will be below the demand.

- Demand is seasonal for some products which creates problems of storage and preservation. Historically, the seasonality of demand has been caused by the seasonal supply of certain products, especially with vegetables and fruit but much of modern seasonal demand is caused by festivals augmented by advertising. Most turkeys are eaten at Christmas. The industry attempts to spread the demand further by heavy advertising campaigns at the festivals such as Easter. To some extent the element of seasonal demand has been disappearing because fresh food is now flown or shipped in from all over the world regardless of season. We can also find frozen or preserved varieties of many types of food.

- Recent experience indicates that demand for particular types of food is susceptible to fads, fashions and health scares. The salmonella in eggs scare is a classic example of how a few ill-judged words can slash demand. The beef and BSE relationship has had a devastating effect on the industry. A few products benefit, for example garlic, red wine and ginseng. You could add your own favourites to this list.

In conclusion, it may be said that demand for foodstuffs in European countries is only slowly increasing because of slow population growth and low or negative income elasticity of demand. The industrial demand, especially for natural fibres and for biomass for fuel is likely to rise rapidly over the next decade. There is some compensation for European producers in exporting rather than in relying on home demand.

Supply factors

- There are many complicating factors in agricultural supply. The national supply for arable products is determined by the annual harvest and will therefore be very inelastic apart from amounts of some products that may be stored. There will, however, be foreign supplies available in most periods and this tends to make the supply less inelastic. In addition there are alternative supplies available from storage in various preserved forms as referred to in the section on demand. The United Kingdom has been heavily reliant on imports of many products for nearly two centuries but recent policies have created a much greater degree of self-sufficiency and even surpluses. There has been a tendency since 1974 to substitute imports from the European Union for supplies from the rest of the world. The overall tendency for agricultural products to have an inelastic supply means that good and bad harvests for a particular product shift the supply curve is such a way that, if the demand remains the same, there will be disproportionately large changes in market price (see Figure 16.1).

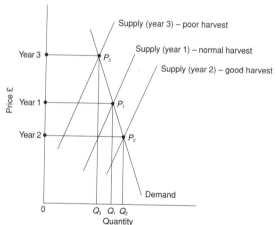

The steep gradient of the curves illustrates the relative inelasticity of supply and demand conditions for this agricultural commodity. Relatively small changes in output produce disproportionately large changes in price.
The figure also illustrates the change in revenue from the sales of this product over the three years. Compare the three rectangles of selling prices multiplied by the quantities $0Q_1$, $0Q_2$, $0Q_3$ in the years 1, 2 and 3.

Figure 16.1   Effects of relative inelasticity of demand and supply on price

- Farmers tend to enter markets where prices have been high in the recent past and to leave those where prices have been low. This may be a movement of 'marginal' producers only or may be a shift of a significant proportion of producers. Not all farmers have the luxury of being able to choose what to produce because their land conditions, expertise and machinery may all be specific to one type of production although transition to new crops has been made easier in recent years by the growth of specialist contractors who provide labour, machinery and expertise for the farmer.

- Farmers who have a limited range of output options tend to respond to falling prices and a fall in their income by producing more of their main product. A typical American midwest wheat farmer, faced by a falling price of wheat and therefore a falling income, can only compensate by growing more wheat. If all fellow producers do the same the aggregate supply expands. If demand fails to rise proportionately, excess supply is generated and prices fall even further. This is followed by another fall in net income unless the farmer has managed to cut costs even more. The possible causes of the initial fall in prices and incomes are many, for example good harvests elsewhere, or falling real incomes of consumers, or a change in the tastes and preferences of consumers.

- There is a supply phenomenon called the *pig cycle* because it is most apparent in that line of production but it can also be seen in some manufacturing areas such as computer chips. The classic pig cycle still operates with under supply and over supply alternating to produce, and respond to, price changes. Pigs reproduce quickly and fatten up very easily for market. The cycle is one of buoyant demand in relation to supply pushing up pig product prices. Farmers see the price rising and the likely profits. Existing producers expand their output and newcomers begin production. The result, if demand fails to rise sufficiently, is excess supply which tends to depress market prices. The fall in prices forces marginal producers out of business and reduces prices for the more efficient. The consequent decline in output creates a deficiency of supply in relation to demand. Prices tend to rise and we are back to the starting point. The cycle is illustrated in Figure 16.2. There are checks on the cycle nowadays. Entry to the market is made more expensive by modern welfare of animals regulations and the costs of housing the pigs. There is also much better information available in the market so that producers and potential producers are better informed about market trends. Periods of heavy losses and business failure are better known and act as a deterrent to entry. The 1995–96 period of very high prices for pig products has led to only a very small increase in the number of breeding sows and the experts are somewhat puzzled and have been asking if the pig cycle is a thing of the past. Some try to explain the failure of output to expand in terms of producers at last learning from past experience and not believing that the high prices will last. Ironically they are more likely to last because of the shift of demand to pork since the BSE in beef scare.

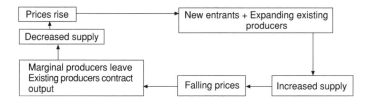

Figure 16.2 The pig cycle

Conclusion

The combined supply and demand conditions of a free market in agricultural products create a situation where there is likely to be great volatility in price. The combination of price inelastic supply and demand and income inelastic demand results in rapid price fluctuations as harvests change from year to year. This is illustrated in Figure 16.1.

Some economists have found some markets in food so unstable that they have asserted that the normal stable price equilibrium predicted by the usual supply and demand analysis does not always operate. They apply a different explanation, the so-called cobweb theorem. The theorem takes into account the way in which farmers respond to current and immediate past market price and to their expectations of future price.

The uncertainty of market price and supplies, together with strategic and political influences have caused most governments of the world to intervene in the agricultural industry and its markets.

Exercise 2

Analyse the effects of the BSE scare on the market for beef and substitutes such as pork and lamb.

BSE – AN ECONOMIC SHOCK

Background

Bovine Spongiform Encephalopathy (BSE) in cattle, mainly diary cows, was first identified in 1985 and by 1997 about 160 000 cattle in England and Wales had developed the disease. This was far more than in any other country; Switzerland was the next largest sufferer with about 350 cases. On 20 March 1996 the Secretary of State for Health announced in the House of Commons that BSE in cattle might have crossed the species barrier and emerged as a new variant of the fatal degenerative disease Creutzfeldt-Jacob disease (CJD). NvCJD was different from CJD in that it affected much younger people. In the year after 20 March 1996 there were 16 confirmed cases of NvCJD.

The announcement caused chaos in the markets and the European Union imposed an export ban on UK beef and beef products such as meat, tallow, gelatine, semen and embryos. In the UK over 1.25 million cattle have been slaughtered in an attempt to eliminate the disease whose cause is thought to be the feeding to cattle in the 1980s of animal protein boosted feed containing scrapie infected meat from sheep.

Case study – The Orkney Islands

There are 20 000 people on the Orkneys and 100 000 head of cattle. The islands have a reputation for high quality beef derived from the excellent grass land there. There is no scope for farmers to diversify into arable farming although there is some vegetable growing. The local economy obtained about £30 million a year from beef farming before 1996. Some of the effects on the local economy have been:

- In 1995 sellers received, on average, 135 pence per kilo for all beef cattle sold. In 1996 this had fallen to an average of 113 pence per kilo.

- Local shopkeepers found that their sales dropped by between 15 and 20 per cent in the three months after 20 March 1996.

- The largest feed, fertiliser and farm machinery supplier on the Islands laid off 10 per cent of its workforce. Their sales of animal protein feeds and beef nuts fell away completely and many sales of machinery and tractors were cancelled or postponed.

1. Consider the long-term implications for the Orkney Islands' economy of the fall in beef prices.

2. What assistance could the UK Government or the European Union provide?

16.2 The Common Agricultural Policy

The CAP was conceived against a background of 80 years of fluctuating supply, demand, prices and rural prosperity. Rural deprivation was one of the mainsprings of political and social unrest in European countries, as the post-war strength of the Communist party in rural France and Italy shows. The immediate backdrop to the CAP, however, was over ten years of food shortages caused by post-war dislocation. The foremost aim of the CAP, therefore, was to remove any threat of food shortages and it has succeeded in this aim and exceeded it in many instances to an embarrassing extent. The objectives explicitly stated in Article 39 of the Treaty of Rome which created the Community were to:

1. remove any threat of food shortages;
2. increase agricultural productivity;
3. ensure thereby a fair standard of living for the agricultural community;
4. stabilise markets;
5. guarantee reasonable prices for consumers.

The CAP began with six nations mainly in Northern Europe, all of whom had, at that time, a large agricultural sector dominated by small family holdings. In 1996 it is a policy that has to apply to 15 members ranging from the Arctic areas of Sweden and Finland to the sunny climate of Greece and Spain. The original policy was agreed in early 1962 after bitter wrangling. The principles on which it was based are a variation on the list above:

- the establishment of a single market and, therefore, of common prices for most agricultural products;
- an assurance that those working in agriculture would enjoy a standard of living comparable to workers in other sectors;
- preference for Community products;
- a common financial system operated through a European Agricultural Guidance and Guarantee Fund (EAGGF).

The new system began operation two years later in 1964 but uniform prices did not appear until 1967 when cereals prices were applied across the Community.

In 1968 Sicco Mansholt who was responsible for the CAP proposed the Mansholt Plan to modernise the Community's agricultural sector. There was another long and bitter wrangle and the main plank of his proposals, income support for farmers, was not adopted, that is not until 1992. The Hague Summit at the end of 1969 did, however, agree on agricultural financing. In the spring of 1984 the CAP was reformed again because the problem of excessive surpluses had become too urgent to ignore and too expensive. These reforms lasted until the end of the 1990 when another round of reforms, called the MacSharry reforms after the then Commissioner for Agriculture was debated, again acrimoniously. His reform package was published as a 'reflection paper' in 1991. It was mauled, modified and agreed in May 1992. The reforms came into effect over the next four years with completion in 1996. Further reforms are currently under discussion but will be probably postponed until after 1997.

The CAP in 1997

It is hard to summarise the latest version of the CAP briefly. Even an outline of the system, *The New Regulation of Agricultural Markets 1/93*, published by the European Commission, is 120 pages long. These are the main points:

1. The core of the system is the EAGGF which is divided into two parts:
   (a) The Guarantee part creates the price and market structures needed to maintain and raise farmers' incomes.
   (b) The Guidance section, which has undergone several transformations since it began, is directed at financing the restructuring of agriculture and helping the less favoured regions. The fund usually provides about 25 per cent of the cost of guidance and the rest comes from national governments. It is this section that has financed the early retirement of thousands of farmers and the amalgamation of holdings, together with education and training programmes to improve production methods.

2. The CAP has its greatest impact in cereals, beef, milk and milk products, wine, tobacco and various types of oilseeds. It has almost no effect on pigmeat and vegetables and relatively little on fresh fruit. The wine, fruit and vegetable regimes were not reformed in 1992 but proposals were being discussed in 1996 and early 1997.

3. The system of managing the internal market and prices differs for each type of product so generalisations may lead to misunderstanding. The broad types of organisation of markets are:
   (a) Crop products – cereals, rice, sugar and isoglucose, olive oil, oil seeds and protein plants.
   (b) Livestock products – milk and milk products, beef and veal, sheepmeat and goatmeat, pigmeat and eggs and poultry.
   (c) Specialised crops – fresh fruit and vegetables, processed fruit and vegetables, wine, raw tobacco, hops, seeds, flowers and ornamental plants and fibre plants and silkworms.

4. The main method of market support for cereals, for example, is to fix a target price for a product which is based on the price that a marginal producer would require to continue production. This high price is to

encourage production and achieve the objective of self-sufficiency and contributed to the excessive surpluses of the 1980s because efficient non-marginal producers could make exceptionally good profits if market price approached these levels. Beneath this target price is an intervention price which is effectively a floor price for a quantity of the produce determined by the annual decisions on the CAP. There used to be no restriction on the quantity that qualified for the intervention price and this fact contributed to surpluses because farmers would simply maximise their output. If the market price falls to or below the intervention price for a certain period then the produce is bought and stored by an Intervention Board in each country. This storage was, and is, very expensive. The stored product is sold in the future if the market price rises to a sufficient level or is exported or even destroyed. Intervention buying is now subject to severe controls on the quality of what is bought into store and there are time limitations. For example, there are time limitations on purchase of cereals which can only be bought in seven months of the harvest year. There are also incentives to beef producers to market their beef at specific times in order to curtail intervention purchases (see Table 16.1).

Table 16.1   Commodity intervention in the United Kingdom: an example

1000 tonnes	Closing/ opening stock*	1993–4 Purchases	Sales	Closing/ opening stock	1994–95 FORECAST Purchases	Sales	Closing stock*
Feed							
Wheat	15	277	–	292	52	279	65
Barley	835	690	246	1286	119	684	720

* The figures, closing/opening stock = opening stock plus purchases = sales, may not always equate because of rounding and stock adjustments as orders from previous years are fulfilled.

Source: Adapted from *Agriculture in the United Kingdom 1994*, London, HMSO, 1995.

5. Competition from imports was dealt with until the Uruguay Round Agreement in 1994 by raising their prices by a set of sliding scale levies that raised the imported product's price to a *threshold price* which was above the target price and took account of transport costs and taxes. The United Kingdom paid more levies than most members because of its higher dependency on imports, especially of North American hard (durum) wheat. The system effectively kept out many imports although some

countries were favoured by membership of the Lomé Agreement that benefited ACP countries. Since 1994 the levies have been replaced by tariffs that will gradually be removed.

6. Until the Uruguay Round Agreement in 1994 the European Community subsidised exports of many surplus foodstuffs particularly cereals and meat with a system of export rebates. In doing so it antagonised Third World producers as well as the USA and Australasian countries. The subsidised exports were harmful to the home producers in countries such as India. Since 1994, however, these export rebates have been phased down and even temporarily replaced, in the case of cereals, with export taxes since early 1995. The reversal occurred because of the cutback in production and the decline of stocks in store. Export rebates returned when prices changed.

7. Since the MacSharry reforms for cereals, the target and intervention prices have been reduced year by year until the 1995/96 harvest year, as the following figures show:

| | ECU per tonne | |
	Target Price	Intervention Price
1993–94	130	117
1994–95	120	108
1995–96	110	100

The threshold price is ECU 45 above the target price.

8. Along side these reductions in price guarantees, farmers were forced to leave some of their land fallow in what is called *set-aside*. The scheme was based on a US model from the 1930s and a pilot voluntary scheme applied in the Community after the 1984 reforms. The details are complex but the percentage of arable land to be set-aside is fixed each year. It was 15 per cent in 1994–95 but was reduced to 12 per cent and was fixed at 5 per cent for 1996–97. A few farmers chose not to participate in the schemes but some chose to stop arable production altogether and receive income compensation instead. As compensation for the set-aside producers are now paid income support, that is money based on the profit they would have received from the set-aside land. The compensation requires a complicated calculation of average yields and prices. The compensation rose each year as the intervention price fell, as follows:

1993–94	ECU 25 per tonne multiplied by the cereal yield calculation
1994–95	ECU 35 per tonne multiplied by the cereal yield calculation
1995–96	ECU 45 per tonne multiplied by the cereal yield calculation

These figures amounted to about £220 per acre in the United Kingdom in 1995.

9. The system for oilseeds was also altered to abolish maximum guaranteed areas and prices and to replace them with aid paid per hectare fixed at Community level and then regionalised to take account of average historic yields. European oilseed production was a major source of conflict with the USA during the Uruguay Round discussions because the old CAP system kept out US oilseeds and subsidised the export of European oilseeds. The changes fit in better with the Uruguay Agreement and the new World Trade Organisation system.

10. The support system for beef, veal, sheep and goats was also changed. The beef system has since been buffetted by the BSE problem. The main new ingredient is premiums paid per head of output. These lump sum payments are subject to a maze of regulations and qualifications. For beef and veal there are also intervention prices and buying. It was intended to reduce the intervention buying of beef year by year to a 1997 total of 350 000 tonnes but this plan has been abandoned because of BSE and the level is going to be restored to at least 750 000 tonnes in 1997. One of the main purposes of the new scheme has been to reduce levels of stocking so there are now calculations of livestock units per hectare of forage area. This general policy is called *extensification*. Sheep are subject to the same sort of regime – ewe premiums, variable slaughter premiums and a distinction between heavy and light lambs. Some buying into private storage is also allowed for. There is also provision for reducing the basic price used to calculate the ewe premium if the number of ewes in the Community exceeds 63.4 million. In the case of both beef and sheepmeat there are extra payments to producers in less favoured areas.

11. The milk market has given a great deal of trouble over the years and a so-called 'mountain' of butter was bought into intervention store and disposed of at great expense. The market has a *guide price* for milk, an *intervention price* for butter, skimmed milk powder and certain Italian cheeses, and a *threshold price* for imported milk products. This latter keeps the price of such imports at levels corresponding to the guide price for milk. In 1984 a system of milk quotas was introduced that limited the output of each country and farm. In the United Kingdom the quotas have become a saleable commodity. There was also, between 1977 and 1993, a *co-responsibility levy* paid by producers according to the level of output and directed at helping small producers and those in less favoured regions. Individual producers now suffer a cut in price, effectively a fine, if their quota is exceeded and if the national quota is exceeded. Milk also has to match quality requirements. There are special regulations that enable milk products to be disposed of from intervention stores.

12. One part of the CAP budgetary system that has been periodically reformed and which is on the verge of being phased out is called, rather dauntingly, the Agrimonetary Compensation Mechanism (ACM). CAP payments and prices are fixed in ECU, and Monetary Compensatory Amounts (MCAs) were designed to compensate for exchange rate alterations and to stabilise prices. They actually created an immensely complex variety of so-called 'green rates', for example, a 'green pound'. These rates were subject to devaluation and revaluation and there was something called a 'switch-over mechanism' whose overall effect was to cause prices to rise over time. MCAs could be negative or positive. In 1995 the problem of MCAs became very serious because of the strength of the Deutschmark and the old system was reformed by virtual abolition. This should help to restrain price increases but reforms of the remaining policy are being considered because there is still a remnant of a switch-over mechanism remaining. There is still a 'green pound' because all CAP payments are calculated in ECU and a conversion rate has to be applied in order to pay UK farmers. If the pound strengthens against the ECU the UK producers are worse off because they get fewer ECUs per pound. If the pound depreciates they receive more.

13. The new system is backed up by new bureaucracy. Farmers submit an annual plan of their cropping proposals and there is satellite surveillance to ensure that they do not cheat.

Conclusions

The new CAP since the 1992 reforms is by no means perfect but it regarded as a success by the European Commission who are in the process of reforming the other areas, particularly wine, fruit and vegetables. By 1994 prices had stabilised and the real incomes of farmers had risen. Cereal stocks had fallen from 33 to 25 million tonnes during the marketing year 1994–95. Beef and veal stocks fell from 1.7 million tonnes in 1992 to 40 000 tonnes in February 1995, an historic low, although they have begun to rise rapidly since March 1996 when the British Government announced that a new variant of Creutzfeldt-Jacob disease was possibly linked to BSE.

The other effect of the reforms has been to keep the agricultural budget within its designated bounds. The 1995 agricultural budget of ECU 36.7 billion was ECU 1 billion less than the guideline. Some of this improvement is due to measures to prevent fraud, some to the higher world prices resulting from poor world harvests and some to the reduced cost of intervention buying and storage. There are more measures being studied to introduce more reforms as well as to cope with the proposed entry to the European Union of several central European countries with large agricultural sectors, for example Poland and Hungary.

Exercise 3

Why has the CAP been given such a bad name? Has it any redeeming features?

16.3 Commodity Markets

As international trade and industry developed there grew up a large number of local commodity markets for cereals and raw materials such as cotton, wool and metals. Many of these have closed and their work has been taken over by exchanges situated in cities such as London, New York and Chicago.

There are several features that commodity markets have in common:

- The product either never appears in material form or is dealt with using samples. (The first market that operated without goods was formed in Antwerp in 1531.) The market trades in defined qualities and quantities of the product, for example, aluminium of 99.7 per cent purity, or gold in lots of 100 troy ounces, crude oil in 1000 barrels, or pork bellies in 40 000lb lots. Many products are graded, for example 'copper grade A'. This type of standardisation enables deals to be made on paper and via electronic dealing without recourse to immediate problems of carriage and storage.

- The market operates spot trading and futures trading in the same way as the foreign exchange markets described in Chapter 15. The existence of futures trading was originally intended to help manufacturers who actually wanted the commodity in the future to buy at a price that guaranteed certainty against fluctuation of prices. It also helped suppliers to manage their financial affairs better. The existence of futures, however, quickly enabled people to hedge against unforeseen movements in prices by both buying and selling futures so that the eventual price paid was predictable and without significant gain or loss. Nowadays the bulk of trading is in futures and much of the trading is speculative. Many of the buyers would be horrified to be left with any of the commodity on their hands, indeed sceptics sometimes wonder if they know what the product looks like. Of course, some of the traders do actually want the commodity for manufacturing purposes and have warehouses and storage areas.

- Many of the markets have developed derivatives markets in options to buy and sell and these enable a greater degree of speculation to take place because of the leveraged nature of their deals. The buyer need only produce a small percentage of the agreed price 'up front' in the deal although there may be calls for extra funds to be provided on a daily basis if the option agreed diverges too far from the spot price. The London market trades options in aluminium, copper, cocoa, coffee and Brent crude oil.

- The markets are to a large extent self-regulating but the state may also introduce a supervisory body for overall surveillance. The general principle is that the outsider needs to be protected against insiders with additional knowledge of the market. The effectiveness of this supervision is called into question when scandals affect the markets.

- The commodity markets create enormous flows of finance of different kinds and generate huge international payments and work for the foreign exchange markets. Certain markets are so important that they effectively determine the world price for given commodities. Examples include the Chicago Board of Trade that fixes wheat prices; London prices tend to follow with a premium for transport and insurance costs and exchange rate or interest rate costs. The London Bullion Market determines gold prices at its morning and afternoon 'fixes'. All of these markets have a great influence on the lives and work of the people, farmers, plantation owners and miners who produce the commodities and on those who derive employment from the use of the products. This fact has led governments to try to control commodity prices by the use of intervention buying and selling. These agreements usually operate quite well for a few years and then break down, sometimes disastrously as in the case of the International Tin Agreement. They usually dissolve because, while people and governments are happy when market prices are raised by intervention buying and stock holding in what are called *buffer stocks*, they become very unhappy when the prices are 'stabilised' downwards by selling stocks from the buffer. There have been commodity agreements in cocoa, coffee and tin. They ebb and flow and the coffee agreement never seems quite to die.

Examples of commodity markets

The London Metal Exchange deals in aluminium, lead, nickel, tin, zinc and copper. It is still essentially a pit method of dealing with face-to-face bargaining and electronic recording of deals and settlement. The London Bullion Market deals in precious metals, gold, silver, gold coins, platinum and palladium. Then there are markets in what are called 'softs', that is cocoa, coffee, white sugar, cotton and orange juice. The various grain markets around the world, especially in Chicago and the London Commodity Exchange, deal in wheat, maize, barley, soyabeans, soyabean oil, soyabean meal and potatoes. Meat and livestock markets deal in live cattle, live hogs and pork bellies. The other important commodities in international markets are crude oil of different sorts, oil products such as jet fuel, natural gas, rubber, palm oil, cotton and wool tops. To reiterate, these are bought and sold in standard quantities and qualities. Without this standardisation a market has to be conducted face to face with real merchandise on view.

The method of dealing favoured in the USA is the open outcry system with floor trading, usually in 'pits' and modern information technology to record and administer the deals. That system was adopted in London for the London International Financial Futures Market but it is dubious how long such primitive methods will survive. The French tend to prefer such a system for share dealing still but the Germans are moving over to electronic dealing. The floor trading systems seem to reach a physical limit on their growth so if trading continues to expand we shall either see new exchanges open or older ones transfer to complete or partial screen trading.

Exercise 4

Buy a *Financial Times*, or read it in a library, and study the commodity market prices. You will learn a great deal from this exercise, although you may need help interpreting some of the abbreviations.

---

17 Trade and the Balance of Payments

Aims of the chapter

To:

- explain why nations trade;
- explain the make-up of the balance of payments' accounts in the context of the United Kingdom;
- describe the measurement of the terms of trade;
- outline the main theory of trade, the theory of comparative cost advantage;
- discuss the arguments relating to free trade and protectionist policies.

17.1 Why Do Nations Trade?

There are simple, commonsense answers to this question as well as reasons based on economic theory, particularly on what is called the *theory of comparative cost advantage* which is explained in some detail near the end of this chapter.

International trade is essentially the same as regional trade but frequently involves cross border formalities and different currencies. None of us finds it odd that we should get our coal from Newcastle (if only we could nowadays) or our woollen goods from Yorkshire, or our financial services from Scotland or London, because we recognise the benefits of regional specialisation that arise from the physical geography of a region and the acquired advantages in terms of skilled labour forces, transport facilities and communications. A region tends to specialise in the production of those things where it enjoys comparative cost advantages over its competitors and these advantages alter over time. In the same way, international advantages change and we see the rise and fall of national dominance in certain areas of production.

There are some products that can only be produced economically in a few places. There are good examples with certain primary products, especially minerals such as bauxite for aluminium production or nickel where deposits are mainly located in Canada, or crops such as cocoa and cotton where the climatic restrictions on where they can be grown are severe. It is obvious that such things will have to be traded but the real question then becomes what determines which goods or services are traded for them and in what quantities?

One of the characteristics of international trade is the fact that developed countries especially frequently import and export the same products or varieties of them. The most obvious examples are cars where, for example, the United Kingdom exports a number of models and also imports very similar models. There are cases of the same model produced in UK and continental factories under different brand names being exported and imported. The reason for this type of trade must lie in the perception of the buyers who think they are getting something different or who feel that the foreign product has some sort of cachet not possessed by the home product. There may also be a perception that the foreign car is better value for money because exported cars often have better quality control and more built-in features. Even so, some of the peculiarities of trade are difficult to explain except by falling back on the assertion that many people do not know what is going on in the market, that is, the old imperfect knowledge argument.

The study of trade is made more difficult by the fact that much of modern industry is an assembling process so that, for example, a computer assembled in Scotland will have components inside that come from umpteen different countries. World trade is awash with products in a state of semi-manufacture. We can only conclude that the buyers of the assembling company have scoured the world looking for the cheapest available supplies and that trade theory is working in practice, that is countries and regions are specialising in the production of those goods and services in which they have the greatest comparative cost advantage or the least comparative cost disadvantage.

Exercise I

In which goods and services do you reckon the United Kingdom has the greatest comparative cost advantage?

17.2   The Balance of Payments

Some students confuse 'the balance of payments' which refers to international payments relating to trade in goods and services and monetary flows with the government's budget and its attempt, if any, to balance its revenue and expenditure. It is advisable to understand the normal usage of the terms.

If you wish completely to comprehend the United Kingdom's balance of payments you should look at the annually published *The United Kingdom Balance of Payments*, which is called the Pink Book. Extracts from it appear in the Annual Abstract of Statistics available in reference libraries. Unfortunately there have been several revisions in recent years of the presentation of the balance of payments figures, mostly for the better, so comparisons that go back too far require many footnotes. The other problem is that the statistics are subject to continual review and may be altered some months or even years later. Many of the problems arise from the fact that payments may be made in different accounting time periods from the original delivery of goods or services. A more recent difficulty arose because of the adoption of the European Single Market from 1 January 1993. What had once been imports and exports to and from the continent now, overnight, became internal trade because borders had, in theory, been abolished. Imports between members have been renamed as 'arrivals' and exports between members are known as 'shipments'. The European Union trade data is now handled by Intrastat, a subdivision of Eurostat.

Another piece of terminology that sometimes puzzles students is the use of initials, particularly f.o.b. and c.i.f. In the UK trade accounts exports are valued 'f.o.b.' while imports are valued 'c.i.f.' so an adjustment is made to convert both to f.o.b. **F.o.b.** means 'free on board' which in turn means that the price of the good is based on the manufacturing cost and does not include the cost of transporting the good to the final consumer. In other words the foreign consumer bears the cost of insurance and freight. **C.i.f.** means 'cost, insurance, freight' or alternatively, 'charged in full'. Since payments for insurance and freight are what are called 'invisibles' they are placed in the part of the balance of payments accounts called services or invisibles and both imports and exports are valued f.o.b. in the tables.

The balance of payments accounts

Nowadays there are two main sections of the balance of payments accounts; **The current account** and **transactions in external assets and liabilities**. The latter is sometimes referred to as 'the capital account'. The pluses and minuses of these accounts are so arranged that the overall account is in balance. There is also something called *the balancing item* which represents the net total of errors and omissions in other items in the accounts. The balancing item can be an enormous figure, for example plus £6.4 billion in 1992 and minus £1.7 billion in 1987 and makes one doubt the overall reliability of the figures or at least the sense of those who place complete faith in them.

The current account has traditionally been divided into (1) visibles and (2) invisibles but the most recent presentation of the United Kingdom's accounts has abandoned the distinction between visibles and invisibles although the statistics are still available separately.

1. **Visibles** are merchandise imports and exports that can be seen and touched. The accounts are presented in the f.o.b. form. This section has usually been called 'the balance of trade' or the 'balance of visible trade'.

The United Kingdom has normally had a deficit on the visible balance with a few exceptions for 150 years although North Sea oil reduced the size of the deficit for a time. The deficit peaked at –£24.6 billion in 1989. The extent of the so-called 'trade gap' depends on many factors such as the price competitiveness of UK exports and home production, the rate of inflation in the UK compared with other countries, the state of world trade and the quality and extent of the UK manufacturing sector. It is in this context that there is heavy criticism of the 'deindustrialisation' of Britain in the 1980s with the assertion that we no longer make things for ourselves and must, therefore, import them. The **terms of trade**, that is the price of exports relative to the price of imports, is also important. This concept is discussed fully below.

2. **Invisibles** are services of different types for which we pay foreigners (invisible imports) or which we supply and are paid for by foreigners (invisible exports). The invisible exports yield credits and the invisible imports create debits. The invisibles are classified into groups as follows:

- Services
- Investment income
- Transfers

Services are classified as follows:

- *General government* which covers all UK government transfers that are not included in other items in the accounts. This figure is always a very large net debit.
- *Sea transport* – that is freight, charter hire, port payments and passage money. In recent years, as the British merchant fleet has fallen in size or been reflagged, this figure has become a net debit.
- *Civil aviation* – relates to payments and receipts for passenger fares, freight, charter hire and airport payments. Until 1985 it was usually a net credit but has become a large debit since then.
- *Travel* – covers personal expenditure by UK residents abroad (imports) and by overseas residents in the UK (exports). The figure is a growing, large net deficit, –£3.3 billion in 1993 despite the impressive record of the British tourist industry.
- *Financial and other services* are the earnings, net of expenses, of UK financial and allied institutions for services and all services transactions not included elsewhere (and the foreign side as well). They amount to an extremely large net credit, +£11 billion in 1993, which reflects the strength of the UK financial services sector and the City of London.

Investment income refers to interest, profits and dividends (IPD) received by UK residents from non-residents or payable overseas, after deduction of local taxes and depreciation, by UK residents. The figures include profits that are kept for reinvestment. The statistics distinguish between credits and debits of: (1) general government and (2) private sector and public corporations. The general government figure is always a net debit, –£1.8 billion in 1993, but the private sector is always a very large net credit, +£4.9 billion in 1993. These receipts and payments of interest, profits and dividends, are very important because they derive from overseas investment. The credits, £72.6 billion in 1993, reflect the enormous overseas investments of the British, individuals, companies and institutions as well as government sector. In the nineteenth century the flow of IPD exceeded the net deficit on visible trade and much of the excess was reinvested abroad. The two world wars saw a serious reduction in the amount of overseas investment and a consequent fall in the flow of IPD until the overseas investments were rebuilt. The debits, £67.6 billion in 1993, under this heading have increased, with some interruptions, over the last 20 years and this reflects the increase in foreign investment in the UK economy. The discovery and exploitation of North Sea oil caused a huge inflow of foreign capital which has inevitably produced an outflow of IPD. Similarly, the inflow of Japanese and Korean money to open assembly plants will, in future, lead to an outflow of profits. Flows of foreign money into the United Kingdom in pursuit of higher interest rates and the chance of capital gains also create a future outflow of money in the form of interest and profits.

Transfers are also divided into (1) general Government transfers and (2) private transfers. The former are mainly grants to overseas countries and payments to or from international organisations. There are also some flows in the other direction especially grants from the European Union. The net debit in 1993 was –£4.8 billion. The private transfers are the value of net assets passing from non-resident to resident ownership or the other way round without there being anything provided in exchange. This figure includes the transfer of assets by migrants other than their personal or household possessions. The balance for private transfers was always a small net credit until 1987 but has been a small net debit ever since, in the region of minus £275 to £300 million.

Exercise 2

Is the distinction between visible and invisible trade worth preserving in the balance of payments accounts?

Summary of the current account

Transactions in external assets and liabilities

At the same time as individuals, companies, the government and institutions are buying and selling goods and services abroad and receiving current income from investments, there are also 'transactions in external assets and liabilities', that is buying and selling assets or reducing or incurring liabilities. These used to go under the name 'capital account'. They explain, among other things, how a deficit on the current account is financed or how a surplus is accounted for. In principle the idea is simple. If you owe money because your current spending exceeds your current income you can do a mixture of three things. You can borrow money to meet the difference; you can take money out of savings; you can sell assets. Similarly, if your spending is less than your income you can lend money, increase your savings or add to your assets. The country's balance of payments is much the same. It is only more complicated because, like you, you could have a current deficit which you make larger by borrowing more and finance the extra debt by taking more of your savings or selling more assets. Or you could increase your current deficit and buy more assets and borrow more. The combinations are numerous as they are for the country where literally millions of people may be making independent decisions that affect foreign payments.

The figures or flows involved are very large as the following statistics for levels of UK external assets and liabilities in 1993 show:

	Assets £ (billions)	Liabilities £ (billions)	Net £ (billions)
General government	43	64	21
Public corporations	1	0.2	0.8
Private sector	1332	1292	40

It is important to remember that the following signs apply in the transactions in external assets and liabilities section of the balance of payments accounts:

Assets: Increase is a minus sign –; Decrease is a plus + sign.
Liabilities: Decrease is a minus sign –; Increase is a plus + sign.

These are logical if you remember that it is an accounting balance that we are discussing. An increase in assets held overseas requires an outflow of funds whereas a decrease creates an inflow. It is normal practice to refer to a decrease in liabilities with a minus sign and an increase with a plus.

Table 17.1   Summary balance of payments, 1984–94

	1984	1985	1986	1987	1988	1989	1990	1991	1992	1993	1994
Current account											
Visible balance	–5 336	–3 345	–9 559	–11 582	–21 480	–24 683	–18 809	–10 284	–13 104	–13 378	–10 594
Invisibles											
Service balance	4 205	6 398	6 223	6 242	3 957	3 361	3 689	3 708	5 051	5 685	3 790
Investment income	4 344	2 296	4 629	3 927	4 566	3 502	723	–574	3 694	1 890	10 519
Transfers balance	–1 731	–3 111	–2 157	–3 400	–3 518	–4 578	–4 896	–1 383	–5 109	–5 239	–5 399
Invisibles balance	6 817	5 583	8 695	6 769	5 005	2 285	–484	1 751	3 636	2 336	8 910
Current balance	1 482	2 238	–864	–4 813	–16 475	–22 398	–19 293	–8 533	–9 468	–11 042	–1 684
Capital transfers	–	–	–	–	–	–	–	–	–	–	–
Transactions in UK assets and liabilities											
UK external assets	–32 189	–50 617	–91 693	–82 722	–57 495	–90 668	–80 439	–18 872	–81 385	–155 818	–39 363
UK external liabilities	23 655	46 897	87 874	90 132	68 342	110 273	98 560	27 399	86 444	169 330	35 802
Net transactions	–8 534	–3 720	–3 820	–7 410	–10 847	–19 605	–18 121	–8 527	–5 059	–13 512	–3 561
EEA loss on forward commitments	–	–	–	–	–	–	–	–	–	–	–
Allocation of special drawing rights	–	–	–	–	–	–	–	–	–	–	–
Gold subscription to IMF	–	–	–	–	–	–	–	–	–	–	–
Balancing item	7 052	1 482	4 684	–2 597	5 628	2 793	1 172	6	4 409	–2 470	5 245

Source: United Kingdom Balance of Payments 1995, Table 1.1. Key Data 95/6 Edition CSO (London: HMSO 1995).

The main headings under the transactions in external assets and liabilities section are:

- *Overseas investment by and in the United Kingdom.* This is divided into two types: (1) *Direct* which is mainly company net investment and reinvestment of retained profits and real estate transactions and (2) *Portfolio* which is net purchases of government, municipal and company securities.
- *Net foreign currency transactions of UK banks*
- *Deposits with and lending to banks abroad by UK non-bank private sector*
- *Borrowing from banks abroad*
- *Official reserves.* Observers watch this figure which is also the subject of monthly reporting with great interest although with less attention than when the pound was not floating. The figure consists of the sterling equivalent at current rates of exchange of drawings on or additions to the gold, convertible currencies and special drawing rights held in the reserves and of changes in the reserve position with the IMF.
- *Other external assets.* This is a bit of a dustbin category and includes inter-governmental loans by the UK and subscriptions to international lending organisations and short-term assets as well as lending and trade credit between unrelated companies.
- *Other external liabilities.* This is the opposite of the last heading and includes loans to the UK government, transactions with the IMF.
- *Allocation of Special Drawing Rights.* The IMF developed a method of allocating a gold equivalent to member states in proportion to their deposits. They are called Special Drawing Rights (SDR) and are occasionally increased.
- *Balancing item.* This has already been described.

The current account and the transactions in external assets and liabilities are very closely interlinked in terms of effects although the various transactions are carried out by millions of individuals and hundreds of thousands of companies. The movement abroad for example of investment funds has a future impact on the levels of interest, profits and dividends in the current account. It also has an impact on the levels of income earned by the financial services sector on the current account.

Does the balance of payments matter?

In the period when the pound was not floating, that is 1947–71, the balance of payments and the size of the deficit or the movement in the deficit on current account was regarded as a vitally important indicator of the nation's economic health. The balance of payments was treated as a sick patient with economic experts vying with each other to explain its problems and to suggest cures. Looking back it all seems so out of proportion. Unfortunately successive governments took it very seriously because they were committed to maintaining a fixed exchange rate for the pound. If the balance of payments moved too far into deficit they reacted by imposing tax increases and cutting government spending and/or imposing various forms of credit restraints or incomes policies. They were also forced into borrowing large sums from the IMF and groups of rich nations, for example the Group of 7 or 10. Such borrowings were only possible if the government of the day promised severe cutbacks to restrict imports and inflation. Such borrowing was repeated even when the pound floated. Indeed, a loan from the IMF in 1978 and the subsequent cutbacks in government spending were the main cause of the withdrawal of trade union support to the Callaghan Government in 1979 and the so-called 'winter of discontent' that contributed to the defeat of the Labour Government and the rise of Thatcherism.

The essence of the United Kingdom balance of payments problem was that each successive deficit was larger than the previous one and took longer to emerge from and each required more draconian measures to reverse. The recoveries lasted for a shorter time on each occasion. There was, however, a fundamental change in the early 1980s. North Sea oil came on stream and the revenues helped to reduce the overall deficit although much of them went abroad to foreign companies who managed not to pay much tax on them. The balance of payments was also helped initially by a huge inflow of foreign capital as it came into the United Kingdom to exploit the oil and gas fields. Unfortunately the inflow also had the effect of driving up the exchange rate of the pound to such an extent that United Kingdom manufacturing industry was decimated and unemployment rose rapidly. The new Conservative Government elected in 1979 abolished foreign exchange controls and thereafter left the balance of payments very much to itself and attributed any changes to the play of free market forces. They basically ignored the balance of payments by saying that, with a floating pound and no controls on capital movements, it was a self-correcting mechanism. This is not to say that there was never any intervention buying or selling and certainly by the second half of the decade there were plenty of people, even in the government, who wanted to join the ERM.

The 'J' Curve
The relationship of the balance of payments and the exchange rate of the pound is complex and there are lags in the impact of exchange rate movements on the balance of payments. This is sometimes explained in terms of what is called the 'J' curve. If the pound is devalued from a fixed parity in order to make exports cheaper and imports dearer, there is a delayed effect before the balance of payments moves from deficit into surplus. If this is plotted on a graph with the balance of payments on the y axis and the years on the x axis the subsequent curve looks like a J. In other words the balance of payments deficit gets worse before it gets better (see Figure 17.1).

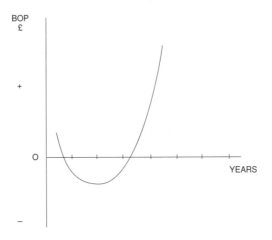

Figure 17.1　The 'J' curve

The 'J' curve is also linked to the relative price elasticities of demand for imports and exports. If the pound depreciates in value or is devalued from a fixed rate, we need the extra revenue from additional cheaper exports to exceed any extra cost of the now dearer imports. The ideal combination is for the export and import demands to be very price elastic and the *Marshall–Lerner condition* summarises the relationship. The condition states that if the sum of the price elasticities of demand for imports and exports exceeds unity, the devaluation will be beneficial and improve the balance of payments.

It is sometimes said that the balance of payments is no problem in itself because it is, after all, an accounting balance and always balances. Economists, however, are concerned with the individual sectors particularly the current balance and investment flows and with the overall question of **how** it is brought into balance. Excessive deficits on the balance of visible trade tend to indicate an inadequate or under-performing manufacturing sector but it could possibly show that industry is stocking up with raw materials, components and investment goods in order to undertake future expansion.

Exercise 3

In 1995 the United Kingdom balance of payments on current account is estimated at a deficit of –£6670 million. Should the government be concerned about this and what could it do about it?

17.3   The Terms of Trade

The terms of trade relate changes in the prices of exports to changes in the prices of imports. The changes are expressed as index numbers and compared with a base year. The formula for measuring the terms of trade is:

$$\frac{\text{Index of export prices}}{\text{Index of import prices}} \times \frac{100}{1} = \text{terms of trade}$$

The current base year for the UK is 1990 = 100. The following figures show how the terms of trade can change. If the index is rising compared with the previous year the terms of trade are improving and if it is falling they are deteriorating. They may be improving compared with the previous year but deteriorating compared with the base year or vice versa but the following figures show continuous improvement.

	1989	1990	1991	1992	1993
Imports	96.5	100	101.4	103.5	114.8
Exports	97.7	100	101.2	102.1	110.5
Terms of trade	98.8	100	100.2	101.4	103.9

The figures are unit value index numbers, 1990 = 100.

The actual prices to which the index numbers relate are determined ultimately by the world supply in relation to the world demand for United Kingdom products and by exchange rates. If the pound is strengthening, other things being equal, export prices will rise and import prices fall. The terms of trade do not tell us anything directly about the volume of trade. We need to know both the terms of trade and the volumes of imports and exports to deduce anything about the balance of visible trade, that is whether it is improving or not.

17.4   The Theory of Trade

International trade is usually explained using the theory of comparative cost advantage which was put forward in the early nineteenth century by Ricardo. The theory is usually illustrated with a two-country, two-commodity model and starts with a number of assumptions about them being closed economies and being in a state of perfect competition and having constant returns to scale. The model usually ignores transport costs and other gritty little problems such as foreign exchange rates. Ricardo himself used the example of Portugal and England and wine and cloth. Modern textbooks use adventurous examples like steel and wheat and the UK and Canada or videos and cloth and

Japan and the UK. You can make up your own example; what matters is the figures that are chosen for the illustration and their application. When the two-country, two-commodity model is explained it is then stated that the principles also apply to a multiple country, multiple commodity world.

The concept of opportunity cost is important because the cost of producing one of the products is expressed in terms of the output of the other product that is forgone if there is a change in output of either. We might, for example, have the following figures:

	Generators	*Vodka*	*Domestic Opportunity Cost Ratio*
Scotland	30	10	3:1
Belarus	16	8	2:1
	7.5:4	5:4	

Scotland has what is called an *absolute cost advantage* in the production of both goods. It is 'better' at generator production and at vodka production. ('Better' here is related to costs of production measured in terms of factors used. Some texts will give complicated labour costings to make it more realistic). But, while Scotland has an absolute advantage in both, it is **comparatively** better at generator production, 7.5:4 as opposed to only 5:4 for vodka. The general conclusions of the theory are:

- If the domestic opportunity cost ratios differ trade is beneficial to both. If they are the same then trade has no benefit because they can each obtain what they want at the same cost from internal substitution.
- It pays each country to concentrate on the production of the commodity in which it has the comparative cost advantage, or to put it another way, the 'inferior' country should produce that good in which it has least disadvantage. In the above example that is generators for Scotland and vodka for Belarus.
- The terms at which they trade and exchange will fall somewhere between the domestic opportunity cost ratios.

In our example the terms of trade will be between 3 and 2 generators per quantity of vodka. Scotland needs to pay less than 3 generators per unit of vodka in order to benefit because her own domestic opportunity cost is 3:1. If the exchange rate fell to 2.1 generators = 1 unit of vodka it would favour Scotland. Conversely, an exchange rate close to 2.9 generators = 1unit of vodka would favour Belarus because she would normally have to give up 1 unit of vodka and get only 2 generators. Textbook examples usually fix the exchange rate halfway between the two domestic opportunity cost ratios and go on to demonstrate the gains from trade which are measured in physical terms, that is additional generators and vodka. The gains arise because of the benefits of specialisation. In practice a country will probably obtain enormous economies of scale if it concentrates on certain types of production and the costs do not remain constant as the simple model assumes.

In our example, if we assumed an exchange rate of 2.5 generators per unit of vodka we would have the following situation:

Scotland would concentrate on generator production and produce 30 and exchange, say, 15 for 6 units of vodka.

Belarus would specialise on vodka and produce 8 units and exchange, say, 6 for 15 generators.

Scotland now has 15 g + 6 v and Belarus has 15 g and 2 v, an overall total of 30 g + 8 v.

If the two countries' original domestic opportunity cost ratios are studied you can calculate that Scotland could have combined 15 g with only 5 v and Belarus could have combined 2 v with only 12 g. The gains from this speciali-sation are, therefore, 3 g and 1 v in total.

In practice the terms of trade between the two nations and products will depend on the relative strength of the world supply and demand of the two products. Except where straightforward barter takes place it would be normal for countries to export a wide range of goods and services to pay for their imports. The prices of these imports and exports are continually shifting and so is the range of goods traded and their quantities. The real world is made much more complex by the fact that, unlike our simple example, there is no need for the trade itself to balance. There may be lending and borrowing and dealing in assets and liabilities as well.

The overall **conclusion** is that free trade maximises the world's economic welfare and the use of resources and that nothing should interfere with it. Needless to say there is a great deal that does interfere and there are many obstacles and barriers to free trade despite the efforts of the World Trade Organisation (WTO).

17.5 **Arguments About Protectionism**

Countries inevitably try to look after their own national interests because their leaders wish to be re-elected and elections can be influenced by pressure groups who demand protection for their own industry or for the national level of employment in general. There have also been, and no doubt will be again, politicians who have shamelessly appealed to the nationalistic or chauvinistic attitudes latent in their population and introduced strong trade barriers against foreigners. In principle, all of the usual 'economic' arguments in favour of protectionism are refuted by the theory of comparative cost advantage. The main arguments are as follows but there are many subtle variations on these themes.

The maintenance of home employment argument. Cheaper imports can quickly erode the home markets of even a well-established industry and the leaders of the industry almost always ask for some sort of protection against them, usually with the argument that it will prevent unemployment. They may ask for taxes in the form of tariffs either on an *ad valorem* basis where a percentage is added to the import price, or a specific tax that is levied per unit imported. They may ask that this is a temporary measure while the industry restructures itself and modernises in order to match the competition. Governments often agree to this argument because keeping unemployment down helps to keep social security payments and taxes down and keeps more of the electorate happy. The industry may also, or instead, ask for quotas on imports from selected countries. These may be quantity quotas if the goods concerned are homogeneous or value quotas if the product is something like cars which can be small and cheap or large and expensive. The UK has some quotas still on toys from Hong Kong and cars from Japan. These are negotiated agreements but the United Kingdom has the whiphand in the discussions. If granted, the tariff or quota raises a protective shield behind which the home industry can shelter and all too often fester into uncompetitiveness.

The free trade argument against this is that the effect in the longer run is more harmful than beneficial. Admittedly the people employed in the industry benefit by keeping their jobs and the shareholders maintain their dividends but everyone else is denied the benefits of the cheaper imports. Moreover, the foreign exporters may shift the goods they would have sold in the UK to other markets where they will compete even more effectively with the exports from the UK. Thus the industry may be protected at home but lets itself in for greater competition abroad so its overall sales may fall. If the home industry does not export it will not lose in this way.

The protection against low wages and cheap labour argument is closely related to the previous discussion. It concentrates on the reasons for the foreign imports being cheaper and the traditional reason has been the low wages of the workforce in the foreign country. These sorts of arguments were very prominent in the 1920s and 30s during the rapid expansion of Asian textile and other industries into export markets. The popular myth was that the workers were paid a bowl of rice a day. There are similar arguments put forward in the 1990s about cheap Chinese labour and the exploitation of children in developing countries. The problem has changed somewhat in many instances; nowadays it is just as likely to be a combination of the latest technology and low wages that produces cheap foreign exports.

This group of arguments is also dismissed by calling in the aid of the theory of comparative cost advantage. If the cheap foreign goods are excluded it simply prevents the people of a country benefiting from the most efficient allocation of the world's resources and the cheapest available goods. Moreover, if they are excluded, the foreign employer is likely to pay even lower wages in order to maintain competitiveness and profit, and once again the excluded goods will find their way into common export markets and compete more effectively there. The better long-term approach, in terms of global benefit, is to accept the cheap imports and watch as the foreign industry becomes prosperous and begins to pay its workers more as it has to compete for labour and other factors. Unfortunately, the home industry may by then have disappeared as it falls into a downward spiral of falling sales, profits and investment. Society as a whole may have had to bear the social costs of its demise.

There is some comfort from the fact that the home industry rarely disappears completely. It may end up as a rump of its former self but it is more likely to restructure itself and contract into a specialised sector where it concentrates on high value-added products. The mass of unskilled, low paid jobs will, however, have gone and been 'exported' to other countries. Some economists argue that there is, in any case, no hope of competing directly with low wage industries in the developing world by trying to cut home labour costs because there will always be another country ready to step into the shoes of the country presently leading in the international low wages stakes. Japan, Taiwan, Hong Kong, Singapore, and Korea have all reached the point where they find that they cannot compete with the low wage levels of Thailand, India and China. Waiting in the wings are the millions of South America and possibly Africa as well as some of the people of Central and Eastern European countries. It produces ambivalent feelings to learn that Korean companies are setting up assembly plants in South Wales because semi-skilled, mainly female labour, is cheaper in Wales than in modern Korea. The efforts of the International Labour Organisation (ILO) to combat the exploitation of workers and children is unlikely to prove more than marginally successful.

The protection against dumping argument is frequently used to justify protection. Dumping is not as easy to define as might be thought. Technically it is selling a product in export markets for less than the cost of production and transport costs, but it is often interpreted to mean simply selling at a lower price than in the home market. A country that thinks a foreign producer is dumping goods can make a case to the World Trade Organisation (WTO) which is the successor to the General Agreement on Tariffs and Trade (GATT). The snag is that such cases take years to be resolved and by that time the home industry may be largely destroyed. The result is that many countries act first and impose import controls. It is reasonably straightforward to detect imports being sold below the cost of production but not always. For example, there was a glut of amazingly cheap Polish suits in the United Kingdom in the 1970s. If you wished to look like a KGB agent you could do so very cheaply. The same suits in Poland were priced at a much higher level. It became apparent, however, that the Poles at home were paying a high price for the suits, well above the minimum cost of production, in order to allow the suits to be exported at a low price to earn valuable foreign exchange. The exported suits were being sold at a price roughly equal to the minimum average cost of production but were not being 'dumped' in the strict interpretation of the word. They were being cross subsidised by the home buyer. The situation described is fairly typical though not always as extreme. Exported cars are frequently sold at a lower price than cars sold on the home market. The pricing of goods at various levels in different markets is part of the normal business activity of companies.

Some dumping is rather blatant and consists of simply selling surpluses on any market that will take them. This may be hard to separate from the concept of remainder sales. The USA has frequently complained of the European Union steel industry dumping some steel products like this and has imposed retaliatory import controls. The USA keeps quiet about its own tendency to 'subsidise' exports of products such as artificial fibre carpets at very low prices which it achieves by pursuing a cheap oil energy policy (to the detriment of the environment one might add). Critics argue that the rise of Japanese industry in the 1960s and 70s was accompanied by the deliberate cut price selling of certain products in selected market that they wished to penetrate. Korea may have followed the same approach. The products mentioned in this context are motor cycles, cars, ships, pianos and heavy equipment.

The infant industry argument is another common justification for import controls. It can be presented with varying degrees of sophistication, but at its simplest argues that a new industry will eventually thrive unaided, although during its early years needs some protection against foreign competition. This view is put forward to support the tariffs that protect many indigenous industries in developing countries. The embryo companies obviously cannot compete against the foreign multinationals who enjoy great economies of scale despite transport costs. Many countries set up airlines for prestige reasons and use the infant industry argument to defend their subsidies. The main criticism of the argument is that the new industries seem to require protection for ever and never lose their infant status. The theory of comparative cost advantage is invoked to argue that the people of the country protecting an infant industry are being deprived of the benefits of free trade, that is cheaper goods and a greater variety to chose from. There are, however, plenty of infant industry success stories, especially in Japan and Korea, some of whose products are now world export leaders.

The essential defence industry or strategic argument is often put forward to justify import controls or subsidies. Almost all countries have done this and still do. There are variations on the methods of support, a favourite being the restriction of purchasing and procurement to home industry. The United Kingdom has long indulged in this practice although new European Union rules restrict the ability to procure government contracts from home suppliers alone. A subsidiary of this argument relates to agricultural protection which is discussed in Chapter 16. Few countries wish to allow their food supplies to be dependent on imports although not many have gone as far as Japan which banned imports of foreign rice until 1995.

Summary. The theory backs the principle of free trade but most countries have means by which they intervene to help or protect their own people. They may use protection as a bargaining counter or as retaliation but they also use sneaky methods such as administrative controls, technical standards and so on to restrict imports. Japan is a past master at these techniques. Some simply pursue aggressive 'buy home products' campaigns'. The WTO exists to try to remove trade barriers and is discussed in more detail in Chapter 18.

Exercise 4

Is it economically wise for one country to pursue a free trade policy when most of its main competitors do not?

---

18 International Institutions

Aims of the chapter

To explain the role and significance of the:
- International Monetary Fund (IMF);
- International Bank for Reconstruction and Development, (IBRD) (The World Bank);
- International Labour Organisation (ILO);
- Organisation for Economic Co-operation and Development (OECD);
- World Trade Organisation (WTO);
- the role of various trading partnerships such as NAFTA (North American Free Trade Agreement).

18.1 The International Monetary Fund

The IMF was set up in 1945 following the 1944 Bretton Woods Conference that had been convened for the Allies to work out ways of preventing the post-war world collapsing into the economic chaos that had characterised the 1918–39 period. It became a specialised agency of the United Nations in 1947 as did the other institution that was established, the World Bank (International Bank for Reconstruction and Development). The main interwar problems had been the hyperinflation of the early 1920s, the great depression from 1929, the financial collapses of 1931, the end of the gold standard in 1931, the adoption of trade protection and 'beggar my neighbour' policies and high and persistent levels of unemployment policies. The IMF's central role has been to:

- promote exchange rate stability;
- encourage international monetary co-operation;
- help the expansion of world trade;
- help the balanced growth of trade;
- to help members correct balance of payments deficits.

Its emphasis in its early days was on short-term balance of payments difficulties and their solution but since the early 1980s it has been more concerned with helping to resolve the world's debt problem.

Members, of whom there were 179 in 1995, make contributions to the fund and to its lending arrangements. Each member's contribution is based on a quota related to its national income, monetary reserves and some other indicators. The quotas are regularly revised and have been payable in Special Drawing Rights (SDR) since they were introduced in 1969. Prior to that they were paid in gold and convertible currencies, mainly dollars, and some national currency. SDRs are an artificial creation that were conceived to relieve the shortage of international liquidity, mainly gold. Initially they were the equivalent of $US but, after currencies began to float, they were denominated on the basis of a weighted basket of 16 currencies, from 1973 to 1981. After that they have been denominated in relation to the $US, the Deutschmark, the French franc, the Japanese yen, and the £UK. SDRs were first issued in 1970 and again in 1971, 1972, 1979, 1980 and 1981 and have not really lived up to the expectations of their supporters. They play a very small part in international payment settlements in relation to the total of such payments. There are some conditions attached to them being used to settle debts between nations which are a slight hindrance to their use. SDRs are also used by other financial institutions.

The IMF was the main instrument for establishing and running the so-called 'Bretton Woods' system of managing exchange rates as discussed in Chapter 15 on foreign exchange markets. Between 1947 and 1971, or 1973 according to one's definition, the IMF ran the fixed exchange rate system where members determined the par value of their currency and allowed only a one per cent range of fluctuation around the par. The par value was expressed in terms of $US which were, at that time, convertible into gold at the rate fixed by the USA. When the USA suspended the convertibility of the dollar in 1971 and devalued it by 10 per cent there was a change to a system of wider fluctuations in place of the par value. This new method, which lasted only to 1973, was called an 'adjusted par value' system and was almost completely jettisoned because the European countries formed their own system after the USA devalued the dollar again in 1973. The present role of the IMF on exchange rate determination is governed by the Jamaica Agreement of 1976 which accepted the system of floating exchange rates and reduced the role of gold in the international system. It also altered the valuation and range of possible uses of SDRs and gave itself the power to sell the gold reserves of the IMF in order to help developing countries.

If members developed balance of payments deficits under the original fixed parity system, they could borrow from the IMF on a short-term basis and pay a low rate of interest on the loan. If they failed to resolve the problem the member could request a devaluation and a replacing of the par value. Occasionally a country would request a raising of its parity in a revaluation. The IMF was supposed to be consulted before devaluation or revaluation but in 1967 the UK does not appear to have notified the IMF until the very last minute. At present, lending to members is governed by so-called 'tranche policies'. These are complex but, in essence, limit the amount that a member can borrow in terms of multiples of their quota and require the member to accept conditions before the loan is made. The United Kingdom, for example, had to sign a 'Letter of Intent' when it borrowed money from the IMF in 1967 guaranteeing that it would curtail public spending and control inflation. There is a variety of schemes within which the assistance can occur.

The guarantees that have to be given concern the adoption of policies towards the balance of payments, economic growth, the creation of jobs, financial rectitude, and structural reforms. There must also be agreement on any restrictions on trade and on the terms of repayments. It is in this area that the IMF comes under the greatest criticism particularly in the manner in which it requires developing countries to run their economies. The IMF's approach has appeared to be a very strict monetarist one with great emphasis on free market economics. Not everyone thinks that these are suitable for many of the poorest, developing countries. Two of the methods of assistance provided by the IMF are, however, specifically aimed at low income countries and their attempts to raise economic growth rates.

The IMF does not only make loans, it also supervises the exchange rate policies of its members. It does this by having discussions with members either annually or biannually. In doing so it is trying to create some sort of consistency in policies throughout the world. The IMF is inevitably criticised for being dominated by the USA, its largest contributor, which has SDR19 billion deposited, but the US Government has usually taken a very enlightened view of the needs of smaller countries and has been very generous in its aid and loan programmes.

The work of the IMF has sometimes become entwined with the role of the dominant world traders and financiers. The press began calling them by titles such as the Group of 7 (G7), the Group of 10 (G10). It began with the Group of 5, USA, Japan, UK, Germany and France. This expanded to the Group of 7 with the addition of Italy and Canada. It became the Group of 10 with the further addition of Belgium, the Netherlands and Sweden. In 1962 the group of 10, plus Switzerland which is an associate of the IMF, made what were called General Agreements to Borrow under which they agreed to provide up to $6 900 million of their own money if the IMF needed it. Until 1983 only these ten plus Switzerland could use the general agreements to borrow, but after 1984 the right was given to the other members of the IMF and the amount increased to SDR17 billion. This was part of the effort, combined with the World Bank, to ease the growing problem of the debt of developing countries.

18.2 The World Bank

The full title of this institution gives a clue to its functions, that is the International Bank for Reconstruction and Development (IBRD). Like the IMF it was set up as a result of the Bretton Woods Conference and also became a United Nations specialised agency in 1947. Its initial role was to provide and allocate finance for the post-war reconstruction of European countries but it relinquished that role once the Marshall Plan (European Recovery Programme) came into effect in 1948.

Since that date the World Bank has concentrated on providing loans to members to finance specific projects on a long-term basis where private finance has not been forthcoming. Since the 1960s it has dealt mainly with Africa, Latin America and Asia and more recently has concentrated on programmes that will benefit the poorest people in developing nations. The loans are long term, usually for 15 years and do not charge interest for the first five or so years. The loans, which are guaranteed by the recipient country's government, are mainly given to developing countries at more advanced stages of economic growth and not to the very poorest. Before the money is lent there is a strict scrutiny of the project by the World Bank and conditions are laid down to make sure that the money is used properly. If the loan is to a private agency the government of the country must guarantee it. The World Bank also supervises the loan via reports from the borrowers and from its own observers. In the 1980s the World Bank put more emphasis on schemes to provide safe water, waste disposal, family planning guidance, housing and education and on small-scale developments in enterprises and agricultural development. There has, necessarily, been an increased emphasis on ecological and energy conservation matters.

The World Bank obtains its funds from three main sources:

1. Members' contributions which are based on their quotas in the IMF.
2. Borrowing on world capital markets by selling interest-bearing bonds and notes.
3. Money from the repayment of earlier loans and from its profits.

The World Bank works through other bodies as well, for example through the UN Development Programme, for whom it conducts feasibility studies and evaluates projects. It continually provides technical advice for members. The World Bank runs the Economic Development Institute which is a staff college for training officials of the members so that they are more effective in implementing programmes. There are three organisations affiliated to the World Bank to complement its work. These are:

1. The International Finance Corporation (IFC) founded in 1956.
2. The International Development Association (IDA) founded in 1960.
3. The Multilateral Investment Guarantee Agency founded in 1988.

The IDA has the role of providing finance from the rich members for members who do not qualify for loans charged at the market rate of interest. These so-called 'soft loans' are for longer periods than normal and bear no interest although there is a small annual administrative charge. The bank has over 150 members and is based in Washington, USA. The five largest subscribers appoint executive directors and the remainder elect a further 16 to serve two-year terms of office. The 21 executive directors elect a president for five years.

Exercise I

The World Bank has been heavily criticised for the effects of its policy towards developing countries. What is the basis of these criticisms?

18.3 The International Labour Organisation

We tend to hear very little about the International Labour Organisation (ILO) probably because it is something of an irritant to those who choose to ignore the evils of unrestricted free enterprise markets and who view any attempt to protect workers as subversive or communist. The ILO is a relic of the old League of Nations formed in 1919 after the First World War. It was adopted by the UN in 1946 and has a world role in trying to improve labour conditions, to raise living standards and to foster productive employment and social progress. It works by promoting Conventions which its 170-odd member nations may voluntarily ratify. It also supplies guidelines for members to incorporate into their laws and receives complaints from bodies concerned with labour conditions, that is governments, trade unions and employers' organisations.

The main areas covered by the ILO and in which it sets standards are child labour, discrimination, the treatment of disabled workers, equality of treatment, human rights, maternity provision, pensions and the prevention of forced labour. In order to achieve these goals the ILO gives technical assistance to members who have ratified the Conventions and wish to incorporate them in their laws. It also provides technical help with co-operation programmes on things such as training, industrial relations, health and safety, working conditions and social security. The ILO operates from Geneva but has field offices in about 40 countries.

The value of ILO lies in its long-term efforts and persistence in trying to maintain and raise standards for workers throughout the world. It acts as a sort of moral watchdog and its responses to the formal complaints made to it are beneficial in setting criteria for others to meet. No-one pretends that it has solved the appalling evil of the exploitation of child labour or the use of forced, coerced or virtual slave labour or eliminated discrimination but governments have been made aware of the extent of the problems in their country and there is significant moral pressure on them to remedy the situation.

18.4 The Organisation for Economic Co-operation and Development

The OECD was set up by a Convention in late 1960 as a broadening of its predecessor, the Organisation for European Economic Co-operation (OEEC), which had been set up to make the Marshall Plan for European recovery effective. The Convention says that the OECD shall promote policies designed:

- to achieve the highest sustainable economic growth and employment and a rising standard of living in member countries while maintaining financial stability, and thus to contribute to the development of the world economy;
- to contribute to sound economic expansion in member as well as non-member countries in the process of economic development; and
- to contribute to the expansion of world trade on a multilateral, non-discriminatory basis in accordance with international obligations.

The membership in December 1996 consisted of the original members: Austria, Belgium, Canada, Denmark, France, Germany, Greece, Iceland, Ireland, Italy, Luxembourg, the Netherlands, Norway, Portugal, Spain, Sweden, Switzerland, Turkey, the United Kingdom and the USA, together with the following who joined later: Japan 1964, Finland 1969, Australia 1971, New Zealand 1973, Mexico 1994, the Czech Republic 1995 and Poland and South Korea 1996. The accession of Mexico was significant because it was the first developing country to join; this was mainly because it had joined the North American Free Trade Area with the USA and Canada.

The OECD comes into the news twice a year when it publishes the *OECD Economic Outlook* which reviews the economic trends, prospects and policies in the member states. The analysis is independent of national governments and is, therefore, highly regarded as an impartial view. The organisation also publishes *OECD Economic Studies* on a half-yearly basis. These have an international or cross country macroeconomic approach. It also publishes surveys of individual countries, not just for the members but also for countries such as Hungary and Poland, under a Partners in Transition Programme. There is also a wide-ranging series of *Working Papers* which disseminates studies that have been produced by the OECD. There is, in addition, a small number of publications on contemporary issues such as Global Warming or Reforming the Economies of Central and Eastern Europe. Overall the OECD is an institution that spreads knowledge, understanding and effective analysis of economic matters and which provides an outstanding statistical service.

Exercise 2

What are the essential differences between the IMF and the World Bank?

18.5   The World Trade Organisation

The WTO emerged in 1994 from an extended 'round' of negotiations under the General Agreement on Tariffs and Trade (GATT). It will eventually replace the GATT, probably at the end of 1997, but they have had a parallel existence since January 1995. The final replacement of GATT will occur when all the signatories have ratified the 1994 GATT Treaty. The WTO is based in Geneva as is GATT and is run by a General Council under the supervision of a ministerial conference. It has many specialist and subsidiary committees. There is a well-developed system for settling the grievances of members against other members who they allege are breaking the GATT agreements although it is slow and ponderous.

The GATT was formed by a treaty signed by 23 nations at the Geneva Conference in 1947 and came into operation in 1948. By 1994 it had 117 members as well as other countries which took part in some of its arrangements. The main purpose of the agreement was to create rules of conduct for international trade and a forum for discussions on trade liberalisation and the elimination of tariffs. GATT allowed protection of domestic industries only by tariffs and therefore prohibited import quotas and other methods of restricting trade. This is not to say that they disappeared. The agreement aimed at two principles, non-discrimination and reciprocity. These principles referred partly to what is called 'most favoured nation' status (MFN) which means that trading partner countries have to give each other the same trading conditions as those given to the 'most favoured nation'. This prevents discrimination. There are exceptions here for customs unions such as the European Union and other free trade groupings such as EFTA.

Over the years GATT conducted eight 'rounds' of negotiations on reducing trade barriers and extending the operation of the agreement to new types of goods and services. These rounds go by the names of the city in which the talks were launched or, in the case of the sixth round between 1964 and 1967, under the name of President Kennedy of the USA. (In 1962 President Kennedy had passed the US Trade Expansion Act which allowed for a 50 per cent reduction in US tariffs.) The Kennedy Round negotiated reductions in tariffs on groups of goods rather than item by item as had been the case at previous negotiations. The Tokyo Round between 1973 and 1979 looked at non-tariff barriers to trade as well as at the traditional tariffs. The Uruguay Round, which opened and closed in Uruguay but was negotiated in Geneva, lasted with severe hold ups, between 1986 and April 1994. It had been scheduled to finish in 1990. The new 1994 GATT Treaty has had, and will continue to have for some years ahead, a profound effect on world trade in both goods and services. Among other things it will lead to the end of GATT and its substitution by the World Trade Organisation. As stated earlier the WTO and GATT will run in parallel until all the members of GATT have ratified the treaty.

18.6 The Uruguay Round Agreement

The main agreements were to:

- cut industrial tariffs overall by one-third over a number of years;
- cut trade distorting subsidies and tariffs on agricultural products over six years and to convert all import barriers to tariffs;
- eliminate by gradual reduction over time non-tariff obstacles to trade;
- extend the role of the agreement to cover intellectual property in order to protect more effectively the owners of the copyright or trade marks against illegal copying and counterfeiting. This area covers patents, computer software, film, music and video rights as well as the traditional rights of authors;
- extend the scope of the agreement to services, including air transport, and financial services. This requires further talks on telecommunications and financial services which began in 1995 but which have not proved very productive yet;
- institute clearer rules for the conduct of investigations and to have better criteria for defining dumping;
- set up the WTO to replace GATT and to endow it with greater powers to enforce agreements. The WTO has been given the power to impose sanctions on a member who refuses to remove legal obstacles or practices that breach their agreements.

Not everyone is happy with the Uruguay Round Agreement and the new, more powerful WTO and there was some difficulty in passing the required Bill through the US Congress. The area of most bitter dispute was over agricultural products but that was eventually resolved when the European Union reformed the CAP after 1992. There has been some concern, however, that the poorest countries will suffer most from the Agreement because they may end up paying more for imported food now that EU export subsidies are being phased out. World Bank studies in 1995 indicate that, contrary to earlier assertions, the poorest nations will do better out of the new system than the richer industrial countries. Other criticism of the Round is that it fails to take enough account of the environmental problems of the world and the rights of workers. Several organisations representing human rights movements, workers and environmentalists campaigned against the final Agreement.

We should always take with a pinch of salt estimates of the effects of proposed change. It is not that the statisticians wilfully distort their predictions by wearing rose-tinted spectacles but that so many things are interdependent and difficult to quantify. There were estimates, however, by the World Bank and OECD, that partial liberalisation of world trade along the Uruguay Round lines would raise world GNP by about $212 billion at current prices by the year 2002. Most of this, $190 billion, would come from agriculture. It is, of course, going to be very hard to separate the effects of the Uruguay Round from the other consequences of other economic events between now and 2002.

Exercise 3

Why did the Uruguay Round 1986–94 take so long to come to an agreement?

18.7 Other Trading Agreements

The most important agreement is the customs union turned political union which is now called The European Union. This is discussed in detail in Chapter 19. Others have waxed and waned on the world scene and include:

COMECON

This existed between 1949 and 1991. Its initials stood for Council for Mutual Economic Assistance. It was the trading organisation of the Communist block in central and eastern Europe and was dominated by the Soviet Union and was effectively a rouble zone with very tight controls over foreign currency transactions. Cuba, Mongolia and Vietnam also joined while China and North Korea had the status of observers. Each member had its own version of a socialist economic regime but there was free, although strongly regulated, trade between them. The need for unanimous decisions limited the effective of COMECON especially as East Germany and Romania tried to have their own economic policies. The Council was dissolved when the member states had their internal political revolutions after 1990.

EFTA and the EEA

The European Free Trade Association was established in 1960 under the sponsorship of the United Kingdom which did not want to join the European Economic Community which had begun in 1957. Six countries joined the EEC and EFTA consisted of the other Western European countries, the UK, Austria, Denmark, Norway, Portugal, Sweden and Switzerland. Finland became an associate in 1961 and a full member in 1986. Iceland joined in 1970 and Liechtenstein in 1986. Members left at various times to join the EEC or European Union as it became called: Denmark and the UK in 1972, Portugal in 1985 and Austria, Finland and Sweden in 1995. The present membership is, therefore, Iceland, Liechtenstein, Norway and Switzerland.

EFTA is, as its name implies, a free trade area, that is it has abolished trade barriers on non-agricultural goods between its members but does not have common external tariffs (CET) as does a fully fledged customs union.

Since 1972 EFTA has had close relations with the EEC and now with the European Union. In 1972 a bilateral trade agreement was signed with the EEC and in 1989 negotiations began on a proposal to form a closer link between the EC and EFTA. In 1991 they agreed to form the European Economic Area (EEA) to formalise relationships between the two organisations. There were delays in the ratification process and a referendum in Switzerland kept it out of the new EEA, so the EEA did not start officially until January 1994, a year later than intended. The 19 members of the EEA constitute the largest and richest trade grouping in the world. The EEA is a tariff free zone for industrial goods and for some processed agricultural products but there are still special arrangements for steel, fish, food, energy and coal. There will be a gradual removal of restrictions on the freedom to supply services, although there will still be some controls on investment in real estate. The EFTA countries will pay ECU 500 million through a 'EEA Financial Mechanism' into the European Investment Bank to assist the less developed regions of the European Union. Figure 18.1 gives the basic statistics of the EEA.

The North American Free Trade Agreement

NAFTA was formed in 1993 by the USA, Canada and Mexico as an organisation to bring about free trade in all goods and services traded between the three countries. It is notable that it does not include free movement of people as does the European Union and this is because the USA does not want unrestricted movement of people from Mexico and other Central and South America states into its territory. NAFTA grew from the USA/Canada free trade agreement (CUSTA).

The Association of South East Asian Nations

ASEAN was formed in 1967 by Brunei, Indonesia, Malaysia, Philippines, Singapore and Thailand to improve cultural links. In 1993 it modified itself into a more formal organisation called The Asian Free Trade Area (AFTA). It aims to cut tarifffs between members to less than 5 per cent over fifteen years. Vietnam joined in 1995 and Cambodia, Laos and Myanmar (Burma) in 1997.

Mercosur

Mercosur is an acronym of Mercado Comun del Sur or 'Southern Market' and was formed in 1995 by four countries, Argentina, Brazil, Paraguay and

Uruguay. Chile and Bolivia are considered joining. Mercosur is a step forward from previous trading arrangements in South America all of which suffered

The European Economic Area	
Total area	3 662 200 km²**
Population	372 million**
Average number of persons per household	2.6*
Life expectancy at birth	men: 72.9 / women: 79.2*
Foreign residents	15.3 million*
Working population	160.6 million*
GDP	7501 (billion US$)**
Annual exports per inhabitant	3878 (US$)**
Net disposable income	15 141 (EC PPS/inhab.)*
Numer of cars	128.9 million*

* 1990 / ** 1992 [PPS = purchasing power in ECU based on EU price indices]

The economic basis of the EEA   **EFTA–EU trade**

EFTA and the EC are each other's largest trading partners and this provides some of the economic rationale for the Agreement.

The European Economic Area 1990	
Percentage of total EFTA exports to the EU	57.9
Percentage of total EFTA imports from the EU	60.8
Percentage of total EU exports to EFTA	10.3
Percentage of total EU imports from EFTA	9.6

If taken as a whole, the EEA countries send over half of their exports to other EEA countries.

Percentage of exports to other EEA countries 1992

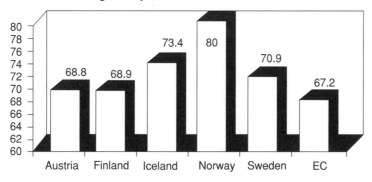

Figure 18.1   Basic statistics of the European Economic Area

from the political rivalries and instabilities of the region. They included the Latin American Free Trade Area (LAFTA) of 1960 that was replaced by LAIA (Latin American Integration Association) in 1980. Mercosur is a customs union with a population of over 200 million. Already about 90 per cent of the trade between members is tariff free and the intention is to make the remainder free by the year 2000. The common external tariff is at an average of 14 per cent. In South America there is also an agreement made in 1969 called the Andean pact. Further north there is CACM or Central American Common Market dating from 1961.

Other regional agreements

There are several organisations in Africa, for example ECOWAS or Economic Community of West African States which was formed in 1975. There is also PTA or the Preferential Trade Area for Eastern and Southern Africa formed in 1987.

Australia and New Zealand formed ANZCERTA in 1983, that is Australia-New Zealand Closer Economic Relations Trade Agreement.

In 1992 some central European countries formed CEFTA, the Central European Free Trade Association. They were previously called the 'Visegrad' countries, Hungary, Poland, the Czech Republic and Slovakia. It began operating in 1993 and Slovenia joined in 1995. A number of other countries were queuing up to join, Romania, Bulgaria, Latvia, Lithuania and Estonia.

The European Union has made several 'Europe Agreements' with countries in central and eastern Europe and these are seen as preliminaries to those countries joining the European Union after 1999 when their economies have converged more with Western Europe. The agreements encourage a swift move to free trade and give financial and technical assistance for restructuring. Much of this is administered through the European Bank for Reconstruction and Development.

There are grounds for hope that these trading agreements, together with the Uruguay Round and the WTO, will help break down trade barriers very quickly over the next decade but there is always a risk that they might turn into self-protection organisations with a consequent detrimental impact on world trade and prosperity.

Exercise 4

Are there any potential threats to world trade posed by the proliferation of regional blocs such as NAFTA, MERCOSUR and ASEAN?

---

19 The European Union

Aims of the chapter

To:

- provide a very brief outline of its development and decision-making process;
- concentrate on post-1992 events and policies;
- examine the following policy areas:
  - the budget and finance,
  - the Common Agricultural Policy (details are in Chapter 16),
  - the Common Fisheries Policy,
  - regional,
  - social,
  - environmental,
  - transport,
  - trade,
  - R&D.

The proposals for European Monetary Union (EMU) and a single currency are dealt with in Chapter 20 on Money. Competition policy is dealt with in Chapter 8.

Note: the chapter will not discuss the political issues such as the attempts at a joint foreign and security policy or the 'home and justice' issues of immigration, crime and policing through Europol. If you wish to study these in depth you should consult the author's *The European Union* (3rd edn 1996, London, Macmillan) which deals with them in depth as well as with the economic issues discussed here.

19.1   An Outline of the EU's Development

The modern origins of the EU stem from the events and aftermath of the two world wars, particularly the second, and from the bitter effects of the interwar recession and the 'beggar my neighbour' policies adopted by most countries.

1951 six countries, Belgium, The Netherlands, Luxembourg (Benelux), France, Italy and West Germany, signed the European Coal and Steel Community Treaty and formed the ECSC which still exists and whose treaty has to be redrawn by 2002.

1957 the same six signed the Treaties of Rome to create (1) The European Economic Community (EEC) and (2) Euratom. The treaties came into operation in January 1958. Since then the European Community and its derivative The European Union have consisted of the three bodies, **1**. ECSC, **2**. EEC (called the European Community since 1987) and **3**. Euratom.

1972 Denmark, Ireland and the United Kingdom acceded with effect from 1 January 1973 ('The Nine').

1979 Greece acceded with effect from January 1981 ('The Ten').

1985 Portugal and Spain acceded with effect from January 1986 ('The Twelve').

1990 the newly unified Germany was incorporated as a single state into the Community on 3 October.

1994 Austria, Finland and Sweden acceded with effect from 1 January 1995 ('The Fifteen').

Other important landmarks are:

1986 The Single European Act (SEA) was signed in February and came into force in July 1987. It established the Single European Market from 1 January 1993.

1991 The European Economic Area (EEA) was formed by an agreement signed in October. It joined the EC to EFTA (minus Switzerland) and came into force on 1 January 1994. Liechtenstein joined late in 1995.

1991 The Maastricht Treaty on European Union was agreed in December and signed in February 1992. After ratification delays it came into force 1 November 1993.

1996 An Intergovernmental Conference proposed reforms to the Maastricht Treaty. It led to the Treaty of Amsterdam, June 1997.

19.2   The EU's Decision-making Process

The European Union has five main institutions: the Commission, the Council, the European Parliament, the European Court of Justice, and the European Court of Auditors. Figure 19.1 shows a simplified outline of decision making and institutional relationships in the EU.

The relationships in the diagram have evolved over time and will change again as the Maastricht Treaty is revised and as new members join. At the moment, decisions are made by the Council, sometimes in conjunction with the European Parliament. The word Council covers several formats for meetings. It can be the heads of government and/or state meeting twice (or more) a year in what is called 'The European Council'. Or it can be the ministers for a particular subject such as agriculture or transport, meeting as 'The Council of Ministers' or it can be 'Council working groups' who are officials from the member states. The term also includes the Committee of Permanent Representatives (COREPER) whose members are senior diplomats and civil servants. They meet weekly and aim to smooth the passage of decisions so that only the final or most contentious issues are decided by their political masters.

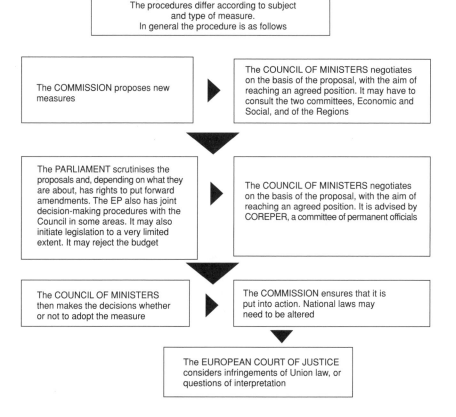

The process of making decisions in the European Union is a complicated one. The procedures differ according to subject and type of measure. In general the procedure is as follows

The COMMISSION proposes new measures

The COUNCIL OF MINISTERS negotiates on the basis of the proposal, with the aim of reaching an agreed position. It may have to consult the two committees, Economic and Social, and of the Regions

The PARLIAMENT scrutinises the proposals and, depending on what they are about, has rights to put forward amendments. The EP also has joint decision-making procedures with the Council in some areas. It may also initiate legislation to a very limited extent. It may reject the budget

The COUNCIL OF MINISTERS negotiates on the basis of the proposal, with the aim of reaching an agreed position. It is advised by COREPER, a committee of permanent officials

The COUNCIL OF MINISTERS then makes the decisions whether or not to adopt the measure

The COMMISSION ensures that it is put into action. National laws may need to be altered

The EUROPEAN COURT OF JUSTICE considers infringements of Union law, or questions of interpretation

Source: Adapted by the author from *Europe Today*, London Offices of the Commission of the European Communities and the European Parliament in cooperation with the Department of Education, November 1994.

Figure 19.1   A simplified version of the European Union's decision-making procedure

Some decisions require the Council and the Commission to consult the Economic and Social Committee or the Committee of the Regions which have an advisory role.

Generally speaking the European Parliament's role is also advisory because it is not a law-making body in the way that other parliaments are, but there are two procedures called *the co-operation procedure* and *the codecision procedure* that give the European Parliament more say and authority.

In practice, the Commission, which is the executive or civil service of the Union, is the most important of the institutions if only because of the continuity of its existence and the sheer quality of its permanent staff. It currently has 20 Commissioners, two from France, Germany, Italy, Spain and the United Kingdom and one from each of the other states. It has about 15 000 staff and is divided into Directorates General (DG). The Commissioners, who are now appointed for five years, are obliged to be completely independent of their national government. The Commission is the main source of initiatives in the EU and the role of President of the Commission is extremely important, as Jacques Delors showed during his period of office to 1994. He was responsible for the Single European Act and for the Treaty on European Union and for the initiatives on European Monetary Union which will lead to a single currency (probably).

When decisions are made they are formulated in different ways. Put simply they are:

- **regulations** which are directly applied and no national measures are needed to implement them;
- **directives** which bind member states on the objectives to be achieved but leave it to the individual government to achieve them through modifying their own laws;
- **decisions** which are binding, in all their aspects, on those they are addressed to, whether individuals, firms or member states;
- recommendations and opinions which are not binding.

Member states vary significantly in the speed and effectiveness with which they implement directives and this difference is a major cause of dissension between members. The process of making European Union laws is long drawn out and full of opportunities for consultation, representation and protest, so there is no real excuse for national governments to talk as if they are being overridden by 'Brussels' which is a short-hand term for the Commission. The United Kingdom Government has developed a reputation for being over-pernickety or over-enthusiastic in interpreting the application of directives and for adopting an excessively bureaucratic approach to changing UK law to comply with them.

A high proportion of European Union legislation requires unanimous agreement in Council but the Single European Act introduced a method of qualified majority voting which was extended by the Maastricht Treaty. There are proposals to extend this majority voting system further but the UK Government of Mr Major strongly opposed the idea. The numbers are modified with each accession of new members but, in 1997, were as follows:

	No. of votes
Germany, France, Italy, UK	10
Spain	8
Belgium, Greece, Netherlands, Portugal	5
Austria, Sweden	4
Ireland, Denmark, Finland	3
Luxembourg	2
Total	87

When a Commission proposal is being considered, at least 62 votes must be in favour. In other cases, the Qualified Majority Vote (QMV) is also 62 but at least 10 states must vote in favour. In 1994 only about 14 per cent of the legislation adopted in the Council was passed by QMV. Whether the proposed legislation is subject to a QMV or not depends on the relevant Act or treaty under which it is discussed and which 'pillar' of the European Union it appears under. Items under the first pillar may or may not be subject to the QMV depending on whether they are designated for that under the Single European Act or the Treaty on Union. Items under the second pillar, that is Common Foreign and Security Policy (CFSP) and under the third pillar, that is Justice and Home Affairs (JHA) are not because they rely on what is called 'intergovernmental cooperation'. See Figure 19.2. for the so-called pillar structure of the EU since the Maastricht Treaty.

When EU laws are passed the Commission puts on its hat as 'Guardian of the Treaties' and makes sure that the laws are implemented according to the original intentions. It may take countries or organisations to the European Court of Justice (ECJ) in order to get a legal determination of an issue. The ECJ is an institution with a growing role and importance and is beginning to have a significant impact on national laws through its interpretations. United Kingdom 'Eurosceptics' want its powers curtailed or even abolished because some of its decisions on social legislation and fishing have upset the UK government. The political argument about the ECJ disguises the more important discussion of the relationship between national laws and EU law. So far the ECJ has established the principle, as did the USA Supreme Court in the relationship of Federal and State laws, that national laws must be subordinate to EU law. Incidentally, you should not confuse, as does the UK media from time to time, the European Court of Justice with the European Court of Human Rights whose decisions also annoy Little Englanders.

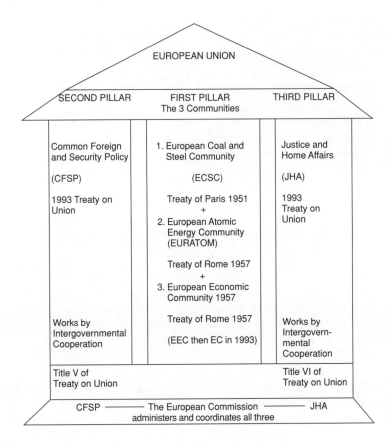

Fig. 19.2   The pillar concept of the European Union

Subsidiarity

There are several interpretations of this term but, essentially, it means that action should be taken in the EU at the most appropriate level, whether it be at community or national or even regional level. The concept is increasingly applied to European Union decision making. The United Kingdom tends to interpret and advocate it as a way of restraining the growth of the Union's federalist tendency but the idea does work both ways. There are, for example, many occasions when joint action by all members is desirable and more effective.

19.3 The Budget and Finance

The annual budget of the EU (technically of the European Community) is fixed by the Council of Ministers and the European Parliament by a process called 'the shuttle' which begins in June when a preliminary draft budget is published. From this preliminary effort the Council draws up a proper draft budget in July which goes to the Parliament for its first reading in October. It returns to the Council which gives it its own second and final reading in November. When the Council has finished with it the budget goes again to the Parliament for its second reading and final adoption, usually in mid-December.

Some of the expenditure allowed for in the budget is designated as *compulsory expenditure* which is defined as such on the basis of whether it results from the European Community Treaty and from acts adopted in accordance with it. The Council has the final say on this type of spending, most of which is agricultural or about half the budget. The Parliament has the final say on most of the remaining expenditure. There is usually some wrangling between the Parliament and the Council over amendments proposed by the Parliament which almost always wants to raise spending.

The annual budget is set up within a framework called *The Financial Perspective* which is a plan incorporating the four years ahead with ceilings laid down for expenditure on the six main categories within the budget. The 1995 budget, for example, included agriculture, structural actions, internal policies, external action, administrative expenditure and reserves. The commitments will lead to actual payments in the future.

Sources of revenue for the Union

The Community has four sources of revenue which together are called 'own resources'. The history of how the EU came eventually to have these own resources is long and tortuous. The four, with 1995 figures, are:

1. **Agricultural and sugar levies**, £1546 million in 1995, are placed on imports of agricultural products from non-members. They raise the price of imports from world price levels to the level of the threshold prices fixed for Community agricultural products.
2. **Customs duties**, £10 187 million in 1995, are received from trade with non-members.
3. **Contributions based on VAT**, £30 973 million in 1995. The calculation of this is complex but each member pays over an amount which is calculated by applying a notional rate of VAT to an identical 'basket' of goods and services in each member state. The amount payable is subject to a restriction or cap based on the size of the member's Gross National Product.

4. **Gross national product (GNP) based contributions**, £17 121 in 1995, which are calculated by taking the same proportion of each member's GNP. This source, which is also called the 'Fourth Resource', is used to make up the difference between the EU's expenditure and the revenue expected from the first three sources, and is subject to an overall own resources ceiling.

The total for 1995 for these four sources of revenue was £59 827 million. The present system of finances was agreed in 1988, 1992 and 1994. Under these there are maximum contributions or own resources ceilings established until 1999:

% of	1993	1994	1995	1996	1997	1998	1999
Community GNP	1.2	1.2	1.21	1.22	1.24	1.26	1.27

The United Kingdom has an 'abatement' on its VAT payments in order to reduce its overall net contribution to the EU budget. Mrs Thatcher spent several years asking for 'our money back' and was partially successful. The abatement is roughly two-thirds of the difference between what the United Kingdom contributes to the EU budget and what it receives from the budget. The repayment is made a year in arrears. The UK's net contribution for 1995 was estimated at £3.1 billion.

The expenditure of the European Union

The expenditure side of the budget is divided into six main categories. The proposed expenditure commitments for 1995 are given with each item:

1. **Agricultural guarantee**, £29 851 million, which is the largest single group and covers the price and market guarantees under the CAP. Great efforts have been made to keep this section under control and to reduce it.

2. **Structural operations**, £20 723 million some of which relates to agricultural restructuring but most applies to regional policy. They are divided into:

   ● Agricultural guidance £2956 million
   ● Regional Development Fund £8338 million
   ● Social Fund £5072 million
   ● Cohesion Fund £1694 million
   ● Other structural operations £2664 million

   This is the next largest area of spending.

3. **Internal policies**, £3980 million, which are a collection of policies such as that for the environment:

- Other agricultural operations £164 million
- Other regional operations £40 million
- Social and educational policies £575 million
- Energy and environment policies £172 million
- Industry and internal market £574 million
- Research and development £2337 million
- Other internal £118 million

4. **External policies**, £3842 million, which cover overseas aid:

- Food aid £667 million
- Aid to Eastern Europe and former Soviet Union £1246 million
- Other development aid £1462 million
- Other external £468 million

5. **Administration**, £3155 million, which is a small percentage of the EU budget in relation to the scale of operations:

- Commission £2039 million
- Parliament £664 million
- Council £242 million
- Court of Justice £91 million
- Court of Auditors £42 million
- Committees, Economic and Social, of the Regions £79 million

6. **Reserves and payments**, £2120

- Monetary reserve £394 million
- Emergency reserve £254 million
- Loan guarantee reserve £254 million
- Repayments £1218 million

The total proposed commitments expenditure for 1995 was £63 670 million which shows a steady increase over previous years: £46 000 million in 1992, £54 000 million in 1993, £56 000 million in 1994.

Figure 19.3 shows how the pattern of EU expenditure has altered in recent years and indicates the degree of success in reducing the dominance of agricultural spending and shifting money to regional and social policy.

The winners and losers

Some countries are net contributors to and some are net beneficiaries from the European Union budget. The largest net contributor over the years has been Germany followed by France, Italy, the Netherlands and the United Kingdom. The Netherlands usually contributes most per head of population. Most of the net contributors see their payments as necessary to raise the overall standard of living in the Union and to create better regional cohesion through the regional and social funds. The United Kingdom has taken a different line and has always protested about being a net contributor. The abatement negotiated by Mrs Thatcher leaves the UK still contributing about £2.5 billion a year net to the Union. Table 19.1 shows contributions/receipts.

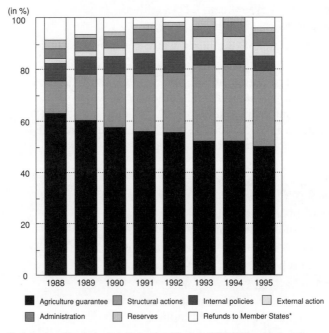

*Includes transitional refunds to Portugal and Spain in 1988–1992 and budgetary compensation to Austria, Finland and Sweden in 1995

Source: *European Community Finances*, HM Treasury, Cm. 2824, London, HMSO, 1995.

Fig. 19.3   Developments in community spending

Exercise 1

There are winners and losers in receipts and contributions to the European Union budget. Why are the losers prepared to be net contributors?

Table 19.1 **Contributions to, and receipts from, the European Community budget,* 1993 (£ billion)**

	Contributions	Receipts[†]
Germany[#]	14.9	5.6
France	9.0	8.2
Italy	8.0	6.8
United Kingdom	5.9	3.5
Spain	4.0	6.5
Netherlands	3.1	2.1
Belgium	1.9	1.9
Denmark	0.9	1.2
Greece	0.8	4.0
Portugal	0.7	2.6
Ireland	0.5	2.3
Luxembourg	0.2	0.3

* From the Court of Auditors Report, 1993

† Excludes £4.9 billion which is mainly development aid and administrative expenditure for the other institutions. The receipts are Community payments to both private and public sectors in member states

As constituted since 3 October 1990

Source: Social Trends 95, London, HMSO, 1995.

19.4   The Common Agricultural Policy

The details of the CAP are given in Chapter 16 so this section is concerned with the place that it has within the economy of the European Union. The CAP was the first of the common policies and by far the most important because it absorbed so much of the revenues of the original EEC and later the Union. It also had a profound effect on the political development of the Union and on the relationships between the members, especially when new states acceded. The CAP has also influenced the foreign relations of the Union particularly with developing countries and with the USA where it has been a persistent source of grievance. The policy has, in addition, had a significant impact on the redistribution of income between member states and within the various regions of the Union. There have been large transfers of income to the areas of marginal farming and important additions to the prosperity of rural areas. Overall the CAP has added to the price of food for the consumer if EU prices are compared with world market prices and the assumption is made that the food could have been bought abroad. If it had been, of course, there would have been high rural unemployment as a consequence and a higher tax burden to pay for that. It is probably better to pay higher prices for food and directly keep farmers and farm workers in jobs. In the longer term the CAP will be an integral part of the European Union's environmental policy and may change radically as agricultural products are used for fuel and when (if?) world demand for agricultural products exceeds supply.

FISHING – PROBLEMS AND SOLUTIONS

1. Bottomless by-catch?

'By-catch' – that portion of the catch that is not specifically being targeted – has recently become one of the most important issues in fishery management. It occurs because fishing vessels are not able to limit their catch to a target species. The fate of by-catch is a function of economic, legal or personal considerations. If there is a market for it, and the price justifies landing the fish, it will indeed be landed; otherwise it is simply discarded at sea. If by-catch is composed of illegal species (undersized fish, for example), they too will be jettisoned. If fishers are allocated a landing quota on a species by species basis, they may choose to cull the more valuable fish and discard what remains (a practice referred to as 'high-grading').

The global volume of by-catch is estimated to be in the neighbourhood of 27 million metric tons, a staggering amount when compared to global landings of about 98 million metric tons. In 'clean' fisheries, where the combination of gear and stock composition result in yields limited to the target species, by-catch can be insignificant. But in others the figures can be startling; in the shrimp fishery, for example, by-catch has been estimated to be in excess of 16 million metric tons.

There is no easy solution to this problem. Some countries require that fishers land all the marine life they harvest. This is a potentially costly undertaking when there is no market for the landed products. It is, furthermore, a difficult measure to monitor without an observer on board every vessel. Other countries place no restrictions on the amount of by-catch and its fate, which can lead to considerable wastage. Advances in the selectivity of gear may also reduce the harvest of non-targeted species. But there is no certainty as to the best way forward: research into this area is costly.

2. Hope for halibut

The commercial Pacific halibut fishery of the western coast of Canada and the United States began in 1888. Until 1990 the fishery was managed by a variety of measures, including limits on the amount of fish that could be harvested on an annual basis, control of the number of licences issued to participants, restrictions on the type of gear used, and closure of fishing areas to protect immature fish. Stock abundance and harvest volumes fluctuated throughout this period, with the fishing season lasting anywhere from the whole year to 65 days (the season ends when the annual quota is harvested).

cont'd

In 1990, because of higher prices for halibut, the fishery – which had very recently provided income and employment on a year round basis – attracted so many vessels that the entire quota was harvested in six days. This 'race to fish' resulted in an over capitalised fleet, loss of gear, increased injuries and market gluts, leading to much lower prices, both for fresh and frozen fish.

Canada therefore introduced individual vessel quotas between 1991 and 1993, whereby boats were allocated a portion of the resource. Because operators were given ownership of a share of the resource, they now had an incentive to harvest it in a manner that maximised the returns on their investment. The result has been an increase in the fishing season from six days to eight months, an increase in fish quality, higher prices, and a reduction in the fleet size. In 1995 the United States introduced individual transferable quotas (ITQs) which can be sold or transferred; the results of the programme are awaited with interest.

The two extracts above are Focus points from an article by William Emerson called Can Private Property Rescue Fisheries? In the *OECD Observer* 205 April/May 1997.

1. Are there any lessons for the UK Government and the Common Fisheries Policy contained in the above extracts?
2. Examine possible methods by which the Common Fisheries Policy could be reformed.

19.5 The Common Fisheries Policy

The CFP is one of the most controversial policies of the Union and is one that is never likely reconcile the national desires for maximum catches and strong fishing fleets with the desperate need to conserve fish stocks. Every time a new member joins the European Union there has to be a renegotiation of the CFP and the allocation of catches and quotas because, outside the narrowly defined coastal territorial waters, the fish stocks are regarded as a joint resource. The accession of Spain, the second largest fishing country in the EU after Denmark, has caused particular anxiety in the UK because Spanish ships were allocated a quota of some species in the Irish Box which impinged on traditional UK waters. Spanish ships were also registered in the United Kingdom in order to take some of the UK quotas and some UK owners sold their quotas to the Spanish. An attempt by the British Government to legislate against the practice was declared illegal by the European Court of Justice. One of the reasons that Norway's referendums have rejected membership of the European Union is the fear of the impact on their fishing industry.

Although the fishing industry employs only 260 000 fishermen in the EU, that is about 0.2 per cent of the working population, it has a much larger impact indirectly by employing four or five times as many on boat building, processing, distribution and so on. It also has a disproportionate importance in less developed regions where there is little alternative employment. Fishing is a term that can be extended to include fish farming, and the collection of shell fish and molluscs.

As territorial waters, or economic zones, have been extended to 200 nautical miles from coasts, the EU fishing fleet has been excluded, except by Treaty and the allocation of quotas for catches, from the old fishing areas off eastern Canada (now almost fished out), Iceland and Norway. The deep-sea fleets now travel further to the warmer waters of the Atlantic, the Indian Ocean and to Africa where agreements have been negotiated with the countries concerned. At the same time there is increasing competition from the former Soviet Union countries and Japan for the dwindling supplies.

The conservation of fishing stocks has led to very controversial decisions, some of which seem to have counterproductive results. The EU has agreed that members should reduce their fleets of certain types of boats by paying the owners to destroy them. The United Kingdom has been rather slow to pursue this policy. At the same time the EU has also had a policy of financing the building of more modern, technologically advanced boats which can stay at sea longer and catch fish more effectively. The attempt to conserve stocks has led to different boats being allocated quotas for specific types of fish. The consequence is that if a boat reaches the quota and then catches more of that species they have to throw the excess back, dead, into the sea. There is a strong temptation to cheat and keep the fish and smuggle it ashore. Another effort to reduce catches is to increase the mesh size of nets and regularly inspect fishing gear and fine defaulters. The most hated method, however, is to limit the number of days in a month that a boat can fish, a regulation that creates all sorts of anomalies and injustices, given the problems of the weather that beset fishing. The final policy is to suspend altogether fishing of certain fish, for example as happened with herring in the North Sea. Governments seem to respond exceptionally slowly to the dire warnings of the conservationists in respect of fish stocks and seem to listen more to their fishing lobbies. Fishermen tend to adapt to shortages of one type of fish by switching to catching other types and by doing so they aggravate the problems. The long-term solution may lie with fish farming but even that is throwing up political problems as Norway is accused of dumping farmed salmon and trout on the European market. Paradoxically there is sometimes a glut of fish, mainly caused by the activities of non-EU boats such as those from Russia, and some fish prices have collapsed at the quay side but not in the shops. An example was in 1995 when such an occurrence resulted in French fishermen staging destructive demonstrations and the EU responded by introducing minimum prices for some species.

It is hard to see how the intractable problems of the CFP can be resolved except, perhaps, by a savage reduction in fishing fleets, draconian imposition of quotas or restrictions on time at sea or a repatriation of fishing policy to each member state and a return to national fishing controls, which is what many nationalists advocate. If this latter policy were adopted it would be a serious breach of the single market concept.

Exercise 2

How could the Common Fisheries Policy be reformed without breaking the idea of a *common* policy and a *common* market?

19.6 Regional Policies

The regional policy of the European Union is closely bound up with other policy areas such as agricultural, social, transport and environmental but the main methods of implementing regional changes are contained in the structural funds. There are four of these and their purpose is to reduce regional disparities and increase economic and social cohesion. The four funds are:

1. The European Regional Development Fund (ERDF);
2. The European Social Fund (ESF);
3. The Guidance Section of the European Agricultural Guarantee and Guidance Fund (EAGGF);
4. The Financial Instrument for Fisheries Guidance (FIFG).

The ESF was set up by the Treaty of Rome and began to operate in 1961. It has been reformed several times, the latest reform being introduced in 1990 when it was modified together with the ERDF and the EAGGF. The FIFG was introduced in 1993 to help struggling fishing communities. These funds have been given **six objectives in the post-1994 framework**:

1. Helping less developed regions that are lagging behind in the sense that they have a GDP per head of less than 75 per cent of the Union average or where there are special reasons for including them in this objective. The regions eligible for aid under this objective are the whole of Ireland, Portugal and Greece, the south and west of Spain, the Mezzogiorno of Italy, the overseas territories of France, one region of Belgium (Hainaut), the Flevoland region of the Netherlands, all the East German Lander, and

in the UK, Merseyside, Northern Ireland and the Highlands and Islands. Three funds supply money, the ERDF, ESF and the EAGGF.

2. The economic conversion of declining industrial areas where the unemployment rate and the rate of industrial employment are higher than average and the rate of industrial employment is falling. The ERDF and the ESF provide money for this objective.

3. Reducing long-term unemployment and facilitating the integration into work of young people and those socially excluded from the labour market. The ESF applies here.

4. Facilitating the adaptation of workers to industrial changes and to changes in production systems through preventative measures against unemployment. The ESF applies here.

5 (a) Promoting rural development and helping to adjust production, processing and market structures in fishing, agricultural and forestry as part of the CAP reform process. The EAGGF and FIFG apply here.
(b) Assisting development and economic diversification in vulnerable rural areas affected by structural decline. Three criteria apply here and two must be satisfied to receive aid. They are a high share of agricultural employment, a low level of agricultural income and a low population density and/or a significant trend towards depopulation. The EAGGF, ESF and ERDF all apply here.

6. Helping regions with a population density of less than 8 inhabitants per square kilometre and meeting certain criteria on GDP. The Arctic and sub-arctic areas of Sweden and Finland will benefit.

Strictly speaking the regional objectives are 1, 2, 5(b) and 6 while the others cover the whole Union.

There has been a major shift of European Union money from agricultural guarantees towards regional policy and the Social Fund since 1985. In the current five-year plan, 1994 to 1999, about 142 billion ECU at 1992 prices will be spent on the structural funds. About 70 per cent of this will go on Objective 1. By 1999 about 36 per cent of expenditure commitments will be on structural funds. Over the years since the accession of Greece, Spain and Portugal there have been special Integrated Mediterranean Programmes to spend extra money in those countries and in southern Italy.

When the Maastricht Treaty on European Union was agreed it included provision for additional funds to be channelled to four members in order to bring them more in line with the other members so that they would be readier for the introduction of a single currency or would suffer less if they did not immediately join. This provision is called the Cohesion Fund.

The Cohesion Fund

The fund is aimed at the four countries mentioned above and they will receive, between 1993 and 1999, ECU 15.1 billion or ECU 16.223 billion in adjusted prices. The aim is to shift resources from the 'rich' north to the 'poorer' south and to remove the excessive economic and social differences between those areas. Each country must have an approved plan to meet the monetary union criteria and will receive these funds only after the projects, costing above ECU 10 million, are vetted by the European Investment bank. The money will only be given for environment and transport projects or for the trans-European Networks schemes. Spain will receive between 52 and 58 per cent of the total, Portugal 16 to 20, Ireland 7 to 10 and Greece 16 to 20 per cent.

The principles behind the allocation of structural funds

In 1989 a set of four principles was established to determine what action should be taken through the structural funds. They were modified in 1993 to produce the following:

1. Action must concentrate on the six objectives.
2. There must be partnership and close cooperation between the Commission and the local, regional and national bodies concerned.
3. The principle of additionality must apply, that is the member state must not reduce its own spending but should use the structural funds to supplement it.
4. There should be proper programming through partnership over a specified number of years.

The United Kingdom has sometimes come into conflict with the Commission because it has not always observed the third principle of additionality and has tried to substitute Union funds for United Kingdom money. There are a large number of programmes applied by the European Union itself and about 9 per cent of the structural funds are spent on those. They have names that are often acronyms such as ADAPT, RECHAR, KONVER and RESIDER that all deal with adjustment to industrial change. These programmes are occasionally upgraded and modified and may be renamed. The remaining 90 per cent of the money goes on national programmes agreed with the Commission and local and regional authorities. In the United Kingdom we shall see the impact of such programmes on Merseyside over the next five years since it now qualifies under Objective 1 for very large sums of money.

The regional policies have been the subject of intense study over the years and of much criticism. It is hard to isolate the effects of the regional policy from the concurrent macroeconomic climate. The conclusions are usually that the creation of new jobs costs a huge sum per job (akin to the £1 million per job of the UK Eurofighter programme announced in September 1996) or that the firms who relocate would have been forced by market pressures to relocate anyway. The bureaucracy of the system is also accused of absorbing too high a percentage of the funds and there are frequent allegations of corruption. There is no doubt, however, that many remote rural areas and declining industrial regions have benefited from the regional funds.

Exercise 3

How could the effectiveness of European Union regional policies be measured?

19.7 Social Policy

The European Union's social policy stems from the original Coal and Steel Community and the need to create jobs to replace those being phased out by technological change and the consequent plant and pit closures. Part of the approach was to promote geographical and vocational mobility. The ESCS pursued these policies to find new work for large numbers of unemployed coal miners. The ESF followed similar lines after 1961 and its role has expanded since into areas such as equal pay for equal work and health and safety at work. Progress was very slow in the 1980s because decisions in Council had to be unanimous unless the proposal could be 'smuggled' through under the Single Market rules of health and safety at work. The United Kingdom was usually the only member to vote against social legislation and in 1989 refused to sign the Social Charter or, to give it its proper title, The Charter of Fundamental Rights of Workers. As a result the other members incorporated a new Social Chapter into the Maastricht Treaty on Union and the UK opted out of it. In practice the other members, now 14, took the Social Chapter into a protocol of the Treaty and ran it using qualified majority voting without the UK having the right to participate in the voting. They removed this anomaly when the Amsterdam Treaty was agreed in June 1997 and the new UK Government signed the Social Chapter. Some social policy matters require unanimity because they still come under the Treaty of Rome and later treaties.

The areas covered by social policy include:

- Free movement of workers;
- Social security for migrant workers;
- Promotion of workers' geographical and occupational mobility;
- Equal pay for men and women;

- Safety at work;
- Health protection in the nuclear industry;
- Working hours and holidays;
- Vocational retraining;
- Handicapped persons, elderly persons;
- Youth unemployment;
- Full and better employment – co-ordinating national policies;
- Redeployment of workers in declining industries;
- Leisure of workers, housing;
- Accident prevention and health protection;
- Integration of migrant workers;
- Help for the neediest – homeless, old, vagrants, one-parent families;
- Industrial democracy, workers' participation;
- Rights of working women.

The United Kingdom Government up to May 1997 had trouble accepting the elements concerning industrial democracy and workers' participation and resolutely opposed the Works Councils that have been accepted by the other members under the Social Chapter protocol. In practice many large British multinational companies that operate in other member states introduced Works Councils despite the objections of the Government. The UK also opposed the Social Charter and Chapter on the grounds that it would commit the UK to introducing a national minimum wage, but there is nothing specifically in the Chapter on this subject so it was something of a bogeyman. The Labour Government elected in May 1997 committed itself to signing the Social Chapter and to introducing some sort of national minimum wage. There has been a very confused and not very illuminating debate about the potential effects of a minimum wage and other social legislation. The Conservative Party argues that the general effect of the Social Chapter is to raise the costs of employing people and thus it contributes to reducing the international competitiveness of the European economy and 'destroys jobs'. Their opponents say that that is not the case and that a minimum wage at certain levels would not raise unemployment and that workers' morale and productivity would rise.

One area in which the European social policies have had a considerable impact on members' economies is in establishing the rights of women to equal pay and conditions and much of the progress in the UK is attributable to rulings of the European Court. The Court has also had a great impact on the rights of part-time workers and on pensions. In all of these changes the UK has been, to say the least, reluctant and often very obstructive until the Court ruling has been made. The accession of Sweden and Finland has shifted the balance of the Union further towards social intervention and the raising of standards of social provision. In September 1996 a conflict developed between the UK and the EU over the Working Hours Directive which limits the working week to 48 hours and its extension to hitherto excluded occupations such as hospital medical staff and transport workers.

Exercise 4

Why did the United Kingdom not sign the original Social Charter and then negotiate an opt out from the Social Chapter?

19.8   Environmental Policy

The European Union has over the years evolved a reasonably coherent policy on the environment through the medium of action plans. The Maastricht Treaty on Union raised environmental action to the status of a policy and replaced unanimity by the QMV in Council on most environmental affairs. The latest action plan, the fifth, is called *Towards Sustainability* and runs from 1992 to 2000. The previous plans were subjected to regular reviews and one such review in 1988 had a big impact because it led to an increased emphasis on energy efficiency through programmes such as *Thermie* which provides money for spreading technological information on energy efficiency, renewable energy sources, clean coal technologies, and oil and gas prospecting and development. The programme is now in its second phase, 1995 to 1998. In December 1991, 45 nations signed the European Energy Charter which aims at exploiting Eastern European energy sources more efficiently after EU nations have installed modern, environmentally cleaner power stations and equipment. A new version of this was signed in 1994 and there are now 48 nations involved including the USA, Japan, Canada and Australia. One important aim is to modernise the energy industries of the former Soviet bloc, many of whose plants were appallingly harmful to the environment. Part of this policy includes shutting down the remaining reactors at Chernobyl which were still being used in late 1996.

The early Community policies began as early as 1972 and were intensified after the Single European Act of 1986 which established legal requirements in the environmental sphere. By 1993 over 200 directives had been approved on improving air and water quality, controlling waste disposal and monitoring industrial risk. Many of the measures were aimed at the protection of nature, that is flora and fauna. In general the approach to improving quality was based on prevention via the setting of standards and the prosecution of defaulters. This approach underwent a major change after 1992 when the *Towards Sustainability* action programme was adopted. This now concentrates on prevention and on the control and management of growth. The new action plan incorporates environmental considerations into the basic agricultural, social, regional, transport and economic policies. In many instances, for example the building of new major roads, an environmental impact study has to be made. Another example of the application of the policy is the Cohesion

Fund mentioned above under Regional Policy, which incorporates the environmental dimension into part of the allocation of funds. The new programme is in accordance with the 'Earth Summit' held in Rio de Janeiro in 1992, that is the UN Conference on the Environment and Development which adopted the Agenda 21 aimed at achieving international co-operation in the twenty-first century.

In 1989 the Commission issued detailed proposals for the setting up of a **European Environmental Agency (EEA)** and it came into being in late 1993. It is based in Copenhagen and the hope is that it will become an international agency and not just a European one. Its job is to provide reliable data, objectivity and the information needed to monitor the application of European laws on the environment. The EEA is the culmination of a programme called CORINE that lasted from 1985 to 1990 which collected information on an experimental basis. In pursuit of the aim of making sure the public is properly informed on environmental matters, the EEA is setting up a European Information and Observation Network. To begin with it will concentrate on air quality and atmospheric emissions, water quality, resources and pollutants, the state of the soil, flora, fauna, and use and natural resources, waste management, noise emissions, chemical substances harmful to the environment and coastal protection. The Commission says it will 'give special consideration to transfrontier, pluri-national and global phenomena and the socio-economic dimension'.

There has been a long-running debate in the European Union on the question of how to 'make the polluter pay'. Several ingenious schemes have been suggested but all rely eventually on the state creating a very effective inspection, supervision and monitoring service whose cost, if it worked properly, would fall on the taxpayer rather than the polluter because polluters would stop their bad practices and cease paying 'fines'. Another solution to some environmental problems associated with excessive or inefficient use of fossil fuels is the 'carbon tax'. This proposed tax has been at the heart of the Commission's attempts to reduce carbon dioxide emissions and it began as a serious and potentially effective measure. It turned out to be much too bold for the average politician, however, and the final measure is a much watered down one. The United Kingdom led the opposition to the detail of the scheme although it accepted the principle. The plan required the other major users of carbon fuels, the USA and Japan, to follow suit and would have put $10 on a barrel of oil in AD 2000 after an initial $3 in 1993. Other taxes would have been cut to compensate for the rise in the price of industrial coal of about 60 per cent, of petrol by 6 per cent, of domestic heating oil by 17 per cent and electricity by 14 per cent. The final decision, made in December 1994, was a feeble compromise. The Environment Council decided that the Commission should draw up a framework for members to apply a carbon tax in their own country if they wished. Sweden, which already had a version of such a tax, has been left looking very lonely because the other members are frightened to follow suit in case they anger their motoring lobby. They seem to believe that the public would not understand that other taxes would fall to compensate for the rise in carbon fuel taxes.

One of the main purposes of the proposed tax was to help the European Union meet its self-imposed targets for maintaining carbon dioxide emissions at 1990 levels in the year 2000. (The UK set itself the year 2005 as a target date.) Only Germany and Belgium are anywhere near reaching their targets and the Commission has recommended more efforts to curb vehicle emissions and improve energy efficiency. There is great opposition to these suggestions from vested interests on the grounds that costs of production will increase. The poorer member states who cannot afford the energy price rises or the technological improvements necessary to achieve the suggested improvements in efficiency also object.

In December 1995 the Commission adopted what it calls a 'landmark' White Paper entitled 'An Energy Policy for the European Union'. The paper follows on from a Green Paper issued for consultation in January 1995. The White Paper says that the future energy policy will be based on three pillars, **overall competitiveness**, **security of energy supply** and **environmental protection**. It says that the policy will be implemented mainly by means of integration of the market, management of the external dependency, promotion of sustainable development and support of energy research and technology. There will be a programme for the Commission to follow accompanied by a two-yearly updating process. A basic assumption of the policy is that European energy use will increase. The integration of the market will take place on the foundation of a liberalised internal market for gas and electricity backed by 'an efficient monitoring tool in order to analyse and understand market developments and to ensure that structural and technical changes are not in conflict with energy policy goals'. In other words there will be a regulated market because monitoring on its own would be ineffective. As far as possible the intention is to make policy decisions neutral in their effect on the energy market and investment.

Another main thrust of the policy is to 'internalise external costs as far as possible'. This means that producers and presumably users of energy will, in the medium term, be subjected to fiscal tax measures that make them bear the external costs of the pollution and other environmental disbenefits that they create. The environmental aspect would also be approached through the promotion of renewable energy sources and support for energy efficient technologies. All of these aims will be the subject of a five-year Work Programme so we can expect a stream of Commission initiatives.

In September 1996 Eurostat published a report on the rising demand for energy and land in the context of 'sustainable mobility'. It revealed that transport now consumes more energy than industry in the European Union and that road transport is responsible for over 80 per cent of the transport consumption. The price of fuel in relation to disposable income has fallen significantly between 1980 and 1994. In 1994 the proportion of disposable EU income per head needed to buy 1000 litres of a weighted mixture of fuel was

4.9 per cent compared with 7.7 per cent in 1980. Needless to say, consumption has increased. The other gloomy fact is that emissions of carbon dioxide and particulates are continuing to rise despite the tougher controls on exhausts and higher fuel standards. Moreover, emissions of sulphur dioxide continue to rise in almost all member states. The report also says that the fall in lead emissions has been caused mainly by regulation rather than by the price differential in favour of lead-free petrol. It casts doubt on the benefits of the price differential in favour of diesel fuel which has stimulated the rise in demand for diesel vehicles because of the growth in output of particulates and oxides of sulphur that has resulted.

Exercise 5

Why is there a need for a European Union environmental policy?

19.9 Transport Policy

Strictly speaking, there is not yet, in late 1996, a European Union transport policy. There is an attempt to achieve one and there are many EU aids to transport investment and development but the full policy will probably take until AD 2000 to emerge. In 1992 the Commission published a White Paper 'The Future Development of the Common Transport Policy'. The Maastricht Treaty marks the beginning of a Common Transport Policy (CTP) because it set the goal of further development of the single market together with sustainable growth which respected the environment and improved safety and quality in the infrastructure of the Union. The Treaty incorporated decisions for the finance of trans-European Networks or TENS as they came to be called, the first 14 programmes of which have already begun.

The White Paper was followed by a debate and the Commission then published its CTP Action programme for the years 1995–2000 which will contain a number of initiatives. The three objectives of the programme are:

1. improving the quality of transport systems in terms of competitiveness, safety and environmental impact;
2. improving the functioning of the single market to promote efficiency and choice;
3. broadening the external dimension by improving links with third world countries.

Improving the quality will be achieved under the fourth R&D framework programme by setting up four task forces to target and co-ordinate R&D. The task forces will work on 'The Aircraft of the Future', 'The Car of the Future', 'The Trains and Railways of the Future' and 'Transport Intermodality of the Future'. The TENS programmes will also serve this objective. Their aim is to develop integrated, efficient, and interconnected transport systems across the Union and into neighbouring countries. This requires the co-ordination of investment, the promotion of partnership between public and private bodies and the convergence of technical standards. In the first 14 TENS and four other large traffic management projects, over 80 per cent of the finance will be spent on rail-related developments.

The Commission is also trying to improve the public service passenger networks and published a Green Paper called 'The Citizens' Network' in November 1995. This was the first time the Commission had issued a policy document on public transport and its central theme is the provision of attractive alternatives to the private car. Another future publication is likely to be on 'intermodal freight transport', that is transport by different modes, say road to canal or rail to road. The Commission published a short document in July 1995 on the development of short distance sea shipping which it concludes is underutilised in some countries. In August 1996 a White Paper was published on 'A New Strategy to Save Europe's Railways from Extinction' which contains a proposal for rail 'freeways' for freight, where freight would be given priority and administrative delays minimised at frontiers. The problem of different technical standards such as loading gauges would be tackled so that large containers and full height road vehicles could be transported by rail easily throughout the Union.

The initiatives on safety will include ones on roll-on, roll-off ferries and a single, fully unified Air Traffic Management System for Europe. In July 1995 the Commission published a review of methods of overcoming air traffic congestion. Some nations have proved very dilatory or even obstructive in previous attempts to create a unified air traffic control system in Europe. Even the United Kingdom has been less than co-operative.

The Single Market objective will be based on the liberalisation of markets. Road freight has already gone a long way in that direction and there will be proposals on coach transport and a third package for air transport. Rail transport and inland water transport are also due for further liberalisation. In this context the Commission intends to hold a debate on transport pricing, so that member states can no longer give their own transport companies unfavourable advantages by charging differently for infrastructure use or allowing extensive cross subsidisation of services. In December 1995 a Green Paper called 'Towards Fair and Efficient Pricing in Transport' was published to start this debate.

The external dimension objective will include policy initiatives on further development of bilateral links for road, rail and air with Central and Eastern European states. It will also include working via the World Trade Organisation to negotiate maritime liberalisation. There will be another effort to reach an air transport agreement with the USA.

19.10 R&D Policy

There is considerable variation among the members in their spending on R&D. There are differences between their sectors, industries and, within their own borders, between regions. Data on R&D can be hard to collect or collate because of problems of definition but in 1991 about 2 million people were engaged in R&D in the EU, about 1.33 per cent of the labour force. There were great variations in expenditure as a percentage of GDP as Table 19.2 shows. All members except Germany and Sweden spent a lower percentage of their GDP on R&D than the USA (2.65 per cent) and Japan (2.87 per cent) in 1991. The UK spent 2.1 per cent.

Table 19.2   R&D Input by Member State in 1991

	R&D expenditure as % of GDP	R&D personnel as % of labour force
Belgium	1.67	1.46
Denmark	1.69	1.43
Germany	2.65	1.87
Greece	0.46	0.57
Spain	0.87	0.77
France	2.42	1.77
Ireland	1.04	0.88
Italy	1.24	0.75
Netherlands	1.92	1.39
Austria	1.74	1.05
Portugal	0.56	0.34
Finland	2.07	1.69
Sweden	2.86	1.72
United Kingdom	12.13	1.30

Source: Eurostat, *Europe in Figures*, 4th edn, Luxembourg Office for Official Publications of the European Communities, 1995.

Most of the funding by governments in the EU goes on three types of research:

1. research carried out by universities;
2. specific technological objectives such as exploration and exploitation of the earth and space and into energy use and distribution;
3. defence.

The European Union began to apply its own policy in the mid-1980s although there had previously been programmes for energy research. It created framework programmes and specific programmes within them. The Single European Act was a stimulus for these and the Maastricht Treaty continued them, but put the job of proposing programmes in the hands of the Commission and their adoption in the joint hands of the Parliament and Council of Ministers. Currently the fourth framework programme (1995– 98) is spending about ECU 3.1 billion a year which is a huge jump from the paltry ECU 280 million in 1980. The framework targets key sectors rather than spreading the money thinly over many areas. Table 19.3 shows how the priorities have changed over the years. The latest programme adds two new areas, transport policy and socioeconomic. Within this, the specific programmes are on three areas, technology assessment, education and social exclusion.

Table 19.3   Changes in R&D priorities between framework programmes

Field of research	Framework programmes			
	1984–87	1987–91	1990–94	1994–98
Information and communications technology	25	42	38	28
Industrial and materials technology	11	16	15	16
Environment	7	6	9	9
Life sciences and technologies	5	7	10	13
Energy	50	22	16	18
Transport	0	0	0	2
Socioeconomic research	0	0	0	1
International cooperation	0	2	2	4
Dissemination and exploitation of results	0	1	1	3
Human capital and mobility	2	4	9	6
Total %	100	100	100	100
Total amount (million ECU)	3 750	5 396	6 600	12 300

Source: Eurostat, *Europe in Figures,* 4th edn, Luxembourg Office for Official Publications of the European Communities, 1995.

There are three main ways of implementing the specific programmes:

1. The most important is on a shared cost basis where the Commission generally provides 50 per cent of the total costs for industrial partners and 100 per cent of the marginal costs for other partners. The rest of the

money comes from the members of the private consortia. The partnership is usually universities, public research centres and large firms and small and medium-sized enterprises (SMEs), often across several countries.

2. The Community has its own Joint Research Centre (JRC) which has eight institutions in six countries. In 1993 it had a budget of ECU 272 million and employed 2000 staff. It also acted as host for over 200 visiting scientists.

3. The Union operates through concerted actions and networks. In the former, the EU provides the money only for co-ordination which may also include the costs of meetings, travel and publications. In the networks, the EU begins with the aim of co-ordination but may provide money for research by members of the network.

The three methods of financing programmes referred to above are the most significant but there are special methods for projects such as the Joint European Torus (JET) used for fusion research and for money spent on training and dissemination of information such as CORDIS which is a database, as well as fellowships. In addition there are many other schemes conducted in co-operation with other countries, such as CERN for nuclear research. They spawn acronyms such as EMBL, ESO, ESA, ESRF, ILL, and COST. Some of these have subsidiary programmes which also have acronym titles or clever plays on words such as Eureka. ESA is the European Space Agency which is responsible for the Ariane satellite launching system. COST is 'European cooperation in the field of science and technical research' which has 25 members for whom the EU provides the Secretariat services. You can award yourself a prize if you can find out what the others mean!

Most economists would agree that R&D is a vital component for economic growth and many would argue that, other things being equal, more is better. The European Union still has some way to go to catch up with the USA and Japan and, for example, Singapore, in the percentage spent in relation to GDP. But economists will also want to look at the detail of the figures and see how the money is spent, because the indications are that expenditure on defence R&D is less valuable in contributing to economic growth than other types. There is also some conflict about state intervention in R&D. Some argue that it is absolutely essential because of the huge sums of money involved and because of the co-ordination needed. In the case of the EU there is also the need to make R&D multinational. Others argue that the state (or Commission) is too bureaucratic and ponderous and too insensitive to market forces and may waste money on spotting 'winners' that turn out to be duff runners. This argument tends to ignore the many ignoble failures of private enterprise R&D.

Note: The proposed single currency is dealt with in Chapter 20.

20 Money

Aims of the chapter

To explain:
- what money is;
- what its functions are;
- the process of the creation of credit;
- the role of banks;
- the role of the monetary authorities;
- the proposed single European currency.

20.1 What is Money?

Money can be defined as anything that by law or custom is accepted in exchange for goods and services. Some definitions also add 'acceptable in settlement of debts'. In most countries, in normal circumstances, it is the law which says what is legal tender and that is abided by. In abnormal circumstances such as defeat in war, civil war or hyperinflation the official money is replaced by barter, that is swapping, or by foreign money of greater stability such as the US dollar or Deutschmark as in the Ukraine in 1992–96. In some closed institutions such as prisons tobacco may be the customary money. The defining quality is, therefore, acceptability in exchange.

There have been, and are, many items used as money. The most common have been metals, originally iron, bronze and then silver and later gold. Notes became a substitute for coinage on a wide scale in late seventeenth-century Britain but only achieved proper status when the Bank of England's note issuing function was given formal recognition. In 1844 it was given the right to issue a limited number of notes called the fiduciary issue. All of the present United Kingdom note issue is 'fiduciary' now because its backing is government gilt-edged securities. In other words, the value of our notes is backed or guaranteed by the Bank of England holding an equivalent amount of government promises to pay. Until 1914 it was possible to take a Bank of England note into a bank and ask for cash, that is gold, in exchange for it. Nowadays the issue of notes is regarded purely as creating enough liquidity or lubrication for the economy to function. If a high street bank requires more notes and coin it simply withdraws some from its account at the Bank of England.

Money replaced barter for most purposes but swapping is still prevalent in developing countries and as part of the 'black economy' of countries such as Britain. Barter is sometimes still used in international trade especially with oil which is swapped for other items. The great problem of barter is what is called 'the lack of a double coincidence of wants'. For example, I may have a cow that I wish to dispose of and want some sheep instead. It may prove impossible to find anyone who has sheep and wants a cow. They may not like my cow even if they do want one. I may end up trading my cow for wheat, then for goats before I can find someone who wants goats for sheep. Barter is impossible on any extensive scale where there is division of labour and specialised production.

Bank money. Most people think of money in terms of notes and coin but, in a modern society, most money is in the form of bank deposits of various types. We treat our bank deposits as money because other people will usually accept our cheques or credit transfers such as 'switch' payments as if they are money. This type of money, which is often called bank money, is entries in ledgers or electronic records. In June 1996 the amount of Bank of England notes in circulation was £20 483 million; the amount of sterling deposits was £698 628 million. The latter figure includes mainly sight and time deposits in UK banks and overseas, together with deposits in TESSAs and certificates of deposit (CDs). We behave as if we have nearly £700 billion of money yet there is only £20 billion of notes in circulation. The process of creation of bank deposits is explained later in this chapter.

Exercise I

How does the economy keep running when there are only about £20 billion of notes and coin in circulation?

The functions of money

The functions of money are usually divided into four:

1. **As a medium of exchange**. We exchange our goods and services through the medium of money. We work for money and change the money into what we want. The money removes us from the restraints of barter.
2. **As a unit of account**. This means that we can do our sums in money and keep accounts in money values. A pound comes to represent a wide range of possible combinations of goods and services but we normally treat it as an abstract entitlement. A small child may see a pound coin as four

chocolate bars but adults usually see it as a contribution towards any number of unspecified payments.

3. **As a store of value**. People accept money as a payment because they expect that it will retain its value and be usable in the future for further purchases. If it loses this quality, as in periods of hyperinflation, people resort to using other methods of payment or foreign money.

4. **As a standard for deferred payments**. This is not a completely essential function of money but it is convenient to be able to use it to decide future payments for such things as loans. It becomes a sort of unit of account for the future.

20.2   The Process of Creation of Bank Deposits

Most textbooks explain this process with a detailed multi-page, numerical example based on first one bank and second on a number of banks. The example is based on several assumptions about the percentage of assets that are kept as cash. Let us try a variation on this approach. If I ask my bank for a loan of say £1000 they will say, after making arrangements for me to repay it with interest, 'that's OK, you can now draw that amount from your account'. I might go hotfoot to the counter or the cash machine and withdraw the whole amount in notes but I am much more likely to write cheques or use my switch card. In other words I, like most people, use very little cash for significant, large transactions. Think about the nature of my deal with the bank. They have said that they have put into my account an amount that I can immediately use, that is it is a very liquid deposit or promise by them to pay. In return I have promised to repay over a longer period of time, say two years. My promise to repay is much less liquid than the bank's promise to pay.

There are two elements in the above transaction that enable the banking sector to 'create deposits'. The first is the fact that only a small percentage of financial transactions is conducted with cash. The second is that a bank's deposit or promise to pay is regarded by everyone as the equivalent of cash. The combination of the two means that, if a bank receives a cash deposit, it is able within the bounds of prudent banking, to lend a multiple of that cash deposit. Before 1914, for example, UK banks kept a ratio of cash to total assets of about $12\frac{1}{2}$ per cent; after 1914 it fell to 10 per cent; in the 1960s it fell to 8 per cent where it remained until a different set of definitions and ratios was adopted. The 8 per cent ratio meant that if banks received an additional £100 deposit in cash they could lend or purchase assets such as bills and bonds up to $12\frac{1}{2}$ times that amount, that is they could in theory end up with £1250.

Their balance sheet might appear as follows:

Liabilities:	Current and deposit accounts of customers	£1250;
Assets:	Cash	£100
	Money at call	75
	Bills	200
	Investments in gilt-edged securities	250
	Advances (loans) to customers	625
	TOTAL	£1250

The above example is intended to illustrate the process and not as an up-to-date representation of present practice which is discussed below. In the above example the banks kept 8 per cent of their assets in cash and 30 per cent in the top three forms, that is as liquid assets, cash, money at call which is lent to the money or discount market, and bills which are very liquid. Their loans to customers are 50 per cent of the total, a figure which fluctuated and still does depending on market circumstances. The practicalities of the system meant that they did not use this $12^1/_2$ times multiplier to the full.

Exercise 2

What sort of 'practicalities of the system' mean that banks cannot use their theoretical credit multiplier to the full?

To return to the element of liquidity, if all the bank's depositors turned up at this bank and wanted to withdraw their deposits in cash the bank would fail but it would, over a period of years, be able to pay its depositors because it would sell off its assets and collect the repayments on loans. After twenty years it might have repaid everything. Banks that fail and do not eventually pay their depositors have usually been corruptly managed. Banking is, therefore, an exercise in the manipulation of liquid assets so that the bank can make profits for its shareholders and provide security to its depositors. At the centre of this balancing act is liquidity because the most secure asset is cash but cash earns no profit. Advances to customers are generally the most profitable but are also the most risky or insecure. The bank holds its assets in such a form and in such proportions as to enable their liquidity to balance out security and profit maximisation. Gilt-edged securities, for example, have varying terms to maturity and are completely secure because they are issued by the government, so banks hold a mixture of them according to their yields and date of maturity (liquidity).

Some countries still insist on their banks maintaining minimum cash and liquidity ratios, a system which may be called 'monetary base control' but since 1981 the United Kingdom has abandoned that in favour of minimalist requirements and supervision by the Bank of England. Banks in the United Kingdom (banks are defined by the Bank of England as explained in Chapter 13) are required to deposit 0.35 per cent of their liabilities at the Bank of England (October 1995). This money, which is non-interest bearing, is effectively used to finance the Bank of England's running costs in respect of the accounts that all banks are obliged to keep at the Bank. In June 1996 these compulsory 'cash ratio deposits' amounted to £1763 million; the banks also kept an additional £286 million there voluntarily.

The banks find it very convenient to keep accounts at the Bank of England because it enables them to make payments to each other at the end of each day when the various cheques and credit transfers between them are cleared. Another benefit is the ease with which they can obtain cash if there is an increased seasonal demand, as at Christmas. At this point it is worth mentioning that an individual bank is unable to adopt a much more expansionist lending policy than the others because it would suffer a continuous drain on its resources each day at the clearing. If, for example, Barclays Bank were to attempt to expand its lending by aggressive interest rate cuts or advertising and were successful, more cheques and credit transfers from Barclays would be generated and it would find itself having to transfer money to the other banks at the end of each day. It might maintain this for a short time but not for very long.

Table 20.1   Bank assets. Banks in the UK: Balance sheet of reporting institutions

Sterling Assets	£ million	Sterling Liabilities	£ million
Cash	6 372	Notes outstanding	2 387
Bills & Market Loans	216 542	Sight deposits	248 600
Claims under sale and		Time deposits	350 457
repurchase agreements	27 768	Liabilities under	
Advances	450 581	sale and repurchase	
Miscellaneous £ assets	28 687	agreements	19 896
		Certificates of Deposit	79 674
		Miscellaneous	99 316
A. Total Sterling Assets	805 687	Total Sterling Liabilities	800 330
B. Other Currency Assets	1 077 905	Other Currency liabilites	1 083 262
Total Assets A+B	1 883 592	Total Liabilites	1 883 592

Source: Adapted from Bank of England *Quarterly Bulletin* August 1996, **36**(3), London, 1996.

The manner in which banks hold their assets has become more varied over recent years as can be seen from Table 20.1 which shows a simplified version of the situation in June 1996 relating to what are called 'reporting institutions', that is a list of banks and building societies that fit certain criteria as 'banks'. Notable additions are certificates of deposit (CDs) which originated in the USA in the early 1960s and came to the UK as sterling CDs in 1968. They are documents issued by banks to confirm that someone has deposited money with them. The CD is, in effect, a promise by the bank receiving the deposit to repay it at a future date which is given. The CD becomes a highly liquid, negotiable instrument, that is it can be sold and traded on the money markets. CDs have a maturity date of between three months and five years. The Bank of England has also begun separating out claims and liabilities 'under sale and repurchase agreements' as a heading in the statistics.

20.3 The Role of the Banks

Banks are:

- Financial intermediaries who accept deposits which they will repay on demand or at short notice.
- Purchasers of assets such as bills and bonds.
- Lenders of money in the form of overdrafts and loans.
- Institutions that operate payment systems between themselves, for example the London Clearing House which settles inter-bank debts and payments arising from cheques and credit transfers.
- Providers of specialist services to commerce and industry, for example advice and tax and investment services. Some provide, through subsidiaries, direct investment.
- Providers, usually through subsidiary companies, of mortgages, investment and unit trusts and insurance of property and possessions as well as life assurance.
- Operators in the foreign exchange markets and/or provide foreign currency services.
- Suppliers of many services such as legal and trustee services and storage of valuables.

The above list is by its very nature generalised and there is considerable difference between the role and functioning of a high street branch bank such as Lloyds operating at the retail level and merchant banks or a foreign banks which tend to operate at what is called a wholesale level. The high street bank does also operate as a wholesale bank from its City location. Some banks, for example the Hong Kong and Shanghai Bank (HKSB), which owns the Midland Bank in the UK, are global organisations; Barclays Bank is also global in its world wide operations but is centred in the United Kingdom.

There have been important changes in the functioning of banks in recent years, particularly since 1980; one example is the growth of bank activity in the mortgage market and another is the development of telephone banking. The entry of the traditional building society into the world of banking is also important and some are now classified as banks. The role and classification of banks is discussed in more detail in Chapter 13 in the context of capital markets.

20.4 The Role of the Bank of England

The Bank of England was founded in 1694 as a commercial bank with private shareholders. Its original capital was the beginning of the national debt. Over the following years the national debt, operating through the issue of gilt-edged securities (bonds), became a very significant repository for the savings of the growing middle classes and joined investment in land as the normal, secure refuge for accumulated wealth. The bank also issued notes against its deposits and these are the ancestors of the present note issue. The process of banknote issue and use was speeded up in the late eighteenth century because of the suspension of payments in gold during the wars against France. After the 1844 Bank Charter Act the Bank of England gradually assumed the right of sole issue of notes and coin in England and Wales. Other banks forfeited the right when they merged and the last independent issuer disappeared in 1921. Banks in Scotland still issue their own notes. The Act established the fiduciary issue of notes, that is notes not backed by the Bank's holdings of gold. Technically any increase in the note issue requires the approval of Parliament but this is a mere formality and the current issue is not backed by gold but, as stated earlier, by the Bank holding government stock. After 1844 the Bank of England, although still privately owned, developed the functions of a *central bank* but it was not until 1946 that it was taken into public ownership, that is nationalised, by the Bank of England Act. Since then there has been a shift of emphasis in its functions as a result of several acts, particularly the Banking Acts of 1979 and 1987 and the Building Society Act of 1986. The so-called 'Big Bang' changes in the City in 1986 have affected the volumes of stock dealings and the settlements systems. Other important influences have been the failure of various 'fringe' banks in 1973 and the Johnson Matthey problems of 1984 which contributed to big changes in the Bank of England's supervisory role.

The functions of the Bank of England

These can be classified in several ways, for example as follows:

It is the sole issuer of notes and coin. This function has already been discussed.

It acts as the banker for the banks. This is a useful role because it facilitates the payments system between banks and helps the supervisory role of the Bank.

It is the Government's bank. The Bank holds the various accounts of the government that are incorporated into the Consolidated Fund Account into which all receipts are put and from which all government payments are made.

It supervises the banking system. The Bank has a major role in maintaining a stable financial system. The 1979 Act gave it the power to authorise and supervise all deposit taking institutions, although building societies are supervised by a Commission. The 1987 Act strengthened these powers. The main aim is to protect depositors and there is a Deposit Protection Fund which pays limited compensation if an authorised bank fails. The supervision simply reduces risk of failure, it does not prevent it. The Bank takes part in international efforts to increase the stability of the world banking system. There are several other types of institutions other than banks that the Bank helps to supervise. These are brokers and market makers in the wholesale financial markets such as in gilts, bullion and foreign exchange. The function and effectiveness of the Bank of England in supervising the financial system is under constant criticism but more attacks are directed at the Securities and Investments Board (SIB) which covers the general areas of investment and the various self-regulatory bodies. The new Labour government announced in May 1997 that the supervisory system is to be reformed.

It launches the 'lifeboat' or does sometimes. If a bank nears collapse the Bank of England may try to get some of the other bodies in the City to contribute towards a rescue package that will stave off an escalation of a collapse of confidence. It last attempted this in 1996 during the Barings collapse but was criticised for being half-hearted about it. In the past the Bank of England was always called '*the lender of the last resort*' which was a specialised function whereby the Bank would lend money to a discount house, or buy bills from it, when it could find no other source of loans. The lending might be at the usual discount rate or at a penal rate. The function has been very important historically, especially in certain money market crises, but is not normally relevant to day-to-day operations.

It manages the National Debt. This is, to a large extent, simply a massive clerical operation that keeps track of ownership of stock and arranges for the quarterly payment of interest. There are over one million stock accounts and over half a million transfers each year. The Bank operates a Central Gilts Office that makes automatic gilt transfers via computer between the major participants in the market. There are, however, very important ramifications of the management because the debt is continually churning over, that is old debt is being redeemed and new debt issued. The volumes involved and the timing of the issues and reissues are of great potential importance because of their impact on interest rates and on perceptions of government monetary policy. Each year the Bank has to issue enough stock to replace maturing stocks and to fund the Public Sector Borrowing Requirement (PSBR). Occasionally the sums are such that debt can be repaid so that there is Public Sector Debt Repayment as in the late 1980s. The market watches the terms of each new offer and the degree of oversubscription with keen interest and reacts in a manner that can have consequences for bond and share prices.

It operates the Exchange Equalisation Account in the context of the foreign exchange markets. The account was set up in 1931 to hold and manage the United Kingdom's reserves of gold and currencies for the purpose of intervention, if appropriate and desired, in the markets. The EEA has been very important at certain times when the pound was kept within certain foreign exchange rate limits, for example between 1946 and 1972 and between 1990 and 1992 when it was a member of the European Union's Exchange Rate Mechanism (ERM). If the United Kingdom joins the proposed single European currency, the euro, the account will be subsumed into the new European Central Bank that will be set up on the foundations of the European Monetary Institute.

It manages monetary policy with and on behalf of the government. Monetary policy covers a wide and ever changing range of activities but the present system is probably the simplest for decades. All manner of methods of control have been jettisoned or put into cold storage and we are left with one straightforward objective and one main weapon, interest rate changes. The objective of monetary policy in mid-1997 is:

An explicit inflation target of 2.5 per cent on the RPIX measure. Until the June 1996 Mansion House speech of the Chancellor it was expressed as 2.5 per cent within bands of between 1 and 4 per cent. In June 1997 the new Labour Chancellor announced a target of 2.5 per cent and placed an obligation on the Bank of England to write a letter of explanation if the level rose to 3.5 or fell to 1.5 per cent.

In pursuit of this end the Bank of England monitors ranges for what are called narrow money and broad money but it no longer tries to modify them directly; it simply observes them as indicators of what is likely to happen to the future rate of inflation. The terms are explained in Figure 20.1

- **M0** Notes and coin in circulation + bankers' balances (banks' non-statutory deposits with the Bank of England)

- **M4** Notes and coin held by the private sector;
    - + Private sector £ non-interest-bearing sight bank deposits;
    - + Private sector £ interest-bearing sight and time bank deposits;
    - + Private sector holdings of £ certificates of deposit;
    - + Private sector holdings of building society shares and deposits and £ certificates of deposit;
    - − Building society holdings of bank deposits and bank certificates of deposit and notes and coin.

Source: Bank of England Fact Sheet *Monetary Policy in the United Kingdom,* October 1995.

Figure 20.1   Official monetary aggregates

The jettisoned and suspended methods of monetary control include:

- Direct controls such as telling banks who they could lend to and where;
- Special deposits which forced banks to put a proportion of their eligible liabilities at the Bank of England, that is they were 'frozen', although an interest rate was paid on them equal to the bill rate.
- Supplementary deposits, or 'the corset' which forced banks to deposit a proportion of any excess growth of their eligible liabilities at the Bank of England, that is they were 'frozen'.
- Monetary targets. There were a number of targets set, especially in the early and mid-1980s but, since the United Kingdom left the ERM in 1992, they have been abandoned because they required active manipulation of the money supply. As the 1980s progressed the targets became more and more indicators rather than requirements. In 1987 formal broad money targets were abandoned in favour of the Medium Term Financial Strategy (MTFS) although a target was retained for narrow money. An early example of a monetary target is the 1979 £M3 (sterling M3) which the government wanted to be kept within the range of growth of 7–11 per cent. It turned out to be over 16 per cent. Other targets were M0, M1 and M4, all of which are different measures of the money supply (see Figure 20.1).

Exercise 3

There has been a long debate on whether the Bank of England should be more independent of control by the Treasury and Chancellor. What would be the benefit arising from a more independent central bank?

20.5 The Bank of England and Interest Rates

The starting point for explaining the Bank of England's ability to fix and influence short-term money market interest rates is the fact that all the banks and the government keep money in accounts at the Bank. There is, therefore a flow of money, for example tax revenues and government expenditure, between them. The Bank is able to keep a close eye on the balance between these flows of money and can act each day to smooth out any inequalities. If more money flows from the banks than in the other direction the banks find that their holdings of liquid assets fall, that is their accounts at the Bank decline. If more money flows from the government account into the banks' accounts than in the other direction there will be an increase in the banks' holdings of liquid assets. Normally, there is an imbalance that gives the Bank of England an edge because there is usually an excess of payments to the government account so there tends to be a shortage of cash in the markets each day. This gives the Bank a certain leverage because it acts to remove the shortage but can, in so doing, raise the rate of interest at which it is prepared to lend or supply the required liquid assets. If there is a surplus of funds it may choose to reduce the rate of interest.

The second point in explanation is the fact that the Bank of England does not work directly on all the banks, all 450 odd of them, but operates through the discount market and the discount houses as intermediaries. (See Chapter 13, 'Money Markets'.) The Bank keeps in close touch with the discount market during each day providing figures and details on the state of surplus or shortage in the market. When it has decided to raise interest rates it will only help to relieve the shortage at a discount rate (interest rate) that is higher than before. It does this by asking for the higher rate when it lends cash directly to the discount houses or provides money by buying bills from them. The moment that the discount houses have to pay a raised rate of interest the rest of the financial markets begin to adjust their own rates upwards. All or almost all of the banks raise their base rates and eventually the building societies will follow suit. There may some differences between the initial rise in rate to the discount market and the final change in long-term lenders' rates.

If the Bank of England wishes to cut interest rates it will lower the rate at which it supplies money to the discount market, and again the rest of the market follows.

Decisions to change the rate of interest were taken until June 1997 after discussions between the Bank of England and the Chancellor of the Exchequer, usually after their monthly meeting but according to need if there was a crisis. The minutes of their meeting were published a month after the actual meeting and threw some light on the Bank's thinking about inflationary pressures compared with the Treasury's. The impression is given that the monetary authorities are masters in their own house but, of course, interest rates have an important international dimension and the United Kingdom can rarely stand for long against the international tide of rates. In May 1997 the new Labour Chancellor announced that, in future, a 9-member Monetary Policy Committee of the Bank of England would take decisions at monthly meetings by majority vote on the level of interest to be set. It did this for the first time in June 1997 when it raised rates by 0.25 per cent. The Committee's decisions are announced immediately. The minutes and details of the voting are published within six weeks of the meeting. This change enhances the independence of the United Kingdom central Bank and increases the credibility of the government's anti-inflation stance.

The effects of interest rate changes

Changes affect the cost of borrowing as opposed to saving and the benefits of spending today rather than in the future. A rise will tend to reduce present spending on consumption and investment depending on how interest rate elastic they are and on how high existing rates are.

Alterations in interest rates also affect the incomes of both borrowers and creditors. Many people and businesses are both at the same time. Rising rates tend to persuade people to reduce their borrowing. Companies are usually net borrowers but the high interest rates of the period 1990–94 caused them to reduce their borrowing massively.

Any change in interest rates affects the value of some assets, particularly real estate, housing and stocks and shares. These movements influence people's borrowing and expenditure.

The above three influences will affect demand for both consumer and investment goods and modify company profits. The assumption is that there will also be an effect on wage pressures.

Interest rate changes have an impact on the foreign exchange rate because higher rates tend, other things being equal, to attract more funds into the United Kingdom and this causes the pound to appreciate. If interest rates fall, funds tend to flow out and the pound depreciates. Such movements in the value of the pound affect the price of imports and exports and, eventually, consumer expenditure and the price of imported materials and components. The official view is that a rising pound will increase export prices and reduce import prices and thereby increase competitive pressures which will bolster the downward pressure on inflation resulting from weakened demand. Conversely, a falling pound will cut export prices and raise import prices and tend to boost the inflation rate because of stronger demand. In practice, much depends on what the levels of change are and the time lags involved in the economy's adjustment. Above all the effects depend on what is happening in the rest of the world; other things do not stay the same.

Exercise 4

How much impact do interest rate changes have and how long do they take to become effective?

20.6 The Proposed Single European Currency

European monetary union was first formally proposed in the Werner report of 1970 but EMU as it came to be known, that is Economic and Monetary Union, was delayed by the upheavals of the foreign exchange market in the 1970s. The European Economic Community as it was then called adopted a monetary system instead. That is described in Chapter 15 in the context of the Exchange Rate Mechanism and the ECU, European Currency Unit.

In 1986 the Single European Act (SEA) included economic and monetary union as a formal objective and imposed on member states the obligation to work towards a convergence of domestic policies in order to achieve it.

In 1989 the then President of the Commission, Jacques Delors, headed a committee of mainly central bankers and produced a very important document that is known as 'The Delors Committee Report'. It was accepted by the Madrid summit in June 1989. The report defined monetary union as 'a currency area in which policies are managed jointly with a view to obtaining common macroeconomic objectives' and it laid down three conditions for achieving this. These three points have remained central to the proposal ever since. They are:

1. Total and irreversible convertibility of currencies;
2. The complete liberalisation of capital markets;
3. The irrevocable locking of exchange rate parities.

The report argued that once these had been achieved national currencies would become substitutes and interest rates would equalise in each country and then it would be possible to have a single currency. It added that a single currency would be desirable but not a necessity. The report went on to argue the need for a common monetary policy with a new institution to implement it, that is a federal European System of Central Banks with a high degree of independence and whose functions would gradually replace most of those of national central banks such as the Bank of England.

The report included a list of the four basic elements required for economic growth:

1. a single market with free movement of goods, services, persons and capital;
2. a competition policy and measures to strengthen markets;
3. common policies aimed at structural change and regional development;
4. co-ordination of macroeconomic policies including binding rules for budgetary policies. This last was very controversial.

Finally, the committee suggested a timetable for EMU, in three stages. Stage 1 actually began in July 1990 and was completed when Stage 2 began on 1 January 1994. Stage 1, which is now history, concentrated on completing the single market by the end of 1992 and on increased monetary co-operation. Some members moved into the narrow bands of the ERM and the United Kingdom joined until 1992.

Stages 2 and 3 were incorporated into the Maastricht Treaty on European Union which came into force in November 1993. The treaty was the result of the work of two Intergovernmental Conferences, one on political union and the other on EMU. The United Kingdom signed the treaty but opted out of a part of it called the Social Chapter and out of commitment to Stage 3 of EMU.

Maastricht and EMU

The Treaty fixed the timetable for EMU and established certain convergence criteria for members to meet if they were to join the single currency. It gave alternative dates for Stage 3 to begin, that is the adoption of a single currency by qualifying members, but the European Council has since decided on 1 January 1999 as the start date for Stage 3.

Stage 2. The Treaty decided that Stage 2 should begin on 1 January 1994 and it did. During this stage a European Monetary Institute (EMI) has been set up based in Frankfurt and its job is to prepare the way for Stage 3 and to oversee the continuation of the ERM and the financial support system that goes with it (see Chapter 15). It also issues and supervises the ECU. When Stage 3 begins it will be transformed into the European Central Bank (ECB) as part of the European System of Central Banks (ESCB). The EMI has members from each state on its board. It is working on a uniform system of measuring various economic statistics such as inflation rates and government debt as well as other indicators. It will be very influential in deciding which members have satisfied the convergence criteria for membership of the single currency.

The convergence criteria set by the Treaty are as follows:

1. *Inflation.* The country must have had an inflation rate which is no more than 1.5 per cent higher than that of the three members of the ERM with the lowest rates in the previous year.
2. *Interest rates.* The country must have had long-term interest rates (long bond rates) no more than 2 per cent higher than the lowest three members in the previous year.
3. *Exchange rate.* The country must have been in the normal band of the ERM for two years and not to have realigned (devalued) in that time.
4. *Budget deficit.* The country's budget deficit must not exceed 3 per cent of its Gross Domestic Product.
5. *Debt stock.* The country's outstanding stock of public debt must be less than 60 per cent of GDP.

In order to help some members meet these criteria the Treaty set up a Cohesion Fund for Spain, Portugal, Greece and Ireland. There is continuing speculation about which members will meet the criteria by early 1998 when decisions will be made on who is fit to proceed to Stage 3. There was concern that the criteria may be fudged or that members will 'fiddle' their budgets in order to reduce debt percentages. Some became very concerned that efforts to meet the criteria were leading to cuts in public expenditure and to unemployment, especially in France and Germany.

The United Kingdom's opt out from Stage 3 is contained in a protocol to the Treaty. It says the UK 'shall not be obliged or committed to move to the third stage of economic and monetary union without a separate decision to do so by its government and parliament'. Denmark has a similar option.

Recent events

In May 1995 the Commission published a Green Paper for consultation called *On Introducing a Single Currency*. In June 1995 it was a adopted by the European Council. It contained a timetable for the introduction of the single currency. In December 1995 the Madrid summit adopted the name euro for the proposed currency and confirmed 1 January 1999 as the starting date for Stage 3. These agreements followed the publication in November 1995 of the EMI's proposals called *The Changeover to the Single Currency*. The four critical benchmark dates that follow are taken from the EMI proposals that were adopted:

- **As soon as possible in 1998**, the Council will confirm which member states fulfil the necessary conditions to participate in the euro area. As early as possible thereafter the ECB and ESCB will be established and will prepare for their operation at the start of Stage 3 of EMU.
- **On 1 January 1999, the starting date of Stage 3**, the exchange rates between the currencies of participating member states will be replaced by irrevocably locked conversion rates. The national currencies and the euro will become different expressions of what is economically the same currency. National bank notes will remain the only notes with legal tender status until the introduction of euro bank notes. The ESCB will start conducting its single monetary policy in the euro.
- **By 1 January 2002 at the latest**, the ESCB will put euro bank notes into circulation and start exchanging national bank notes and coins against them.
- **At the latest, six months after the first day of introduction of the euro bank notes and coins**, the changeover to the single currency will have been completed for all operations and all agents. National notes and coin will lose their legal tender status and the euro will be the only currency to have the status of legal tender within the euro area.

The adoption of this timetable places a great burden on potential members to adapt their payments systems, initially between financial institutions, to the euro. Then businesses will have to prepare for conversion. The intention is for the business and commercial worlds to have adopted the euro into their systems, presumably on a parallel currency basis, before the issue of notes and coin.

The benefits of a single currency

These are summarised in the Green Paper on *Introducing the Single Currency* of May 1995 and are also in the Delors Committee Report:

1. A more efficient single market without disruptions to trade and investment caused by exchange rate fluctuations;
2. A stimulation to growth and employment arising from greater price stability and the integration of financial markets. Borrowing conditions should be improved;
3. The removal of currency conversion costs between member currencies;
4. Greater international stability following from the new currency's inevitable role as a world reserve currency equal to the dollar and yen;
5. Collective management by a single monetary authority will enhance the sovereignty of the Union beyond that possible for a national currency. The single currency will be one of the strongest and best in the world.

The report *One Market, One Money* of 1990 which put a statistical framework to the Delors Report argued that a single currency would stimulate economic growth, cut transactions costs, stimulate production and raise employment. The statistics need to be treated with caution but are as follows:

- Costs of exchanging currencies could be cut by between ECU 13 and ECU 19 billion, depending on who joins;
- Production would increase by up to 5 per cent of the GDP of the 12 members because of greater business confidence;
- The convergence of inflation rates would stimulate real output growth by 0.3 per cent of the 12's GDP;
- There would be great savings because the need for each country to keep monetary reserves in relation to other members' currencies would be reduced. It estimated the savings would be about ECU 160 billion.

A subsequent report from the Commission in October 1995, called *European Strategy for Employment*, argued that if the Maastricht criteria were adhered to and if investment led growth of between 3 and 3.5 per cent per year were maintained there would be a fall in unemployment from 10.7 to 5 per cent by the year 2000.

Criticisms of the proposed single currency

Some reject the idea out of hand because it would, they say, undermine national sovereignty over monetary policy and be a step towards a federal European Union. Anyone who believes this extreme point of view cannot be convinced by economic reasoning but may use the anti arguments to bolster their position.

- The efforts to achieve convergence are said to be too costly and are blamed for the rise in European unemployment and for cuts in public spending. In other words, the alleged gains from a single currency are not worth the costs of achieving it.
- The convergence criteria do not include all the items they should, particularly the criterion of unemployment. Efforts have been made under the leadership of Sweden to address this criticism and the Treaty of Amsterdam contains a commitment to employment.
- Some economists argue that the European Union or even sections of it are not what is called an 'optimum currency area' (OCA) and that there is insufficient convergence of economies to enable a single currency to work without massive shocks in terms of economic adjustment. That is, they say there will be serious problems of unemployment and migration of workers, capital and investment. Some fear an adverse effect on the 'strong economies' and others fear detrimental effects on the regions that already have high unemployment.
- Many of the arguments against are encapsulated in the phrase 'fear of the unknown and unpredictable'.

Exercise 5

How would you personally benefit or suffer from the replacement of the pound by the euro after 1999?

Note. It may be said that many economists were predicting the complete collapse of the EMU project, especially after the ERM problems of August 1993 when the bands were widened to plus or minus 15 per cent. Since then, however, Chancellor Kohl of Germany and President Chirac of France have reaffirmed their determination to press ahead to the agreed timetable and more member states have begun to take action to meet the criteria. It looks, at this stage in mid-1997, that several members will meet the criteria, and more if they are liberally interpreted, and be ready to start in 1999. The United Kingdom is still keeping its options open but, even with the change of government in 1997, it looks increasingly unlikely that the United Kingdom will be among the first group of nations to form the euro zone. This likelihood has given rise to an anxious debate about the relationship between the 'ins' and the 'outs' of the euro zone. In late 1996 a 'stability pact' was agreed to regulate this relationship (see Box). It includes proposals for a revamped ERM for those who are not in the euro zone, a system of penalties for those who are in but who allow their performance as measured against the convergence criteria to fall behind and a code by which to conduct relations between the euro members and the non-euro members (see Box). The City of London is becoming increasingly concerned about the consequences for its pre-eminence if the United Kingdom is not in the first group of members of the single currency.

THE STABILITY AND GROWTH PACT FOR THE EURO

1. ECOFIN will be able to impose severe fines on a member state if its budget deficit exceeds the ratio of 3 per cent of GDP.

2. Fines will be automatic if the growth of GDP is positive or has declined by less than 0.75 per cent.

3. If GDP has declined by between 0.75 and 2 per cent the excessive deficit member is liable to sanctions but it may claim that the excess was beyond its control and thereby avoid fines.

4. If the deficit results from 'severe recession' there will be no fine. Severe recession is defined as an annual decline of 2 per cent or more of GDP.

5. Decisions on action will be made by ECOFIN minus the alleged transgressors on a Qualified Majority Vote basis, that is 62 votes out of 87.

- What are the implications for an independent national budgetary policy of this pact to which the UK government has agreed?
- Why are exceptions to be made for deficits resulting from severe recessions?

---

21 Public Finance

Aims of the chapter

To explain:

- government objectives;
- changes in emphasis in recent years;
- the broad outline of government expenditure;
- the broad outline of the taxation system;
- the system of local government finance.

21.1 Government Objectives

From 1945 to 1979 it was the consensus that government budgetary objectives could be summarised, with occasional variations of order or content, as follows:

- **Full employment** which was defined along the lines laid down by Lord Beveridge in his report 'Full Employment in a Free Society' as a level of unemployment of about 3 per cent of the insured workforce. In the light of interwar experience unemployment was regarded as the great evil which had the potential to destroy the social order and open the way for extremism such as fascism or communism. The objective of full employment was the first aim of all governments until 1979.

- **Stable price levels** became the next most important objective of most governments because excessive inflation was seen as the enemy of full employment and inimical to the achievement of the other objectives listed below. Ironically, most governments were pretty keen on low levels of inflation and did not want to get rid of it completely because having low levels tended to stimulate economic growth and make the job of taxing and spending easier to manage. This objective of controlling inflation did not become dominant until after 1979. It should be noted that there was no real agreement on the desirable level of inflation but most governments became uncomfortable if it rose above 3 per cent (until the rapid price rises of the 1970s) but the usual criterion was its level in comparison with the UK's major competitor nations. If UK inflation was higher it usually boded ill for the foreign exchange rate and for the balance of payments.

- **A healthy balance of overseas payments** was another important objective especially in the period 1945 to 1972 when the pound operated under a fixed exchange rate system. If the balance of payments moved too far into deficit the government felt moved to correct the situation to avoid devaluation of the pound by raising taxation and/or cutting government expenditure. The United Kingdom did not have the problem of excessive surpluses so it did not have to take corrective measures and cut taxes and/or raise government spending. (In the early 1980s when oil revenues and capital inflows raised the pound to very high values the government might have reacted by cutting taxes and/or raising government spending but, by then, it was adopting a 'let the market sort it out' philosophy and was obsessed by the need to cut the level of inflation.) There was little agreement in the period before 1979 as to what constituted an unhealthy balance of payments because the current account movement was often at variance with that of the capital account and the overall equilibrium or disequilibrium was disputable. The practical test was what the foreign exchange markets felt about the balance of payments.

- **Economic growth** became an important objective as politicians realised that if it could be achieved at a high enough level they could have their cake and eat it, that is they could promise to increase spending on all sorts of popular programmes and not have to increase taxation to pay for them. Along the way the people would end up possessing all manner of consumer durable goods and enjoy a multitude of life-enhancing services. Raising the standard of living of the mass of low earners through economic growth was also the answer to the persistent problem of how to improve the distribution of income without removing some of the income of the rich and above-average income groups by confiscatory taxation in order to give it to the 'poor'. If the national 'cake' could be made bigger the increase could go mainly to the lower income groups without taking anything from the higher income groups. It is no surprise that economic growth was and still is a popular idea with politicians. It was only later that others began to ask 'what are the costs of growth?' or 'what is the content of the growth?' or 'what is the impact on the developing countries?'. It has still not occurred to some that not every family can expect to enjoy a car per head, a detached house and a second home in the country, a boat, a caravan, a TV in every room, holidays abroad three times a year and so on without an impossible strain being placed on the infrastructure of roads and services and resources in general, in the United Kingdom at least. It may be possible in more spacious countries. It is necessary to ask the question 'what is the growth for?' Asking it may lead to the concept of *sustainable growth.* In the background of the quest for higher rates of economic growth is international rivalry. The best performing economies have been the ones with the highest rates of growth although measures of growth need to be treated with great caution.

- **A regional balance of economic development** has also been an important aim of governments until 1979 and there has been an ever-changing mixture of subsidies, grants, incentives and prohibitions in order to keep the less affluent areas of the United Kingdom closer to the levels of income of the better off regions. Areas have been designated and redesignated as being in need of extra assistance from central government or from the European Union. Some of these attempts to influence the location of industry have been relatively successful; others have had little impact; most policies were changed frequently in their detail and application; the mobility of the workforce was affected or rather its immobility was often reinforced. In general the policies have been a messy series of expedients driven by electoral pressures and expediency rather than a coherent philosophy. Since 1979 the government has, in practice, thrown in the towel in the face of the largely self-inflicted decline of manufacturing industry, and left things to the usual 'market forces'. It had no real option, given its policies, because the level of unemployment rose rapidly even in the previously prosperous areas of the South and Midlands. The pre-1979 regional and location of industry policies have been superseded by a mixture of European Union aid and a vague policy of stimulating small and medium-sized enterprises mainly by exhortation and a fairly superficial attempt at 'deregulation'.

- **The redistribution of income** has been a policy of post-war governments but it is one that has usually been left in the background as a series of pious hopes or has been brought out as an additional argument to justify a tax increase. Few governments, even the limited number of Labour governments with working majorities, have pursued this policy actively and Conservative governments have followed contrary policies that redistributed income to the higher income groups on the grounds that it encouraged enterprise and had a trickle-down effect. An effective redistribution policy requires a progressive system of taxation, especially income tax, and an effective charge on wealth and the inheritance of wealth. It also needs a positive effort to spend money in a differential manner to help the lower income groups. These two sides could be combined in a negative income tax, a policy that was once supported by all major parties. Instead, the politicians have ducked the issues of poverty and the poverty trap and tried to escape via the outcomes of economic growth which they hope will raise living standards generally without anyone having to sacrifice anything.

The incompatibility of these objectives became evident as governments tried to reconcile them when inflation, the level of unemployment and the balance of payments' deficit all rose and the foreign exchange rate came under pressure. The fixed exchange rate demanded that action be taken to attack the perceived causes of the balance of payments problem. This was seen as excessive inflation in comparison with international competitors and the cause of inflation was usually seen as excessive pay increases although this was a very superficial analysis. The true cause was just as likely to be rising costs of production caused by rising costs of imported raw materials, or rising energy and distribution costs. It may even have been attributable to a built-in 'cost plus' attitude to pricing goods and services on the part of sellers. Later it became fashionable to attribute much of the inflation to excessive growth of the money supply caused by government borrowing via bill and bond issues and to excessive government spending. Government reactions followed very predictable courses. They harangued the public to accept lower pay settlements; they raised taxes; they cut government expenditure or tried to; they rephased capital expenditure programmes; they tried to manipulate the quantity of money via monetary policy and the demand for money through interest rate changes. In desperation they frequently resorted to some form of incomes policy to restrain employees' incomes and, occasionally, to control prices as well. The main vehicle for their restraints was the public sector, especially public employees' pay and the nationalised industries' investment and pricing policies. They completely failed to control the incomes of the self-employed and could not control payments in kind and rarely had a sensible impact in controlling prices other than in the public sector. Even there they simply created a log-jam effect so that, when the restraints were removed, there was an accelerated rise in prices. The more successful nations, Germany and Japan, managed to control the growth of incomes within the growth of national output so their inflation rise was usually much lower than the UK's. There was very little easing of the situation when the pound was allowed to float after late 1971 because the oil price rise induced inflation when OPEC forced their prices up.

Other objectives which many people would have liked to have appeared closer to the forefront of government objectives included some more positive approachs to the environment and sustainable growth. A few visionaries were worried about these issues from the 1960s. Another was a more coherent policy towards the developing world and aid which all too often seemed to be an adjunct of foreign policy. Yet another was a more positive effort to encourage R&D and investment in long-term growth through managing the declining industries and their substitution with new ones.

Note. It should be borne in mind that all of these objectives were subject to the electoral cycle. There is plenty of evidence that governments failed to take appropriate economic action, or delayed it or brought it forward, in order to generate a climate that favoured their electoral chances. In effect they braked when they should have accelerated or accelerated when they should have slowed down.

Exercise I

Are the 1996 government objectives of low inflation, falling unemployment and steady economic growth compatible with one another?

21.2   Policy Objectives After 1979 to May 1997

The Conservative Government of Mrs Thatcher was elected in 1979 with a commitment to push back the boundary of the state and to create more competition. In an attempt to emulate the economics of the advisors of President Reagan in the USA there were promises to balance the Government's budget and to raise revenue by the bold method of cutting the higher rates of income tax in order to generate incentives for entrepreneurs. It is, incidentally, one of the odder paradoxes of the 1980s and early 1990s that it was assumed by right-wing economists that the rich would work harder if they were paid more but that the poor would work harder only if their wages were kept low. There were a number of other pledges that usually accompany elections such as reduced direct taxation, less bureaucracy and less reliance on government borrowing. There was an emphasis on freedom of choice and on home ownership. There was also a promise to curtail the power of the trade unions and to bring the extremely high rate of inflation under control. There was no explicit commitment to maintain the level of employment but an assertion that, if the economy did as well as expected under the new draught of competition, 'real' jobs would be maintained and that economic growth would produce more employment. Medieval philosophers may have stood a better chance of understanding what a 'real' as opposed to an 'unreal' job was than those who swelled the ranks of the 3 million unemployed in 1993.

The new government became devoted to the ideas of monetarism with its emphasis on controlling the money supply and manipulating the demand for money via the interest rate. It also sought salvation in a crusade for what are known as 'supply-side' measures to improve the efficiency and competitiveness of United Kingdom industry and commerce. This produced spates of deregulation, some more trumpeted than real, and privatisation of nationalised assets. Controls on foreign exchange movements were abolished and British capital flowed freely, mainly out of the UK. The exploitation of North Sea oil induced a huge inflow of foreign capital and the pound rose rapidly against the dollar, almost to the old 1967 pre-devaluation rate of £1 = \$2.40. It subsequently fell to almost £1 = \$1. The effect of the high level was catastrophic for British manufacturing industry and it suffered a blow from which it has not fully recovered. Output fell and was not back to the 1979 level until 1989. Imports were substituted for United Kingdom produced goods and jobs were literally exported to the Pacific rim countries, to South America and to Southern Europe. For a time there was a rapid growth of employment in the service industries, particularly in financial services which were expanding in response to deregulation of financial markets and because of the surges of the housing market. As the 1980s proceeded and the level of unemployment rose to 1 million, then 2 million and finally above 3 million and as the unemployment statistics were modified at frequent intervals to reduce the number recorded as unemployed, fears grew as each million landmark approached that there would be mass rioting and civil disturbance.

There will be some interesting theses written explaining why civil unrest was, in fact, minimal. It was obvious, by 1990, that government objectives were a far cry from the consensus list given above for the period 1945–79. They seem to have evolved in a rather stumbling fashion from experience and expediency. The new objectives may be summarised as follows but others might produce a different list when the archives are opened.

Reduction of the government's borrowing became a major self-imposed objective that was later bolstered by the need to match the Maastricht Treaty on Union's criteria for joining the single currency. It was apparent that up to 1979, various governments, especially the Labour Government of 1974–79, had stoked the level of inflation by borrowing too much and then spending the proceeds on current consumption rather than on capital investment in the public sector. They had allowed the current deficit of expenditure over revenue to become excessive and resorted to too much borrowing via the issue of Treasury bills which, because of their liquidity, magnified the money supply. The excessive borrowing was alleged to cause a phenomenon known as 'crowding out', whereby the government could afford to push up interest rates in order to obtain the funds it needed and thereby priced some private enterprises out of the market for borrowing for investment expenditure. Thus the evils of excessive public sector debt were threefold: (1) its effects on inflation; (2) crowding out and (3) the requirement of raising more taxation to pay the interest on the national debt.

The government elevated the Public Sector Borrowing Requirement (PSBR) to the status of tribal totem and pursued policies that were designed to reduce it and even remove it. Indeed, there was a brief period when the receipts from privatisation were so large that it became the Public Sector Debt Repayment (PSDR) and the national debt was actually reduced. Gladstone, who spent so much effort on trying to remove the national debt, must have chuckled in his grave. The main policies adopted were to maintain the overall tax base by shifting the tax burden from direct to indirect taxation, to sell the nationalised industries, to cut the growth of local authority spending and to reduce central government expenditure. The policies were pursued but that does not mean that they were effective. Except for a brief period the PSBR proved to be intractable. It responded more to the moods of the overall economic environment than to the government's efforts. As unemployment rose so did the burden of social security payments and with it the PSBR. As unemployment fell so did the social security burden and, other things being equal, the PSBR. Eventually the government began to try to cut the budget share allocated to social security benefits of different types. Over the years the government put itself in a cleft stick. It announced loudly that it was going to cut public expenditure but failed to do so in almost every case except those of housing and assistance to industry. At the same time it was forced by electoral considerations to argue that it had increased spending on health, education and law and order. There was a tendency for the public not to believe the increased spending line although it was true that it had risen, even in real terms, for education, health and law and order. The issue, of course, was really whether expenditure had risen sufficiently to cope with rising demand and numbers and the ageing population. It had not.

The government found that it was not believed because it raised to a fine art a tactic used by all governments. When it announced cuts in spending it was not, or rarely, reducing a real amount. It was cutting something off a proposed increase which is not the same thing at all. It is as if you proposed spending £10 000 on a new car but then only spent £9000 and announced this as a spending cut of £1000. You should be aware of this device when reading about government cuts in expenditure.

Exercise 2

Why did the government abandon full employment as an objective of economic policy in the early 1980s?

The Private Finance Initiative (PFI) is a recent mechanism to cut government spending and borrowing. This scheme was relaunched in mid-1996 because its early performance was disappointing. Under the PFI the government decides what service it wants and the private sector is invited to design, build, finance and operate the capital assets required. Such services may be railways, rolling stock, roads, bridges, hospitals, prisons and so on. There are three types of project:

1. financially free standing such as toll roads and bridges;
2. services sold to the public sector such as prisons where the private company builds and runs the prison and charges the state for the use of cells;
3. joint ventures where funds are provided jointly by the public sector and the private firms but the control rests with the private sector, for example the Channel Tunnel Rail Link or the Croydon Tramlink.

The government expressed the hope that over £14 billion of deals would be made under the PFI by the end of 1998/99 and is trying to make the scheme more attractive to the private sector. Experience so far indicates that they are being over-optimistic unless the bureaucracy and risks are reduced. The central belief behind the PFI is that the private sector should bear the risks of the enterprise and that it is the risk bearing that will lead to efficiency. The PFI was again subject to review in June 1997.

Reduction of inflation was another objective that came to dominate especially when inflation rates had reached lower levels under the discipline of membership of the exchange rate mechanism from 1990–92. Once they were down the government was able to make the maintenance of low rates of inflation, which incidentally are a requirement for membership of the European single currency after 1999, a main plank of its policies. Some commentators would place the achievement of low inflation at the centre of the policies but the evidence does not support the many government utterances to this effect. An example is the persistent shift of taxation to indirect taxes on expenditure which consistently had an inflationary effect. Another is the benign encouragement of the house price inflation of the 1980s which underlay general inflationary tendencies. The persistent inability to meet the various and changing monetary targets of the 1980s is also indicative of a failure of will in respect of the control of inflation. It is, of course, possible to argue that one national government, especially of a major trading nation, is unable to control international inflationary pressures but governments do not like to admit such weakness. The reader should note the tendency of governments to deny responsibility when inflation is rising and to want the plaudits of the people when inflation falls. We should also remember that there have been changes in the presentation of the inflation statistics, mainly for the better, and their subdivision into RPI, RPIX and RPIY. Unscrupulous politicians tend to emphasise the one that most favours their interpretation of recent events.

A balanced budget became a desirable objective following the aspirations of American economists of the so-called Reaganite economic school. This is closely linked with the first objective of reducing the PSBR but stems from a fundamental belief that the Keynesian approach to the government's budget was wrong. Keynes argued that a budget could and should be deliberately unbalanced in order to achieve economic objectives. Thus a deficit financed by borrowing was legitimate when there was high unemployment in order to generate expenditure and to compensate for deficiencies in private sector investment. The balanced budget concept stems partly from a belief that the national budget is based on the same principle as a good housekeeping budget although most households borrow money. It is more sensible to argue that future generations should help pay, via interest charges, for long-term capital assets such as hospitals and schools provided by the state. A balanced budget concept implies that only the present generation, in one year, should pay. Some economists argue that a balanced budget should be a long-term objective and that short-term deficits or surpluses do not matter provided that they are not excessive.

This objective is allied to the notion that the tax system should be neutral, that is that no-one should behave differently because of the tax regime. There have been some historical nonsenses created by taxation and licence systems, for example the continued existence of three-wheeled cars and the odd application in the United Kingdom of tax on adults' clothes but not on children's. In practice any tax has some distorting effect on the allocation of resources and sometimes the state wishes to shift consumption towards merit goods and away from demerit goods.

Economic growth has remained an objective but in a modified form. The government is keen on growth and has anticipated growth rates within historic parameters when planning its expenditure but it is not, apparently, taking any active steps to raise growth rates. It seems to assume that if it gets the economic climate right in terms of low inflation and interest rates that the growth will follow automatically. It does consult the chicken entrails as would ancient soothsayers in the sense that it analyses whether the growth that occurs is attributable to exports, investment or consumption or to a mixture of all three, but there is no evidence of a determined attempt to intervene to stimulate the known agents of economic growth such as R&D, private sector investment, education and training or even public infrastructure investment. It regards such interventionist behaviour as ineffective or, even worse, as detrimental. It is not completely certain that the happy, perhaps temporary, conjunction of low inflation and low interest rates will stimulate growth, indeed the United Kingdom economy in 1995–96 was showing a growth rate below its historic trend.

Unemployment or its reduction disappeared from the government's objectives between 1979 and 1997. The change occurred gradually with ministers initially paying lip service to the Beveridge concept of full employment. Eventually they failed to refer to it as an immediate aim and then took the position that, while they preferred low levels of unemployment because it made them more popular with the electorate, it was not their job and nor could it be in a free market enterprise economy, to do anything about it apart from deregulate the market. The unemployed were somehow persuaded that it was their fault if they were unemployed and that the government would be committing a great economic sin if they attempted the 'old-fashioned' Keynesian techniques of demand management to create or maintain employment. It was frequently asserted that the government could not create jobs and there was reference to 'real jobs' of a long-term nature. This approach was rather at odds with the large recruitment into the police forces and prison services to combat the crime wave associated with poverty, social breakdown and deprivation. It was also at odds with the renewed growth of expenditure on defence in the early 1980s that maintained many jobs in the defence sphere.

At the root of the changed government attitude to the full employment objective was its desire to reduce the power of the trade unions. The rapid increase of unemployment and the uncertainty that it generated sapped the ability of unions to organise their membership to resist effectively the new legislation that was introduced. Once unemployment had reached certain levels and was not apparently having too-destabilising an effect on the social and political scene, the government also awoke to the fact that it could be used as a lever to reduce wage demands and even the level of real wages. Some economists thought that such a reduction was the key to the control of inflation and to economic growth when it was part of a mixture of 'supply-side' measures. They supported the reduction in scope and then the abolition of the Wages Councils that partially protected the wages and employment conditions of low paid workers and changes in the payment of social security benefits to the unemployed. These policies were pursued in the hope of maintaining international competitiveness through low wages and labour flexibility with scant regard to the alternative which is a more skilled and better trained workforce with better technology from R&D expenditure.

The redistribution of income as an objective was gradually turned on its head as the shift from direct to indirect taxation and the reduction of higher rates of income tax, together with an assortment of other changes to tax and benefits, altered the distribution of income in favour of the better off. The analysis of income distribution figures is beset with problems but, stated very crudely, over the years 1979 to 1996 the top decile of income recipients became better off, the bottom decile became worse off and those in the middle remained in the same position. There is an argument about whether the changes are in absolute terms or relative terms. It is possible that some politicians believed in the 'trickle-down effect', whereby making the rich richer benefits the poorer sections of society because of the increased spending. This tends to ignore the fact that the 'rich' have a much higher marginal propensity to save than the lower income groups. In the light of post-war history it is unlikely that any change of government would have much immediate impact on the distribution of income.

A balanced regional development was also neglected as a government policy after 1979 partly because the very high levels of unemployment have made it much more difficult to direct firms to certain regions or to prevent firms from developing in the previously prosperous areas. Present policy has devolved into assistance for investment projects undertaken by foreign firms within European Union guidelines and to applications of the European Union's regional policies in a rather half-hearted manner. There has been a major shift away from grants towards financial incentives related to reductions in taxation on profits and subject to complex criteria. Since 1979 the government has strongly rejected any idea that it should try 'to pick winners' and subsidise them in the short run or even help companies in temporary difficulties.

Low interest rates have become a clearly stated objective of government. As with the rate of inflation, governments tend to accept no responsibility when they are high but would like praise when they are low. Governments like to give the impression when rates are falling that they can control interest rates but will always argue that it is international factors that are causing them to rise, unless they see advantage in appearing strong and determined in the fight against future inflation by raising them. One problem with having a too-strongly stated interest rate policy is that there is a time lag of up to two years between changes in interest rates and subsequent impacts on the rate of inflation.

Policy changes since May 1997

A Labour Government was elected in May 1997 with a large majority. It promised to give priority to the reduction of unemployment but also promised to maintain strict budgetary and monetary discipline. It gave operational responsibility for fixing interest rates to a new Monetary Policy Committee of the Bank of England and set an inflation target of 2.5 per cent within a margin of fluctuation of ± 1 per cent. The government fixed its first budget for July 1997 and a study of that will reveal what policy changes are likely over the next few years.

Exercise 3

Should future generations help to pay for assets such as roads, schools and hospitals bought now from borrowed money?

21.3   The Annual Budget Process

The Labour Government elected in May 1997 may make changes to the budget process introduced in November 1993 when the first 'unified budget' was produced which combined proposals on public expenditure with those for taxation. Prior to that the budget was simply an explanation of how the government intended to raise the taxation needed to cover its expenditure for the following period. (There have sometimes been more than one budget in a year, particularly election years.) The proposals for expenditure were dealt with separately in the period from late autumn to the spring of the following year and the budget was usually in March.

The main work on the budget goes on in the three months before it is due to be presented. The Chancellor of the Exchequer supervises the Treasury in its work on the tax system and is also Chairman of the Cabinet Committee on public expenditure. This committee looks ahead three years in its expenditure plans. Throughout the process the Treasury is subject to pressure from various sources that want spending raised or cut and from the departments, especially the large spending ones. There may come a point where a Cabinet committee has to arbitrate between the conflicting requests of the departments and ultimately the Prime Minister may be appealed to.

The budget speech is made and is accompanied by a flood of documents. The speech itself is essentially a political statement reviewing the economy in as favourable a light as possible and then going on to outline the proposed expenditure programmes and the changes in direct and indirect taxation that are needed to finance them. Many of the documents are press briefings but others are detailed explanations by the Inland Revenue and Customs and Excise of proposed changes. The detail in these is much studied by taxation specialists and financial advisers because they often put a less rosy gloss on some of the Chancellor's alterations. The main document issued is *The Financial Statement and Budget Report* or FSBR or 'Red Book' as it is commonly known. This puts flesh on the bones of the speech. It usually:

- summarises the budget;
- sets out the government's medium term financial strategy (MTFS);
- contains an economic forecast (a second is published in June);
- gives an analysis of the public finances including projections for the PSBR;
- gives more detail of the budget's tax and national insurance changes;
- covers public expenditure in more detail.

The budget gives the plans that have been agreed for public expenditure but the full details of departmental spending are not available until March. In late March each department publishes a Departmental Report which contains the full explanation of their aims, objectives and an assessment of their performance and the criteria against which it is measured. The Treasury co-ordinates the publication of these reports and itself produces the 'Statistical Supplement to the Financial Statement and Budget Report'. As soon as the Departmental Reports are published the Main Estimates and the Summary and Guide to Estimates are also published. In 1995 a new format was adopted in an attempt to make them more intelligible.

Some taxes are defined as permanent, for example all indirect taxes, petroleum revenue tax and taxes on capital, but some have to be renewed each year, for example income tax, corporation tax and advanced corporation tax. The measures announced in the budget may take effect before Parliament has passed the Finance Bill in which the proposed tax changes are embodied. Budget resolutions have to be passed to put the measures into effect before the Finance Bill is finally enacted by 5 May of the following year (before the unified budget this date was 5 August). The debate that follows the speech is on these resolutions. The parliamentary procedure for the budget and Finance Bill is very complex although it has been simplified since 1995. The Finance Bill itself is not actually published in detail until after its formal first reading where only the main title is read out so it does not now appear until January, over a month after the budget speech.

One of the oddities of the British budgetary process is that the financial year runs from 1 April to 31 March whereas the tax year runs from 6 April to 5 April. The reasons for this anachronism lie in the obsession with tradition of the ruling elite and the inertia of the United Kingdom system of government. In 1752, 1 January was adopted as the start of the year instead of Lady Day on 25 March. The calendar was changed to the Gregorian and 11 days were 'lost' but the government decided to keep a tax year of 365 days and extended the tax year to 5 April. In 1854 the financial year's start was altered to 1 April. You may well ask 'why is the system not modernised?'

Indexing. The budget process is affected by a 1977 amendment to the Finance Bill which now has the effect of indexing the personal allowances for income tax to the change in the rate of inflation as measured by the Retail Price Index in September (it used to be December). This 'Rooker-Wise' amendment applies also to the thresholds for the higher rate of income tax and inheritance tax and the capital gains exemption levels for trusts and individuals. It can be overridden and is if the Chancellor wishes to alter allowances and thresholds by more than the change in the RPI.

Regulators. The budget process gives the government the power to use what are called regulators of which there are three. They provide the ability to alter tax rates of VAT and most customs and excise duties in the course of the year. They are:

- **the economic regulator** whereby the Treasury can put a surcharge on, or give a rebate on, the main duties on alcohol, oil products, betting and bingo. The change may be up to 10 per cent;
- **the tobacco products regulator** which applies the same principle;
- **the VAT regulator** whereby the Treasury can alter the rate of VAT by $1/4$ of the rate in force, that is currently $17\frac{1}{2}$ per cent.

21.4   Public Expenditure

The government publishes an annual review called the *Public Expenditure Survey* which reviews its existing expenditure intentions for the following two years and draws up plans for a new third year. The basis of the government's plans in 1995–96, and earlier, has been the desire to reduce public expenditure as a percentage of national income and to obtain better value for money from its spending. This review is a gold mine for economists and financial analysts because it reveals the extent to which the government's policy is deviating from its intended route and the extent of the probable corrective measures.

In 1992 some significant changes were made in the method of planning and controlling expenditure. The major alteration was the replacement of the planning total by a **Control Total** and the setting up of a **Cabinet Committee on Public Expenditure** (called EDX) with seven members.

The control total relates to about 85 per cent of government spending and is a system of annual ceilings which are expressed in cash. The exclusions from the control total are cyclical social security spending, proceeds from privatisation and debt interest. The total does, however, include local authorities' self-financed expenditure. The cyclical social security expenditure that is excluded is unemployment benefit and income support paid to non-pensioners. The reason for the exclusion is so that the effects of recession in terms of higher spending on benefit do not have an impact on other programmes' spending. When unemployment falls the exclusion prevents the 'savings' on benefit leaking away into other programmes. The total level of expenditure is fixed in advance by the setting of these control totals so the purpose of the annual Public Expenditure Survey is to allocate spending among the various programmes within these control totals. Such an attempt to allocate scarce financial resources is bound to cause interdepartmental rivalry so the EDX has to play a part.

The Committee on Public Expenditure is a successor to similar bodies but much more detail is known about it. In May each year the departmental ministers responsible for expenditure report to the Chief Secretary of the Treasury about any scope for savings and any pressures to spend more and he then makes a report to the Cabinet. On the basis of this the committee is given its instructions by the Cabinet and reports back in early November. Most of its work consists of interviewing the ministers in charge of the main spending departments after studying their programmes and after an analysis by the Chief Secretary of the Treasury. The committee is very busy in the two months before the budget.

The pattern of public expenditure

The long-term trend this century has been for public expenditure to rise in absolute terms and as a percentage of national income despite attempts to restrain it. The Conservative Government from 1979 gave great importance to reducing the role of the state but had had little success by 1996 in cutting the percentage of GDP spent by public authorities, despite the privatisation programmes and other measures to reduce the civil service. Its policies were derailed by the deep recession and growth of unemployment. Among the causes of the growth of public expenditure are:

- wars and the cold war;
- state pensions;
- the assumption of responsibility for health services;
- the assumption of responsibility for other social services;
- population growth and the increased number of the elderly;
- the provision of merit goods such as education and the extension of their provision;
- the increased cost of labour intensive services;
- the growth of assistance to industry and the provision of transport infrastructure.

Table 21.1 International public sector comparisons of government expenditure

	Current General Government Revenue % of GDP	Current General Government Expenditure % of GDP	Total	Defence	Public Order and Safety	Education	Health	Social Security and Welfare	Housing & Community Amenities	Government Employment % of total Employment
Belgium	50.90	54.60	16.80	2.6	1.6	6.2	0.5	1.0	0.2	19.3
France	46.80	51.00	17.90	3.0	0.8	4.6	3.1	1.4	1.1	24.8
Germany	45.70	45.60	18.30	2.2	1.5	3.5	5.6	2.2	0.3	14.9
Italy	44.90	50.90	17.80	1.9	1.9	4.7	3.7	0.7	0.5	16.2
Japan	32.90	26.90	9.70	0.9	–	3.2	0.5	0.6	0.7	5.9
Netherlands	52.00	53.20	15.30	2.7	–	4.6	–	0.7	–	12.7
Spain	40.10	43.70	15.60	1.5	1.2	3.0	3.7	1.7	0.9	15.1
United Kingdom	36.80	42.70	22.00	3.8	2.2	4.4	5.7	1.8	0.6	16.9
United States	31.70	35.80	17.10	–	–	–	–	–	–	14.5

Note: These figures are for an assortment of dates, mainly 1993 in columns 1, 2 and 10 are for general comparison only.

Source: National Accounts, OECD Paris 1996 adapted from OECD in Figures 1996 edition.

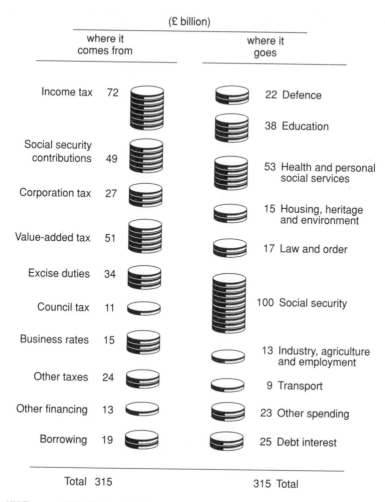

(£ billion)

where it comes from		where it goes
Income tax	72	22 Defence
		38 Education
Social security contributions	49	53 Health and personal social services
Corporation tax	27	15 Housing, heritage and environment
Value-added tax	51	17 Law and order
Excise duties	34	
Council tax	11	100 Social security
Business rates	15	13 Industry, agriculture and employment
Other taxes	24	9 Transport
Other financing	13	23 Other spending
Borrowing	19	25 Debt interest
Total 315		315 Total

Source: HM Treasury 1996, 'Budget in brief'

Figure 21.1   Public money 1997–98 – where it comes from and where it goes

Table 21.2   General government expenditure: by function

United Kingdom						Percentages
	1981	*1986*	*1991*	*1992*	*1993*	*1994*
Social security	27	31	32	33	34	34
Health	11	12	14	14	13	14
Education	12	12	13	13	12	13
Defence	11	12	10	10	9	8
Public order and safety	4	4	6	5	5	5
General public services	4	4	5	5	4	4
Housing and community amenities	6	5	4	4	4	4
Transport and communication	4	2	3	3	2	2
Recreational and cultural affairs	1	2	2	2	2	2
Agriculture, forestry and fishing	1	1	1	1	2	1
Other expenditure	19	16	11	11	12	13
All expenditure (=100%) (£ billion in real terms[1])	224.6	241.0	250.9	268.1	278.3	285.7

[1] Adjusted to 1994 prices using the GDP market prices deflator

Source: CSO, *Social Trends*, **26**, London, HMSO, 1996.

21.5 Taxation

The traditional distinction between, or classification of, taxes is to call them **direct** or **indirect** but it is probably better to classify them as **income, expenditure** or **wealth** taxes because there is more clarity in the application to examples.

Direct taxes are ones where the individual who pays the tax to the revenue authorities also bears the loss or incidence of the tax. Income tax is the clearest example but there are problems with the classification and it is not very useful. Vehicle excise duty is, for example, a direct tax on a private car owner who pays for the car out of his or her own pocket but if the tax is paid by a business it can be recovered wholly or in part via the prices charged to customers and is indirect. Even the government has had problems with the direct/indirect classification and reclassified employers' social security contributions from a 'direct' tax on the employer to an 'indirect tax' on expenditure on employees because it was likely to be passed on in the form of higher prices to customers.

Indirect taxes are ones where the individual or firm that pays the tax to the revenue authorities can pass on some or all of the burden, loss or incidence of the tax to other people. For example, whisky becomes liable for excise duty as it leaves the bonded store in which it has been maturing. Thus the distiller pays the tax but recovers some of it from the distributors, wholesalers and retailers, who in turn raise their prices so that the final customer bears some of the incidence. The public often believes that the whole of the tax burden is passed on but if there is any elasticity of demand at all, that is the demand curve is not vertical, the manufacturer and distributors suffer a loss of sales and profit when they try to raise their prices to recoup the tax. Thus the incidence, or loss, of an indirect tax is normally shared by the three groups, manufacturer, retailers and wholesalers and final purchaser. As a generalisation:

- the more inelastic the demand relative to supply, the greater the incidence borne by the buyer;
- the more elastic the demand relative to the supply, the greater the incidence borne by the manufacturers and distributors.

Figure 21.2 illustrates the sharing of the incidence of an indirect tax according to the relative elasticities.

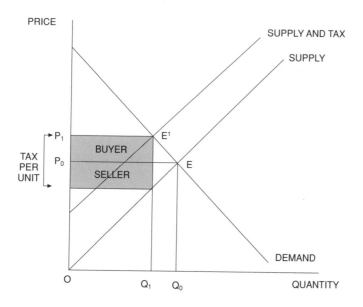

Figure 21.2   The incidence of an indirect specific tax

The expenditure, income and wealth tax classification is much more straightforward than the direct/indirect distinction but even here some arbitrary decisions have to be made. For example, many people live off their capital gains and treat their gains as income. Indeed attempts have been made to tax such gains in the United Kingdom but only the small fry get caught since the big fish use their expertise to avoid such taxes. In such a case the decision is made to treat the tax as a tax on income but it could in some circumstances be seen as a tax on the accumulation of wealth.

Principles behind the tax system

It is usually asserted, following Adam Smith, that **an individual tax should be certain**, that is the payer should be clear as to what is liable to be taxed, how much the tax bill is and when and how to pay it. The payment arrangements should also be convenient to the payer. One of the unfortunate characteristics of the modern United Kingdom system is that it has spawned an army of tax accountants who advise people on how to minimise their tax liability by legal means. Tax avoidance, which is legal, as opposed to tax evasion which is illegal, reveals the extent to which our system does not possess the quality of certainty. Tax laws are often written in an opaque fashion and are frequently trying to close previous loopholes. They result in complex legal test cases and uncertainty.

Another principle is that **the cost of collecting a tax should be minimal**. Modern taxes are usually very productive in the sense that their collection cost is only a very small percentage of the total raised. There are some exceptions to this and some taxes such as the capital gains tax are maintained nowadays as a gesture to the old concept of equality of tax burdens, that is the idea that the rich should bear the greater share of tax. The inheritance tax thresholds are subject to indexation mainly because they are expensive to collect when small sums are involved as well as to mollify the public. The very rich, of course, tend to avoid inheritance tax in any case. In contrast income tax is very economical to collect. One of the retrograde steps in the substitution of VAT for the old purchase tax was the fact that it is much more expensive to collect.

The principles mentioned above are important but a much more fundamental, and controversial, one is that of **equity**. It is controversial because it is interpreted in different ways. The consensus used to be that an individual tax or the whole system was equitable if it contained a strong element of progression, that is the higher income groups paid a larger percentage of their income in tax than the lower income groups. Some modern commentators think that the disadvantages of a progressive system in terms of being a deterrent to enterprise and work are such that the principle of equity should be superseded by the principle that people should pay tax mainly on their expenditure where they are alleged to have some choice and discretion.

Technically, a tax is **progressive** if the proportion of *income* taken in tax rises with income. This usually results from having a rising marginal rate of tax as income rises. The UK income tax, for example, is essentially progressive with three rates of 20, 24 and 40 per cent in 1996. It used to be more progressive with a top rate of 83 per cent. A tax is **regressive** if the proportion of *income* taken in tax falls as income rises and this includes most indirect taxes on expenditure. It is possible for a tax to be **proportionate** if the percentage of income taken in tax remains the same as income rises, for example a flat rate 10 per cent income tax without any allowances. As usual the picture can be more complicated. It can, for instance, be argued that the United Kingdom VAT system has a progressive element despite being an expenditure tax at a rate of $17^{1}/_{2}$ per cent and with some goods and services zero-rated. This is because people on higher incomes increase their expenditure on goods and services liable to the tax so that the VAT payments on their incomes become a higher percentage than does the VAT burden on the incomes of other groups. Even if this is the case VAT is not normally thought of as a progressive tax especially in those countries where it is applied almost universally with few exemptions.

Another principle that is important is that **taxes should not distort the economy** to any serious extent unless that is the deliberate intention as when demerit goods are taxed. Economic decisions frequently have to take tax matters into account particularly on investment expenditure where the system of depreciation allowances against tax is crucial. Taxes also affect pricing policies, especially in alcohol, tobacco and petrol markets or in foreign trade if tariffs are levied. A badly designed tax system can seriously affect the allocation of resources within a country and one nation's tax regime can have an adverse impact on the world economy. An example of the latter effect is the USA whose low tax policy for fuel oil and gasoline leads to the profligate use of scarce world resources.

One important application of the principle of non-distortion is that **taxation should not adversely affect the willingness of people to work, to save or to take risks** in their enterprise. There is a great amount of economic literature available debating the impact of taxation on work and enterprise. It is generally acknowledged that the individual will often have a 'backward bending' supply curve for their labour because they come to a point where they value extra leisure above the additional income from working longer hours. The level at which they reach this point will be affected by their marginal rate of tax. One argument is that if marginal rates are high (whatever that means) people will be less willing to work longer hours or harder. The other side of the argument is that some people, if not all, will work harder if marginal rates are high in order to make up their post-tax incomes to the level they want. This general debate has been important in the approach of both the USA and UK governments to marginal rates of income tax. President Reagan introduced large tax cuts in order to stimulate enterprise and reward work. Mrs Thatcher followed the same policy in the UK. Their efforts were based on what is called the 'Laffer Curve' which is shown in Figure 21.3.

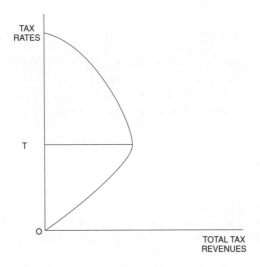

1. Tax revenues would be maximised at a tax rate of T.
2. The exact shape of the Laffer curve is not known.
3. The curve can be drawn with the axes reversed.

Figure 21.3   The Laffer curve

Other considerations which can be elevated to the status of principles are:

- minimum impact on the rate of inflation. Alteration in most taxes on expenditure affect the RPI and the rate of inflation. The raising of VAT to 15 per cent in1979 had a noticeable impact on the already high inflation rate. Fuel tax increases are particularly inflationary.
- ease of alteration. The tax mechanism must lend itself to easy and administratively cheap change.
- contribution to economic stabilisation. Some taxes aggravate a recession while others fail to help restrain a boom. Indexation of some taxes helps to prevent this tendency but not all taxes can be indexed.
- encouragement to saving. This may be achieved by the differential taxation of savings and expenditure or, in the company sector, by taxing distributed profits more highly than retained profits.

The sources of tax revenue in the UK are shown in Figure 21.1.

Exercise 4

Why is there pressure to adopt more uniform rates of VAT across the European Union member states?

21.6 Local Government Finance

Relations with the Central Government

Central government decides:

- the structure of local authorities in the United Kingdom;
- what services they will provide;
- how the services will be financed in overall terms but not always in specific detail;
- how the provision of services will be audited and inspected;
- the qualifications required for many local authority posts and the establishment (numbers to be employed) of, for example, the police force;
- the amount of money available from central funds for pay increases of local authority employees each year;
- how the local authority allocates contracts;
- how the proceeds of the sale of council housing are used;
- what planning regulations are and applies an appeal system.

This is by no means an exhaustive list but the message is clear – the modern local authority is the creature of central government particularly in the control of its expenditure in the context of macroeconomic policy. Governments have steadily strengthened their grip on local authority expenditure because they found in the 1960s and early 1970s that while central government was tightening its purse strings, local government was not. The PSBR is central *and* local government borrowing not just central so if a government places great store by controlling the PSBR it is bound to want to control local authorities.

There is another motive for central control and that is the fact that the main source of local government spending is grants from the centre, and local government is very labour intensive. The government, therefore, uses its power to control local authority revenues to help limit the pay rises of public sector workers. This is an important part of its anti-inflation policy although the Conservative Government from 1979 to 1997 has always denied that such incomes policies worked in the past.

Central government contributes to the revenues of local authorities in the following ways:

- formula grants that are based on complex formulae related to population factors such as numbers, age distribution, and percentage aged over 80 and under five, road mileage and various weightings related to averages of the national figure. These grants are to be spent on a variety of services but predominantly education;

- specific grants that are for a given service only. The best example is the police grant which is 51 per cent of the amount spent, but the overall total that can be spent is capped. This type of grant was once used to encourage spending;
- unit grants are given to a local authority to encourage it to spend money on items such as training places in disabled workshops or for the elderly in specialised homes. The major unit grant used to be for each council house built.

The local authority has additional sources of revenue and has a greater degree of control over these:

- **revenues from the council tax**. This is called a hybrid tax because it is based partly on the property – one tax per dwelling based on its banding valuation – and partly on the number of people living there. The tax is based on two people per dwelling so if there is only one a rebate may be had. The council tax replaced the community charge in 1993 which was basically an old-fashioned, not to say mediaeval, poll tax, that is a fixed sum per adult head with rebates for special categories. The community charge was a foolish attempt by Mrs Thatcher to resolve the dilemma that government inaction had created. The old rating system, which was regressive but familiar and accepted by most people apart from a few moaners and intellectuals on the right wing, required revaluations every five years in order to keep the rate in the pound at a sensible level. Otherwise it soared faster than the rate of inflation. Successive governments from 1963 failed to conduct these revaluations so that if one had been done (as one was eventually in Scotland) the cries of outrage would have been unbearable for the politicians whose chickens had come home to roost. So Mrs Thatcher, acting on advice, quelled the misgivings of some of her senior ministers and went for the appealing simplicity of the community charge.
- **revenues from selling services, renting, licensing and inspecting**. Once upon a time many of these services were provided free but the new regimes in the 1980s forced local authorities to charge for things such as planning permission and passing building regulations applications. The rents and licence fees are from things such as markets, property and crematoria. This area of activity has become exceedingly complex since the introduction of compulsory competitive tendering (CCT) whereby local authorities had to seek tenders from external bodies for many services that they hitherto provided for themselves, such as refuse collection and disposal, road mending, house repairs, architects' and lawyers' advice, or payroll services. There was a general retreat from the old policy of a local authority

employing its labour directly in a Direct Labour Organisation (DLO). CCT has probably gone beyond what is sensible and there is considerable doubt about whether it saves money in the long run or delivers good quality services. The government persistently argued that it gave value for money. CCT is one reason the government was keen not to have a national minimum wage and why it partly deregulated the labour market because many of the workers employed on contracted-out services are low paid and without adequate job guarantees. The new Labour Government announced that CCT is to be abandoned from mid-1997.

- **rents** from the ownership of council housing and property are another important source or revenue. The housing accounts are now ring-fenced in that they cannot be subsidised by money from outside the accounts so there is no longer any possibility of non-council tenants subsidising the council tenants – not that this was common or normal and it ignores the fact that owner occupiers with mortgage interest relief are heavily subsidised by other tax payers.

- **miscellaneous** is another category and includes all sorts of odd money from investments, some fines, parking meters and so on.

The following Tables 21.3 and 21.4 give examples of one local authority, a county council and one of the districts within it in 1996–97.

Table 21.3   Hertfordshire County Council budget analysis, 1996

1995/96		1996/97	
Gross	SPENDING (£m)	Gross	Net
470.6	Education	485.2	389.6
153.0	Social Services	176.8	134.3
64.4	Transportation	70.1	44.5
21.4	Fire & Rescue	23.2	22.7
6.8	Planning	6.4	4.9
16.3	Libraries	15.4	13.9
7.0	Refuse Disposal	9.1	8.5
46.7	Other services	49.7	38.4
786.2	**TOTAL**	**835.9**	**656.8**
INCOME (£M)			
61.5	Fees and charges etc	79.8	–
257.0	Revenue Support Grant	251.9	251.9
100.7	Other Government Grant	99.3	–
181.7	Non Domestic Rates	206.6	206.6
168.0	Council Tax	179.0	179.0
3.5	Collection Fund	3.9	3.9
13.8	Use of Reserves	15.4	15.4
786.2	**TOTAL**	**835.9**	**656.8**

Source: Hertfordshire County Council, *Council Tax 1996/97 Update*, Hertford, 1996.

Table 21.4   A District's budget, 1996/97

Dacorum's spending plans in 1996/97 are:

		1995/96 £ million	1996/97 £ million
A:	Community and leisure	9.1	9.8
B:	Transport and highways	2.8	2.9
C:	Town and neighbourhood centres	2.6	2.7
D:	Other customer services	2.1	2.2
E:	Highways and sewerage agencies	2.6	2.1
F:	Planning	1.9	2.0
G:	Environmental health	1.8	1.8
H:	Refuse collection & recycling	1.6	1.7
I:	Improvements in services		2.2
	Total spend:	**24.5**	**27.4**

This will be largely financed from:

		1995/96 £ million	1996/97 £ million
A:	Government grants	8.3	7.7
B:	Fees & charges	7.0	7.4
C:	Council tax	4.0	4.0
D:	Agency income	2.6	2.1
E:	Interest	1.4	1.4
F:	Financial reserves	1.2	1.3
G:	Transfer from housing		3.5
	Total Income	**24.5**	**27.4**

Note: Dacorum Borough Council is one of the districts into which Hertfordshire County Council is divided.

Source: Dacorum Borough Council, *Working for You*, 1996.

Exercise 5

Justify the central government's efforts to control the expenditure of local authorities.

22 Introduction to Macroeconomics

Aims of the chapter

To explain:
- the basic concepts of macroeconomics;
- the terminology usually applied to this field;
- the simplified models of the macroeconomy, that is the circular flow of income;
- the concepts of the multiplier and accelerator;
- the problems associated with the idea of a business cycle;
- briefly, the interrelationship of unemployment and inflation;
- the techniques of government intervention in the economy.

22.1 What is Macroeconomics?

Macroeconomics is the study of the economy as a whole and deals with aggregates such as the general price level as opposed to the price of potatoes which is a matter for microeconomics. Macroeconomics includes the levels of aggregate demand and supply, money supply, the levels of inflation, employment and growth as well as analysis of the business cycle and foreign trade and payments.

The basic concepts include the following:

Consumption expenditure (C) which is the aggregate level of spending on consumption goods and services in a given time period. Its main determinant is the level of income. An associated concept is the marginal propensity to consume (MPC) which is the percentage of a change in income that is spent on consumption. There is also the term average propensity to consume (APC) which is the percentage of total income that is spent on consumption. MPC tends, other things being equal, to fall as income rises. In crude terms, the rich spend less and save more of any increase in income than do lower income groups.

Saving (S) which is best regarded as money that is not spent, that is it represents abstention from consumption. Again there are concepts of marginal propensity to save (MPS) and average propensity to save (APS) which are the percentage of a change in income that is saved and the percentage of total income that is saved respectively.

Government expenditure (G) has a specific meaning in the equations of macroeconomics, that is **(1)** expenditure by government departments on goods and services either in the form of subsidies or directly. This first type adds to the level of aggregate demand. The other two types are not part of what is defined as G, that is **(2)** transfer payments such as social security and welfare benefits and **(3)** expenditure by nationalised industries on capital investment because this is treated in the same way as private investment expenditure.

Taxation (T) is the counterpart of government expenditure. There is a concept of the marginal propensity to tax (MPT) which is the percentage of a change in income that goes in tax.

Export expenditure (X) and **import expenditure (M)** are two other important factors in macroeconomics. Export expenditure is regarded an addition to, or injection into, the circular flow of national income and expenditure on imports is regarded as a leakage from it. There is a concept of the marginal propensity to import (MPM), that is the proportion of a change in income that is spent on imports.

Aggregate demand (AD) normally refers to the sum of **C+I+G+(X-M)**, that is consumption plus investment plus government expenditures plus difference between export and import expenditures.

Aggregate supply (AS) is a more complex idea and refers to the quantity of net national product that would be supplied at each general price level if there were expectations of constant prices. Put simply it is the total quantity of domestically produced goods and services supplied by businesses. It consists, therefore, of both consumption and capital goods. There is more about AS, both short term and long term in the next chapter.

22.2   Models of the Circular Flow of Income

Economists delight in making models of the economy which start off very simply and then become more complex as variables are added or as the assumptions underlying the model are changed. Over time, research is carried out that points to the relationships between the variables, for example between income and saving or between income and consumption. More research may show the relationship between the rate of change of a variable and another. For example, what is the relationship between the rate of change of national income and changes in investment or taxation or imports? Ultimately a full model of the economy based on these relationships can be created and run on a computer. The Treasury has such a model and so have other research institutions. The Treasury macroeconomic model is used to forecast future trends and the Chancellor of the Exchequer may be presented with a set of predictions based on possible alterations in taxation and expenditure of different degrees. Since other bodies such as universities may also use this model they can make predictions as well. Thus the budget becomes an area of speculation with experts basing their ideas on the outcome of computer simulations.

The circular flow model can be drawn with squares, rectangles, circles, ovals or any shape that can be generated. Let us use diamonds for a change! What matters is what the lines signify and the direction of the arrows. One direction is a flow of goods, services and the factors of production, land, labour, capital and enterprise through markets for factors and goods and services. The other line is a flow of money in payment for goods and services and in the form of wages, rent, interest and profits as the payment for the factors supplied by households. Many textbooks build this model up in stages but Figure 22.1 below is a version of the complete model for a country with a government and foreign trade. The four-stage model building that you may see is as follows:

1. Only households and firms with no leakages (withdrawals) (W) or injections (J) so the flow never changes. All income is spent. There seems little point in this model except for its use as a stage in teaching.
2. Households and firms and one leakage (savings) and one injection (investment). This can be a final model depending on the definition of terms but it is not usually used as such nowadays.
3. Households and firms and a government so that there are two leakages (savings and taxation) and two injections (investment and government expenditure).
4. Households and firms and a government and foreign trade so that there are three leakages (saving, taxation and import expenditure) and three injections (investment, government and export expenditures).

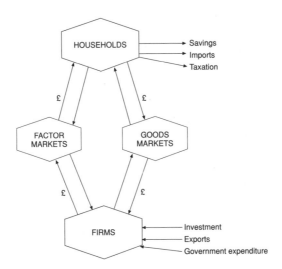

Figure 22.1   The circular flow of income

The concept of equilibrium in the national income

This is defined as the level of national income where there is no tendency for it to change, or the level to which it will tend if it is not already there. In terms of what has been said above about the model of the economy introduced by Keynes using withdrawals and injections the equilibrium level is where withdrawals equal injections or to put it fully where:

$$S + M + T = I + X + G, \text{ or more simply } W + J.$$

This is often shown on a diagram such as Figure 22.2.

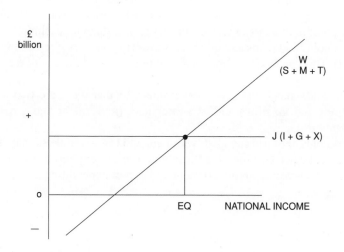

Figure 22.2   Equilibrium in the national income

There is, however, more to the concept of national income equilibrium. We need to know whether it is at the level that ensures full employment. If it is then it is called a **full employment equilibrium** and if not it is an **unemployment equilibrium**. There is some dispute among economists about this area of the subject. The so-called neoclassical school argues that equilibrium is possible at full employment level only whereas Keynes argued that national income could be at an unemployment level for long periods of time and would not necessarily correct itself.

If we pursue the Keynesian approach it is evident that if the national income is not at equilibrium and there is unemployment, the government can do something about it by trying to alter either the withdrawals or the injections or both. The practice is much more difficult than the statement of the theory but, in principle, if there were unemployment the government would deliberately budget for a deficit or larger deficit by cutting taxes and/or raising government expenditure. The increased expenditure would generate a demand for more labour and unemployment would be reduced over a period of time. If there was inflation with an excess demand for labour the opposite would be advisable, that is taxes would be raised and expenditure reduced in order to remove a deficit, or to make it smaller or even budget for a surplus. The crux of all this is that the government would be expected to pursue these interventionist policies and this is what was done in the United Kingdom until 1979. After 1979 the same approach was adopted, but mainly with the intention of controlling inflation or cutting government borrowing, not with the intention of reducing unemployment. Indeed the long-run aim appears to be a balanced budget and any deficit is regretted.

The practice of this type of Keynesian 'counter-cyclical policy' proved very difficult given the imperfection of the available data and of the politicians who ran the system. They succumbed too often to the demands of elections and the level of expenditure was raised too fast or for too long and cuts in it were delayed or were insufficient to be effective. As has been stated before, the accelerator was applied beyond the time that braking was called for. This, and the practical problems of finding suitable schemes for government capital expenditure and the time lags involved in altering taxes and spending, caused the whole method of counter-cyclical policy to fall into disrepute in some countries such as the UK. At this point it should be explained that any change in the level of injections, I or G or X, would have a multiplied effect on the level of national income if there were unemployed resources such as labour and capital. An increase in injections if full employment already existed would have an inflationary effect.

Exercise I

If injections I + G + X are increased when the economy is near or at full employment level, inflation develops. Why is this the case?

22.3 The Multiplier and Accelerator Effects

The idea of the multiplier is based on the simple fact that if we spend money it becomes someone else's income. They will then proceed to spend most of that extra income but will probably save some of it, pay some tax and buy some imported products. Thus, when they spend what remains, they pass on less than they received, that is there has been a leakage or withdrawal from the flow of income. The people and businesses who receive the money that they have spent will, in turn, spend less than they received because they also pay tax and save and buy imports. This process continues until the amount being passed on dwindles away to nothing. The process can be analysed using just one withdrawal, saving, or two, saving and taxation, or three, saving, taxation and import spending. Which we choose depends on the model we are using. In all cases we are dealing with a geometrical progression which gives us a **formula for the multiplier**:

the multiplier $= \dfrac{1}{S + M + T}$

where S, M, and T are the marginal propensities to save, tax and import.

The multiplier can be expressed in a number of ways such as

$\dfrac{1}{MPS}$ or $\dfrac{1}{1 - MPC}$

It should be noted, if it has not already been obvious, that MPC + MPS = 1, if saving is the only withdrawal.

It should be apparent that the smaller the marginal propensities to save, tax and import the larger the multiplier because a higher proportion of income is passed on as expenditure at each stage. The following Figure 22.3 is a very simple mathematical explanation of the multiplier in action using a MPS of $\frac{1}{2}$, a MPC of $\frac{1}{2}$ and, therefore, using the formula above, a multiplier of 2. We start with an initial new injection of £64 million being spent on new signalling system for the west coast main line from London to Glasgow (we can always fantasize!) This example gives us a final level of national income (expenditure) of £128 million which consists of £64 million of the original investment spending and an additional £64 million of income which is spent on consumption. The process generates £64 million of savings which is equal to the original investment expenditure. The process therefore could go ahead with bank created credit in the expectation of society as a whole producing enough saving to pay for it. We end up with what is called realised saving equal to realised investment even though the original intentions of the different groups in society were not matched and intentions to save could be very different from intentions of entrepreneurs to invest. The act of investment spending generates higher income, savings, taxation and imports. It is obvious why the stimulation of investment expenditure is a priority with governments that accept the notion of intervention.

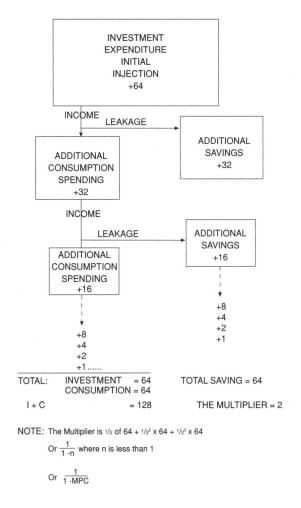

Figure 22.3   The investment multiplier simplified

Exercise 2

Calculate the investment multiplier if the only injection is investment and the only leakage is savings if: MPC = (a) 0.8; (b) 0.9; (c) 0.5; MPS = (d) 0.3; (e) 0.25. Assume there are unemployed resources.

The idea of the accelerator is based on the fact that as the multiplier effect occurs there will be, in certain circumstances, such a large increase in consumption demand that the entrepreneurs in those industries will consider new investment expenditure in plant and equipment in order to expand their output. If they decide on extra investment there will be a further boost to incomes, savings, taxation and imports as this additional investment takes place. There will, of course, be a time lag in the impact of this accelerator effect. An important point about the accelerator is that it is a function of the change in incomes and consumption expenditure and the desire of entrepreneurs to maintain a fixed ratio of desired capital stock to their level of anticipated output. Another is that it is the accelerator effect that largely explains the volatility of the output of capital goods industries because it leads to future surges in demand for replacement equipment. The accelerator theory can be expressed in several ways and there is much argument among economists about the various versions and their assumptions.

The accelerator effect may be dampened by several influences. First, there may already be plenty of spare capacity in consumption good industries making any further investment unnecessary. Second, entrepreneurs may hesitate and wait until they are certain that the growth of consumption is permanent before investing in new plant. Third, the increase in demand may be satisfied by importers who are quick to seize the opportunity. This happened in the case of the United Kingdom machine tools industry which failed to keep sufficient stocks to meet demand when it rose. Fourth, manufacturers may keep sufficient stocks to meet the extra demand or, alternatively, make the customer wait longer. This latter is a dangerous strategy if there are predatory foreign suppliers as mentioned above in the case of machine tools. Keeping stocks is, of course, expensive so the interest rate is important. Apart from the four factors mentioned the entrepreneur is still subject to the normal constraints governing investment decisions, that is the expected rate of profit and the cost of the investment, that is the rate of interest.

Note. The multiplier and accelerator are explained in most textbooks using lengthy numerical examples and complex diagrams. The numerical examples are often unrealistic in that they have multipliers of up to ten, presumably to make the arithmetic easy (but not as easy as 2 and £64 million!). Figure 22.4 shows the multiplier with a withdrawals and injections schedule. There are, of course, efforts to measure the real multiplier in the United Kingdom economy and one measure is fed into the Treasury computer model of the economy; it is 1.32 which is a surprisingly low figure. The importance of the multiplier–accelerator relationship is also the subject of academic debate but it is accepted by many as an explanation of the three-year business cycle.

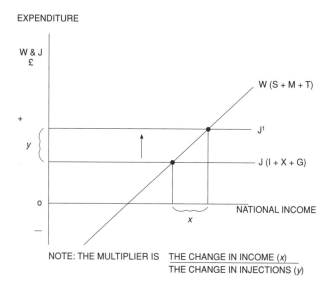

NOTE: THE MULTIPLIER IS $\dfrac{\text{THE CHANGE IN INCOME } (x)}{\text{THE CHANGE IN INJECTIONS } (y)}$

Figure 22.4   The multiplier, withdrawals and injections approach

22.4   Business Cycles

There is an enormous literature on the business cycle or the trade cycle as it is often known. Until the 'industrial revolution' after approximately 1750 there had only been an agricultural cycle based on the weather and harvests. After 1750 there emerged what was originally called the trade cycle and more recently the business cycle. At one time economists seemed to be obsessed with what they perceived as the regularity of the cycle and numerous theories of varying degrees of credibility were propounded to explain the cycle's existence and the alleged regularity. There has also been much analysis and argument about the existence, nature and form of an *international* trade cycle and the extent to which individual national cycles conformed to it. Post-1945 experience, and particularly that of the 1980s, indicates that the major economies' business cycles may no longer be synchronised but there is much disagreement on this.

The technical definition of the trade cycle is the short-term fluctuation of total output around its long-run trend path. Another term for long run is secular so you may read references to secular trends. The definition means that we are not talking simply about fluctuations in activity which we would expect to occur anyway. The simplified outline of the cycle shows an expansion of economic activity which is usually measured in terms of national income, followed by a contraction and then another expansion. Different writers have given different names to these phases and there is some disagreement both about the regularity of the cycle and the time period between the troughs or the peaks. The usual terminology is to talk about the peak, trough, expansion and contraction of the cycle as is shown in Figure 22.5 but you may see references to boom, slump, recession, upswing, downswing, recovery, depression and turning points. There may also be reference to false upturns or downswings or 'bumping along on the bottom' which occurs when there is a series of shortlived upturns when the cycle is at its lowest.

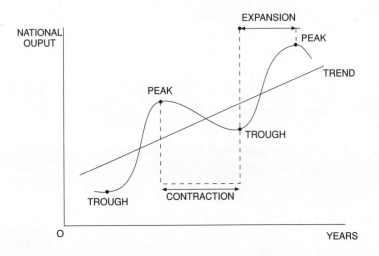

Figure 22.5   The business (trade) cycle

Exercise 3

The existence of the accelerator is often used to explain the business cycle. How might it influence the cycle?

Problems of counter-cyclical policy

In the context of macroeconomics the significance of the business cycle is the policies that could be adopted to counteract it. Keynes proposed what are called counter-cyclical policies and these lay at the heart of post-war efforts to prevent the trade cycle plunging the world economy into a rerun of 1929–33.

The main thrusts of counter-cyclical policy are to alter injections and withdrawals in order to raise or lower the level of aggregate demand to a level where it is at the equilibrium at which there is full employment. The problems associated with this policy are:

- The size of the gap between the level of expenditure at equilibrium and that which exists is very difficult to estimate. In other words, it is hard to know by how much to raise or cut taxes and expenditure. The estimate is a problem because of the continual changes in the economic climate as none of the main variables, interest rates, price levels, wage levels, foreign exchange rates, employment and balance of payments stay the same. Budgeting for an appropriate change in deficit or surplus is like shooting at a moving target. The Treasury model of the economy should be a help but its output is only as good as the data fed into it and the correctness of the assumptions on which it is constructed. The consequence of this initial problem is the danger that the alteration of aggregate demand may be too large or too small, with the associated risk of not eliminating the gap in aggregate expenditure.

- Another major problem is that of the timing of the changes in taxation and government expenditure. There are almost always time lags in the implementation of these changes despite attempts to have spending schemes ready. The government can keep pigeon holes full of plans for new hospitals, naval ships, bypasses, schools and so on ready for putting out to contract but they still take a long time before any extra money is flowing through the economy. This, by the way, is why we sometimes end up with new roads that were planned years ago and are inadequate from the day of opening or hospitals that were conceived against a different background of medical needs. On the other side, the disruptive effects of reductions in planned government expenditure can be appalling. The classic example is the way in which the electrification of the west coast main line was completed in four phases over several years, instead of in one fell swoop, because of cuts in government spending. Housing programmes suffered especially from this sort of on/off scheduling. It makes planning by construction companies very difficult and leads to the inefficient use of plant and labour.

- Unless any planned increase in expenditure is carefully managed in relation to the regional needs of the country it can have the effect of producing what is called 'overheating' or inflationary tendencies in some regions, usually the southeast and parts of the Midlands, before it has any significant impact on the areas with the highest unemployment. The government then puts on the brakes and the result can be an even worse regional imbalance than before.

- There is a temptation for governments to cut taxation whenever they can even if increases in government expenditure might be more appropriate or effective. There is, therefore, a danger of creating a consumer-led boom rather than an investment-led improvement in productive capacity.

- The United Kingdom economy does not operate in a vacuum and there are bound to be balance of payments consequences of attempts to raise or reduce the level of aggregate demand. It may be the intention to cut the balance of payments deficit via a reduction in the rate of internal inflation or to strengthen the exchange rate of the pound but the effects are fairly unpredictable and depend to a large extent on the market evaluation of expectations of interest rate changes and the size of the PSBR and the methods of financing it.

- It is rare for a government simply to adjust injections and withdrawals without any modification of monetary policy as well so interventions to alter aggregate demand will usually be accompanied by changes in interest rates and perhaps a change in credit restrictions if they are appropriate. Interest changes have an unsettling effect on markets and eventually may affect real investment expenditure. If the policy creates a larger public debt there may have to be considerable rises in interest rates to induce people to lend to the government. This, according to some economists, produces the 'crowding out' effect whereby the private sector is unable, or unwilling, at the margins to pay the high interest rates for investment borrowing.

- In some ways the biggest problem of Keynesian counter-cyclical policy is persuading the politicians not to use it for electoral advantage. There is good evidence from modern British experience that most governments have used it for this purpose and it brings the system into disrepute as well as producing undesirable macroeconomic effects.

22.5   The Relationship Between Unemployment and Inflation

This is a complex relationship. Inflation is defined as a sustained rise in the general price level. In periods of very high inflation, or hyperinflation as it is often called, there is also very high unemployment and there are plenty of examples to illustrate that fact, ranging from Germany in the early 1920s to the Ukraine and Bulgaria in 1997. The government is literally printing money to meet its debts and there is a breakdown of normal financial arrangements and jobs disappear or only survive when barter becomes the norm or a foreign currency is used instead of the national one.

There is, however, evidence that reasonably low rates of inflation, say below two to three per cent per year, are actually a stimulus to economic growth and to employment because entrepreneurs have optimistic expectations about the future in terms of market demand and profit. This state of affairs typified the United Kingdom economy in the period from 1945 to about 1965 (you can argue about this date in favour of an earlier one).

There was a short period, between 1958 and the late 1960s, when it appeared as if the relationship between unemployment and inflation had been established in the British context. This was when A. W. Phillips published a statistical analysis of the relationship between the rate of change of money wages (inflation) and the unemployment rate in the UK between 1861 and 1957. The conclusion which is usually known as the Phillips curve shows an inverse relationship between inflation and unemployment. The basic diagram is Figure 22.6.

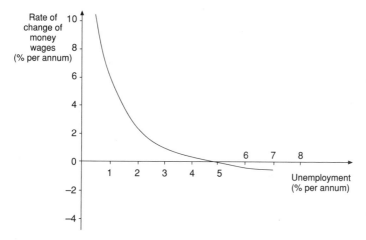

Source: A.W. Phillips 'The relationship between unemployment and the rate of change of money wages in the UK 1861–1957, *Economica*, 1958.

Figure 22.6   The Phillips curve

The implications of the curve were absorbed by the people in the Treasury who made economic policy. They realised that there was what is called a *trade off between inflation and employment*, that is, if they chose to reduce unemployment there would be a rise in the inflation rate and if they chose to cut inflation they would incur a rise in unemployment. If you look at the curve carefully you can see that it cuts the x axis between 5 and 6 per cent which means that there would be zero inflation when there was that percentage of unemployment. The other point to note is that the closer the unemployment rate is to zero the steeper the curve which means that inflation accelerated as unemployment fell. The explanation for this is that there would be competition for labour as the unemployment level fell and that would bid up the level of wages and costs.

Running the economy on the basis of the Phillips curve, among other things, proved successful for a time but it became obvious that the relationship was breaking down after 1966. The explanations are usually based on the growth of knowledge by trade unions and employers that this was the policy approach of the government. They therefore began to anticipate a certain rate of inflation and began to build it into their price rises and wage demands. In other words, it was expectations of future inflation that broke down the Phillips curve relationship. To explain further, trade unions would anticipate a rise of inflation of say 3 per cent in the coming year so they would take account of that in their pay claims and ask for that 3 per cent plus more for other things such as productivity increases. The trade unions were concentrating on the growth of their members' real wages. Employers, for their part, began to incorporate the expected level of wage increases or inflation into their pricing and costing strategies. There developed an expectation and understanding in the nation that prices would rise annually by a certain percentage. Indeed the budget began to incorporate inflation assumptions. The old Phillips curve gave way to an analysis that is called the 'expectations added' or the 'augmented Phillips' curve. It should be noted that the original Phillips curve deals in *money* wages which is its weakness because it can be argued that people negotiate for *real* wages; the modified versions incorporate real wages. Economists sometimes refer to something called the *money illusion* which is a short-term phenomenon where workers accept wage increases based on the money involved but in the long run the illusion disappears and they want real wage increases above the rate of inflation.

The conclusion of the new analysis was very depressing. It argued that any attempt by the people making policy to cut unemployment by the traditional Keynesian methods was doomed to a temporary short-run success followed by a long-run return to a combination of inflation and unemployment that was worse than the original combination, either higher unemployment or higher inflation or both. This is usually explained using a Phillips curve with additional curves (expectations added) to the right of the original and a series of arrows showing the movements over time. In the years that this realisation was percolating through the system the relationship of unemployment and inflation took on a different manifestation. The United Kingdom began, in the 1970s, to suffer both rising unemployment and rising inflation. At this point we should look at the possible causes of inflation and unemployment.

Exercise 4

Why should high rates of unemployment be associated with high rates of inflation when falling prices are also associated with rising unemployment?

22.6 The Causes of Unemployment

It is possible to produce several different classifications of the types and causes of unemployment but it is probably best to stick to Lord Beveridge's on the basis that he knew what he was talking about! There have, of course, been new insights since he published *Full Employment in a Free Society*. He talked about *cyclical, structural, frictional and seasonal* and some modern authors like the sound of 'technological' but that is really incorporated into frictional. If we deal with the simplest first:

- **Seasonal unemployment** is endemic in certain industries and there is not a great deal that can be done about it except to diversify or to adopt new technology that obviates seasonal factors. The most affected industries are agriculture, construction and tourism but seasonal demand does affect many consumer durable goods industries such as the motor industry. Students usually volunteer Christmas card manufacturing as a seasonal industry but greetings card manufacturers diversify their output to achieve a reasonably smooth output through the year.

- **Frictional unemployment** arises from the natural changes of the economy in response to short-term alterations of demand and to new technology. Within reason it is essential to the health of an economy because labour needs to be able to change jobs in search of new experience and qualifications and employers need to be able to alter their mix of workers when new methods arrive. The assumption behind this definition is that the unemployed will be able to get new jobs that suit them. The distinction between frictional and structural may become a little blurred when there are high levels of unemployment.

- **Structural unemployment** arises from a permanent fall in demand for the good or service provided by an industry. As economies grow and develop they shed industries or sectors of them. Newly developing countries tend to start with certain industries such as textiles, iron and steel, shipbuilding and small consumer durable goods and eventually move on to automobiles and larger and more technologically advanced consumption goods. This process of development and change may cause those industries in developed countries to fall into decline. We can see this at work in the United Kingdom shipbuilding industry where world dominance has given way to a small industry producing naval vessels, some very specialised ships and oil industry vessels. The industry has shed many thousands of jobs permanently. There are similar examples in textiles, motor cycles and coal. In some cases industries disappear because of new technology, for example the old metal typewriter and cash register industries which have been replaced by computerised, mainly plastic, machines. The cure for structural decline is education, retraining, research and development and government intervention to assist in redevelopment and managed decline. (The industry often asks for a protective tariff.) The European Union regional policy, especially for the iron and steel industry is a good example of such policies to combat structural unemployment.

- **Cyclical unemployment** is sometimes called demand deficient unemployment which gets to the core of the problem. When the trade cycle passes its peak and moves into the downswing or recession it is accompanied by rising unemployment because demand has fallen or ceased rising as quickly as before. If the cycle is synchronised internationally the problems are aggravated. Keynes was very concerned about cyclical unemployment because of the experience of the interwar years and his counter-cyclical policy proposals were aimed at preventing, reducing or removing it.

22.7 The Causes of Inflation

Inflation can be caused by different factors or by a mixture of elements. Sometimes the cause is very clear – a government tries to remove its debt by printing money. It may do this in the aftermath of a war or during a war to finance its purchases or it may do it during extreme political upheavals such as during the transition from a command economy to an enterprise system. Even responsible governments may contribute to inflation by excessive short-term borrowing using very liquid assets whose existence affects the volume of credit creation. It is also possible to accelerate the rate of inflation if a country such as the USA removes large quantities of gold from its accumulated stock and spends it over a short period.

There has been a debate in recent years about two types of inflation, demand-pull and cost-push but they may be viewed as simply different approaches to the same thing because it is extremely difficult to separate cause and effect when dealing with inflation. Some economists would insist, however, that at certain time periods the inflation was of one type or the other.

Demand-pull inflation arises if there is an excess demand in relation to the ability of the economy to produce. This raises the question of where the excess demand comes from. If a predominantly Keynesian approach is taken the most likely culprit is government expenditure and, probably, an excessive budget deficit. Additional sources could be a combination of consumption demand and investment demand but again both of these need to be explained. Excess consumer demand might arise from the anticipation of future income by extra borrowing and the use of credit. Excess investment expenditure, if such a thing is possible, might arise from the accelerator effect or from the inability of the capital goods sector to meet the demand because of under-capacity or inefficiency. There is also the possibility of a change in the savings ratio with reduced savings stimulating demand but this does not fit the assumptions of some versions of the theory which argue that savings are determined by income and are, therefore, a passive element. The Keynesian view is that there is an autonomous increase in demand and that the money supply adjusts itself to fit. If a monetarist approach is taken the argument is that the excess demand springs from an expansion of the money supply that is not matched by a growth of the productive capacity of the country. The question then arises of where the expansion of the money supply comes from. Once again the government may be the culprit with excess borrowing (PSBR) and excess expenditure. To some extent the excess money might be in the form of inflows of foreign money as when North Sea oil was exploited in the late 1970s and early 1980s. Demand-pull inflation is usually illustrated by an inflationary gap diagram as in Figure 22.7 but it can be illustrated, as in the next chapter, by aggregate demand and aggregate supply curves,

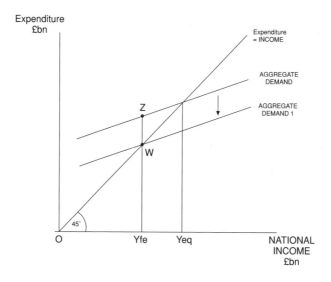

The economy reaches full employment level of national income (Yfe) before it can reach equilibrium level (Yeq). There is, therefore, a gap of ZW.

Figure 22.7   The inflationary gap: demand-pull approach

Cost-push inflation is the other type of inflation that is distinguished. This is defined as a sustained rise in the general price level arising from an autonomous increase in costs. There are three possible causes of such a rise, higher real wages demanded by workers, raised profit margins on the part of firms and a rise in import prices. The most extreme versions of the cost-push theory attribute the whole of the inflationary pressure to the pressure of trade unions for higher wages for their members. Right-wing politicians and the tabloid press usually accept this version unquestioningly. They call it 'wage inflation'. The second cause, rising profit margins, is less popular but is favoured by left wingers and some trade unionists who point to the monopolies and oligopolies that dominate our economy and accuse them of operating a cost plus system of pricing so that they always ratchet upwards their prices to absorb any cost increase whether it be wages or other costs. This is sometimes called an administered price theory of inflation. The third cause, rising import prices, is associated with the rapid oil price rise created by OPEC in the early and mid-1970s, but it can arise from a fall in the foreign exchange rate which may raise the price of almost all imports. Needless to say, if there is cost-push inflation it probably results from a mixture of all three. There is a problem here in that there has to be an explanation of how the higher prices induced by higher costs are absorbed by people and firms. The inference is that they are able to meet the price rises because of higher incomes. How do we know which came first, the higher income or the higher price? Cost-push inflation is usually shown with a shift of the aggregate supply curve as on Figure 22.8.

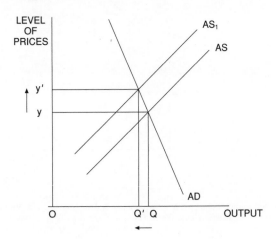

Figure 22.8   Cost-push inflation

When all the arguments about the causes of inflation are over we still have the problem of how it is that the United Kingdom has had a very high rate of unemployment and a high rate of inflation. An attempt to answer this is given in the next chapter.

22.8 How Can the Government Deal with Inflation?

There are three main methods and a combination of all three is usually used:

1. budgetary policy which is manipulating taxation and public expenditure. This is often called fiscal policy;
2. monetary policy which is using interest rates to influence the demand for money and attempts to control the supply of money;
3. direct controls which includes price controls and incomes policies and extremes such as rationing.

Direct controls and incomes policies. Budgetary policy and monetary policy have been discussed in Chapter 4 so this section will concentrate on direct controls. In the context of the control of inflation the most frequently used method has been some sort of control over the rise of incomes occasionally with some form of price control. Some countries such as Germany have managed to control their inflation levels by strict controls over monetary expansion and an annual national agreement on the level of income rises that could be accommodated within the expected growth of the GNP. The United Kingdom in contrast has applied a series of *ad hoc* and largely ineffective, unfair or partial policies whenever all other budgetary and monetary options seemed not to work. If you asked a Conservative Government spokesperson in 1997 if there was an incomes policy in the United Kingdom they would say 'no, we believe in the free market forces in the labour market'. Indeed, one reason Mrs Thatcher was elected in 1979 was that she vehemently decried the effectiveness of incomes policies and vowed not to interfere in labour markets by this method. In practice, however, like most governments, it operated a very tough incomes policy over its own employees and those employed by local authorities. Each year the government arbitrarily decided what it thought it could afford in terms of a percentage increase and communicated this figure as a ceiling which it was prepared to finance to the various negotiating bodies. If they made awards above this figure they had to find the extra money from their own sources or from 'efficiency savings'. The result of this policy was similar to previous incomes policies – it caused the affected employees to suffer a fall in incomes relative to other groups in society whose incomes were not restrained. Thus average earnings might rise by say 4.5 per cent while public sector earnings rose by only 2.6 per cent in a given year. The effect might also to be produce a fall in real incomes if the inflation rate was, say 3 per cent.

Incomes policies. A study of post-war incomes policies in the United Kingdom makes very depressing reading because of their repeated failure and repetition of previous error. It is difficult to escape the conclusion that they were polices adopted in desperation and without a coherent philosophy. Despite this, one of the last efforts, the 'social contract' of March 1974 to July 1975 was very successful in that it helped to cut the inflation rate from 27 to

12 per cent in two years, although it did create a backlog of pay claims. The nature of the policies can be seen from their names, the first being the Cripps–TUC pact of 1948. (Cripps was a famously austere Chancellor of the Exchequer.) Others are: The Pay Pause; the Guiding Light; the Statement of Intent; the Freeze; Severe Restraint; Continued Restraint; Reserved Restraint; Stages 1, 2 and 3; the Social Contract; Compulsory Non-Statutory Incomes Policy. There were 13 in all between 1948 and 1979 with only the periods between 1950 and 1961 and 1970–1972 free of them. There have been three main types:

1. Freezes on pay increases for the employed. The self-employed may not be affected or those on commissions and fees or unearned income.
2. Voluntary norms where the government set a figure which might be a percentage increase or an absolute money amount or a range of either. Such norms tend to erode traditional pay differentials and store up trouble when the restraint is removed.
3. Statutory norms where the government passed laws imposing ceilings on pay rises for groups. The figure might be zero or a small percentage but there were always exceptions for special cases such as where there was an increase in productivity or for cases of scarcity of skilled labour.

Incomes policies sometimes had price controls attached or even a rein on profits but these were exceptionally hard to monitor and administer. The whole system created injustices because only those whose income fell under the net suffered pay restraint. Profit restraints were particularly hard to enforce. There was inevitably much evasion and a resort to payments in kind. The unhealthy British obsession with company cars and other perks is partly the result of the succession of incomes policies. The main problem of the policies, however, was that although they might be temporarily helpful they built up accumulated wage demands for the future. They also eroded established differentials and relativities and encouraged trade unions to play a game of 'restore the differential' when the policy was relaxed. There were, however, some bright points of co-operation and effectiveness and there are still some economists and politicians who think that a properly thought out, universally applied, policy of annually negotiated norms along the lines of the German model would work. Some British observers, however, think that the German model began, in 1996, to show signs of breaking down.

Exercise 5

What lessons can be learned from the United Kingdom's past experience with prices and incomes policies?

22.9 An Alternative, Supply-side Policy

The methods discussed above proved inadequate in many respects in controlling inflation in the mid to late 1970s although it might be reasonable to blame the politicians or world economic forces rather than the methods. Monetarist economists of that time argued that prices and incomes policies were bad because they had an adverse effect on the aggregate supply of the economy and shifted it to the left. They advocated policies that would improve aggregate supply and these have become known as *supply-side policies*. Their overall effect is supposed to increases aggregate supply and shift the AS curve to the right as in Figure 22.9.

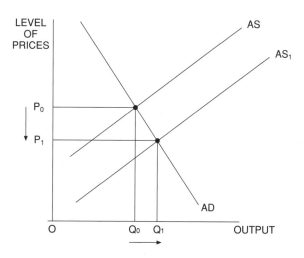

Figure 22.9   Intented effects of supply-side policies

Supply-side policy has become a broad term with widening ramifications. The essentials are:

The main determinant of the growth of national output is based on the efficient use and allocation of the factors of production, especially labour and capital. Pareto's ideas of allocative efficiency are relevant here.

Labour markets should be liberalised to allow free market forces to operate. This belief results in efforts to deregulate the labour market by such acts as the abolition of wages councils, the adoption of local as opposed to national pay bargaining in the state sector, the reduction of the powers of trade unions, the reduction of workers' protection from dismissal, resistance to European Union labour legislation to protect workers (the Social Chapter opt out), opposition to a national minimum wage and the removal of restrictions on women's working hours. In the background also is the war against anyone who becomes unwilling to work because they are better off drawing social benefits, that is against the poverty trap. In principle the method adopted here is to remove benefit so the people concerned are forced back into the labour market or into crime. An example is the removal of benefits for young people aged 16 to 18. There are attempts also to improve labour mobility and to make it easier for small firms to employ workers without incurring excessive social benefit payment costs. This set of policies is summed up by its critics as a cheap labour policy which favours the bad employer at the expense of the good. In May 1997 the new Labour Government said it would sign the Social Chapter. It may take up to 2 years for it to be put into effect.

Capital markets, it is believed, **should be liberalised** to allow the free flow of capital nationally and internationally. There should also be, it is argued, freedom of financial markets, privatisation of nationalised industries, compulsory competitive tendering for local government contracts, agencies in central government departments, and general deregulation of transport and other areas of enterprise. Most of this sounds fine but we end up with a complex and possibly ineffective system of regulation and supervision of markets and the privatised sector. The final enemy of such policies is the tendency towards monopoly and the corruption of entrepreneurs as well as market imperfections.

The tax system, it is argued, **should be reformed** to stimulate initiative, entrepreneurial skills and effort. This takes the form of cutting taxes on income and on higher income earners, and on capital gains, in the hope or belief that there will be a surge in enterprise and work and a trickle-down effect that raises the number of jobs and the incomes of the lower income groups. The tax burden is shifted from income taxes to expenditure taxes. As has been mentioned before, this analysis is founded on the Laffer curve analysis (see Chapter 21) and on the possibly unfounded belief that the rich work harder if they are offered more money whereas the poor need to be paid low wages to induce them to greater effort.

The next chapter discusses inflation and unemployment again in the context of economic growth and aggregate demand and aggregate supply.

23 Price stability, employment and growth

Aims of the chapter

To:
- apply aggregate demand and supply analysis to the problem of inflation;
- discuss the relationship between the control of inflation and price stability;
- explore the relationship between price stability, growth and employment.

23.1 Aggregate Demand and Supply

The Keynesian-style analysis of demand-pull inflation was clear and straight-forward when there was an inflationary gap, that is a level of aggregate demand (C+I+G+(X-M)) which was beyond the capacity of the economy to fulfil, that is above the full employment equilibrium. Keynesian analysis was also fine for studying the problem of the deflationary gap where national income equilibrium was reached before full employment level, that is when there was a deficiency of demand. It became unsatisfactory for analysing the new situation of rising unemployment and high levels of inflation which characterised the late 1960s, 70s, 80s and much of the period since. In 1986 for example, when there were over 3 million unemployed (11.2 per cent) the inflation rate was at its lowest level of the 1980s at 3.4 per cent. Aggregate demand and aggregate supply analysis helps to tackle the question of rising unemployment and high inflation but it does involve controversial areas about something called the 'natural rate of unemployment' and 'voluntary unemployment'. These will be discussed later.

Aggregate demand

Aggregate demand (AD) curves relate the demand for real output to the price level so they are not the same as the demand curves for individual goods which relate the quantity demanded to price changes. The AD curve is drawn up from a schedule which gives the quantity of net national product that would be bought at each general price level. When we have drawn the curve it shows combinations of output and price where the goods markets and money markets are in equilibrium at the same time. The conclusions to be drawn from the AD curve are that when there is inflation the demand for real output of goods and services will fall. If the price level were falling, deflation, the demand for real output would rise. The reasons for it sloping as it does are that rising prices raise interest rates because the real money supply has fallen, that is there is a rise in the demand for money in relation to its supply. Another reason is that there is a fall in investment because of the higher interest rates. Moreover, if the inflation rate is higher than that of competitor countries there will be a fall in demand for exports until the foreign exchange rate falls enough to redeem the situation. The other reason is often called the *wealth effect* or the *real balance effect* which some economists think is theoretically acceptable but weak in practice. The argument here, very simplified, is that as prices rise people feel that their money assets are worth less and they therefore spend less. Conversely, if prices fall they feel that their accumulated money assets are worth more and they spend more. The AD curve can be seen in Figure 23.1 together with the AS curve.

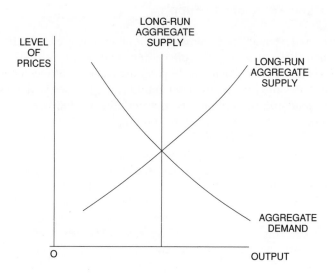

Figure 23.1   Aggregate demand and supply

Aggregate supply

In the case of the aggregate supply curve a distinction has to be made between the short and the long run. Aggregate supply is the quantity of net national product that would be supplied at each general price level if people's expectations of price were constant. The short-run aggregate supply curve slopes upwards to the right, that is it has a positive slope. The reason for this is that it is expected that inflation produces a rise in real output but this assumption is based on the idea that firms expect to get higher profits and that will only happen if prices rise faster than costs of production, particularly wage costs. This implies that real wages are cut by inflation but this is not the case if workers are building inflationary expectations into their wage bargaining. In practice most workers' real wages rise in periods of inflation because their nominal wages rise by a higher percentage than the rise in prices.

The long-run aggregate supply curve is the subject of much debate in modern economics, or rather the assumptions behind it are, especially with regard to the relationship between nominal wages, rises in prices and real wages. The general agreement is that the long-run aggregate supply curve is vertical above the level of real output where there is full employment because the economy has limitations on its ability to expand real output. There is, after all, a restriction on the amount of land, labour and capital available and a limit on the ability to improve their combination to expand output. In brief, the classical model concludes that increases in aggregate demand will, to begin with, raise both prices and output but that after a time, as prices continue to rise, output will fall. In the long run the only effect of the increased aggregate demand would be to raise the price level without any increase in aggregate supply. The long-run equilibrium will have the same level of output but a higher price level. In contrast, the Keynesian model, which is drawn in Figure 23.2, indicates that the effect depends on where the increase in aggregate demand occurs in relation to the level of real output on the long-run aggregate supply curve.

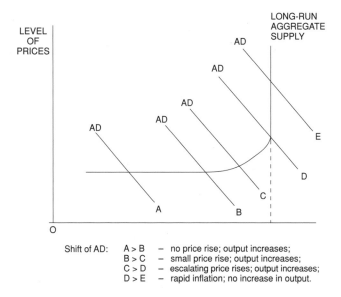

Shift of AD: A > B   – no price rise; output increases;
               B > C   – small price rise; output increases;
               C > D   – escalating price rises; output increases;
               D > E   – rapid inflation; no increase in output.

Figure 23.2   Long-run equilibrium: Keynesian version

The conclusions of the Keynesian model are that, if there is a serious deficiency of demand, then an increase in AD can produce an increase in AS without a rise in the price level. If, however, the economy is close to the point where there is full employment of labour, land and capital there will be some increase in real output but also a rise in the price level. At or beyond the point of full employment any increase in AD will force a rise in the price level, that is create inflation, without any rise in real output. There is no 'trade off' between inflation and unemployment beyond that point. If the long-run aggregate supply could also be shifted to the right the price rise would be less or non-existent.

Exercise I

What measures could be adopted by an interventionist government to increase aggregate supply in the economy?

23.2   The Natural Rate of Unemployment

This is a term that has many explanations, some very long and complicated and some so brief that they do not mean a great deal. Here are a couple:

1. The natural rate of unemployment is the rate of unemployment that would exist if we had 'full employment', that is mainly some frictional and perhaps some structural unemployment.
2. The natural rate of unemployment is the level determined by frictional and structural factors and which cannot be reduced by raising aggregate demand.

It is a long-run concept and is usually related to the Phillips curve, that is the vertical version. It is used to explain why any effort to reduce unemployment below its 'natural rate' will produce accelerating inflation. The natural rate of unemployment is sometimes called NAIRU or non-accelerating inflation rate of unemployment.

The Bank of England in its *Quarterly Bulletin* of May 1993 (p.174) contains a reference to an article by R. Cromb which surveys different authors' estimates of NAIRU. The estimates are given in Table 23.1 together with figures for what the actual level of unemployment was in the relevant decade. They make rather gloomy reading and partly explain why the government seemed to adopt such a helpless posture towards unemployment. If it believes in the application of a natural rate or NAIRU it becomes resigned to high levels of unemployment. There are some economists who think the concept should be ditched because it takes insufficient account of the growth that could be achieved in real output if the unemployed were back at work with adequate training and skills, capital and modern technology to help them. It is also hard to place much credence on estimates that vary so much.

Table 23.1 NAIRU estimates for the United Kingdom (claimant definition)[a]

| | Period within which the estimates fall | | | |
	1969–73	1974–80	1981–87	1988–90
NAIRU range	1.6–5.6%	4.5–7.3%	5.2–9.9%	3.5–8.1%
Actual U rate	2.5%	3.8%	10.1%	6.8%
Number of estimates	11	13	15	5

[a] R Cromb, 'A survey of recent econometric work on the NAIRU', *Journal of Economic Studies* (1993, forthcoming).
Source: The Bank of England, *Quarterly Bulletin*, May 1993, London.

At this point it is helpful to refer to the term **involuntary unemployment** which may, as usual, be defined in different ways. Much of the modern debate about unemployment is conducted in terms of whether it is voluntary or involuntary. Involuntary unemployment exists if workers are prepared to work at the going rate of pay but are unable to find jobs. The conclusion is that this unemployment could be removed by an increase in aggregate demand without a rise in the price level. **Voluntary unemployment** is that which arises from people voluntarily searching for jobs, that is they choose not to work at the wage rate offered. They wish to be in the labour force but not at the prevailing wage rate. The natural rate of unemployment consists of people who are in this category of the voluntarily unemployed, that is the percentage of the labour force that is unemployed when the labour market is in equilibrium.

It is possible, therefore, to divide unemployment into two categories:

1. The natural, or equilibrium, rate which is the voluntarily unemployed whose numbers are determined by the usual turnover of the labour market, by trade union activity in pressing for excessively high wages and a failure of incentives to readjust the distribution of workers. There may also be some problems arising from structural change in the economy. This type of unemployment may only be removed by 'supply-side' action which usually means creating a climate where workers are willing to accept lower wages and/or more flexible working practices;

2. Involuntary unemployment which has a variety of names – Keynesian unemployment, demand deficient unemployment or cyclical unemployment. As the names imply it is assumed that this type could be removed by short-term government measures to adjust aggregate demand in order to raise the demand for labour.

Exercise 2

Why is demand deficient unemployment so called?

23.3 Price Stability

United Kingdom governments since 1945 have all stressed the need to restrain inflation and emphasised the benefits of price stability. Their motives have been based upon the desire to maintain the price competitiveness of UK exports and the exchange rate of sterling, especially if the pound was in a managed system such as the Bretton Woods (1945–71) or the ERM (1990–92). They were also influenced by the perceived evils of inflation which are briefly summarised below. It is important to remember that inflation actually benefits some sectors of industry, commerce and society. In practice most of us gain and lose from inflation so it is a matter of personal circumstance whether we gain or lose overall. Having said that, it is probable that most would be even better off if inflation were very low. There are, however, some gains from low levels of inflation because it may be a stimulus to investment and growth. The case against inflation depends on its level, its persistence and whether it is anticipated or unanticipated but it can be summarised as follows:

● **There are considerable administrative costs associated with persistent inflation**. There is a constant need to reprice goods and services and to relabel them; manufacturers' price lists have to be revised at regular intervals; coin in the slot machines need frequent conversion; computerised laser scanning pricing systems in supermarkets require constant updating although this is easier than relabelling every can and packet. These administrative costs are usually called *menu costs* after the analogy of constantly changing the prices on a menu. If the inflation is anticipated these 'menu costs' become an additional cost of production or supply as well as being a nuisance. It may be that our society has become so adjusted to inflation that we have made the administrative process of changing prices too easy. When resale price maintenance existed on a wide range of packaged products and the price was printed on them the costs and impact on consumers of changing the printed price was very large and, therefore, a deterrent.

- **Inflation is normally accompanied by higher interest rates** than occur when prices are stable. These higher nominal interest rates alter the way people regard their savings and money balances. Higher interest rates raise the opportunity cost of holding money in liquid form and there is a stronger incentive to spend time and effort seeking the best manner in which to hold financial assets. Such expenditure of time and effort is usually called the *shoe-leather cost* of inflation because it takes up resources that could be spent on productive enterprise. Are all the people who are employed by the media to advise us on the best things to do with our money part of this shoe-leather cost?

- **Inflation adversely affects those members of society who are on relatively fixed incomes**. They need not necessarily be the 'poor' but tend to be pensioners who have a fixed income from an occupational pension or people who have saved lump sums for retirement intending to live off the interest on the capital. The income of the latter group can easily fall behind if real interest rates become low or even negative, that is the rate of inflation exceeds the nominal interest rate received. There may be some degree of indexation built in to pensions as in the state system in the United Kingdom but the British method now is to use the index of retail prices, a special pensioners' version, rather than as used to be the case, an index of average earnings. Thus, although the pension keeps up with one version of the RPI and inflation, it falls behind most of the wage earners in the country whose incomes are likely to be rising faster than inflation. The pensioner, therefore, becomes relatively poorer. Those on relatively fixed incomes may be those employed by the state, such as nurses, teachers, civil servants and so on, whose incomes are controlled as part of an anti-inflation policy. While the employees in the private sector may keep ahead of inflation the public sector worker may fall behind absolutely and relatively. Some economists refer to inflation as an *arbitrary redistribution* of income between groups in society. This redistribution is, to some extent, between income receivers but also between borrowers and lenders (although most people may be both).

- **Inflation or the expectation of it may affect the real markets for goods and services**. It may persuade people to hold real physical assets such as property, land, gold, diamonds and works of art instead of financial balances. Even pension funds have 'invested' in works of art instead of stocks and shares and there has been a constant toing and froing into and out of land holding by institutional investors. The anticipation of inflation of property values contributed to the house price boom of the 1980s and to a distortion of the housing market.

- **Inflation creates uncertainty** and the higher its level the greater the problem. Contracts have to incorporate inflationary expectations. The longer the period of the contract the greater the risk that the prediction is wrong. The main impact is probably on investment decisions and that affects economic growth.

- **The government is affected by inflation** in many ways, both in its expenditure plans and in its revenues. Inflation is not uniform among the various sectors of the economy and government services may be more affected because of their labour intensive nature. The history of defence contracts in the United Kingdom with their constantly escalating costs is a sharp warning about the problems of inflationary accounting. One of the difficulties for the government is called *fiscal drag* which has several manifestations but consists, in the main, of pushing people into higher tax brackets because their nominal incomes have risen. If the government wishes to prevent this rise in the real tax burden it has to index the various allowances and thresholds. If it does not do so the rising tax revenues act as a drag on the level of aggregate demand.

- **The experience of hyperinflation destroys the basis of society's economic stability**. Debts are quickly written off with worthless paper money and only those left holding real assets end up better off. The middle classes, especially retired groups and rentiers, suffer a loss of income and social status. The poor become desperate and respect for property may give way to anarchy. The scene is set for political extremism, revolution or a military usurpation of power.

- **The measures taken by the state to counteract inflation may be more harmful than the inflation itself**. It may be that mild, below 2 per cent, inflation is not very harmful or even beneficial. The frequent changes in taxation, the switching of public expenditure and the drives for economy may all have adverse economic and psychological effects. The cure, if it works, may be worse than the disease.

Exercise 3

Are you personally a net gainer or loser from United Kingdom inflation over the last five years?

Price stability as a policy since 1992

The United Kingdom was forced to withdraw from the European Exchange Rate Mechanism (ERM) in October 1992 and had to search for a policy that replaced the discipline of membership. During the two-year period of membership the rate of inflation had fallen steeply, the level of unemployment had risen fast and interest rates were tied to (above) those in Germany. Not all of the rise in unemployment was the result of membership of the ERM and the high exchange rate of the pound against the mark; most of it was due to the recession which had begun before the UK joined.

Inflation (a)

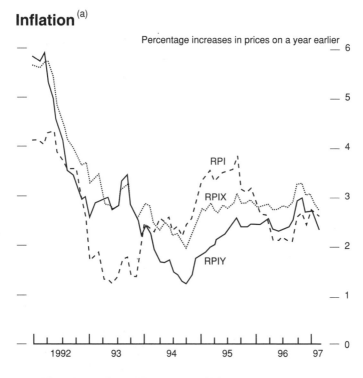

(a)   Adjusted by the Bank of England for an ONS error in under-recording aggregate price indices between February and May 1995.

Source: Bank of England, Quarterly Inflation Report, May 1997

Figure 23.3   Inflation, 1992–97

The new policy included for the first time an *explicit inflation target* which was to keep inflation at or below 2.5 per cent as measured by the Retail Price Index excluding mortgage interest (RPIX). Although 2.5 or less was the target figure the Chancellor accepted that there might be problems caused by unpredictable external shocks and fixed a range of 1 to 4 per cent within which the target operated. The success of this policy can be judged from Figure 23.3. It can be seen that RPIX inflation fell from late 1990 to the fourth quarter of 1994 after which it began to rise again because of 'adverse supply shocks' from the rise in relative import prices aggravated by a falling exchange rate of the pound in early 1995. By mid-1996 RPIX, measured on a three-month annualised basis had fallen below 2.5 per cent. The average rate of inflation in the United Kingdom over the last 30 years to 1996 has been 8 per cent, whereas in the three years 1993 to 1996 it was below 3 per cent. The August 1996 Bank of England Inflation Report concluded that a 'tightening of monetary policy was necessary at some point to achieve a better than even chance of keeping inflation below 2.5 per cent in the medium term'. This meant that interest rates would be raised because changes take some time to have any effect on the level of spending and inflation.

The rate of interest is, therefore, at the centre of government monetary policy as implemented by the Bank of England and is set in relation to expectations of the future trend of inflation. The indicators that are used to assess the future are demand, output, money and credit growth, asset prices and the exchange rate. This is a departure from previous practice; for example in the early 1980s the growth of the money supply as measured by a changing measure or group of measures was very important and was sometimes a specific target. In the late 1980s the foreign exchange rate became the most important target while the UK was in the ERM. The monetary authorities now *monitor* narrow and broad money measures but not as targets. Ranges are set for each as indicators for the future course of inflation.

The Medium Term Financial Strategy (MTFS) was introduced in 1980 with the objective of ensuring that monetary and fiscal policies complement one another in a coherent framework in the attack on inflation. Thus the basic aim has been price stability and the main weapon has usually been changes in short-term interest rates. The MTFS has, however, changed in many ways since it was introduced. To begin with it worked within a framework of monetary aggregates set as intermediate targets and with a broad money target as well. There are two official monetary aggregates in the UK, M0 and M4. The MTFS fixes monitoring ranges for these two only. M0 is notes and coins in circulation plus bankers' balances at the Bank of England (the non-statutory deposits). M4 is M0 plus a list of other private sector holdings which are essentially bank and building society deposits and certificates of deposit which are liquid and are regarded as money by their owners.

The early targets were abandoned as it became obvious that they were not being achieved and that the broad money figures were misleading because of the deregulation and increased competition in the financial services and banking industries. During the mid-1980s the monetary authorities set a range of indicators rather than a single monetary aggregate although a broad money target was published until 1986. Since 1984 targets or monitoring ranges have been set for M0 or narrow money as it is called. More recently there has been much more concentration on the weekly measure of narrow money because it is a good short-run indicator of consumption spending and is a reasonably good leading indicator of future events. After 1986 the broad money, M4, targets were abandoned and the emphasis was on the narrow money target range and on the exchange rate with a view to possible entry into the ERM. After entry into the ERM in 1992 the exchange rate became the central target for monetary policy because the pound had to be kept within its six per cent wide bands range on either side of the central par value against the Deutschmark of £1 = DM 2.95. Membership of the ERM helped (not caused) the United Kingdom interest rates to fall from 15 to 10 per cent in the first year and a half and the rate of inflation fell from 12 to 4 per cent but both falls were accompanied by a rise in unemployment from 5.8 to 9.9 per cent (standardised rates).

The episode of membership of the ERM raises the problem of the compatibility of different policy objectives. The dilemma is often stated in terms of what is called **the impossibility theorem**. This says that the bodies responsible for economic and financial policies cannot simultaneously and continuously follow the three objectives of:

1. free mobility of capital;
2. fixed exchange rates;
3. an independent monetary policy.

The reason for the incompatibility is that world capital markets are now integrated and flows of money will establish more uniform interest rates, given differences in national circumstances, and will frequently modify exchange rates against the wishes of governments. In practice, therefore, the United Kingdom monetary authorities try to obtain the best possible trade-off between exchange rates and domestic monetary independence. Unanticipated movements of the sterling exchange rate have an impact on the price of imports and exports and alter the costs of raw materials and semi-manufactured goods with a consequent knock-on effect on the rate of inflation. These changes may impinge on domestic monetary policy by affecting the interest rate.

Confidence and credibility are two words that accompany many government statements about monetary policy. The use of an inflation target will only be effective if business and commerce – 'the markets' – believe that the government will stick by their policy. If their credibility falters business confidence is eroded and the markets respond in a manner that makes the achievement of the target much more difficult or impossible. This is why the government and Bank of England tried to make their policy-making more 'transparent' by publishing the minutes of the previous month's meeting between the Chancellor and the Governor of the Bank. These efforts are encouraging and the inflation target is very clear for all to see in comparison with the obscurities of the 1980s but the British Government's credibility is by no means as strong as that of the Deutsche Bundesbank. Confidence is a word that is never fully defined but probably means that the stock market and sterling would fall sharply if dealers did not like a policy; alternatively it means that there will be an increase in uncertainty and private sector investment will fall and growth will decline. Credibility has been increased by the May 1997 decision to hand over interest rate determination to the Monetary Policy Committee of the Bank of England.

Exercise 4

Why did the Chancellor of the Exchequer set a target rate for inflation of 2.5 per cent *and* a range of 1 to 4 per cent?

23.4 Price Stability, Growth and Employment

Fine tuning

These three have a very complex set of relationships even after we have defined the terms. The theories of several economists and schools of economists have come into fashion and moved into obscurity over recent years. From 1952 the most frequently adopted approach was that of Tinbergen who laid out a theory of fixed targets, that is conditions for the simultaneous achievement of fixed targets for a number of objectives. He produced what is called *Tinbergen's rule* which says that if these fixed targets are to be achieved simultaneously there must be as many instruments of policy as there are targets. In other words you cannot expect a tool to do two or more jobs at the same time. His theory was fairly simple to follow and encouraged a fine tuning approach to the macroeconomy, that is the development of new policy instruments and frequent budgets or mini-budgets.

Tinbergen's ideas on fixed targets were, to some extent, superseded by the work of Thiel in 1956 in which he analysed flexible targets. He worked on the assumption that not all targets could be met simultaneously so that a choice had to be made by compromises. Such compromises involved a welfare loss so policy became a matter of minimising the welfare loss of any choice made (not an easy task). This flexible target approach also favoured fine tuning of the economy but the technique came under increasing criticism as the problems of the late 1960s and 70s developed. There emerged a new approach by Mosley in 1976 called 'a satisficing theory'. Mosley's theory sees the policy maker as trying to achieve satisfactory levels of performance not the best possible at all times. His research showed that policy makers, that is the government, Bank of England and Treasury had different standards of 'satisfactory' for various objectives. For example, they wanted a positive balance of payments or at least no deficit, whereas over the years they modified their 'satisfactory' level of unemployment from below 1.6 per cent in 1953 to below 2.5 in 1965 and to below 3.6 in 1971. Over the course of the 1970s all of these approaches, fixed and flexible targets, satisficing and fine tuning were replaced as new theories, or revamping of old, began to stress that the economy was inherently stable and that what the policy makers should do was to look at the medium term and abandon the quest for short-term remedies. This was quite a popular shift for many politicians who could now fall back on the argument that they could not be blamed for inaction in the face of an appalling rise in unemployment and that market forces would restore equilibrium if only they were allowed to work.

The demise of fine tuning

As the Keynesian approach to the management of aggregate demand and its associated fine tuning fell into disrepute among some groups of economic authorities the rate of both inflation and unemployment rose rapidly. There was a resurrection of theories that gave prominence to money and the money supply. Two groups rose to the forefront, the monetarists and the Cambridge Economic Policy Group (CEPG). Although they disagreed on the way the economy worked and on the policy measures that should be adopted they did agree that that the use of short-term intervention was either harmful or of no consequence. In the period 1974–84 the CEPG approach became well established. It was strongly against fine tuning and argued that it was harmful and that the economy is relatively stable in the medium term. It recommended as an appropriate policy the application of a fiscal rule within a medium-term strategy so that the required targets for employment and balance of payments could be achieved. The fiscal rule was a composite tax rate that would only be altered if there were great economic shocks in the world economy or the targets themselves were changed. The monetarist approach accepted that change in the stock of money does not affect the level of real output in the long run but that prices are affected although short-run alterations in money supply could affect both output and prices. They thought that output and employment would be determined at what was called their natural levels by aggregate supply affected by microeconomic influences. From this view developed the emphasis on improvements on the 'supply side' to shift the aggregate supply curve to the right as efficiency and productivity improved. The monetarists also proposed certain rules, the most important of which was to control the rate of growth of the money supply particularly in the long run.

Short-run measures were not usually advocated. Monetarism accumulated some extra baggage along the way with reductions in the size of the public sector and of the government borrowing requirement prominent. Another policy accessory was cuts in direct taxation. Monetarism reached respectability when the first monetary targets were set in 1976 as part of the effort to meet the requirements of the IMF loan. It was from this period that we began to get to know of such measures as sterling M3 (£M3) because the 1976 target was set against that measure. It is easy to be wise after the event but these measures changed so often over the next decade that they ceased to carry much weight.

New policies after 1979 – supply-side measures

After 1979 economic policy was made in relation to the new ideas emanating from Friedman's monetarism and the new interpretations of the 'expectations added Phillips curve'. Policy, therefore devolved into trying to control the money supply and thus aggregate demand, and to improving the supply side of the economy. The supply-side measures were supposed to reduce the level of the natural rate of unemployment (NAIRU). With hindsight it is difficult to avoid the conclusion that the so-called policy makers, that is the Treasury and the Bank of England, were behaving like small children poking an ant hill and waiting to see what would happen. They changed their minds so often about monetary targets and so many of their tax policies seemed to be inconsistent except insofar as they benefited the rich, that they appeared to be drifting aimlessly in the economic current (to change the analogy) without a paddle or with only the paddle of the interest rate. Apart from ever-changing monetary targets the main objective of policy was the Medium Term Financial Strategy which placed emphasis on controlling public expenditure and the PSBR and on ending 'crowding out'. These policies were macroeconomic; the other, supply-side policies are usually thought of as microeconomic. The central aim was to control inflation which was thought to generate unemployment through a wage-price spiral – a version of the cost-push theory of inflation.

An assessment of the new policies

It is difficult for even a rabid supporter of the policies adopted to argue that they were successful. Unemployment doubled between 1979 and 1982 although interest rates fell. The monetary targets were completely missed and overshot. The emergence from the deep recession came after tax cutting budgets and an expansion of consumer demand from 1982–85 when earnings rose faster than inflation. The monetary targets were expressed in a different form as the previous ones became obviously unattainable or failed to measure what they had been thought to measure. PSBR targets were also altered when it became apparent that to achieve them was impossible if the government wished to be re-elected. The government eventually, by 1985, accepted a target inflation rate of 5 per cent. After 1985 the policy makers shifted their attention away from the money supply towards the foreign exchange rate. After an initially very high rate against the dollar which caused considerable problems and destruction of United Kingdom manufacturing industry, the pound fell to almost one for one dollar in 1984. It was reckoned that the low exchange rate stimulated inflation via high import prices. Thus, after 1985 monetary policy was used to control the exchange rates rate rather than the money supply, a policy that lasted until 1988. £M3 was reduced in status to a range to be monitored rather than targeted and M0 became the only targeted variable. The period 1985–88 saw a boom and interest rates were at first lowered but had to be raised again as the inflation rate rose in early 1988. The sudden drastic end of the boom in mid-1988 left monetary policy in a mess. The rapid rise in interest rates cut consumption spending and ended the house price boom. The government persisted with the exchange rate objective, still believing that the discipline of the exchange rate would control inflation and restore equilibrium. In October 1992 the United Kingdom entered the ERM and remained in it until forced to withdraw in September 1994.

Post-ERM policy

Membership forced the government into a renewed effort on the fiscal side to control government spending and borrowing. These efforts were frustrated, and are still being so in 1997, by the high level of unemployment and the subsequent increase in benefit payments and reduction in tax revenues. During the period of membership the government had one policy, to keep the pound within the wide bands of the ERM and it had only one important instrument to achieve it, interest rate changes. It was called 'the one club policy' by its critics.

After 1993 there were further policy changes to fill the vacuum left by the failure of the previous policy. These, to some extent, are a return to something like the approach suggested by Thiel, that is flexible targets. As mentioned before, the government set an explicit inflation target of 2.5 per cent as the main objective in the range of one to four per cent measured by RPIX and a monitoring range for M0 and M4 measures of the money supply. There has also been a renewed emphasis on the PSBR and the nation's ability to sustain the debt incurred by governments. In the background, although for political reasons the government has been loathe to admit it, are the requirements for European monetary convergence. Even if the United Kingdom exercises its opt out and does not join the single currency euro zone in 1999 it will still be adversely affected if its economy diverges too far from that of the other states who do join. It might be able to enjoy the dubious benefits of depreciation of the pound but that would make it even harder to join at a later date. If the

United Kingdom Government genuinely wishes to keep its options open it must maintain an inflation rate and interest rate within the convergence criteria.

23.5 Would Economic Growth Resolve the Problem?

UK governments have usually shied away from setting targets for economic growth with the short-lived exception of the Labour Government's National Plan (The Economic Plan) of 1965 which set a target growth rate of 3.8 per cent per year. It was abandoned in the face of balance of payments problems and the need for a counter-inflationary policy. The only Conservative reference to any figure was the hope of a doubling of the standard of living every twenty-five years uttered by R. A. B. Butler in 1954. The 3 per cent per year required for that was well above what the United Kingdom economy normally provided. It is an interesting speculation as to why there has been this wariness about growth targets. It may be that failure to achieve them is too obvious and potentially damaging politically. Some politicians believe that everything of that nature should be left to the market and that government intervention is doomed to fail. The other, more economic, reason is that in the United Kingdom experience economic growth even at low levels appears to bring inflation with it.

If we go back to a basic point, economic growth is the rise over a period of time of real net national product per head. The determinants of growth, which vary in significance according to the level of development of a country, are

- **An increase in the stock of factors of production**. As land is relatively fixed in quantity most of this increase will come from a growth of the labour force via a rise in population and from an increase in the quantity of capital goods. It is, of course, rare for the stock of these things to rise without some change also in their quality, especially in the skill of the workforce or in the nature of the technology of the capital employed. Any increase in the stock of factors will, other things being equal, shift the production possibility frontier outwards. There will be various reasons over time, and in different countries, why the supply of these factors will increase. The supply of capital depends on levels of savings as well as upon the stimulus of new inventions. The supply of labour depends on social as well as demographic trends. If we define land as natural resources then a discovery of new minerals or oil, or the use of new methods of exploitation will increase the effective stock of factors. Examples include the discovery of North Sea gas and oil and the methods of mining old coal tips to recover 'waste' coal thrown away by our ancestors.

- **An improvement in the quality of the factors of production**. Over time the quality of the land is improved by the addition of capital so agricultural waste land is put into profitable use; buildings are erected and the land becomes more productive; higher percentages of ore are recovered as metal; forests and water are managed better to produce greater benefits and so on.

- **An improvement in the combination of the factors of production.** This arises from the development of better management and from the availability of economies of scale as output is expanded. As population rises and grows richer, assuming that it does, the level of demand rises and makes more likely the availability of greater economies of scale.

- **Improvements in technology and technical knowledge.** Some of the points about the factors of production above depend upon progress in technology and knowledge. The world economy has shown bursts of development over the centuries in response to new technology. New inventions and new applications of technology create a demand for capital goods and, through the multiplier effect of increased investment, generate incomes and employment. There may be a transitory drop of employment in some occupations and some jobs may disappear altogether, but overall the effect will stimulate economic growth.

- **Research and development** (R&D) are extremely important as a basis for improvements in technology and may be seen as one of the most important contributors to economic growth. Any analysis of the impact of R&D must include a division between the percentage spent on civilian and defence projects. The United Kingdom for example spent only 57.4 per cent of its national R&D expenditure in 1992 on civilian research. It should be added that the term R&D is a blanket phrase to cover both fundamental research and methods of improving existing techniques and products. Innovation needs to be accompanied by laws on patents and copyright that protect the original developers and reward them otherwise the incentive to innovate is much reduced. Most societies also look to their governments to finance certain types of investment in R&D, not just in defence but also in such things as road safety and health.

- **Improvements in education and training** are another major contributor to growth although they are sometimes classified as improvements in the labour force or factor supply. The better skilled labour force is more productive and more able to adapt to new technology.

- **The accumulation of capital** is often thought to be at the root of increased economic growth. Most of the modern analysis of long-run growth of output stems from the writings in the late 1950s of Robert Solow who received a Nobel prize in 1987 for his neoclassical growth model. The surprising conclusion of his initial model is that savings and investment are not determinants of growth. They set the capital–labour ratio and the output per head but not the growth of output. Solow found that four-fifths of the USA's growth of output per worker was due to technical progress. Later research on his theory gives more emphasis to capital growth as a contributor to economic growth. In this context there is often a distinction made between *capital widening* which is simply having more in total so the capital–worker ratio is constant and *capital deepening* which is having more per worker so the capital–worker ratio is rising. **Technical progress** leads to growth by its effect on improving or augmenting the output of labour.

Note: It should be noted that more developed countries tend to show economic growth which is slower than that of developing countries. This is sometimes called the *convergence hypothesis* which envisages a catching up process as poorer countries expand faster and converge with the richer. The evidence seems to be that developing nations derive some advantages from savings on R&D by importing foreign technology and therefore have more resources to devote to production of goods and capital equipment. An analogy with the racing car or motor cyclist who moves along in the slipstream of faster vehicles is often quoted here. It is instructive to consider the comparative effects of different growth rates on incomes per head over time. This is like an exercise in compound interest. A one per cent growth rate doubles income per head in 72 years; two per cent in 36 years; three per cent in 25 years. The United Kingdom's low trend growth rate of 2.4 per cent therefore explains why it has slipped in the international league table of income per head.

Growth as a solution

If inflation results from an excess of aggregate demand over aggregate supply it would seem that an increase in aggregate supply would be a way of resolving some if not all of the problem. There have been more than two million unemployed for all the years from 1979 to 1996 and over three million at times, even by the most charitable of measures, which is the number of benefit claimants. In early 1997 the number of benefit claimants fell below 2 million but the Labour Party was quoting 4.4 million as the 'true' figure. It would appear that, in a well-ordered society, these unemployed could be trained to make a productive contribution to the GDP instead of being dependent absorbers of other people's output. The demand for the capital equipment required to employ them would be a welcome addition to the order books of the capital goods industry. Government revenues would benefit from the extra taxation from the newly employed and public expenditure would fall as their benefit payments declined. What are the snags behind these ideas?

- The first is that it requires a government that believes it could achieve such a reduction by these methods. The philosophical thrust of the Conservative Government from 1979, together with its theoretical economic underpinning, was against such interventionism. Moreover, if your economic gurus tell you, as they told the government, to expect a natural rate of unemployment of 8 per cent, you do not believe that you can do anything. If they add that short-term intervention makes things worse you have a good reason not to do anything. You fall back on the mantra that the market will find its own equilibrium. You may even concoct a new form of economic 'social Darwinism' to justify competition as a form of natural selection for the survival of the fittest. If, at the same time, your own incomes and capital gains rise significantly as the tax system and privatisation policy operate in your favour, you may well think that you have discovered the best of all possible economic systems.

- The second is that the United Kingdom economy is so heavily dependent on foreign trade that any attempt to expand output runs a risk of balance of payments difficulties that push the exchange rate down and import prices up with consequences for the domestic economy and inflation.

- The third is that such a policy requires expenditure 'up front' on the training and education of the workforce and probably pump-priming financial measures for industry. The likelihood is that borrowing would have to increase with consequences for the size of the PSBR and interest rates as well as 'confidence'. At this point we might question the basis of the obsession with the PSBR and 'confidence'. It can be argued that the size of the PSBR is nowhere near as important as is alleged by right-wing economists and that 'crowding out' is also either non-existent or not significant. The question of confidence is more of a problem because it has a great impact on stock and share prices and upon the willingness to invest. Moreover, loss of confidence might cause a flight out of sterling and a serious outflow of capital. This would depress the exchange rate and the inflationary effects would probably outweigh the beneficial effects on exporting industry.

Exercise 5

Suggest some reasons for the United Kingdom's economic growth rate having a trend rate of 2.4 per cent which is below that of our main competitors. (Long books have been written on this!)

Potential output

The above discussion again raises the issue of the potential output of the economy and what it means. Potential output is defined as the output that the economy would produce if all factors of production are fully employed. This is not the same as the maximum possible output but the maximum that could be achieved and sustained if all the markets were in long-run equilibrium. Thus the potential output includes 'normal unemployment' or, to put it in the terms previously used, it is the long-run equilibrium level of real output embracing the natural rate of unemployment. This natural rate of unemployment may be as high as 10 per cent in some economies or as low as 5 per cent. If actual output is below the potential output it is possible to expand output without inflation but the smaller the 'output gap' the more likely it is that inflation will rise. The monetary authorities use measures of the output gap to help judge inflation pressures and seem to welcome the existence of the gap. In other words they might not be too keen on measures to remove too many unemployed from the register if they thought that real output or potential output would not rise as well. The output gap is defined as the gap between actual output and the level of output consistent with a constant rate of inflation. There are very wide estimates of the size of the output gap and two main methods of calculating it. The first uses extrapolations based on previous output growth. The second, as used by the OECD, tries to take account of changes to productive capacity over the cycle, that is production functions for labour and capital in terms of inputs and output. In June 1995 the OECD estimated the United Kingdom's output gap at –2.1 for 1995 and predicted –1.6 for 1996, that is the gap defined as the deviation of actual GDP from potential GDP as a percentage of potential GDP. The output gap in the United Kingdom may be between 1.5 and 7 per cent which is enough to exert a downward pressure on inflation. The question remains, what about the unemployment level and what about the missed production opportunities? There must be some way in which the reduction of unemployment could be speeded up without raising the rate of inflation if output could also be increased commensurately.

Table 23.2   Changes in real GDP of the G7 countries 1970–96

	Average 1970–77	1978	1979	1980	1981	1982	1983	1984	1985	1986	1987	1988	1989	1990	1991	1992	1993	1994	Projections 1995	1996
United States	3.0	4.8	2.5	-0.5	1.8	-2.2	3.9	6.2	3.2	2.9	3.1	3.9	2.5	1.2	-0.6	2.3	3.1	4.1	3.2	2.3
Japan	4.4	4.9	5.5	3.6	3.6	3.2	2.7	4.3	5.0	2.6	4.1	6.2	4.7	4.8	4.3	1.1	-0.2	0.6	1.3	2.3
Germany	2.7	3.0	4.2	1.0	0.1	-0.9	1.8	2.8	2.0	2.3	1.5	3.7	3.6	5.7	5.0	2.2	-1.1	2.9	2.9	2.7
France	3.5	3.3	3.2	1.6	1.2	2.5	0.7	1.3	1.9	2.5	2.3	4.5	4.3	2.5	0.8	1.3	-1.5	2.7	3.0	3.2
Italy	3.4	3.6	5.8	4.1	0.6	0.2	1.0	2.7	2.6	2.9	3.1	4.1	2.9	2.1	1.2	0.7	-1.2	2.2	3.0	2.9
United Kingdom	2.2	3.5	2.8	-2.2	-1.3	1.7	3.7	2.3	3.7	4.4	4.8	5.0	2.2	0.4	-2.0	-0.5	2.2	3.8	3.4	3.0
Canada	5.1	4.6	3.9	1.5	3.7	-3.2	3.2	6.3	4.8	3.3	4.2	5.0	2.4	-0.2	-1.8	0.6	2.2	4.5	3.9	3.4

Source: Adapted from OECD *Economic Outlook 57*, June, Paris, OECD, 1995.

24 World Development and the Environment

Aims of the chapter

To:

- put economic growth in the context of world development;
- discuss the roles of aid and trade;
- outline the world debt problem and the efforts to find solutions;
- link economic growth to the economics of the environment.

24.1 Economic Growth and Developing Countries

We have discussed economic growth in the context of the United Kingdom in Chapters 21 and 23 and referred to the debate about the costs of growth with particular reference to developed countries. This chapter links together the economic problems of growth in developing countries with the world problem of the environment. We have defined economic growth as 'an increase in the real level of Net National Product' (NNP) with the added 'per head' to take better account of the distribution of the growth. The term *developing countries* has largely replaced terms such as 'backward', 'less developed' and 'underdeveloped'. The United Nations would classify a country as 'developing' if it had an income per head less than one-fifth of that of the USA.

The core of the relationship between growth and relative poverty is clearly seen from the calculation of how many years it would take to double a nation's standard of living (NNP) at specific annual rates. The following figures are rounded. At 1% 72 years; 2% 36; 2.5% 28; 3% 25; 4% 19; and 5% 14.5 years. It can be seen clearly from these figures that developing countries must raise their growth rates if they are to overtake the developed world rather than to fall further behind in relative terms. The United Kingdom's trend growth rate has been approximately 2.4 per cent this century. As a measure of relative poverty and affluence, according to the *Human Development Report* of the UN Development Program, in 1990 the richest 20 per cent of the world's population had 59 times the income of the poorest 20 per cent. It is such disparities that led to the coining of the phrase 'rich north, poor south' when talking about the global distribution of wealth. The 'north' includes Japan and Australasia. It is possible to measure the widening gap between north and south and the UN found that it widened between 1960 and 1990 in certain objective criteria and narrowed in others. It widened, for example in relation to years of schooling, tertiary education, expenditure on research and development, numbers of scientists and technicians per 1000 of population, and the possession of some durable goods like radios. It narrowed on the more important criteria of life expectancy, infant and child mortality, access to safe water and adult literacy.

If we dropped the word *relative* and considered *absolute* poverty instead we would discover some very disturbing facts about the levels of income of the countries with the lowest income levels, that is some of the countries in Africa, Central America and South Asia. In 1993 an average Canadian enjoyed an income of over US $20 000 while an average Tanzanian had $110 as measured in GNP per head. Even if an adjustment is made for barter, payments in kind and purchasing power parities the figures show a similar disparity of US $19 200 in Canada and $572 in Tanzania measured in Purchasing Power Standards (PPS).

Apart from the inequality of wealth and income between nations there is, of course, inequality within a nation between its higher income groups and lower. These differences can be measured by combining two mathematical techniques, the Lorenz curve and the 'Gini coefficient'. As a generalisation, the distribution of income in developing countries is much less even than in developed countries, that is there are greater extremes of affluence and poverty. This phenomenon is partly related to land ownership which accumulates in a few hands, for example in Mexico and Brazil. It is also partly explained by membership of the ruling elites that can exploit employment in the bureaucracy or by family connection to it and by the absence of any sizeable middle class. The old Victorian saying is also appropriate, 'the rich get richer and the poor get children'. Ruling elites ensure that the tax system on income, wealth and inheritance favour them.

Exercise I

Why should a relatively affluent citizen of the United Kingdom be concerned *economically* about the inequality of incomes in the world, that is between developed and developing nations?

24.2 The Causes of Inequality Among Nations

There is an assortment of reasons for unequal development and standards of living:

Natural resources differ enormously. Other things being equal the countries with extensive resources are likely to enjoy a higher income per head than those without. But other things are not equal and there are plenty of examples of countries with inadequate natural resources who have triumphed over their handicap and become rich while there are others that are plentifully endowed who are in poverty. Japan, Switzerland and the Scandinavian countries are examples of the former while Angola, Uganda and even Russia and Brazil are examples of the latter. Thus differences in natural endowment are not the sole answer and we must consider the use to which the resources are put and the skill and enterprise of the human resource.

Capital deficiency or shortage is an extremely important cause of lack of development. It can be remedied in three main ways:

1. The first remedy is from increased savings but this may be extremely hard to achieve in a low income society because savings represent an abstention from consumption. Some command economies such as Russia and China achieved increased savings by centralised purchasing and resale at a higher price. The Chinese government, for example, would buy the surplus food produced by the peasants at fixed prices and resell it in urban areas at higher, state controlled prices. The revenue generated could then be channelled into investment in capital projects such as railways, steel works and housing and factory development. The method worked well in some countries but was not very successful in others such as Albania and North Korea. It is not appropriate for many more democratic states.

2. Another remedy is to receive aid from foreign governments and international organisations. Some of this aid is **emergency** or **humanitarian aid** and is frequently channelled through non-governmental organisations (NGOs) as well as specialised United Nations agencies. The European Union has its own emergency aid system, the European Community Humanitarian Office (ECHO). Although it is very important in the short run to help reduce the impact of famine, flood, earthquake and drought it is not the remedy for low long-term growth. It may even have undesirable effects if it undermines the local market economy by placing free food alongside locally available food. In the longer term the aid from governments needs to be directed at cost effective schemes that educate and train local people as well as improve the infrastructure and basic farming techniques. The aim behind the aid, experience shows us, is to develop self-sufficiency and independence rather than dependency.

   The history of post-1945 aid is very cheering in some ways but extremely depressing in others. Some aid programmes such as those to Europe under the Marshall Aid system and to Japan and South Korea have proved highly effective. Others have produced grandiose, out of scale, public construction programmes such as great dams, power and irrigation systems which do not address the main problems of the country. Other aid has been corruptly absorbed by the ruling elite or spent on extravagant public works systems. But lessons have been learned and most official aid schemes are now thoroughly vetted and assessed before approval is given. There is much more emphasis on local co-operation and implementation and less on central government. On a more gloomy note, however, some aid appears to be given on a bilateral basis between countries and is spent on armaments rather than on infrastructure projects. It may not be directly spent on arms but is used as a substitute for revenues from taxation that would otherwise have been spent on arms, that is the aid is not additional but a substitute.

Some aid is **bilateral**, that is the two countries make an agreement directly. This type of aid tends to have strings attached of the type that insist on the donor country's contractors supplying the plant and machinery or technical expertise or servicing of the project. Aid with strings attached is much easier to 'sell' to the donor's electorate. Bilateral aid is often linked to orders for arms.

Other aid is **multilateral**, that is a number of donors supply aid to one or more other countries. The usual instrument for this is the World Bank whose work is discussed in Chapter 18. Another agency is the United Nations Children's Fund (UNICEF). The European Union has a special agreement called the Lomé Convention which is the fourth of its kind running from 1991 to 2000. Lomé IV aims 'to promote and expedite the economic, cultural and social development of the African, Caribbean and Pacific (ACP) states,' 70 in number, 'and to consolidate and diversify their relations in a spirit of solidarity and mutual interest'. Most of the money is channelled through the European Development Fund (EDF) whose current eighth programme will provide aid 15 billion ECU over the remaining five years of Lomé IV.

3. The third remedy for capital deficiency is to accept and encourage investment from foreign private sources. This is a very complex field and generalisations are more dangerous than usual. There is little doubt that foreign direct investment (FDI) is a stimulus to economic growth and employment and that it has considerable multiplier effects on the local and national economy. It does, however, often produce an initial inflow of imports that affects the developing country's balance of payments adversely, although that may eventually be corrected by raised exports. Much of the early FDI received a bad press because it was aimed at the extraction and exploitation of local resources. Modern FDI has shifted more in favour of investment by multinationals who bring the latest technology and want to exploit the low labour costs of the typical developing economy. The 'globalisation' of the world economy has accelerated this process but the result is not all sweetness and light. Such development is often at the expense of production in the developed countries, China instead of Essex, or The Czech Republic instead of Germany. The unemployed workers of the developed world lose incomes and are reluctant or unable to buy the products of the developing world. There is also a real problem of what happens to the profits of the multinationals who naturally

wish to take them home wherever that may be. The developing country would prefer most or all of them to remain and finance new development. If they restrict the outflow of foreigners' profits they will tend to deter inward investment. Another source of friction with FDI is the inevitable inflow of foreign managers and alien management techniques. Over time the local people may be trained to take over but it is a slow and uncertain process.

Labour forces differ in their education, skill, training and productivity. These differences are the product of a complex interrelationship between the economic, commercial, social, and religious history of the country concerned. It is easier to have the desirable characteristic of a skilled, educated and productive workforce if the economic environment can afford the investment required and the opportunity cost involved. Modern aid programmes place much greater emphasis on training and education than those of thirty years ago.

Foreign investment contributes to economic growth and many countries receive very little. They may have a political climate that is inimical to FDI or they may simply lack exploitable resources. There is a tendency for FDI to concentrate on economies that are already well into the process of development with growing incomes and markets.

Trade affects nations in various ways. For some it is a great opportunity to maximise the potential of their resources both human and physical. Historically the richest nations have been great traders, Greeks, Romans, Phoenicians, Venetians, the Dutch, the British and more recently the Japanese and Singaporeans. Trade is based upon comparative cost advantages based on resources and upon geographical location as well as on political influences. Economic growth is strongly related to the growth of trade. There is a tendency for developing countries to try and protect their industry, either on the grounds of the infant industry argument or out of a belief that protectionism is advantageous against the might of competition from the developed world. Some developing countries have suffered because of the trading practices and tariff and non-tariff barriers of developed countries. This leads to the often made statement that fairer trade would benefit developing nations more than aid.

Political factors have a great impact on whether foreign aid is given and on whether foreign direct investment takes place. The great deterrent is not so much the political colour of the regime but the degree of uncertainty. A stable, completely noxious, military dictatorship may attract considerable FDI and foreign aid because of its stability. An unstable, uncertain, embryo democracy may be left to struggle with little foreign assistance. It is clear also that internal strife, especially civil war, has a devastating effect on economic growth and can ruin even relatively prosperous economies; look no further than Yugoslavia.

Overpopulation may be a problem and reduce growth. Technically 'overpopulation' in economics means that the average output per head is falling, not that there is a high density of people per square kilometre. Rapid expansion of population gives many developing countries a very large proportion of young people to support, that is it increases the dependency ratio. It also leads to swift urbanisation and the concomitant problems of urban pollution, transport problems, mass unemployment and high infant mortality rates. If the expanded population remains in the rural areas it may lead to soil and forest depletion, over-grazing and water problems. Sensible and culturally sensitive programmes to restrict the birth rate are usually regarded as an essential accompaniment to policies to increase economic growth. The countries that have succeeded in controlling the growth of their population, such as Japan, have reaped the benefits. Others which have not, sink deeper into poverty either relatively or absolutely.

Exercise 2

How do you explain the rapid emergence from relative poverty of the economies of Taiwan, Singapore, Malaysia and South Korea in such a short period?

THE SAHEL – A MAJOR AID EFFORT, THOUGH NOT AN EXCEPTIONAL ONE

Aid to the Sahel increased by a factor of 4.6 in constant terms beween the early 1970s and the mid-1990s. It rose in particular in the periods after two major droughts in the Sahel in 1973–74 and 1984–85. In 1994, the volume of aid to the Sahel remained comparable to that received in 1986.

Since the mid-1970s, the share of total official development assistance (ODA) accounted for by the Sahel has remained relatively stable, at around 5%. In contrast, the region's share of ODA to sub-Saharan Africa has declined, falling from over 25% after the 1973–74 crisis to around 15% since the early 1900s.

Over the period 1900–94, external aid amounted to 17% of the region's GDP. This share had been under 10% in the early 1970s but was over 20% in the late 80s. Per capita aid followed a similar trend, although at a slower pace, rising from $35 in the early 1970s to $63 in the early 90s. These figures should nonetheless be treated with caution since, in many respects, aid volumes and data relating to specific recipient countries are not readily comparable because of non-material flows, expenditure in donor countries, differences in aggregate prices, and so on.

Although volumes of aid to the Sahel are relatively high, an international comparison shows them to be consistent with the resources and

cont'd

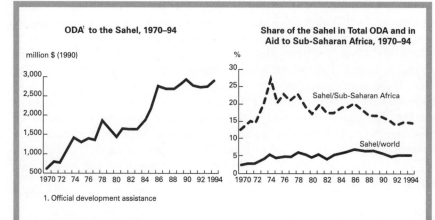

ODA[1] to the Sahel, 1970–94

Share of the Sahel in Total ODA and in Aid to Sub-Saharan Africa, 1970–94

1. Official development assistance

Source: Club du Sahel, OECD

Figure 24.1　Official development aid to the Sahel

size of Sahelian countries. Although the Sahel receives a substantial amount of aid, it is because the region is made up of small countries with low incomes and not because of any specific characteristics of a political, ecological or other nature.

As part of a steady long-term trend, aid is increasingly being directed towards 'services': financial services (debt, balance-of-payments support), management assistance (programme aid), social services. At the same time, the more 'material' aspects of aid are becoming relatively less important: food aid, infrastructure, support for productive services (including agriculture).

Aid accounts for almost all of the financial flows to the Sahel. Remittances from emigrants, about which very little is known, and income from a limited number of exports are the only other external resources. At the current stage in globalisation, this situation means that external aid has a highly specific role to play in the Sahel region.

1. How could the 'steady long-term trend' outlined in the penultimate paragraph be explained?
2. Can you detect from the extract any particular problems of the Sahel and any particular thrust in the aid programmes so far?

Source: David Naudet and Jean-Marc Pradelle *A Verdict on Aid to the Sahel,* OECD, *The OECD Observer,* **205,** March/April 1997, Paris 1997.

24.3   The World Debt Problem

1. In 1995 the external debt of the developing countries was $1750 billion. The world debt problem emerged in the late 1970s and became very serious in the 1980s. Although it is no longer as newsworthy in the 1990s it remains extremely serious as a threat to the stability and growth of world trade and development. The total external debt of developing countries rose by 27 per cent in money terms over the five years to 1995.

2. The difficulties began to emerge after the 1974–75 OPEC oil price rise which raised most prices and reduced world trade. Developing countries, apart from the ones with oil, suffered particularly badly and began increasing their borrowing, not only for new projects but also to meet the increasing burden of interest rates on earlier loans and to service (that is repay capital) their debt. By the early 1980s there was great concern that some major countries would default on their loans, the most likely candidates being in South America, Mexico, Argentina and Brazil, although Nigeria, despite its oil, also figured here. In 1992 Nigeria had an external debt 108 per cent of its annual GDP.

3. In the 1970s the IMF helped countries out with their short-term balance of payments problems, which included interest rate repayments, but not to any great extent so they turned to borrowing from the private sector which responded with what now seems considerable rashness. The banks of the developed world were, at that time, heavily involved in recirculating the enormous revenues from oil that the OPEC countries were earning. Profitable opportunities nearer home were declining so they were looking for secure borrowers such as governments and lent vast sums with what turned out to be insufficient attention to what the money would be used for and how it was to be repaid. Much of the lending was short term with floating rates and this magnified the subsequent problem because rates floated upwards rather than down. In 1982, as an example, the annual debt interest of Brazil, Argentine and Mexico was $13 billion. The crisis came to a head in 1982 and a variety of methods have been adopted for dealing with the problem. In the process banks in the USA, Europe and Japan have written off billions of pounds of debt. In 1989–90 United Kingdom banks wrote off more than £5 billion in bad debts to developing countries.

4. The first step in tackling the problem was after 1982 when the IMF and the banks co-operated with each other to reschedule debt. The IMF insisted on the lender country agreeing to conditions relating to their macroeconomic policies and to austerity programmes and the banks agreed to accept new conditions for existing loans and sometimes gave new ones. In 1983 and 1984 the IMF lent about $20 billion to 70 countries. This lending, together with the banks' debt rescheduling, helped to overcome the immediate crisis. A drop in oil prices helped the debtor nations but was damaging to

Mexico and Nigeria. The IMF policy was seen as too restrictive and excessive and by mid-1988 it was receiving more money in repayments from the debtor nations than it was lending. This was portrayed as the rich exploiting the poor.

5. An informal forum of creditor nations, called the Paris Club, which has no fixed membership or institutional structure, rescheduled $48 billion of debt of 39 debtor nations between 1982 and 1987.

6. The Brady Plan, named after the US Secretary of the Treasury, was adopted in March 1989 to replace the previously unco-ordinated measures of government and banks. It helps banks, the World Bank, the IMF and governments, especially the US Government to work together to resolve the problems of debtors and creditors. Debtor nations sign a 'Brady Agreement' which is really a series of agreements with the IMF, World Bank and commercial banks. The earliest agreements were with Mexico, Venezuela, the Philippines and Costa Rica. The techniques used to implement the Brady plans are very imaginative and intricate. In some cases the debt has been turned into bonds or, to use the jargon, 'securitized'. In the case of Mexican debt, much of it has been sold for as little as 33 cents for the dollar . Debts have been replaced by new debts on favourable terms with lower interest rates and at a discount. In the case of Chile, which came into a windfall when the price of copper rose, it has bought back a large slice of its debt for cash at a 40 per cent discount. The creditors have been taking the view that any repayment is better than none. In some instances the debts have been replaced by equity (shares) in local companies but this is not popular because it transfers ownership in part to foreigners. Some clever schemes, called 'asset backed debt', secure loans against the revenues from such things as telephone charges or credit card interest as well as against physical assets such as buildings or aircraft.

7. The above measures have been effective in removing the immediate threat of wholesale reneging on debt that would cause a domino collapse of some of the world's banking system but the problem has not gone away. Indeed, in some ways it is worse because it is now a major problem in the old Soviet bloc as well. Table 24.1 indicates the problem of world debt.

Exercise 3

What impact has the world debt problem had on the United Kingdom economy since 1980?

Table 24.1   The problem of world debt

	Net present value of external debt as a % of GNP		Total debt service as a % of exports of goods and services	
	1990	*1993*	*1990*	*1993*
Low income countries	30.0	37.1	10.4	16.4
excluding China and India	63.9	75.6	12.4	18.2
Lower middle income countries		36.8	18.8	18.3
Upper middle income countries	24.9	26.3	32.1	19.4
Low and middle income countries				
Sub Saharan Africa	50.0	47.4	11.6	17.1
East Asia and Pacific	23.1	28.5	13.4	14.4
South Asia	20.3	31.1	11.9	24.4
Europe and Central Asia		26.5		12.4
Middle East and North Africa	26.7	57.7	16.5	23.1
Latin America and Caribbean	38.8	34.0	36.9	28.1
Severly indebted economies	39.0	35.6	35.1	25.3

Source: World Development Report, 1995

24.4   The Environment

Economic growth is accompanied by rising population, urbanisation, industrialisation and pollution. Land and sea resources are exploited to their utmost with too little concern for their long-term welfare. Growth is also attended by the expansion of human wants and mass consumption of both durable and non-durable goods. Increased trade and vastly increased demand for raw materials are also evident. If no account is taken of externalities or social costs the only arbiter of whether and how resources should be exploited is private profit. If no money value is placed on the externalities they are not incorporated in the market price. Some economists argue that the essential problem of the environment in economic terms is that there are no property rights over the environment so no-one has the legal right to take action to correct the harm caused by others. The state can, of course, assume some 'property rights' on our behalf.

If private profit is the only criterion on which society operates there is very little incentive to rectify the destruction caused by the extraction and processing of minerals. The disposal of waste becomes a matter of choosing the cheapest private option which is usually indiscriminate dumping and disposal by pumping effluent into rivers. Evidence of this can be clearly seen in any industrial area of the United Kingdom that was developed in the eighteenth and nineteenth centuries. Left to itself nature may cover some of the worst scars but it is usually left to governments to pass laws to force mining companies to set aside money from current profits to restore abandoned sites or, if the perpetrators are long gone, to pay for the work themselves from taxation. Some of the worst excesses of extraction companies were committed in the USA in the great era of unrestricted capitalism between 1875 and 1914 but some are still being committed in the developing world, for example in some uncontrolled Brazilian gold mines, and black market tin production in several countries.

Apart from population size and density and incomes per head, the most important influence on the environment is the demand for energy. It is the rapid growth of demand for energy for industry, commerce, housing and transport that has produced some of the worst environmental problems. Readers are, no doubt, familiar with the issues of global warming, acid rain, ozone layer depletion, carbon dioxide emissions and the greenhouse effect as well as with the general issues of deforestation, pollution and waste disposal. These are all issues that have an international aspect rather than a purely local impact so co-operation between nations is essential if environmental disasters are not to follow.

In June 1992 the United Nations held a Conference on the Environment and Development in Rio de Janeiro. It is usually called 'The Earth Summit' and produced an action plan called the '21st Agenda' or 'Agenda 21' referring, of course, to the twenty-first century. In April 1995 the G7 held an Environment Conference in Hamilton and made further progress. The main, original agreement was the Montreal Protocol of 1987 which has been augmented by subsequent agreements such as the Copenhagen Agreement of November 1992. These international agreements are often criticised by environmental lobby groups as being unambitious, lacking in urgency and too considerate of the manufacturing lobby's interests but they are all we have. Many nations are taking them very seriously and achieving their targets; others have set themselves fairly soft targets. Some developing nations such as China and India are resistant to applying what they see as an imposition by the nations that are already rich and who contributed so much to pollution in the past, of standards and costs that will make their own development harder.

24.5 Solutions

Recycling is a start. If it is efficient and cost effective it goes some way to solving the problem created by the first law of thermodynamics, that is that matter cannot be destroyed or created – we simply convert or assimilate it by some means. Recycling reduces the level of output or extraction of raw materials and the amount of energy required so it is doubly effective. If a recycling policy is to be implemented it requires state intervention through the law, inspection, taxation and possibly subsidy. Some economies such as

Germany have adopted recycling as a major plank in their environmental strategy. Strands of the policy include redesign of products, less packaging, more environmentally appropriate packaging, labelling and classification of materials and laws governing the proportions of products that must be recyclable. There are also efficient administrative frameworks in place to facilitate the collection and processing of recycled materials. The adoption of such policies may have temporary, adverse effects on the industries affected and there may be bottlenecks or surpluses in the process but, overall, the long-term benefits are worth the short-term costs.

Technological approaches are very important in the long term. Products and processes can be designed from the outset with an environmental consideration in mind. Their manufacture, distribution, use and recycling can be conducted against an environmental specification. Programmes such as the European Union's 'eco-label' or individual manufacturer's schemes such as the almost completely recyclable BMW cars are examples. Another way to apply technology is in increased efficiency of energy use. Simple examples are house insulation, more efficient boilers and low energy light bulbs. In the context of energy use, the European Union's Fifth Environmental Action Plan called *Towards Sustainability* which runs from 1992 to 2000 contains many elements to economise on the use of energy. The European Energy Charter of 1991 and 1994 aims at the installation of environmentally clean power stations and equipment in Eastern and Central European countries. The EU and 48 countries together with the USA, Canada, Australia and Japan have signed this charter.

Conservation is another basic approach. It is necessary to consider whether the renovation and conservation of, for example, buildings and large plants is more effective in terms of energy use than replacement with new ones. Conservation is an obvious necessity in the natural world and highlights the need for environmental impact studies before major changes are carried out in the form of building works, new roads and so on.

Regulation is an often tried and reasonably effective method of preventing the worst excesses of dumping, pollution and environmental degradation. The United Kingdom, for example, has adopted a policy of Integrated Pollution Control (IPC) which recognises that all the elements in the environment are linked. The British Inspectorate of Pollution and National Rivers Authority is reckoned to be among the most vigorous pollution control bodies in Europe. Such methods are expensive to operate, however, and rely upon a persistent bureaucracy and deterrent punishments. Moreover, it is not always easy to detect the original offenders and prosecute them.

Taxation is another approach favoured by many economists because it holds out the hope of 'making the polluter pay' or to put it more economically, to make the producer incorporate the external costs of the production process into the price. Inevitably, if the selling prices are raised to incorporate taxes that add some or all of the external costs to them, there will be a reduction in demand and the consumer will bear some of the burden of the tax. The most discussed tax is a so-called carbon tax which has been discussed in the European context for many years but whose effectiveness would rely on other major users of hydro-carbon fuels such as Japan and the USA also applying a similar tax. Since this joint application has appeared unlikely there has been opposition within the European Union from countries such as the United Kingdom. A feeble compromise was adopted whereby member states could adopt a carbon tax if they chose. In principle the tax would have been placed on any hydro-carbon energy source such as oil, gas and coal in proportion to their carbon content in order to force users to economise on use. In return taxes on other products would have been reduced by similar amounts so that the overall tax burden remained constant. The details of the proposals are very complicated but many economists thought that the proposed tax was a good idea; it may still happen but the pressure groups against it are very strong.

Other taxes have been introduced, for example, the UK introduced a new tax in October 1996 on deposits into landfill sites. The hope is that it will provide incentives for recycling; the fear is that it will encourage fly-tipping and end up with local authorities having to clear up the mess and raise local taxes to pay for it.

Fuel duties may be used in a differential manner to encourage the use of cleaner fuels. The clearest example is the lower duty on unleaded petrol in the UK and in some countries lower duties on diesel fuels. There is now some doubt as to whether the shift to diesel is a good thing because of discoveries about particulate emissions. Doubt is also cast on the extent to which the shift to unleaded petrol was caused by the tax differential and how much by the manufacturing firms changing their engine technology. New forms of petrol or fuel made from biomass are being given favourable tax treatment and some legislative backing in terms of target outputs by the tax and subsidy systems of France and Austria.

New policy approaches to public transport and private transport can yield large savings in fuel use and cuts in emissions. Some countries are pursuing the public transport option vigorously by heavy state investment in trains and buses that are much more energy efficient than private vehicles carrying the same number of people. Even Los Angeles, the spiritual home of the private car, is financing the development of more urban transit systems and revitalising urban railways. The private motoring and road construction lobby is extremely powerful politically and has to be handled carefully. This fact helps to explain the great multitude of schemes that have been put forward to reduce or control the use of private vehicles. Many of the proposals include some form of road pricing using sophisticated modern technology such as transponders and meters on vehicles. The main criticism of road pricing is that it will normally favour the rich or those who can find someone else to pay, that is their employer. Another is that it is not likely to work unless there are acceptable public transport alternatives in terms of price and availability. Any state sponsored schemes to substitute public for private transport probably involve some degree of cross subsidisation of users by non-users. Some economists see this as unacceptable but it is possible to make a case that the non-users of public transport do benefit from others using it because the roads are less congested. Some private transport controls become arbitrary as in the example of central Athens where motor vehicles are banned when pollution is too bad, or in the Netherlands where vehicle use is restricted at weekends according to the registration number of the vehicle.

Some attempts have been made to come to terms with the existence of the motor vehicle, to make it more fuel efficient, to make it quieter, to make it depreciate more slowly and to make it recyclable but the latest vehicles are more complex, more demanding of most resources except basic steel, faster and more over-powered than their predecessors. There is some progress towards viable electric and renewable energy vehicles but it is too slow to have much impact on the emissions problem. A far-sighted society might go back to persuading people to live close to their work and return to living, shopping and working in the urban centre instead of on the peripheries.

Licensing polluters is another possible tactic that can be adopted. The USA introduced a clever version of this in its Clean Air Act with what are called 'tradable permits'. Electricity generating companies receive licences for a certain tonnage of emissions of the main pollutants such as carbon dioxide and sulphur dioxide and can trade them, buy and sell, between themselves. Thus a very 'clean' generator can sell surplus licences to pollute to a 'dirty' generator. Over time the total of licences, tonnages, is being cut and the price of the now scarcer permits will rise. There is, therefore, a financial incentive to adopt the latest technology and reduce emissions. The less favourably placed 'dirty' producer bears higher costs and presumably lower profits but has time to adjust to the new technology by buying licences. Eventually there will be an extremely low level of permitted pollutants and the permits that exist will be very expensive depending on how well the industry has coped with the change to low emission production. An alternative to such a scheme is simply to issue quantitative restriction on producers and to reduce the permitted limits year by year.

Setting of quality standards is another device that can be adopted by governments particularly in respect of the water industry. There has to be a time scale set for such standards and a comprehensive system of inspection. The inspectorate must also be backed by an efficient legal machinery and punishments that are an adequate deterrent to repetition of the breach of standards. The European Union has strong and reasonably effective, though tardy, standards. It has also developed an environmental policy that is covered in some detail in Chapter 19 and much of its early efforts were in the area of improving water quality.

Population control is, according to many observers, the key to a successful global environmental policy but the whole issue is overladen with social and religious disputes.

Exercise 4

Can financial incentives and penalties solve the problems of pollution without statutory inspection and control systems alongside them?

24.6   The World Bank, Growth and the Environment

The World Bank has come in for heavy criticism over the years for, among other things, being 'weak' on the environmental aspects of the projects it helps to finance in developing countries. Some of its infrastructure programmes such as helping to build roads into inaccessible areas of forest have allegedly helped unscrupulous logging companies destroy the rain forest and the local ecology. Some of its assistance has helped to turned self-sufficient mixed crop peasant farmers into producers of a single cash crop who are at the mercy of fluctuating international market prices. Since the Rio de Janeiro 'Earth Summit', however, the World Bank has developed as a major proponent of sustainable development. It now has an environmental department and in 1996 was financing 68 countries in their efforts to reform their environmental policies. Over $11 billion has been lent specifically to improve environmental conditions. About 100 countries have national environmental strategies and around half of them have made decisions to reverse the decline of their environments. All the recent lending decisions have been taken after environmental factors have been built into the investment proposals.

Addendum: A model of the economy with environmental linkages

The macroeconomic model can be augmented by the addition of sections to include the natural environment, as in Figure 24.2

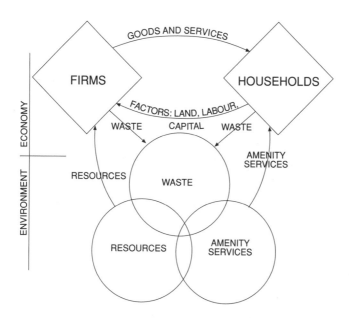

Figure 24.2   The economy with environment linkages

Answers to Exercises

Chapter 1

1 The fact that it uses evidence and data and tries to avoid normative statements (value judgements). It proceeds via hypothesis and theory and testing with an attempt to control variables.

2 The entrepreneur has to make choices based on costs on how to combine the factors of production in the least cost combination. Choice involves opportunity cost.

3 Partly because of the centralised authoritarian rule of Stalin and his successors; partly because of the exigencies of the war and its aftermath; partly because it worked tolerably well or appeared to until the Soviet people and its leadership became fully aware of the divergence between their standard of living and that of West Germany and the USA.

4 Partly to cover things they have not thought of that might alter the validity of their case; mainly to save writing out a long list of all the other variables that might alter their conclusions if they did change. The 'other things' are usually income, prices of related goods, consumer preferences, interest rates and so on depending on the context.

Chapter 2

1 The conventional statement of the opportunity cost would be the other public spending projects that could take place instead such as hospitals and roads but you should also consider what the taxpayers might have done with the money if they had retained it. The benefits are in terms of employment in the defence industry, potential export orders, regional employment, technological progress and research and development spin-offs.

2 The external costs might be tiny and would be borne by future generations of marine life and possibly fishermen and those who consume any of the long-term residues consumed by products in the human food chain. The external benefits would be enjoyed mainly by those who would be spared the noise and pollution near where the inshore dismantling takes place.

3 This could fill many pages but you should consider the construction and operating costs, the depreciation, the interest charges and the external costs to residents and firms during construction and operation (things like traffic delays and pollution). On the benefits side you should consider revenues from operating the line plus the various savings of all sorts of groups from reduced travel time and reduced congestion.

4 National income statistics do not tell us how the income is distributed or on what it is spent in any detail and money does not measure the intangible 'quality of life'.

Chapter 3

1 The birth rate is very unpredictable compared with the other elements such as death rates. Historically, sudden changes in the birth rate have sparked off significant future changes in demand.

2 The balance of argument is currently moving against the excessive removal of older workers because they are skilled, experienced and loyal to their employers. They also embody the collective knowledge of the firm and remember past mistakes and wise choices so they can circumvent problems more quickly or avoid repeating past mistakes. Younger replacements may have more innovative approaches and be more thrusting.

3 The reason lies in the lower productivity of the United Kingdom worker because of inferior levels of skill training and overall education and in the lower provision of capital equipment and modern technology.

4 The discoveries introduced a whole range of new technologies to the United Kingdom with large-scale investments. Much of the work to provide capital goods went abroad as did much of the R&D but there has been a significant increase in employment and wealth in the UK and a developing export trade.

Chapter 4

1 You could measure the proportion of GDP accounted for by the government sector and the percentage of the workforce employed by the public sector. You might also look at the percentage of R&D expenditure attributable to the government. An analysis of the tax burden would help as well.

2 (a) The awful record of pre-war privatised industries such as the railways and coal; the desire to control natural monopolies; the desire to stimulate investment in some areas; the wish to control the macroeconomy more effectively; the hope of redistributing wealth.

(b) It produced revenue for the government so that taxes could be cut; to save the government having to make decisions about investment and pricing policy in the industries; sales enabled the PSBR to be cut; there was a belief in the benefits of competition; it was hoped that share ownership would be widened; the City would make a great deal of money out of it.

3 If they could be measured you could judge the effects on saving, enterprise, work effort, willingness to work, risk taking and investment, tax revenues and government expenditure.

4 You could apply the points in the answer to exercise 3 plus an attempt to measure the impact on different income groups in terms of pre- and post-tax incomes.

Chapter 5

1 More people have been leaving the labour force than joining it. People have withdrawn from the claimants list for the job seekers' allowance.

2 Most economists now probably think it has gone too far and that it does matter because manufacturing has a profound impact on the other sectors and on regional development. Most services depend ultimately on having a healthy manufacturing base.

3   You probably found that there was. The exceptions might be firms with very large family ownership of shares and representation on the board.

4   The cynical answer is that United Kingdom managements are victims of fashion and succumb to the demands of the City institutions for quick and ever-growing rises in share values. Perhaps the earlier trend was often a big mistake and they are rectifying it. Occasionally it is an effort to repel aggressive takeover bids.

5   There is no right or wrong answer to this. I might chose international as opposed to national markets in, for example, cars, computers, insurance services, shipbuilding, steel. Some are competitive because they suffer from overproduction; others because of ever-changing products and technology; some because of new entrants from the Pacific rim or East Asia.

Chapter 6

1   As it links wants with the ability to pay. The wants become valid in the market.

2   (a) salt has a very inelastic demand because of the lack of substitutes and the habitual nature of its use;

(b) new cars in a particular range will be elastic because of the substitutes available in the price range and purchase can be delayed;

(c) skiing holidays of one seller will be very elastic because of the large number of alternative suppliers;

(d) air travel to the USA is almost certainly price elastic within existing price ranges because the business class traveller whose demand is inelastic is only a small proportion of the total market. The others, tourists and so on, have a more elastic demand.

3   OPEC tries to control the output of its members by allocating production quotas and aiming at a target price range. It is unsuccessful if its members 'cheat' and overproduce or if OPEC controls too small a percentage of total world output to determine prices. It is weak if world demand is static in relation to supply.

4   The balance of payments was weak and this exerted a downward pressure on sterling; speculators thought the pound was overvalued; United Kingdom inflation was too high compared with competitors; the UK had insufficient reserves to manage the markets; the government was not believed when it made statements about maintaining the exchange rate in the long term.

Chapter 7

1   It is incorporated because it can be regarded as the cost of having an entrepreneur. Probably some early computer applications that had no substitutes; games consoles where there is effectively a duopoly; early entrants into mobile phones and satellite TV; the early commercial TV companies had what Lord Thomson called 'a licence to print money'.

2   There are eight in my town centre; the banks also provide mortgages. You could study the details of the terms and conditions of loans and interest rates given and charged. If they vary considerably they are not a competitive market but a segmented market where firms compete through non-price elements.

3 There are plenty. Among them are a reduction in safety standards and quality of goods and service to customers. Expensively trained workers may be shed. The other common problems are cuts in training budgets and R&D. The long-term health of the firm suffers.

4 The ability is restricted by the presence of some degree of price elasticity of demand which is also the main limitation on monopoly power. The threat of new entrants and of government regulation are both limitations.

Chapter 8

1 Most people recognise the Coca-Cola bottle and the McDonalds logo. Most multiple retailers have a corporate image including shop fitting and décor so you would probably recognise all the major ones.

2 Both prices and shares of the market have fallen. The Channel Tunnel was claiming over 50 per cent of the car traffic by the autumn of 1996. The price competition era may tail off now that the ferry companies have government permission to organise some rationalisation of services. This may not be a full-blown cartel but may exhibit cartel characteristics. P and O is a very diversified company and can make up ferry operating profit reductions elsewhere so its share price may be more resistant to fluctuation.

3 It should be convinced that benefits to users outweigh the 'disbenefits' and that the public interest is served.

4 There is a complex argument here. There are now quite a large number of firms selling similar sized cars if we include the new Asian and central European manufacturers, but the UK market is still dominated by Ford, Vauxhall and Rover if market share is taken.

5 If there is a single market there needs to be a level playing field with relation to competition. This includes having a common competition and merger control policy. National polices still exist.

Chapter 9

1 You have probably seen the closure of many small, family owned shops and their replacement by multiples or financial services such as building societies. There may be many empty units awaiting redevelopment or charity shops. Food retailers may have closed as they move to the outskirts.

2 They appear to be quick and cheaper and do not need personal interaction. They are alleged to 'cream skim' or 'cherry pick' so they reject many applicants who have what they consider to be poor credit ratings.

3 They are bought in bulk at discounted prices (commercial economies of scale) and their specification and quality can be adjusted to the selling price. They give the buyers choice which they prefer and cater for different elasticities of demand which may raise profits.

4 Obviously to increase its profits. It will use its customer base to sell financial services. It may extend its loyalty card affiliated bonuses and discount opportunities to people who use its banking services.

Chapter 10

1 Advertising reflects business confidence so movements in expenditure indicate sentiments about future markets or their current state. Sensible firms may increase advertising expenditure during recessions.

2 Travel agencies also try to sell holiday insurance, car hire, foreign currency and organised tours with their holiday packages.

3 They cut costs by reducing overheads and reducing paperwork. They can employ flexible workers who work hours convenient to the business on short-term contracts and part time. Their central offices can be anywhere away from expensive city centres.

Chapter 11

1 You could discuss your supply curve of labour with your friends and see how their curves differ.

2 Most people seem to make an automatic assumption that longer training and education should be rewarded by higher pay and it becomes true for the majority. But there are exceptions.

3 You can apply the principle of economic rent of ability based on an extremely scarce talent which is in high demand. Footballers also retain some value in the transfer market, barring injury, so the £15 million should be reduced by the final transfer fee away from the club and divided by the number of years he stays. The annualised fee does not seem too bad if gate receipts increase and other merchandising of team strips rises. You may also want to consider the opportunity cost of the £15 million and the interest revenue forgone on the capital sum.

4 Most benefits seem to keep workers where they live and reduce geographical mobility but some may assist movement and help retraining and thereby increase occupational mobility.

Chapter 12

1 You could measure their earnings in relation to national averages and compare the divergence in the United Kingdom with similar foreign countries. If the UK rate diverges much more that the average of foreign countries there may be cause for concern. You might also consider whether the income of farm workers is a 'living wage', if you could define that term.

2 Recent opinion seems to indicate that firms have gone too far in this direction and some have harmed themselves and lost invaluable corporate experience and what may be called the company 'memory' of what to do in unusual or different circumstances such as recessions.

3 Mainly because of the immobility of labour. If labour were perfectly mobile the differentials would be eroded over time. There is also imperfect information in the labour market.

4 One view is that they are not bad in themselves but may be harmful if they are set too high and are excessively 'bureaucratic'. From the viewpoint of low-paid workers or firms that face 'unfair competition' from cheap labour producers, the minimum wage may be a good thing.

Chapter 13

1 £1.75 over £98.25 x 100 , multiplied by 4 times a year = 7.1246%.

2 The most important source of finance is ploughed back or retained profits. Bank borrowing comes a poor second and share issue is of relatively little importance overall.

3 It is the basis of the security of the institutions; they must be able to meet demands for 'cash' settlements and must keep adequate amounts of assets in relatively liquid form so that they can meet demands for cash.

4 The liberalisation of capital markets and the foreign exchange markets, together with London's position in the international time zones, attracts them. Another major incentive was to US institutions when the stock market was altered in the 'big bang'. The high degree of self-regulation may be another inviting feature.

5 People may be unaware of the differences; it takes time and trouble to change cards; many people prefer to stay with the institution they know. They are not behaving as textbook theory says they will!

Chapter 14

1 House price inflation meant that it was sensible to buy rather than rent because the physical asset, the building, showed a percentage capital gain each year higher than the rate of inflation of retail prices. Earnings were also rising in real terms. Mortgage debt was being repaid in depreciating money.

2 Very little except to manage their existing stocks prior to gradual disposal and to provide social housing; and to help the homeless as defined by parliament. Their role as builders of ordinary family homes has virtually disappeared.

3 Opinion used to favour the wholesale demolition of old urban housing because of the simplicity and speed of the operation. There was considerable contempt for the old housing, much of which was badly decayed. More recent sentiment is in favour of modernising and improvement and keeping the community together. The buildings have to be basically sound for this to be viable.

4 You should send your answers to the political leaders of the nation! They seem to have run out of ideas. Some revision of the system of housing benefit for the young is needed but the root of the problem is lack of employment. Solve that and many of the homeless would find their own homes in the market.

Chapter 15

1 Most of it appears to belong to institutions such as pension funds and unit and investment trusts and to various fund managements who are investing revenues from a great variety of sources. Much of it is bank money buying and selling on behalf of commercial organisations. Some belongs to governments.

2 Did the effective index diverge much from the rates of the individual currencies?

3 Its internal rate of inflation was high compared with other countries for a variety of reasons; the balance of payments was very weak; international events affected confidence in the pound; the government was not firm enough in controlling budget

deficits; speculators decided they could force a devaluation and make a quick profit; foreign assistance was limited and so were UK reserves.

4 The ERM is a purely European system and is based on a grid backed by co-operative intervention to maintain rates within the bands. The Bretton Woods system was an international one which was not based, usually, on co-operative efforts except via the IMF; it was dominated by the USA and the fixing of the price of gold.

Chapter 16

1 Agriculture does have problems peculiar to itself and it does provide considerable employment in non-urban areas so it is probably beneficial to society to subsidise it and maintain rural prosperity. It is also essential to maintain food supplies. If you are opposed to any state intervention you would strongly oppose aid to agriculture and to industry.

2 The overall market for beef fell by about 15 per cent in the UK but by more in Germany in the year from 20 March 1996 when the possibility of a new variant CJD was announced. There has been a significant shift to pork and lamb whose prices have risen. Beef prices in the UK have not fallen much at the retail end.

3 Mainly because of the large surpluses built up in the 1980s and press exaggeration of its imperfections. It has some good features especially in the way it has helped to ensure supplies and stabilise prices and maintain rural and less favoured areas' incomes and jobs.

4 You will have seen the importance of futures markets, the predominance of Chicago in many commodities, the significance of Rotterdam in oil pricing and of London in gold, metals, freight and insurance.

Chapter 17

1 If you look at the Annual Abstract of Statistics, at the pages on exports you will see that visibles are dominated by items such as whisky, transport goods, defence and aerospace equipment, petro-chemicals and pharmaceuticals while invisibles are dominated by financial services.

2 No, which is why it is being removed from new presentations of the balance of payments.

3 Yes, because it is too large for the present stage of the business cycle at which the UK is. If it is too large it has a downward pull effect on the pound which may have implications for the inflation rate and the price of imports.

4 Probably not because it may be exposed to indiscriminate dumping without reciprocal recourse to easy entry to foreign markets. It needs to negotiate a common reduction and possibly to have its own trade barriers to negotiate away, or the threat of imposing some.

Chapter 18

1 It is criticised on the grounds that it has increased the dependency of the recipient nations and has pushed some of them into mono-cultural agricultural practices.

Individual projects for which aid has been given have been heavily criticised for their environmental impact.

2   The IMF is concerned with short-term balance of payments problems and their resolution whereas the World Bank is concerned with long-term development and reconstruction. Their sources of funds and methods of operation differ considerably.

3   Mainly because of clashes between the USA and the European Union over agricultural issues; failure to agree over financial services and intellectual copyright; arguments about the new WTO's role.

4   Yes. They may dissolve into protectionist blocs pursuing regional protectionism which would harm world trade.

Chapter 19

1   The main 'loser' is Germany which regards its net contribution as the price it pays for European unity and economic cohesion. It probably receives much of the money back in trade. Others such as the Netherlands take a similar view. The UK is the odd man out and resents its net contribution, or at least some political leaders choose to say they do. They do not do a lot about getting it reduced. The UK also benefits from trade arising from the better off beneficiary countries' contributions to the less well off members.

2   It may be impossible to do this and if you can work out how you should again tell the leaders of the EU. The answer may lie in even more decommissioning of ships and paid abstention from fishing along the lines of farm set-aside. More rigorous inspection of boats and net sizes might help. We will probably end up with temporary suspension of all fishing in some areas because of depleted stocks.

3   By studying the changes over time of average GDP per head on a regional basis and comparing it with overall EU averages. Recent work indicates that the Cohesion Fund has had a marked beneficial effect in Ireland, Spain, Portugal and Greece.

4   The reasons given were that the UK Government wanted to retain a flexible labour market and keep costs competitively low. It also wished to continue to restrain trade unions. Specifically it resisted the idea of a national minimum wage and works councils.

5   Because international co-operation is needed to deal with cross border issues such as pollution; and because the costs of environmental policies must be borne equally by firms in each country, otherwise those with lax policies could obtain competitive advantages.

Chapter 20

1   It is supported by the enormous amount of bank created 'money' which exists because people make most of their financial transactions with cheques and credit transfers rather than cash.

2   Some of the money in the system does not pass through banks so when a bank lends to its customers not all of the money returns to the banking system. This limits the quantity of cash returning to the bank and reduces the credit multiplier. The theoretical example assumes it is all returned.

3   The City and financial markets would believe the newly independent central bank about its intentions to control inflation. The model given is usually the extremely independent German central bank. In a word, it would increase the bank's *credibility*.

4   There is much debate about this. They have an immediate effect on the money markets but a slower or delayed effect on the longer term markets such as the mortgage market. They may have a longer term effect on investment decisions but this may be muted. A lot depends on the extent of the change and its timing in relation to the business cycle.

5   I would gain by not paying commission every time I go abroad. Prices on ferries would also exclude foreign exchange commissions. We are told that we would all benefit from firms having similarly reduced transactions costs and that business confidence would increase and economic growth with it. But, someone will have to pay the costs of conversion of tills and accounting systems. Guess who?

Chapter 21

1   Yes, because other countries have achieved them for some periods of time. The UK is concentrating on the inflation target and seems to be hoping that unemployment will continue to fall as a result of the natural recovery from recession associated with the business cycle. It is not actively pursuing growth except via supply-side measures which are of dubious effectiveness.

2   Probably because the rise in unemployment seemed inexorable and it was expedient to argue that market forces would restore equilibrium; possibly because it wanted to use unemployment as a means of disciplining the trade unions; possibly because it helped to push wages down or restrict their rise with benefits for production costs; possibly because unemployment was an inevitable consequence of their other policies to maintain a high exchange rate for sterling. They may not have wanted to be blamed for failing to achieve what they knew they could not deliver. The opposition was feeble?

3   This issue is about what is called inter-generational spending. It is obviously sensible that future generations should help pay for facilities that they use and that the burden on the present generation of tax payers should be shared with those in the future. It is possible, however, for the burden on the future to be made excessive and some modern commentators argue in favour of financing capital expenditure from the currently available revenues and not by borrowing.

4   More uniform rates would help to reduce the distortions to prices and trade caused by differential rates. It pays, in some circumstances, to cross borders to buy certain goods and services because the VAT rates are different in the same way that it is cheaper to buy beer and wine in Calais because the taxes on alcohol are lower in France.

5   The central government controls its own spending and provides a high proportion of local authority funds so it is only natural that it wants to control their spending as well; otherwise its macroeconomic demand management policy may fail. However, many commentators think that the present controls are too stringent and are close to destroying local democracy.

Chapter 22

1 The economy is incapable of producing the extra goods and services and capital goods required given its existing combination of factors and technology so there is upward pressure on prices.

2 (a) 5; (b) 10; (c) 2; (d) 3.3; (e) 4.

3 The accelerator, unless it is heavily 'dampened', creates sudden surges and falls in the investment goods industries because of the impact of new demand combined with replacement demand. The investment goods industries are, therefore, subject to greater fluctuations in output and prices than consumption goods industries.

4 The high inflation/high unemployment scenario is usually associated with a long process of economic mismanagement and decay or serious economic shocks. The rising unemployment/falling prices situation is associated with the lower points of the business cycle.

5 In order to work effectively they need consensus and a general acceptance that they are fair. They require a longer time period to work properly and should not be adopted in desperation when all else appears to have failed. New attitudes need to be adopted over a long period. Wage bargaining and profit expectations need to be modified within the projected growth of the overall economy.

Chapter 23

1 In principle a non-interventionist government would leave things alone and concentrate on deregulation. An interventionist government would try to direct government spending into training, research and development and into investment in potential 'winners' such as advanced technology industries.

2 It is assumed to be caused by a lack of consumption demand and/or investment demand. It might be remedied by increased government expenditure on current consumption or on public sector investment. Taxes might be cut to stimulate consumer spending.

3 If your income has risen faster than the rate of inflation you are better off in real terms unless your spending pattern is completely different from that embodied in the Retail Prices Index. In order to be a full-blown net gainer you need to have had physical assets such as property that has grown in value much faster than the RPI and to have realised your gains. If you have not realised your gains you are only better off on paper although you could have borrowed against the security of the inflated real asset value. If your income has been static or has risen less fast than the RPI you are a net loser.

4 Mainly because he would receive less stick from the critics if he failed to meet the absolute figure of 2.5 per cent. It is more practical to set a range as a target because it allows for temporary economic shocks that may distort the short-term figures. Only a fluke could keep the rate on 2.5 for any length of time. Since June 1996 the 2.5 has been regarded as a desirable maximum.

5 It is deep rooted in the structure of our economy, society and form of government. It may relate to the UK's international trading position and the constraints of the foreign exchange rate or to the huge outflow of investment funds that could have been retained in the UK. It may be due to the persistent failure of government to combine with organised labour and enterprise to construct some form of consensus

and national economic objective. Perhaps we value the non-material things of life more highly and do not exert ourselves for purely economic ends.

Chapter 24

1 Because low incomes elsewhere reduce the demand for United Kingdom exports and create poor opportunities for investment. Low incomes also tend to reflect or generate economic instability which is bad for world trade. Having said that, the moral objections to extremes of affluence and poverty are the overriding ones.

2 Once again long books have been written on this subject. It seems to be the result of a powerfully directed consensus between government, private enterprise and sometimes labour to drive their economies in certain directions. Although private enterprise may be the main engine of growth it is stimulated or protected by the state which helps to provide a legal and institutional framework to protect home industry and to target export industries. Civil liberties tend to take a back seat and regimes tend to be authoritarian.

3 Several banks have had to write off extremely large bad debts and this has affected their business. The Midland Bank was reduced in strength by bad debts so that it had to look for a partner and was taken over by the Hong Kong and Shanghai Bank. The flow of interest income failed to reach expectations and interfered with the financial markets' normal operations. Some bad debts eventually had an impact on firms that had won contracts overseas as work or payment failed to materialise.

4 Almost certainly not because inspection is required to judge if penalties are appropriate. The existence of both incentives and penalties creates a financial motive for cheating. You cannot trust a potential poacher to act as a gamekeeper.

Further Reading

More advanced and detailed economic theory is available in a large number of textbooks. A readable and relatively compact one is:

D. Begg, S. Fischer and R. Dornbusch, *Economics* (McGraw-Hill, 1994) 4th edn.

Applied economics is dealt with in a very thorough and interesting manner in:

P. Curwen, (ed.) *Understanding the UK Economy* (Macmillan, 1994) 3rd edn.
A. Griffiths and S. Wall (eds) *Applied Economics – An Introductory Course* (Longman, 1995) 6th edn.

Macmillan produce an exceptionally good series called *Macmillan Texts in Economics*. The following books from that series will take you more deeply into various areas of economics:

P. Ferguson, G. Ferguson and R. Rothschild, *Business Economics* (Macmillan, 1993).
D. Sapsford and Z. Tzannatos, *The Economics of the Labour Market* (Macmillan, 1993).
K. Pilbeam, *International Finance* (Macmillan, 1992).

Almost all applied economics now has a European Union dimension and the following is a very up-to-date coverage of the economic and political issues facing Europe and the United Kingdom:

S. F. Goodman, *The European Union* (Macmillan, 1996) 3rd edn.

If you prefer an approach that contains a lot of stimulus material in the form of newspaper cuttings and data or an investigative angle you could use:

Economics and Business Studies Association, *Core Economics* (Heinemann, 1995).
A. Anderton, *Economics* (Causeway Press, 1995) 2nd edn.

I strongly recommend the purchase of an economics dictionary. There are a number in print published by Penguin and Collins for example. Macmillan publish a very well presented and extremely well cross-referenced one:

D. W. Pearce, (ed.) *Macmillan Dictionary of Modern Economics* (Macmillan, 1992) 4th edn.

There are a number of useful Internet sites, for example:

Bank of England: http://www.bankofengland.co.uk
OECD: http://www.oecd.org/std/
Office for National Statistics (ONS): http://www.emap.co.uk/ons/
European Commission; http://europa.eu.int

Index